Civil Society's Democratic Potential

Organizational Trade-Offs between Participation and Representation

Nicole Bolleyer

Great Clarendon Street, Oxford, OX2 6DP,
United Kingdom

Oxford University Press is a department of the University of Oxford.
It furthers the University's objective of excellence in research, scholarship,
and education by publishing worldwide. Oxford is a registered trade mark of
Oxford University Press in the UK and in certain other countries

© Nicole Bolleyer 2024

The moral rights of the author have been asserted

Some rights reserved. No part of this publication may be reproduced, stored in
a retrieval system, or transmitted, in any form or by any means, for commercial purposes,
without the prior permission in writing of Oxford University Press, or as expressly
permitted by law, by licence or under terms agreed with the appropriate
reprographics rights organization.

This is an open access publication, available online and distributed under the terms of a
Creative Commons Attribution—Non Commercial—No Derivatives 4.0
International licence (CC BY-NC-ND 4.0), a copy of which is available at
http://creativecommons.org/licenses/by-nc-nd/4.0/.

Enquiries concerning reproduction outside the scope of this licence
should be sent to the Rights Department, Oxford University Press, at the address above

Published in the United States of America by Oxford University Press
198 Madison Avenue, New York, NY 10016, United States of America

British Library Cataloguing in Publication Data

Data available

Library of Congress Control Number: 2023944407

ISBN 9780198884392

DOI: 10.1093/oso/9780198884392.001.0001

Printed and bound by
CPI Group (UK) Ltd, Croydon, CR0 4YY

Links to third party websites are provided by Oxford in good faith and
for information only. Oxford disclaims any responsibility for the materials
contained in any third party website referenced in this work.

To Jonathan

Acknowledgements

This book is based on research conducted in the context of two ERC projects, the Starting Grant STATORG (Grant agreement ID: 335890) completed a few years back and the still ongoing Consolidator Grant CIVILSPACE (Grant agreement ID: 101001458). It could not have been completed without either, and this repeated support by the European Research Council is gratefully acknowledged.[1] Many issues dealt with in this book were discussed with my former STATORG team, especially Patricia Correa (now Aston University) and Milka Ivanovska Hadjievska (now Lund University). Without them the bulk of the data collection this book benefited from could not have been implemented and central arguments would not have been sharpened. Many thanks go to the interviewees who—in 2017 and 2022— were willing to talk about the evolution and internal workings of the three membership organizations whose long-term trajectories this book explores to substantiate the statistical findings. My brilliant team at the Chair of Comparative Political Science at LMU, including Vanessa Boese, Valentin Daur, Juan Ignacio Dupetit, Adam Eick, Marlien Heibrock, Michael Neureiter and Sabine Zwerger helped to get the final manuscript submitted. Special thanks go to Philipp A. Schroeder who repeatedly commented on theoretical and methodological elements of the book and to Leonhard Grevesmühl, Vivien Schachtner, and Celina K. Schneider who conducted background research for the case studies. Thanks also go to my LMU colleagues Katrin Auspurg, Klaus H. Goetz, Martin Gross and Heidi Stöckl for making the return to German academia after a decade in the UK much easier. Without their support this already much delayed project would have been delayed even more.

The book benefited from the input of many friends and colleagues who offered constructive criticism and advice on individual arguments that were presented as papers at various international conferences over the last years. There are too many to mention them all. They include Joost Berkhout, Jan Beyers, Gabriela Borz, Fabrizio Di Mascio, Zsolt Enyedi, Justin Fisher, Bert

---

[1] This research was funded by the European Union; the views and opinions expressed are, however, those of the author only and do not necessarily reflect those of the European Union or the European Research Council Executive Agency. Neither the European Union nor the granting authority can be held responsible for them. See for information on the CIVILSPACE project: https://cps-lmu.org/civilspace.html.

Fraussen, Darren Halpin, Anika Gauja, Marcel Hanegraaff, André Kaiser, Dick Katz, William Maloney, Amy McKay and Anne Rasmussen. Special thanks go to Gabriel Katz, who provided input on the statistical analyses, to Edgar Grande and Swen Hutter, who invited me to the WZB in Berlin in spring 2022, and to Michele Crepaz, who invited me on behalf of the PSAI to give the Peter Mair lecture at their annual conference in Belfast in fall 2023. The WZB event allowed me to give my first lecture on the overall framework that holds the empirical elements of the book together. It also provided me with a last round of valuable feedback before conducting some last interviews and completing the manuscript in summer. Preparing the Peter Mair lecture made me rethink central arguments of the book from the perspective of party scholarship, which led me to sharpen some final points when going over the already copyedited version.

Many thanks go, as always, to Dominic Byatt, my OUP editor, for his critical input as well as his patience. The same applies to the OUP referees who commented on various aspects of the book project but, in particular, pushed me to broaden its empirical foundations (as planned initially) and add a qualitative pillar to the quantitative one. This not only made the empirical analysis more robust but the overall study hopefully more interesting to a wider range of readers. Individual arguments that now form part of quantitative chapters of the book have been tested in separate, empirical analyses that were published as journal articles in *Comparative Political Studies*, *European Union Politics*, *Political Studies*, and *Social Forces*.

The usual suspects have provided support and advice—professional and other—along the way. I cannot thank enough Tanja A. Börzel, Patricia Correa, Atina Krajewska, Diana Panke, and Christine Reh.

Last but not least, this book is dedicated to my husband Jonathan Barry, without whom this whole project would have been—from start to finish—unfeasible.

Munich, 14 September 2023   Nicole Bolleyer

Contents

List of Tables	xii

1. A Multidimensional Framework on Civil Society's Contributions to Democracy   1

Civil Society's Contributions to Democracy: Between Potential and Reality	3
Disaggregating the 'Transmission Belt': Three Normative Yardsticks Demarcating CSOs' Potential Contributions to Democracy	8
Membership Organizations as Venues for Participation	11
Membership Organizations as Vehicles of Representation	16
The Ambiguity of Interest Representation Behaviour: Expression of Assumed, Consultative or Surrogate Representation?	18
Adding Societal Responsiveness of CSO Behaviour as Third Normative Yardstick	26
From Normative Yardstick to Comparative Analysis	27
Conclusion and Chapter Overview	31

2. The Distinct Internal Logics of Associations and Professionalized Voluntary Organizations   36

Why Study the Discrepancies between Democratic Potential and Organizational Realities in Membership-Based Voluntary Organizations?	38
The Diversity of Organizational Forms and Its Consequences for CSOs' Democratic Contributions	44
Intra-Organizational Trade-Offs and the Conflicting Priorities of Leaders, Members, and Managers	44
How CSOs Respond to Intra-Organizational Trade-Offs: The Different Logics of 'Voluntary Associations' and 'Professionalized Voluntary Organizations'	52
Conclusion	56

3. Methodological Choices and Data   59

Measures Used in the Quantitative Analyses	64
The Dependent Variables: How to Measure CSOs' Diverse Contributions to Democracy	64
Central Explanatory Variables: CSOs' Governance Characteristics	68
Control Variables Central to the Functioning of CSOs Generally	70
Control Variables Relevant to Specific Dimensions of CSOs' Democratic Contribution	71

x Contents

CSO Diversity and Why the Voluntary Association and the
Professionalized Voluntary Organization Are Not Treated As
Counter-Images 73
The Advantages of a Mixed-Methods Design 77
The Selection of Three UK CSOs for In-Depth Study 78
Conclusion 81

4. **The Distinct Roles of Members in Civil Society
Organizations: Trading Member Control against Leader Autonomy** **82**
A Governance Perspective on Member Activism in Civil Society
Organizations 84
Hypotheses on Member Activism in Professionalized Voluntary
Organizations 85
Hypotheses on Member Involvement in Voluntary Associations 89
Expected Impacts of CSO Type on Patterns of Member Activism 92
A Quantitative Analysis of Member Activism in Civil Society Organizations ... 94
Conclusion 101

5. **When Managers Take Over: Drivers of Staff Control
in Civil Society Organizations** **106**
A Governance Perspective on Staff Control in Civil Society Organizations ... 109
Hypotheses on Staff Control in Professionalized Voluntary
Organizations 109
Hypotheses on Staff Control in Voluntary Associations 112
A Quantitative Analysis of Staff Control in Civil Society Organizations ... 114
Conclusion 121

6. **From Voluntary Association to Professionalized
Voluntary Organization: The Evolution of Member
Activism and Staff Control in Civil Society Organizations** **124**
Intra-Organizational Dynamics and Decision-Making Power in a
Service-Oriented, a Political, and a Partisan Organization 128
The National Activity Providers Association (NAPA) 128
Surfers Against Sewage (SAS) 138
The Green Party of England and Wales (GPEW) 149
Conclusion 167

7. **CSO Goal Reorientation in Individualizing Societies:
Between Commitment and Change** **171**
A Governance Perspective on CSO Goal Commitment and Reorientation ... 175
Voluntary Associations and Professionalized Voluntary
Organizations: Hypotheses on Responsive Goal Commitment
versus Instrumental Goal Reorientation 175
Bringing in Market and Constituency Pressures: External
Sources of Instrumental and Responsive Goal Reorientation 178
A Quantitative Analysis of CSO Goal Reorientation and Commitment ... 181
Conclusion 184

Contents **xi**

8. **CSOs' Political Engagement: Between the Logic of Membership and the Logic of Influence** — 187

A Governance Perspective on CSO Political Engagement — 192

Hypotheses on the Political Engagement of Voluntary Associations and Professionalized Voluntary Organizations — 194

Expected Impacts of CSO Type on Political Engagement — 198

A Quantitative Analysis of Political Engagement of Civil Society Organizations — 199

Conclusion — 204

9. **From Voluntary Association to Professionalized Voluntary Organization: CSO Goal Reorientation and the Evolution of Political Engagement** — 207

Tracing Change in CSO Goals and Political Engagement Qualitatively — 210

Intra-Organizational Dynamics, Goals, and Political Engagement of a Service-Oriented, a Political, and a Partisan Organization — 213

The National Activity Providers Association (NAPA) — 213

Surfers Against Sewage (SAS) — 219

The Green Party of England and Wales (GPEW) — 229

Conclusion — 245

10. **Disaggregating the Transmission Belt and the Study of CSOs' Democratic Contributions** — 248

The Democratic Contributions of Voluntary Associations and Professionalized Voluntary Organizations: An Overview — 249

CSOs as Changing Configurations of Participation and Representation and the Growing Importance of Hybridization — 254

The Professionalized Voluntary Organization: Better Than Its Reputation — 259

The Three Faces of Membership Organization and Avenues for Future Research — 268

Some Final Remarks — 274

Bibliography — 279
Index — 304
An online appendix is available at www.oup.co.uk/companion/Bolleyer

List of Tables

1.1. CSO Configurations of Participation and Interest Representation and Their (Likely) Democratic Contributions   19

1.2. Theorizing and Analysing CSOs' Democratic Contributions   28

2.1. Dimensions of CSOs' Potential Democratic Contributions, Related Organizational Trade-Offs, and Orientations of Leaders, Members, and Managers   47

2.2. Two Types of CSOs and Their Defining Characteristics   53

2.3. Two Governance Templates and Central Theoretical Expectations Regarding CSOs' Democratic Contributions   58

3.1. Macro Characteristics of Long-Lived Democracies and Case Selection for Surveys   61

3.2. The Relative Importance of Different Income Sources by Type of Organization   75

4.1. Theoretically Expected Patterns of Member Control and Involvement   94

4.2. Heterogeneous Choice Models for Member Control and Member Involvement (With Multiple Imputations)   96

5.1. Zero-Inflated Count Regressions with Poisson Distribution (With Multiple Imputations)   116

7.1. CSO Goal Reorientation and Commitment: Drivers and Their Behavioural Rationales   179

7.2. Logistic Regression on Drivers of CSO Goal Reorientation (With Multiple Imputations)   182

8.1. Drivers of CSO Politicization and Their Political Action Repertoires (With Multiple Imputations)   200

10.1. Summary of the Statistical Findings on How CSO Features Relate to Their Democratic Contributions   250

1

A Multidimensional Framework on Civil Society's Contributions to Democracy

Which civil society organizations (CSOs)[1]—whether partisan, advocacy- or service-oriented—contribute to democracy, how, and why? Organized civil society composed of membership organizations is traditionally considered a cornerstone of democracy. Constituting the organizational fabric between government and society, it encompasses a wide diversity of structures and entities[2] thought to fundamentally contribute to participation and representation in a democracy. Despite this widely held conviction, CSOs' readiness and ability to serve either as venues for participation or as vehicles of democratic representation (or indeed both at the same time) have remained a matter of ongoing debate across the social sciences. As we will see in the course of this study, some research in politics and sociology has tended to treat certain contributions of CSOs to democracy as starting assumptions, which as a consequence have been 'more celebrated than scrutinized' (Alexander and Fernandez 2021: 368). Others have questioned traditional expectations regarding CSOs as unrealistic (e.g. Jordan and Maloney 1997; 2007).

These debates have gained salience as membership-based CSOs' *actual* contributions to democracy in Europe—regimes whose stability could long be taken for granted—have been put into question by fundamental changes and shocks, notably societal individualization, digitalization, financial crises, populism, the increasing state dependency and professionalization of CSOs,

---

[1] In this study organization is understood as 'a system of formalized social relationships involving a distribution of tasks and a distribution of authority' (Schmitter and Streeck 1999: 65). Civil society organizations (CSOs) are defined as organizations with a voluntary membership (be those individuals or corporate actors) that are private, separate from government, self-governing, non-profit-distributing, and generally have a formalized infrastructure (e.g. Wilson 1973; Salamon and Anheier 1998). While a detailed discussion of the suitability of this analytical category follows in Chapter 2, it is important to note right away that individual actors (e.g. firms, hospitals, local governments) or completely staff-run, member-less organizations (LeRoux and Feeney 2015: 10–12; Jordan et al. 2004) are not considered in this study. These organizations might well have non-profit status and engage in advocacy activities. But they do not have to manage similar intra-organizational trade-offs affecting their functioning and activities (that, in turn, systematically shape their respectively democratic contribution) as CSOs dependent on voluntary members. The same goes for government-created CSOs (e.g. Doyle 2018).
[2] E.g. Wilson 1973; Rosenblum 2000a; 2000b; Lang 2013; LeRoux and Feeney 2015; Heylen et al. 2020; Bolleyer and Correa 2020a; 2022a.

Civil Society's Democratic Potential. Nicole Bolleyer, Oxford University Press. © Nicole Bolleyer (2024).
DOI: 10.1093/oso/9780198884392.003.0001

2 Civil Society's Democratic Potential

and, most recently, the Covid-19 pandemic. Constitutive for prominent notions such as 'democratic linkage' or 'transmission belt', CSOs' role as central intermediary structures organizing members and societal constituencies and thereby channelling collective voices into the political process is put into question as outdated, costly, inefficient, and sometimes even normatively undesirable. The individualization of Western societies, weakening group affiliations and enhancing societal heterogeneity, has long been highlighted as a challenge for the formation and maintenance of organizations dependent on the ongoing support of voluntary members.[3] Consequently, membership organizations are widely considered to be in decline. Building such structures has been portrayed as outdated, a costly form of organizing ill-equipped to compete with a growing number of completely staff-run (increasingly memberless) organizations as well as much more permeable structures experimenting with new (often virtual) forms of organizing. Relatedly, digitalization has multiplied channels through which individual voices can be expressed directly and unmediated, without the constraints of a formal organizational infrastructure and the need to compromise or even interact with others.[4] Meanwhile, a populist discourse has gained prominence, normatively rejecting the mediated character of long-established structures such as parties, interest groups, and associations altogether, accusing the latter of fundamentally biasing, if not suppressing, the 'real' voice of the people (e.g. Ruzza and Sanchez Salgado 2021). Such outright rejection of traditional forms of interest representation as 'detached' or 'unauthentic' has fed into a long-standing disillusionment with CSOs. The latter's interest in and ability to engage citizens and represent societal interest has been questioned in different subfields for quite a while. Notions such as the 'NGOization' of civil society (prominent in civil society research as well as in international relations) and the 'cartelization' of political parties (prominent in comparative politics research) have problematized organizations' increasing state dependency and professionalization, two central developments shifting organizational priorities away from societal values towards instrumentally driven self-maintenance.[5]

In essence, a range of disparate as well as partially interconnected developments have contributed to questioning CSOs' participatory role, their

---

[3] Processes of de-structuring and the decline of collective identities have affected political parties, interest groups, and associations, e.g. Heelas et al. 1996; Katz and Mair 1996; Koole 1996; van Biezen et al. 2012; Ford and Jennings 2021.

[4] Bolleyer et al. 2015; Margetts et al. 2015; Fitzpatrick 2018; Lynn et al. 2022

[5] See, for instance, Skocpol 2013; Alvarez 2009; Hwang and Powell 2009; Larsson 2011; van Deth and Maloney 2012; Saurugger 2012; Choudry and Kapoor 2013; Lang 2013; Borchgrevink 2020; Della Porta 2020; Arda and Banerjee 2021; Sayan and Duygulus 2022.

contribution to democratic interest representation, and, relatedly, their willingness or ability to behave in a way responsive to societal needs or demands. These developments jointly underpin a powerful critique of 'traditional forms of organizing' long considered constitutive for European civil societies. This critique has only gained in forcefulness since democracies have been hit by the recent Covid-19 pandemic. This fundamental crisis made face-to-face meetings for long periods difficult, if not impossible, meetings widely considered essential for membership organizations' very functioning and the realization of their full democratic potential.[6]

Civil Society's Contributions to Democracy: Between Potential and Reality

These real-world developments bring out with particular clarity the puzzle at the heart of this study that has been present in the literature on organized civil society (broadly defined) for a long time. This puzzle still needs to be addressed both theoretically and empirically: the discrepancies between CSOs' *democratic potentials* (as ascribed to CSOs from different normative angles) and the *actual and very diverse contributions* individual membership organizations make to democracy in terms of the processes they cultivate and the activities they engage in. It is these discrepancies that make it paramount to assess to what extent and in what ways the wide variety of membership organizations contributes to contemporary European democracies and what drives existing differences.

Such assessment requires in the first instance the formulation of a theoretical framework specifying the overall democratic potential that can be ideal-typically ascribed to membership-based CSOs, based on some (widely accepted) normative yardsticks. These yardsticks need to be translated into analytical benchmarks suitable for empirical analysis. On their basis, we can then capture and systematically compare processes and behaviours through which different CSOs' actual contributions to democracy become manifest. This can enable us to understand why some membership-based CSOs make certain contributions to democracy in practice, while others do not.

---

[6] While arguments have been made that the pandemic incentivized innovation with regard to the enhanced usage of online channels for exchange and collective action, channels enabling CSOs to reach a wide range of members and constituencies more easily and with fewer costs, the capacity of CSOs to develop such an infrastructure varies significantly. It is doubtful that this development might result in a significant equalizing effect in the CSO sector (e.g. FRA 2021; Rasmussen 2020; Junk et al. 2022).

4 Civil Society's Democratic Potential

So why does such a framework not yet exist? One likely reason is simply the growing tendency towards specialization in contemporary research, a tendency which—more often than not—is a strength. There are a number of flourishing strands of research on parties, interest groups, and non-profits dealing with these organizations' functioning, behaviour, and their consequences for modern democracy. There is also little disagreement that CSOs *can* fulfil important political and social functions in democracies. However, whether, when, and why CSOs *do fulfil such functions* is a different matter entirely. It is a central contention of this book that there has been too little dialogue across these subfields and that a synthesis of the work on different types of membership organizations that is scattered across political science, sociology, public administration and voluntary sector research will help us shed some light on the discrepancies between widespread normative expectations we tend to have towards these organizations and the often contradictory realities that materialize in empirical studies.

The contention that such dialogue is useful is based on several remarkable parallels that emerge when assessing the various literatures concerning the ways that groups and parties might or do benefit democracy. The first parallel concerns the nature of the challenges or even crises identified in these works that fundamentally affect how membership-based organizations operate in contemporary democracies and the latter's impact on their readiness and ability to perform the roles frequently ascribed to them. The second parallel concerns similarities in organizational responses to these challenges and how they are problematized regarding their implications for democracy. The third one concerns the centrality of how groups and parties organize for the roles they can play in contemporary democracies.

Starting with the parallels in the challenges confronting CSOs, transformations through major technological advances, such as digitalization, or crises, such as the Covid pandemic, impact on many types of organizations operating in a variety of domains of a political system. However, membership-based organizations constituting the civil society sector are—given their own constitutive nature—particularly affected by the increasing individualization of societies in advanced democracies. This fundamental vulnerability has been stressed in group as much as party research. This is because individualization has made societal support, on which these organizations by definition depend, more volatile.

This leads us to the second parallel, concerning organizational responses to those challenges and their 'democratic downsides'. The increasing volatility of societal support is one important reason why membership organizations including groups and parties have increasingly looked elsewhere to secure the finances necessary to maintain their operations and ensure their survival, one much discussed source being state funding. The growing dependency on such funding (and exposure to state regulation related to it) has been problematized in party, interest group, non-profit, and civil society research alike. It has been associated with declining member participation, mission drift, and the weakening of ties to societal constituencies.[7] Similar tendencies have been linked to membership organizations' growing professionalization constitutive for a 'new model of association building'. This model is said to generate 'democratic deficits', substituting membership-based associational activities with professional management assumed to prefer a passive membership.[8] Synthesizing arguments prominent in different subfields, the following broader claim emerges: irrespective of membership organizations' primary mission, the strategies they choose to ensure their own survival in increasingly individualized societies invite or reinforce their societal detachment. This detachment is considered unfavourable to internal participation, as well as to interest representation that is responsive to societal interests and concerns.

Finally, influential works on how groups and parties are likely (or increasingly unlikely) to fulfil their 'democratic functions' have stressed the importance of how CSOs are organized.[9] Classical works already highlighted decades ago the tensions membership organizations as a class of organizations face when trying simultaneously to cultivate internal participation and maximize external voice, activities both central to the role that CSOs play in a democracy (e.g. Olson 1965; Wilson 1973; Schmitter and Streeck 1999). A considerable body of research building on these ideas has shown how organizations engage in this 'balancing act' across a range of domains and on different governmental levels—subnational, national, and international.[10] Going back to the societal transformations challenging collective

---

[7] E.g. Katz and Mair 1995; 2002; 2009; Weisbrod 1997; Panebianco 1988; Bosso 2003; Choudry and Kapoor 2013; Skocpol 2003; Jordan and Maloney 2007; Halpin 2010; Toepler 2010; Kreutzer and Jäger 2011; Whiteley 2011; van Deth and Maloney 2012; Brandsen et al. 2014; Scarrow 2015; Poguntke et al. 2016; Scarrow and Webb 2017; Ivanovska Hadjievska and Stavenes 2020.

[8] See, for instance, Skocpol 2003: 204, 265; Kriesi and Baglioni 2003: 4; Fraussen and Halpin 2018: 30; Hwang and Powell 2009; Eikenberry and Kluver 2004; Rogers 2005; Kohler-Koch 2010; Larsson 2011; van Deth and Maloney 2012; Saurugger 2012; Lang 2013; Schlozman et al. 2015; Alexander and Fernandez 2021.

[9] See, for instance, Jordan and Maloney 1997; 2007; Ganz 2014; Ahlquist and Levi 2014; Halpin 2014; Han 2014; Bentancur et al. 2019; McAlevey 2016; Heylen et al. 2020.

[10] See, for instance, Bennet 2000; Ganz 2009; Kohler-Koch and Buth 2013; Lang 2013; Han 2014; Ahlquist and Levi 2014; Klitzke 2017; Behrens 2018; Bunea 2019; Heylen et al. 2020; Bolleyer and Correa 2020a; 2022a; Bolleyer 2021a.

6 Civil Society's Democratic Potential

organizations, it has been argued that these trade-offs have become more pronounced in recent decades. As the number of politically active organizations engaged in interest representation has multiplied, the way these CSOs increasingly organize suggests an enhancement of advocacy without a cultivation of civic engagement. This, in turn, points to a growing discrepancy between organizations' ability or willingness to function simultaneously both as venues for participation and as vehicles for democratic representation (e.g. Skocpol 2013; Maloney 2012; Lang 2013; Alexander and Fernandez 2021). Alongside this rather pessimistic diagnosis, we find research on both groups and parties (though sharing a focus on organizational adaptation) arguing that the real puzzle lies in the diversity of CSO responses. Shifting from the sector level to the level of individual organizations, it emerges that trade-offs play out in a variety of ways. Rather than pointing to a broader trend, these studies highlight the differences in how CSOs operating in similar settings try to and do address the tensions between cultivating participation, engaging in political activity, and maintaining constituency linkages (e.g. Walker et al. 2011; Ahlquist and Levi 2014; Han 2014; Bentancur et al. 2019 Albareda and Braun 2019; Grömping and Halpin 2019; Heylen et al. 2020).

To date, research has rarely picked up on these various parallels in group and party research.[11] This study argues that these parallels allow us to develop a framework to account for how tendencies towards, for instance, professionalization and bureaucratization in modern societies (that affect parties, interest groups, and service-oriented CSOs alike) might shape why membership organizations fall short of normative expectations applied to them (or not as the case might be). To achieve this, this study takes as its foundation research highlighting CSOs' organizational diversity and its importance for understanding CSO choices when confronted by conflicts of self-maintenance and goal attainment. On this basis, it theorizes how central CSO traits feed into CSOs' varying democratic contributions (see for a similar approach, for instance, Lang 2013).

When developing this framework, this study takes a deliberately broad perspective regarding the organizations it is interested in. It aims at accounting for when membership-based organizations generally—encompassing different political organizations as well as predominantly service-orientated ones—generate internal participation, external interest representation, and maintain linkages to societal constituencies, and when they do not.

---

[11] But see Katz and Mair 1996; Koole 1996; Jordan and Maloney 1997; Skocpol 2003; Fraussen and Halpin 2018; Bolleyer and Correa 2020a; 2022a; Bolleyer 2021a; forthcoming.

Though analyses (especially cross-national ones) that look at membership organizations in general have become rare,[12] this study can build on a tradition of by now decades-old studies, some of them empirical, some of them theoretical (e.g. Olsen 1965; Hirschman 1970; Wilson 1973). It shares with them two basic outlooks: first, the functioning and behaviour of collective organizational structures is considered a central building block of democratic regimes; second, organizations constituted by voluntary members able to withdraw support and exit at any point—whether political, social, or economic—can be theorized and analysed under the same theoretical framework.

There is something to be gained from studying political and social, as well as partisan and non-partisan, organizations jointly. For one thing, it can help us to address some caveats that contemporary research has unintentionally generated. Research on organizational 'hybridization' shows that an increasing number of organizations mix political and 'non-political' activities without clearly prioritizing one over the other, while non-profit research highlights that many service-orientated CSOs engage in political advocacy.[13] Both observations call for a holistic perspective on membership-based CSOs' contribution to democracy. We also do not know for certain to what extent different funding pressures or professionalization affect parties, interest groups, and non-profits—e.g. their ability to cultivate participation internally and engage in interest representation externally—similarly or not. This question is highly salient in face of ongoing debates around political party decline and 'cartelization'—initially leading to the expectation that parties (becoming more and more detached from citizens) might be replaced by more issue-specific forms of organizing as central venues for citizen engagement. However, many interest groups and non-profits as alternative venues were found to be devoid of much internal democracy, with citizen-run organizations—much like parties—increasingly transforming into staff-dominated organizations competing for state funding. This raises the question of whether what is still often perceived as a crisis of political parties and, relatedly, party democracy should be approached more

---

[12] Although this is the case, by now we find excellent comparative work that integrates party and group research, predominantly but not exclusively directed towards understanding the relationships between different types of organizations such as parties, movements, unions, and interest groups (e.g. Hasenfeld and Gidron 2005; Allern and Bale 2012; Rasmussen and Lindeboom 2013; Renzsch et al. 2015; Otjes and Rasmussen 2017; Farrer 2017; Fraussen and Halpin 2018; Lisi and Oliveira 2020; Muldoon and Rye; Berker and Pollex 2021; Berkhout et al. 2021; Borbáth and Hutter 2021; Martin et al. 2022a; 2022b; Heinze and Weisskircher 2022).

[13] E.g. Minkoff 2002; Billis 2010; Kimberlin 2010.

broadly as a crisis of membership organizations and, with this, of traditional forms of organizing 'democratic voice' in established democracies.[14]

To address these questions, this introduction proposes a multidimensional approach to theorize and empirically study the discrepancies between CSOs' *potential* and *actual* contributions to democracy. To do so, I disentangle three normative yardsticks—participation, representation, and societal responsiveness of organizational behaviour. These yardsticks are not only applicable to party organizations, interest groups, and service-providers alike. They can be translated into concepts measurable on the level of the individual organization, which, in turn, allows us to capture and systematically compare different CSOs' actual contributions to democracy.

Disaggregating the 'Transmission Belt': Three Normative Yardsticks Demarcating CSOs' Potential Contributions to Democracy

Defined as the organizational fabric between government and society, organized civil society encompasses a wide diversity of entities (e.g. Minkoff et al. 2008; Larsson 2011; Lang 2013; Heylen et al. 2020). Putting this diversity centre stage, this study's approach to CSOs' (potential and actual) contributions to democracy rests on two basic observations: first, in order to make participatory contributions to democracy, membership-based CSOs—in terms of their external activities—need neither be politically active nor public good–orientated; second, external contributions to democracy in terms of interest representation activity can be generated by internally 'undemocratic' or 'non-participatory' CSOs. All this has been long stressed by the literature on civic associations and NGOs on the one hand and on interest groups and political parties on the other. But it has—to my knowledge—not yet been translated into a study that takes these insights as one of its starting points. Doing so means that neither a 'political mission', 'public good orientation' nor a 'democratic governance structure' should be used as defining characteristics of CSOs and thus demarcate the conceptual and empirical boundaries of how one might study the diversity of CSOs or, relatedly, their democratic contributions. Instead, we need to focus on membership organizations that, in principle, have the *potential* to make contributions deemed relevant to

---

[14] E.g. Lawson and Merkl 1988; Mair 1994; Katz and Mair 1995; Jordan and Maloney 1997; 2007; Norris 2002; Billis 2010; Halpin 2010; Larsson 2011; Bloodgood and Tremblay-Boire 2017.

democracy, in order to then theorize and examine whether and, if so, why some of them realize such potential, while others do not. To decide which organizations possess such potential, we first need to define which democratic functions or contributions to democracy discussed in the literature are relevant to CSOs as membership organizations *in general* (as opposed to those that are specific to particular types).[15]

The democratic functions or roles ascribed to non-profits, NGOs, interest groups, political parties, and civic associations are manifold. Already the choice of terminology for the organizations studied is linked to specific frames expressing distinct normative concerns. Studying 'NGOs' implies concerns around the pursuit of public interests and governance; 'interest group' around representation and pluralism; and 'civil society organization' around democratic deliberation and participation (Schoenefeld 2021: 593). For political parties alone, Dalton et al. distinguish three *sets* of democratic functions—functions they serve 'within the mass public', 'as organizations', and 'within government' (2011: 6). Functions attributed to parties 'as organizations' concern interest representation and intra-organizational participation. They are directly paralleled in the group and non-profit literature (Knoke 1990: 21; Jordan and Maloney 2007: 2; van Deth and Maloney 2012: 4) and can be considered to be relevant to membership-based CSOs in general.[16] As already indicated, one important concern articulated in various subfields is whether, when, and how parties, interest groups, or civic associations can 'perform' as venues for participation and as vehicles for democratic representation *simultaneously* (van Deth and Maloney 2010: 5; Bernhagen and Maloney 2010: 100–1; Kriesi and Baglioni 2003: 10; Ahlquist and Levi 2014; Bentancur et al. 2019; McAlevey 2016).

Two tensions in particular have been discussed across various subfields, each underpinned by conflicting normative yardsticks considered essential

---

[15] This is a central specification. As illustrated by vast literatures that study parties, interest groups, and service-orientated organizations separately, many questions that relate to the roles or central activities of these organizations are unique to or dominated by organizations with a particular functional orientation. They are better addressed through a more specialized approach than adopted here. This means that functions ascribed to political parties due to their special role as 'governors' (e.g. Gunther and Diamond 2001; Biezen 2004; Kölln 2015) that are not applicable to non-party organizations are not dealt with. The analysis aims at being (relatively) encompassing in terms of the spectrum of social and political membership-based organizations it looks at. It does not, however, consider the full range of possible functions particular types of organizations might fulfil in a democratic setting.

[16] As Berry put it (1969: 196) early on, if party membership can be regarded 'as a form of voluntary association participation', we can apply theories of voluntary associations to party membership, see also Lawson 1980; Binderkrantz 2009; Uhlin 2009; Hwang and Powell 2009; Halpin 2010; Albareda 2018; Webb et al. 2019.

10   Civil Society's Democratic Potential

to CSOs' democratic contributions. The first tension highlights the constraints generated by member control over organizational decision-making (participation) on an organization's leadership, which in effect might weaken CSOs' ability to forcefully engage in interest representation.[17] More recent studies stress a second tension. Organizations might forcefully engage in advocacy or partisan activities in their outside behaviour thanks to their increasing professionalization. These activities, however, might be driven by strategic considerations (electoral success or the maximization of donor support) and be detached from the needs of societal constituencies.[18] If interest representation by CSOs can no longer be assumed to be responsive to the needs and interests of societal constituencies, standards of democratic interest representation are no longer met.[19] This second tension – which Aula and Koskimaa discussing party scholarship recently called "the perils-of-professionalization" narrative (2023: 3) - is crucial for this study in two ways. In a substantive sense it suggests diminished CSO contributions to the democratic process due to weakening CSO–constituency linkages (i.e. declining responsiveness of CSO behaviour), irrespective of CSOs' (possibly more) active involvement in interest representation. In an analytical sense it highlights that developing a framework able to account for CSOs' varying democratic contributions (especially one that is applicable to political and social membership organizations alike), requires breaking down the normative yardstick of *democratic interest representation* into two. We need to distinguish external *engagement in interest representation activities* (through lobbying, protest, etc.) from the *propensity towards societally responsive behaviour* reflecting some sort of CSO–constituency linkage (irrespective of whether such behaviour is politically oriented or not). Building on these initial thoughts, the following sections will discuss intra-organizational participation, interest representation, and societal responsiveness as three separate normative yardsticks to assess membership organizations' contributions to democracy.

---

[17] E.g. Schattschneider 1942; Hirschman 1970; Wilson 1973; Schmitter and Streeck 1999; Barakso and Schaffner 2008).

[18] See, for instance, Katz and Mair 1995; Skocpol 2003; Hwang and Powell 2009; Larsson 2011; van Deth and Maloney 2012; Saurugger 2012; Lang 2013; Alexander and Fernandez 2021., see for critical perspectives on these claims Heylen et al. 2020; Bolleyer and Correa 2022a; Aula and Koskimaa 2023.

[19] There is a debate around the extent to which this does matter from a citizen perspective as the number of CSOs that citizens can choose to join has significantly increased over the last decades. This means that although a growing number of CSOs might not provide an effective voice to members internally, unsatisfied members gained power in expressing their dissatisfaction through exit instead (for a discussion of this line of argument see Barakso and Schaffner 2008).

Membership Organizations as Venues for Participation

Though research has shown that the roles members play in membership organizations such as parties, interest groups, or associations differ widely[20], organizations composed of members by definition have the *potential* to have an active membership.[21] Hence, CSOs, including interest groups, parties, non-profits, and associations, have been long considered as possible *venues for participation*. One reason for this role to be considered immediately beneficial to the democratic process is linked to its implications for social integration. Knoke has defined social integration as non-authoritarian integration of society empowering individuals as collectives and providing a bulwark against centralization and bureaucratization of state administrations and the tyranny of the majority (1990: 218; see, for a similar rationale, Jordan and Maloney 2007). Importantly, for these processes to be generated does not require groups to be predominantly politically orientated or partisan in their *external* activities (though they can be). Instead, groups need to be 'substantially self-governing'. This means intra-organizational practices need to emulate democratic procedures (Knoke 1990: 10–12) rather than members just joining a CSOs' social activities, doing work for the organization. This form of participation in membership organizations—*member control over decision-making*—can be (irrespective of an organization's political or social mission) considered beneficial for democracy, as involving members in 'democratic' procedures helps to enhance members' capacity for self-governance and collective action, while fostering their political skills (Dekker 2009: 228; Skocpol et al. 1999).[22] Furthermore, if intra-organizational decision-making is controlled by members—whether a CSO engages in electioneering, interest representation activities, or service provision—we can assume organizational

---

[20] E.g. Jordan and Maloney 1997; Skocpol 2003; Evers 2014; Scarrow 2015; Gauja 2015; Schlozman et al. 2015; Heylen et al. 2020.

[21] There is a debate around whether already passive membership (as compared to non-membership) is democratically beneficial in terms of individual-level perceptions and behaviour (for an overview see Aggeborn et al. 2021). Taking an organization-centred perspective on different types of membership-based CSOs, I focus on the implications for democracy of different forms of active membership.

[22] An insightful literature concerned with the implications of democratic as compared to more hierarchical governance structures on social capital is the one on cooperatives—member-owned business organizations characterized by democratic and inclusive governance structures. While cooperatives—due to their for profit character—do not qualify as CSOs as defined here, studies that assess how the changes from capitalist firm to cooperative enhance levels of cooperation, trust, and participation (Saz-Gil et al. 2021: 7) are insightful. This is because they avoid the problem of self-selection of citizens into associations that makes the effect of associational membership on social capital and political participation in cross-sectional studies difficult to assess (see below). That said, to date the knowledge about how and when social capital generated within cooperatives spills over to the societal level has remained limited (Saz-Gil et al. 2021: 12).

behaviour to be broadly in line with member interests (or with those constituencies' interests members care about, which, in public interest groups, may not necessarily be their own). Assuming such correspondence, member control establishes a direct linkage between the organization and its societal base.[23]

Although intra-organization democracy—giving members direct control over central domains (e.g. the selection of CSO personnel, the formulation or alteration of central rules) as a specific form of member participation in organizational life—is widely considered beneficial from a normative perspective, its desirability in practice is still controversial. Prominent voices in party research consider intra-party democracy (IPD) as unnecessary for democracy on the state level or even detrimental to inter-party competition at the heart of the latter. Intra-organizational participation in the form of member control over decisions is thus contested as a yardstick for CSOs' democratic contribution to the extent that it might hinder or even undermine important external political activities a CSO might engage in, including those related to representation. Sartori has prominently argued that '[d]emocracy on a large scale is not the sum of many little democracies' (1965: 124; see also Schattschneider 1942: 60). What really matters, so the argument goes, is meaningful *inter*-party competition, with parties' internal lives being of little relevance as long as parties provide clear-cut choices to voters.[24] To the extent that IPD—by enhancing intra-organizational pluralism—makes it *more difficult* for parties to represent the interests of their core electorate in a coherent and unified way, the party as an organization might gain legitimacy, while weakening its position in inter-party competition. Such scepticism is further underlined by the fact that intra-party decisions by members do not necessarily cater to the interests of voters a party aims at representing (e.g. Rahat et al. 2008; Cross and Katz 2013), an issue that equally applies to public interest groups (e.g. Halpin 2006). Finally, some party organizations using IPD extensively have found it difficult to function—both inside and outside of public institutions. They suffered from intense internal conflict, especially when wide-ranging member rights were granted, while asking for little or no organizational commitment from incoming members (e.g. Bolleyer 2013a; Bolleyer et al. 2015).

---

[23] Jordan and Maloney 2007: 6; Albareda 2018: 1217; Dalton et al. 2011; Webb at al 2019; Alexander and Fernandez 2021.

[24] Echoing this scepticism, leading group scholars have argued that intra-organizational democracy is not necessarily a sensible standard to apply if CSOs represent wider societal rather than member interests (e.g. Halpin 2006).

This debate is important. It shows that internal participation is neither welcomed *by all*, or *in all its forms*, nor is it considered problematic or undesirable *in itself*. It is problematized in light of various *intra-organizational or external costs* that participation might generate, which brings us back to prominent arguments by group researchers pointing to CSOs' difficulties in reconciling participatory and representative roles discussed earlier (e.g. Schmitter and *Streeck* 1999; Skocpol 2013; Jordan and Maloney 2007). Intra-organizational participation in terms of member control over decision-making can generate *trade-offs* with other organizational activities or goals considered equally or more important by the CSO itself or by some of its audiences. Consequently, in some organizations the costs of intra-organizational democracy might outweigh its benefits, and they might not cultivate such processes as a consequence.

Nevertheless, there is little disagreement that internal participation—if 'affordable'—has *some* internal and external benefits. For instance, depending on the culture or ideology of an organization, it can strengthen members' commitment and loyalty and enhance the CSO's internal legitimacy, hence benefiting its functioning. This leaves aside that, everything else being equal, a participatory organizational culture is widely considered more *normatively* desirable than the cultivation of and socialization of members into authoritarian decision-making, which is why such practices help to enhance a CSO's external legitimacy.[25]

Of course member control is not the only form of member activism. There are others that are compatible with a much wider range of governance structures including hierarchical and leader-centred models. Members can participate in solidarity activities offered by the organization, such as meetings or events, in order to simply enjoy group life with others. They can engage in organizational work such as supporting fundraising activities, participating in member recruitment, or mobilizing support for petitions, whether organizational leaders are held accountable by members or not. Also, 'mere' member involvement (akin to volunteering in non-profit research[26]) has been associated with a range of social benefits. These include the cultivation of well-being and life-satisfaction through social interaction,

---

[25] E.g. Bosso 2003; Kittilson and Scarrow 2003; Barakso and Schaffner 2008; Allern 2010; Grömping and Halpin 2019).

[26] Unsurprisingly, the non-profit, group and party literatures use different labels when referring to similar categories of actors. Party researchers refer to 'activists' rather than 'volunteers' or 'volunteer staff' when unpaid organizational members take on organizational roles or posts, i.e. are *not* merely fee-paying members. This is presumably because *party* activities are, by default, considered politically motivated, which is not the case for volunteering (whose political or apolitical character is debated controversially). Yet leaving aside election-related activities such as running for office, there is wide overlap in the tasks that

14 Civil Society's Democratic Potential

the enhancement of human capital, the prevention of social atomization, trust, the mobilization and detection of unmet social needs, and collective efforts to meet such needs (Hustinx et al. 2010: 417–18, 422; Geys 2012). While arguments have been made that some of these beneficial effects are more pronounced when members have an influence on the goals of the organization and the nature of its activities (Barasko and Schaffner 2008: 188–9), the cultivation of involvement activities (without granting members a say in decision-making) still has positive repercussions for democracies' societal fabric.

Whether or not such involvement activities—especially when taking place in organizations that do not engage in political activities—create 'politically relevant' social capital in line with Putnam's influential work (2000) has—for some time—been subject to debate, a debate that cannot be resolved here.[27] What is fair to say is that the effects of associational engagement found in empirical studies were diverse. Consequently, socialization effects of associational engagement that positively feed into participants' identification with democratic values and, in turn, directly or indirectly enhance involvement in the democratic process on the state level, are difficult to take as a given (e.g. Stolle and Rochon 1998; Welzel et al. 2005; Walker 2008; Tschirhart and Gazley 2014). One central account in the literature on the 'democratizing effects' of associational membership links the positive relationship between associational membership and social capital to socialization effects. The other stresses processes of self-selection, with associational membership *and* participatory behaviour being driven by the same individual orientations and characteristics (e.g. political interest, resources, enjoyment of discussions, trust in others) rather than those orientations and characteristics that are cultivated by individuals' associational membership (Hooghe 2008: 587–8).

In methodological terms, scholarship on the theme has increasingly stressed the difficulty of 'isolating' the actual effects of such membership on political participation, given that those more politically active citizens might be more likely to join (hence self-select into) particular types of CSOs in the first place (e.g. Bekkers 2012; Paxton and Ressler 2018). Recent studies based on panel data suggest socialization effects are overstated. Positive correlations between associational membership and political participation appear to be driven by membership in organizations close to the political sphere where the highest degree of self-selection is expected, as significant effects

---

unpaid members contribute in different types of membership organizations (e.g. related to administration, fundraising, or campaigning). This is why I will use the broader term 'volunteer staff' to denote the group of CSO members actively involved in the running of their organization.

[27] See, for a recent overview, Aggeborn et al. 2021.

of membership on participation are found only in those groups (Aggeborn et al. 2021). Focusing on whether and how associational engagement fosters policy representation (i.e. the correspondence between public opinion and policy in a range of issue areas), Rasmussen and Reher found significant positive effects stressing the democratic relevance of associational engagement. However, their study focused on political CSOs (whose goals and purposes are related to a policy issue) to start with. Also, they did not find a positive effect of overall engagement on the link between public opinion and policy. Rather, it was the strength of issue-specific associations that mattered to the responsiveness of public opinion to group preferences (2019: 1666–7). Clearly, any arguments that *any* affiliation or engagement in *any* type of association is likely to have direct positive repercussions for democracy are difficult to sustain.[28]

This brings us back to more modest claims, namely that member involvement—requiring members to be active—is (at least) indirectly beneficial to democracy by strengthening the social fabric underpinning a democratic regime through individual and social benefits mentioned earlier. This is important even if direct spillovers into the political domain are absent, or beneficial effects are predominantly of a reinforcing nature, presupposing that members already bring certain dispositions with them. For instance, the enhancement of human capital through the learning of valuable skills in an organizational setting can help to qualify organizational leaders for political positions, should they decide to pursue them. Similarly, associational engagement enhancing trust in others, in turn, can have a positive knock-on effect on people's interactions with representative institutions, if they decide to engage politically. Finally, social welfare organizations—by providing services to members or societal constituencies—help reduce demands on the state, which otherwise might have been asked to provide those services (Knoke 1990: 218; Diamond 1994: 10–11; Barakso and Schaffner 2008; Saz-Gil et al. 2021).

While those implications for democratic regimes are less immediate than the implications commonly attributed to member control, they highlight that a study interested in CSOs' participatory contributions should not be restricted to organizations that emulate democratic governance structures. Even if member involvement had none of the individual or social benefits discussed above and only contributed to CSO self-maintenance, it still remains relevant to democracy, conditional on the goals and activities of the

---

[28] Instead, studies stress these effects' context-dependent nature. See, for instance, Hooghe 2003; Quintelier 2008; and Wollebæk and Selle 2010.

16 Civil Society's Democratic Potential

organizations in which it is cultivated. If member involvement solely helps a CSO to maintain its core activities in a purely functional sense, this by default becomes directly relevant to the democratic process if the organization in which such participation takes place (also) pursues external political goals.[29] Hence, to fully grasp the range of democratic contributions of member activism, we need to consider more than the nature of such activism itself. We also need to take into account whether a CSO that cultivates (whatever form of) member activism is politically engaged or not. This brings us to the second, widely used yardstick for CSOs' democratic contribution: their engagement in interest representation.

Membership Organizations as Vehicles of Representation

Interest representation can be defined—drawing on Salisbury's seminal work (1984: 64–5)—as organization-level activity that involves the articulation of 'politically relevant' interests, i.e. interests that are created in response to perceived or anticipated effects of government action or inaction.[30] Research has long stressed the complementary roles that parties, groups, and non-profits play in the aggregation and channelling of societal interests into the political and public sphere generally and the democratic process more specifically. Especially with regard to parties and interest groups, there is general agreement that both types of organizations are central vehicles for interest representation in a democracy.[31] This is the case whether the preferences they aggregate are highly particularistic or represent fundamental interests of the wider public, whether they are directed towards shaping government policy or criticizing its actions, and whether their activities predominantly take place inside or outside political institutions.[32] What receives less attention outside the respective specialist literatures is that service-oriented CSOs

---

[29] That a political orientation can be taken as a given in political parties might be one reason why party researchers studying the drivers of member activism (e.g. Whiteley and Seyd 1998; Pedersen et al. 2004; van Haute and Gauja 2015)—as compared to scholars of intra-party democracy and scholars studying interest groups and non-profit organizations—usually do not tend to distinguish members' 'support roles' from their 'political activities'.

[30] This is a minimalist definition in that it does not require an active bottom-up aggregation process of societal interests or that the constituencies represented actively control representatives.

[31] E.g. Diamond 1994: 7–8; Saurugger 2012: 74; Olson 1965; Wilson 1973; Panebianco 1988; Gray and Lowery 1996; Jankowski 1998; Burstein and Linton 2002; Jordan and Maloney 2007; Beyers et al. 2008; Salamon and Lessans-Geller 2008; Saurugger 2008; Maloney 2009; Heaney 2010; Bawn et al. 2012; Allern and Bale 2012; Schlozman et al. 2015.

[32] For opposition parties, the representation of supporters' interests usually involves criticizing the government and thereby holding it to account, corresponding to the watchdog function assigned to CSOs. Such activities, however, presuppose that organizations are politically active in the first place, which is why this function is not treated as a primary dimension of the analysis.

are also often politically active. Though advocacy remains a secondary mission, these organizations often contribute to interest representation, which is all the more important in terms of 'democratic voice', as they often serve the needs of marginalized groups.[33] Consequently, engagement in interest representation can serve as a yardstick for CSOs' contributions to democracy that is applicable to CSOs with partisan, political, and social missions alike.

Of course, political parties—thanks to their unique role in public institutions, notably parliament and government—are more often than not treated as more than 'mere associations' (Bonotti 2011: 20). This rationalizes—regarding many themes and questions—their separate study. Nevertheless, they are, like other CSOs, 'channels of expression [...] for representing the people by expressing their demands' (Sartori 1976: 27).[34] Similarly, Berkhout stresses that the empirical boundaries between interest organizations and political parties as organizational types are blurred (2010: 20):

> The exclusion of political parties seems straightforward. It is, however, not fully consistent with a functional, behavioral definition of interest organizations. Political parties also engage in lobbying, demonstrations, or public consultations: we find quite some representatives of national parties in the EP lobby register, for example. Further, interest organizations may be deeply involved in elections as well, especially in referenda where an interest group acts like a party, seeking votes for one specific side of an issue.

To consider both types of organization is especially appropriate when moving away from the major parties constituting parliamentary party systems that have a realistic chance of entering government (which form only a small subset of electorally active parties). The majority of party organizations, in contrast, 'endeavour to influence the political agenda without pursuing actual control of the government apparatus' (Bonotti 2011: 19). Considering the universe of electorally active party organizations, only a few enjoy institutional access that is per se unavailable to groups. Vice versa,

---

[33] E.g. Minkoff 2002; Chaves et al. 2004; Guo and Musso 2007; Billis 2010; Kimberlin 2010; Alexander and Fernandez 2021).

[34] Traditionally, parties are considered as mobilizers of majorities, while interest groups merely mobilize minorities (Schattschneider 1942: 193). However, with the advent of Kirchheimer's catch-all party (Krouwel 2003) and Panebianco's electoral-professional party (1988) this integrative capacity through the representation of 'general requests for defense/transformation of the social and political order' (alongside specific group and sectoral interests) is considered in decline, if not lost, with parties becoming direct competitors to interest groups in the transmission of political specific requests (Panebianco 1988: 268–9). A similar line of argument can be linked to the increasing fragmentation of party systems (making outright majorities unlikely) that incentivizes the representation of (more) particularistic interests by parties (Bolleyer and Ruth 2018). Both lines of argument suggest that interest representation by parties and interest groups are not *as such* qualitatively different.

18 Civil Society's Democratic Potential

in corporatist systems, employer organizations and unions can enjoy privileged access neither the broader group sector nor minor parties enjoy (e.g. Schmitter and Streeck 1999). Echoing this, a range of theoretical and empirical works on voluntary organizations have considered parties as part of civil society or the broader group sector, or considered them as 'social change organizations' alongside unions and social movement organizations (e.g. Berry 1969; Kleidman 1994; Baer 2007; Jordan and Maloney 2007; Rosenblum 2000a; 2000b; but see Cohen and Arato 1992). They again underline that parties, interest groups, and service providers can be assessed by applying the same normative yardsticks and using the same analytical tools.

The Ambiguity of Interest Representation Behaviour: Expression of Assumed, Consultative or Surrogate Representation?

Having introduced the two prominent yardsticks, participation and representation, it has gradually become clear that their implications for democracy also depend on their interplay. Table 1.1 therefore specifies the democratic contributions associated with CSOs that represent different configurations of interest representation and participation. The horizontal 'participation axis' is defined by the distinction between passive and active members[35]—with the latter category being divided into member involvement and member control. The vertical 'interest representation axis' is defined by the presence of organizations' external engagement in political activity versus its absence. The latter distinction intuitively aligns with the distinction between social and political groups (e.g. Van der Meer and van Ingen 2009; Alexander et al. 2012). However, as stressed earlier, many predominantly social or service-oriented organizations regularly engage in political activities such as lobbying, campaigning, or public education work. Hence, despite their primary goal, they qualify as politically engaged.

Before going through the implications of each configuration, one central assumption underpinning the following framework (and thus the whole study) needs to be emphasized. CSOs categorized and conceptualized in Table 1.1 are assumed not to be anti-democratic or extremist (e.g. assumed not to cultivate intra-group solidarity directed towards undermining the democratic regime, the state, or to repress other groups in society).

---

[35] Both in group and party research, passive membership—unlike active membership—is (usually) restricted to the regular payment of fees—the formal act distinguishing members from followers (Duverger 1964: 90–116; Jordan and Maloney 1997: 187; 2007: 156 and 2007: 33; van Haute and Gauja 2015: 1).

Table 1.1 CSO Configurations of Participation and Interest Representation and Their (Likely) Democratic Contributions

Interest Representation	Intra-Organizational Participation		
	No	Yes	
		Member Involvement	Member Control[a]
No Political Engagement	**Functional Relief Scenario**	**Internal Responsiveness Scenario**	**Democratic Emulation Scenario**
	Organizational activities addressing societal needs, reducing demands on the political system[b]	Organizational activities generating social contributions[c]	Organizational activities generating social contributions and contributing to social integration
	Indirect contributions to democracy	Indirect contributions to democracy	Indirect and direct contributions to democracy
Political Engagement	**Surrogate or Assumed Representation**	**Consultative or Assumed Representation**	**Transmission Belt Scenario**
	Organizational activities feeding into democratic process	Organizational activities generating social contributions and feeding into democratic process	Organizational activities generating social contributions, contributing to social integration & feeding into democratic process
	Direct contributions to democracy → ambiguous	Indirect contributions; direct contributions to democracy → ambiguous	Indirect and direct contributions to democracy

Notes: [a] Member control can be considered a subtype of involvement, suggesting that the benefits associated with the latter are also granted by the former (thus member control is—by default—associated with the generation of social benefits as well). Yet, as the purpose of the table is to identify the distinct implications of each form of activism, they are displayed separately.
[b] An example would be an organization operating food banks (if not democratically run by members).
[c] An example would be the provision of support to members through an inwards-orientated self-help group (if not democratically run by members).

To indicate this caveat, the heading of the table refers to 'likely' democratic contributions. From an empirical viewpoint, it is clear that CSOs are neither necessarily 'civil' (Ahrne 1996: 112) nor inherently democratic (McLaverty 2002: 310).[36] From a normative viewpoint, the possibility to organize around and collectively voice positions hostile to democracy and its core values might be considered as an important expression of a pluralist and tolerant

---

[36] See, for an overview of the possible positive and negative effects of voluntary associations, Driskell and Wise 2017.

20 Civil Society's Democratic Potential

political system. Yet the concrete effects of such CSOs on democracy are not necessarily benign, as highlighted by literatures around 'bad' or 'uncivil' society, democratic self-defence and militant democracy, as well as anti-establishment and extremist groups and parties.[37]

Being focused on established democracies, this study makes the assumption that, numerically speaking, most organizations in such regimes are *not* hostile to the system they operate in or the values constitutive to it. Applied to such regimes, a scheme that expects the cultivation of participation or interest representation activities by CSOs to—*ceteris paribus*—generate *positive* contributions to democracy rather than damaging ones can help advance our understanding of the roles played by the vast variety of CSOs that (want to) form legitimate parts of democratic governance and the society underpinning it (Schoenefeld 2021: 586).

Moving to the implications of the six CSO configurations displayed in Table 1.1 in terms of the democratic contributions they suggest, four of them are given clear labels (e.g. *'Transmission Belt Scenario'*). This is done when—based on the information provided by the defining axes (intensity/type of member activism; political engagement)—the (likely) democratic contributions of CSOs falling into that category can (relatively) unambiguously be specified. In these instances, the respective configurations of participation and representation have clear-cut implications for the likely responsiveness of CSO activities as well. This is not generally the case, as the remaining, ambiguous categories show. They highlight why it is necessary to add societal responsiveness as a separate yardstick.

Starting with the lower/right-hand corner, the beneficial interplay of CSOs' participation and representation activities is most explicit and pronounced in the '*Transmission Belt Scenario*'. Groups and parties in this category provide a 'participation linkage' expected to channel societal interests into the political process (Jordan and Maloney 2007: 6; Albareda 2018: 1217; see also Lawson 1980; Dalton et al. 2011; Webb at al 2019; Christenson et al. 2021).[38] Members in such CSOs have decision-making authority (member control), ensuring that their interests and concerns directly feed into organizational behaviour. The intra-organizational aggregation of member interests and the latter's transferral into the political process are considered as two central ingredients for CSOs to fulfil their intermediary function. Their

---

[37] E.g. Kopecky and Mudde 2003; Warren 2008; Bob 2011; Casal Bértoa and Rama 2021; Malkopoulou and Kirshner 2021.

[38] The provision of linkage has long been considered fundamental to parties' democratic contribution (Lawson 1980; Lawson and Merkl 1988; Poguntke 2002). Though it has been increasingly questioned whether parties can fulfil this role, recent research indicates they still do (Webb et al. 2019).

interplay ensures the responsiveness of a CSO's political engagement, one crucial indication of CSOs' direct contribution to the democratic process (Albareda 2018: 1216). Echoing these arguments prominent in the group literature, the inclusion of citizens into party organizations is considered crucial to enable the former to 'participate effectively in the political process' (Gunther and Diamond 2001: 8). Party and group leaders, in turn, benefit by enhancing their organization's broader legitimacy, being able to claim societal representativeness of its positions and activities (e.g. Jordan and Maloney 2007; Scarrow 2015; Albareda 2018; Grömping and Halpin 2019). These direct political benefits are complemented by social benefits associated with member activism per se (e.g. the cultivation of well-being through social interaction, the enhancement of human capital, the prevention of social atomization, etc., see Hustinx et al. 2010: 417–18; 422).

In CSOs falling under the '*Internal Responsiveness Scenario*', members are actively involved by contributing to organizational activities, yet do not exercise decision-making control as in the 'Transmission Belt Scenario'. These organizations are not politically active, and do not transition CSO interests from the private to the public sphere (Kriesi 1996: 157). Still, organizational activities in these inwards-orientated CSOs are likely to be responsive—at least to some extent—to the interests and concerns of members to maintain the latter's contributions to organizational life. CSOs in this category are expected to generate indirect democratic benefits (e.g. through the enhancement of human capital, the prevention of social atomization) as well.

The '*Democratic Emulation Scenario*' (upper/right-hand corner) contains 'social' or 'service-orientated' membership organizations that are not engaged in interest representation activities. Nevertheless, they are expected to have direct democratic benefits (beyond the indirect ones attributed to member activism generally) by enhancing members' ability to participate in the public sphere as their internal CSO structures emulate the democratic process. This, in turn, is expected to ensure a basic correspondence between member preferences and organizational activities (Knoke 1990: 218; Dekker 2009: 228).

On the upper/left-hand side, the '*Functional Relief Scenario*' covers CSOs defined by a passive membership without external political engagement. These organizations might provide valuable services to members or to societal constituencies, which—as mentioned earlier—can relieve the state by reducing demands on the latter (Diamond 1994: 10–11). Relatedly, they might strengthen marginalized groups by providing support those would not receive otherwise. Analytically, this category is different from the first three in that it is difficult to reason in the abstract whether or not the 'relief' provided by CSOs in this category is likely to be an 'authentic' expression of societal needs (Guo and Musso 2007: 310). Given a passive membership, leaders might tailor and also alter organizational activities instrumentally towards sustaining their CSO's survival (Maloney 2012: 108–12). This might be driven by who is willing to pay for what type of service (e.g. reflecting the extent of service-provision-related funding schemes by governments or foundations that CSOs could tap into), not by who needs a service most. This ambiguity made the label 'functional relief' seem more suitable than 'societal relief', as the latter suggests responsiveness, at least implicitly. One might of course argue that even the maintenance of a passive membership requires that the CSO leadership presents its cause as a worthwhile one to prevent exit (e.g. Wilson 1973). Whether the absence of exit in such a scenario might qualify as meaningful consent to leaders' actions can be debated (Binderkrantz 2009: 660). The formal 'exit threat' of a passive membership might simply require leaders to 'tread carefully' (Maloney 2015: 110). It is probably fair to say that the incentives for CSO leaders are limited to staying committed to a specific cause rather than strategically reorientating the organization to another one as public or government priorities change. This is also the case as the provision of services or goods by such CSOs might not even concern its (anyhow passive) members directly, if there is only limited overlap between those members and the CSOs' beneficiaries (e.g. Halpin 2006).

Taking a broader perspective, it seems of limited importance for this category's relative placement in terms of CSOs' likely contributions to democracy whether societal responsiveness or leaders' strategic manoeuvring drives the nature of organizational activities. Compared to the other configurations in Table 1.1, CSOs falling into this category are likely to contribute least either way. By definition, they score low on participation and representation. Nor are they likely to score highly for responsiveness. Adding to this, functional relief (freeing the state from societal demands) is 'neutral' to the extent that it can support the stability of *any* regime, not only democratic ones.

While we faced a certain ambiguity with regard to the societal responsiveness of CSO behaviour under the 'Functional Relief Scenario', the same problem emerges in a much more consequential fashion when moving to the last two categories. CSOs in the categories *Surrogate or Assumed Representation* and *Consultative or Assumed Representation* (lower/left-hand and lower/middle quadrants) engage in interest representation activities but without emulating democratic processes internally. Meanwhile, they differ in terms of member involvement. These two configurations are not given clear-cut labels, and their direct contributions to democracy are highlighted as 'ambiguous' as it remains unclear whether CSOs falling under these headings contribute to *democratic* representation, i.e. whether or not interest representation activities are underpinned by any meaningful CSO–constituency linkages.

Following Pitkin, representation is 'acting in the interest of the represented, in a manner responsive to them' (1967: 209). Echoing this, democratic interest representation is commonly understood as 'the product of a constituent-leader relationship' that is based on shared preferences between constituents and leaders (Franke and Dobson 1985: 225). Such a relationship finds expression in an 'authentic' articulation of the concerns of a societal constituency (Guo and Musso 2007: 310). It expresses bonds uniting groups (Höijer 2011: 3) whose interests an organization remains committed to even in periods during which the latter's demands are unpopular or not salient.[39] Once organizations engage in political interest representation activities, we know they make public claims to speak on behalf of the interests of others (Halpin 2006: 923; Guo and Musso 2007: 310). But how 'responsive' they are to societal needs or demands of those 'others' when doing so cannot be judged based on whether or not their 'action repertoire' contains external political activities alone (Maloney 2015: 107–8; Zamponi and Bosi 2018).

Both '*Consultative Representation*' and '*Surrogate Representation*' are considered to meet basic standards of societal responsiveness associated with *democratic* representation and thus to transcend the mere articulation of 'politically relevant' interests (Salisbury 1984: 64–5). '*Assumed Representation*', in contrast, denotes that organizations make unilateral claims to represent a certain group or constituency without the existence of stable linkages mediating between the two. Various concepts used in academic work align with this understanding. They include astroturf representation or astroturf lobbying, 'not built on direct personal encounter or on direct mandating' (Kohler-Koch 2010: 111) but simulating (i.e. only pretending to be based on) grassroots support for or against certain policies (Lits 2020: 164). Similarly, astroturf participation is generated by campaign organizations run by consultancy firms formed to create the appearance of an engaged citizenry (Maloney 2015: 107–8). In these scenarios, the observed political behaviour is instrumentally driven and strategically directed towards maximizing an

---

[39] This non-coercive notion of representation used as conceptual underpinning here contrasts with a coercive notion in which the represented put direct pressure on leaders to get their interests represented by the latter (Franke and Dobson 1985: 225) or requires the represented to have mechanisms of control over the representative (Andeweg and Thomassen 2005: 510–12), essentially requiring member control. Using such notions would be too specific and demanding in face of the multitude of CSO–constituency linkages cultivated by the diversity of CSOs covered by this study.

24 Civil Society's Democratic Potential

organization's chances of survival by the unilateral and detached alteration of target constituencies (Houtzager and Gurza Lavalle 2009: 7).[40] CSOs are charged with 'creating' constituencies and 'manufacturing grievances' rather than authentically representing them (Lang 2013: 95; Holland 2004: 119; Zald and McCarthy 1987). If so, responsiveness of the representative to the represented, central to Pitkin's definition (1967), is unlikely to be present.

Analytically speaking, the two ambiguous categories '*Surrogate or Assumed Representation*' and '*Consultative or Assumed Representation*' in Table 1.1 further highlight that the mere absence of a participatory linkage through member control (that defines the 'Transmission Belt Scenario') does not necessarily indicate either the unilateral behaviour of organizational leaders or the absence of a constituency linkage. To equate the absence of democratic governance structures within CSOs with 'Assumed Representation' is as problematic as equating the mere presence of interest representation activities with CSOs' responsiveness to societal constituencies. In other words, the exercise of member control is not the only mechanism to ensure the societal responsiveness of organizational activity. If there is substantial agreement between organizational leaders and members on organizational policies, the interests an organization pursues qualify as 'representative', even when intra-organizational life is procedurally 'undemocratic' (Wilson 1973: 237–8).

Hence, a meaningful CSO–constituency linkage can be given, although a participatory linkage central to the classical '*Transmission Belt Scenario*' is not. Such linkage might be ensured through consultative mechanisms directed at members or supporters.[41] These mechanisms presuppose that those consulted are, on some level, involved in the organization (i.e. at least are willing to give feedback) and not completely passive. Tools to underpin '*Consultative Representation*' are (depending on the organization's target constituency) member or supporter surveys or focus groups involving organizational affiliates that organizations conduct to find out what their constituencies want. As Wilson put it, considering the voluntary nature of

---

[40] Interestingly, Houtzager and Gurza Lavalle themselves 'assume' that political parties or labour unions as central political vehicles in representative democracy *by definition* fulfil an intermediate function, and associate the possibility of 'assumed representation' only with other organizations forming part of civil society (2009: 7).

[41] Albareda argues that members are the 'inner core' of an organization's constituency, irrespective of whether organizations are public- or member-serving (2018: 1218). However, a focus on the interests of supporters rather than members seems more appropriate when organizational members are not representative of organizational constituencies, hence, organizational leaders cannot 'access' the interest of the latter through consulting members (Halpin 2006: 925). A similar argument can be made with regard to political parties which for the same reason might survey voters rather than their own members.

CSOs' support base: 'The formal apparatus of democracy [...] may or may not be present, but the consultative process, one would think, almost surely would be' (1973: 250).

But what about politically active organizations, whose members are passive? The last category *'Surrogate or Assumed Representation'* (lower/left-hand quadrant) suggests that even when constituencies *do not* or even *cannot* speak for themselves (making direct consultation impracticable or even impossible) interest representation activity can be societally responsive. This is the case when groups engage in *'Surrogate Representation'.*[42] CSOs can make public claims on behalf of those who cannot represent themselves,[43] a compensatory form of representation of those who otherwise would remain unheard (Strolovitch and Forrest 2010: 477–8; Maloney 2015: 111).[44] But if constituencies are silent (Imig 1996: 45), what does it mean for organizations to define the contents of interest representation activities in a 'responsive' way? As put by Imig, analysing the US children's lobby: 'Public opinion provides the operating space available to children's advocates by offering a de facto (however vague) definition of children's concerns and suggesting directions for intervention' (1996: 41).[45] Now as '[o]rganizational needs must be addressed for groups to provide political voice', such organizations will inevitably focus on particularly salient issues concerning their core constituency to gain attention and tap into available funding (Imig 1996: 32; 45). At the same time, an organization committed to a cause is unlikely to strategically redirect attention to another constituency or completely redefine the latter's supposed interest (Halpin 2014: 46) if public attention to or interest in the latter declines. Such tendencies would point towards a form of assumed representation instead. For sure, the distinction between *'Surrogate Representation'* and *'Assumed Representation'* is empirically blurred. It is still important to recognize that even CSO leaders without an active or direct relationship with their constituency do *not necessarily* act in an unresponsive fashion and can contribute to the representation of actual societal needs (Mansbridge 2003: 522–3; Imig 1996).

---

[42] According to Mansbridge, surrogate representation, a concept applicable to political parties and other political organizations, can be understood as a mode of representation by a representative with whom one has no relationship (2003: 522).

[43] Such organizations can still have members and organizational affiliates concerned about the CSO's central issues (hence be membership-based CSOs), but it is not their affiliates' interests which the organization aims at representing.

[44] To describe this process, Imig used the notion of 'representation by proxy' (1996).

[45] In group research, Imig has proposed a similar notion of 'representation by proxy' developed in a study on the US children's lobby (1996).

Adding Societal Responsiveness of CSO Behaviour as Third Normative Yardstick

The above discussion highlights that the observation that CSOs' 'action repertoires' contain political activities (i.e. interest representation behaviour) is no clear indication of processes of *democratic* representation, which presuppose societal responsiveness in terms of acting on behalf of others (Maloney 2015: 107–8; Zamponi and Bosi 2018). The *Transmission Belt Scenario* seems to suggest a straightforward link between member control and CSOs' interest representation activities responsive to members. But even this scenario rests on certain assumptions, notably, that at least some members care about the political stances of the CSO. As Franke and Dobson point out, the policy positions advanced by interest groups will only reflect the wishes of those whose membership is contingent upon policy matters. By implication, those joining for other reasons—i.e. economic or social—will not be well represented (1985: 224). This assumption is unproblematic for parties, as at least some members will care about politics. It can be problematic for politically active groups, though. A sports organization might regularly engage in lobbying to maintain public funding for its activities and also select major posts by member ballot. If so, it behaviourally and structurally falls into the 'Transmission Belt Scenario'. Nevertheless, as members tend to join the organization to participate in sporting activities (i.e. to access solidary activities), the organization's lobbying activities are unlikely to be driven by member preferences. Aspirations by the leadership to sustain organizational finances and thus to ensure CSO maintenance are more likely candidates. One can argue that this matters little normatively as members do not care about their CSO's political activities anyhow. The example still underlines that the sole consideration of the nature of intra-organizational participation and whether or not organizations are politically engaged as a means to identify CSOs' democratic contributions appears as too narrow. Doing so would solely focus on the 'whether' and 'how' of interest representation and not its contents (Saurugger 2012: 69).

In essence, the proposed framework needs expansion by a third normative yardstick—the societal responsiveness of organizational behaviour—that needs examination *alongside* participation and representation. This third yardstick is broader and more broadly applicable than the notion of congruence. It essentially captures the match between what organizations stand for substantively or programmatically and what members, supporters, or voters want, i.e. the positional correspondence between represented and representative (Dalton et al. 2011: Chapter 7; Thomassen and van Ham 2014; Rasmussen and Reher 2019).[46] Leaving aside that it is often difficult to establish what the actual 'constituency position' is, data is not available to measure the programmatic congruence between CSO missions and programmes on the one hand and the actual preferences of their members and constituencies across populations of groups and parties in different countries on the other.

That said, a broader notion of CSOs' varying organizational propensities to make societally responsive decisions (reflecting some CSO–constituency linkage) has its own advantages in light of the empirical scope of this study. Notions of congruence used in party and group research defined as 'positional correspondence' are tailored to assessing the behaviour of political and partisan organizations. To these organizations, programmatic position-taking and competition in the political and public sphere are central. The yardstick of 'positional correspondence' does not straightforwardly travel to service-oriented organizations. In contrast, whether CSOs try to act on behalf of some societal constituencies (displaying some commitment to the latter) or not is equally informative regarding organizations not engaged in interest representation that predominantly pursue a service-oriented mission and address societal needs (upper part of Table 1.1). Only a brief look into voluntary sector and non-profit research illustrates this. In this literature, societal detachment, mission drift, and the unresponsiveness of organizations to their members', constituencies' or beneficiaries' concerns have long been problematized.[47]

From Normative Yardstick to Comparative Analysis

Having identified three complementary but distinct normative yardsticks through which membership-based CSOs' diverse democratic contributions can be approached, we need to translate them into analytical dimensions suitable for comparative analysis. This section breaks them down to four analytical dimensions that can be theorized and measured on the level of the

---

[46] The notion of congruence is also used in non-profit research but tends to focus on the correspondence between organizational values and values held by employees, i.e. on 'individual-organizational value congruence' understood as the fit between individual and organizational value systems (Peng et al. 2015: 585; see for a literature review Bandara et al. 2021). Another strand in the literature looks at congruence, e.g. in terms of political orientation or moral values, between organizations and their donors (e.g. Lee et al. 2020).

[47] E.g. Warner and Havens 1968; Grønbjerg 1993; Salamon 1995; 1997; Weisbrod 1997; Froelich 2005; Frumkin and Kim 2002; Cornforth 2003; Minkoff and Powell 2006; Jones 2007; Bennett and Savani 2011.

28   Civil Society's Democratic Potential

Table 1.2 Theorizing and Analysing CSOs' Democratic Contributions

Normative Yardstick Underpinning Analytical Dimension	Analytical Dimension Theorized	Empirical Indicators of Contribution on Each Dimension on Level of Individual CSO
Intra-organizational participation	Member activism	– High member control over CSO decision-making – High member involvement
Interest representation	External political engagement	– Sustained political activity – Wide political action repertoire
Societal responsiveness of CSO behaviour	Organizational accountability of CSO decision-making Stable CSO identities as foundation for constituency linkages	– No/Low staff control over CSO decision-making – Propensity towards goal commitment

individual CSO. Table 1.2 provides an overview of this including empirical indications for CSOs 'performing strongly' on each dimension.[48]

Starting with the *participation yardstick*, this study focuses on two forms of intra-organizational participation that individual CSOs might or might not cultivate. Member activism as the underlying analytical dimension is defined as the range of activities through which members or supporters participate within CSOs. As detailed earlier, the distinction between member control and involvement is central to the implications such activism has for the nature of CSOs' democratic contributions. Members exercise control when they have a direct say over core areas of organizational decision-making such as the allocation of core posts or the change of central constitutional rules that define the authority structure of the organization. Members are actively involved in an organization when they engage in organizational work or provide valuable information and feedback to the organization by expressing opinions or attending meetings. Having very different consequences for organizational functioning and self-maintenance from the perspective of organizational leaders and managers running an organization, they will be theorized and analysed separately when CSO performance on the dimension of member activism is assessed (see Chapters 3 and 4 for more detail on their conceptualization and measurement).

---

[48] 'Performance' is neither referred to as a yardstick to assess 'efficiency' nor 'best practice'. The later analyses will simply assess whether organizations—depending on central characteristics—tend to show *higher* or *lower* levels of member involvement or have a *wider* or *narrower* political action repertoire.

Moving to the *representation yardstick*, whether a CSO engages in interest representation becomes manifest in its external political engagement or its advocacy activities, i.e. in the range of strategies directed towards influencing public policy, directly or indirectly (Pekkanen and Smith 2014: 2–3). CSO political engagement encompasses a wide range of activities, cutting across dichotomies such as unconventional vs. conventional participation or the distinction between self-interested vs. public-spirited activities. It includes (legal and illegal) protest, attending press conferences, publishing reports, educating the public, election-related activities, as well as classical lobbying targeting politicians or civil servants (see also, for instance, Chaves et al. 2004; Beyers et al. 2008; Cinalli and Giugni 2014; Bloodgood and Tremblay-Boire 2017). Using a broad conception is crucial considering the diversity of CSOs studied that might be inclined towards very different forms of external political engagement. It avoids denoting CSOs as 'non-political' or 'not politicized' due to engagement in the 'wrong' type of activity.

Though the concept of politicization has to date been mainly applied to the micro level (see for a recent overview Zamponi and Bosi 2018), a CSO can be considered politicized when it makes regular recourse to any form *of* political advocacy defined as those activities that transition organizational concerns from the private into the public sphere (Salisbury 1984: 64–5; Kriesi 1996: 157; Cinalli and Giugni 2014: 85).[49] Once an organization is politicized, the intensity of such politicization is captured through a CSO's political action repertoire, i.e. the range of advocacy strategies a CSO regularly engages in (Binderkrantz 2005: 694; Kriesi et al. 2007). Both aspects are empirically closely connected but directly relevant to CSOs' contributions to democracy in different ways. When we characterize a CSO as politicized, the organization exercises some sort of 'voice' in the political process, as compared to inwards-orientated CSOs engaging in interest representation only sporadically, if at all. The breadth of CSOs' political action repertoires, in turn, indicates the diversity of channels that a CSO provides for its members, followers, and possibly the wider public, to engage with the political sphere.

Concluding with *societal responsiveness*, i.e. whether a CSO is structurally disposed towards acting responsively towards the interests or concerns of

---

[49] While political goals (as collective solutions situated in the public sphere) can be considered another component of 'politicization' (Zamponi and Bosi 2018), the focus here is on organizational conditions under which those goals become manifest in organizational behaviour rationalizing a focus on the 'action repertoires'. That said, the qualitative analyses in Chapter 9, which cover patterns of goal reorientations, also look at the conditions under which CSOs adopt political goals or broaden their political agenda in the course of their development.

some societal constituencies, this yardstick is captured through two complementary analytical dimensions. They approach the phenomenon from different angles—one intra-organizational and one external.

Internally, patterns of responsiveness are likely to be reflected in the *organizational accountability of CSO decision-making*, i.e. whether decision-making remains in the hands of organizational actors, leaders, or members, or whether it is taken over by (paid) managers. This can be captured through the level of staff control prevalent in different governance domains, i.e. staff defining the organization's ends, rather than being restricted to implement ends defined by organizational actors (Bauer and Ege 2016: 1020, 1025). Importantly, staff control is not concerned with the degree of centralization of CSO governance. It signals the detachment of intra-organizational decision-making not just from the 'grass roots' but also organizational leaders, hence from organizational actors altogether.[50] Reliance on paid staff and a related managerial culture have been frequently associated with the growing internal importance of senior staff and a weakening of both members and volunteer leaders (Billis 1991: 65; Cornforth 2003: 244; Maloney 2015: 102).[51] As argued by Karl, professionals operate in organizations as a 'protected elite', a group to which access is determined based on qualification and expertise as defined by professions, not by 'democratic society' (1998: 249). While delegating certain tasks to staff is bound to be the norm once these actors form part of organizational life (as this is what they are paid for), members or organizational representatives are still expected to define organizational ends, as this maintains ties with the CSOs' societal base. Staff control over decisions is said to shift organizational priorities away from organizational values and constituency interests towards performance and efficiency, as well as the concerns of external funders (e.g. Mason 1996; Jordan and Maloney 1997; Frumkin 2002; King 2017; Salgado 2010; O'Regan and Oster 2005; van Deth and Maloney 2012).

The second lens through which social responsiveness of CSO behaviour is approached, adds a more outward-oriented aspect to capture CSOs' propensity towards societal responsiveness. It looks at whether an organization readily adapts its own identity or, alternatively, ensures its continuity as one foundation for stable linkages to constituencies and central audiences. The stability of a CSO's identity, fundamentally defined by its mission

---

[50] Note that parts of the non-profit literature have associated organizational professionalization with positive effects such as enhanced transparency and accountability towards stakeholders (Lu 2015; Striebing 2017; Stone 1996).

[51] E.g. Panebianco 1988; Schmitter and Streeck 1999; Bosso 2003; Webb and Kolodny 2006; van Deth and Maloney 2012; Suarez 2010b; Striebing 2017.

and, relatedly, its core constituencies (e.g. Halpin 2014), is crucial to sustain supporters' lasting attachment and thus to the societal anchoring of an organization. To the extent that the fundamental interests of constituencies underpinning a CSO tend to change only slowly, goal reorientations appealing to new, wider, or more diverse audiences are likely to weaken established constituency linkages, while goal commitment is likely to reinforce them.[52]

The two empirical indications of staff control and goal reorientation complement each other, as managers are expected to be particularly ready to strategically adapt organizational goals and activities to ensure the organization's self-maintenance. This can be at the cost of organizational values central to an organization's identity (I return to the distinct motivations ascribed to managers, members, and organizational leaders and their implications in Chapter 2). Group research, especially research on the 'NGOization' of civil society, has associated CSO professionalization and bureaucratization with organizations' strategic reorientation towards 'sympathetic' and 'uncontroversial' causes, i.e. representation activities detached from traditional bottom-up aggregation processes. This leads to the 'creation' of constituencies instead of the representation of existing ones (Lang 2013: 95; Choudry and Kapoor 2013). Echoing the notion of 'assumed representation' discussed earlier, staff-driven organizations are characterized as instrumental in (re)defining target constituencies to facilitate fundraising and cater to the interests of resource-rich citizens who are easier to mobilize (Maloney 2012: 108–12). Similarly, Zald and McCarthy (1987: 375) consider 'attempts to impart the image of "speaking for a *potential* constituency"' [italics added to original] (alongside a powerless membership) as one central feature of a 'professional social movement', again associating the dominance of paid professionals with the weakness of meaningful CSO–constituency linkages.

Conclusion and Chapter Overview

In this introduction I tried to highlight the importance of theorizing and of assessing the discrepancies between membership-based CSOs' democratic potentials and these potentials' actual realization in contemporary European democracies. Synthesizing different strands of research, the introduction presented the theoretical foundation for doing so in the course of this study. This

---

[52] Alterations of central organizational goals can of course also be expressions of responsiveness when CSOs are reacting to external pressures (e.g. resulting from societal changes). This counter-perspective will be theorized and empirically considered in Chapter 7, which analyses the drivers of CSO goal reorientation and commitment.

foundation rests on a multidimensional conceptualization of CSOs' potential democratic contributions distinguishing three normative yardsticks: participation, interest representation and societal responsiveness. All three are associated with the classical notion of membership organizations as 'transmission belt'. As existing research has made clear that 'delivering' on all three at the same time has become a major challenge for CSOs, its core elements were disentangled. This makes it possible to use them as benchmarks to evaluate the variety of ways membership organizations might or might not contribute to democracy.

This study deliberately casts the net widely by looking at parties, interest groups, and service providers simultaneously, which makes it distinct from a range of important studies concerned with similar themes (e.g. Jordan and Maloney 1997; 2007; Skocpol 2013; Lang 2013). To the extent that these organizations qualify as *membership-based organizations* (I will discuss in detail their defining features in Chapter 2), they have the potential to function as venues for participation, to be vehicles of interest representation, and to establish meaningful societal linkages. Therefore these organizations will serve as our reference point to theorize and assess which CSOs realize their potential and which do not.

Starting out from this decision, *Chapter 2* presents a governance perspective on CSOs' democratic contributions applicable to membership organizations generally. Based on the multidimensional perspective of CSOs' democratic contributions presented in Chapter 1, it develops the central theoretical arguments informing this study. It conceptualizes the trade-offs that CSOs as membership-based voluntary organizations face when cultivating processes and activities that shape their contributions to democracy. To theorize the connections between organizational characteristics, actor configurations, and the handling of these trade-offs, the chapter specifies the organizational features of two governance templates from which hypotheses on CSOs' varying democratic contributions will be derived later on: the 'voluntary association' and the 'professionalized voluntary organization'.

Chapter 3 provides an overview of the methodological choices underpinning the study and the data used in the various analyses that follow. It justifies the selection of Germany, Norway, Switzerland, and UK for conducting CSO surveys. It explains how organization-level measures of CSOs' varying democratic contributions were constructed. While the choice of the specific statistical models will be rationalized in the context of the individual analyses detailed in Chapters 4–5 and 7–8 (one dedicated to each of the four dimensions capturing CSOs' different democratic contributions), the chapter presents the operationalizations of independent variables used across these analyses. This particularly concerns the central characteristics of the 'voluntary association' and the 'professionalized voluntary organization'. The limitations of using cross-sectional survey data rationalize the mixed-methods design, which combines the latter with qualitative case studies of three CSOs' long-term trajectories. As all three CSOs—one interest group, one service-oriented organization and one party—increasingly resemble the professionalized voluntary organization template, they allow us to capture the evolving interplay of CSO leaders, managers, and members and the impact of these processes on CSOs' evolving 'democratic performance'.

Chapter 4 is concerned with the participation yardstick and the cultivation of the two different forms of member activism—member involvement and control. Member involvement is positively associated with most characteristics of either template. In contrast, a growing reliance on paid staff—a central feature of the 'voluntary professionalized organization'—is positively related to involvement and negatively to control. This not only stresses the importance of the professionalization of organizations' human resources for how members engage with their organizations, it also shows that its implications are not uniformly negative. Vice versa, none of the features defining classical 'voluntary associations' is significantly related to member control, reflecting a diverse associational landscape that not necessarily mobilizes progressive orientations as some more normative studies have assumed.

Chapter 5 maintains a focus on CSO's internal dynamics but moves to the yardstick of societal responsiveness of CSO behaviour. It theorizes and examines to what extent central traits of the 'professionalized voluntary organization' allow for managers to take control over internal decision-making (i.e. to start operating as a group of decision-makers in its own right), thereby displacing organizational members and leaders alike. Vice versa, it examines whether 'voluntary association features' help contain such tendencies by incentivizing the maintenance of organizational accountability structures over the growing need for expertise and efficiency in decision-making. The characteristics of the two templates shape CSOs in opposite ways: as theoretically expected professionalization and bureaucratization (central features of the 'professionalized voluntary organization') increase the propensity for staff control over decisions. In contrast, organizations with multitier structures that strongly rely on volunteer staff (central association features) help contain it.

Chapter 6 presents the first set of qualitative findings generated by the case studies of the National Activity Providers Association (NAPA), Surfers Against Sewage (SAS), and the Green Party of England and Wales (GPEW). These findings widely substantiate central statistical findings in Chapters 4 and 5. Overall, professionalization and bureaucratization were conducive to member involvement and staff control but detrimental to member control despite the three organizations' very different infrastructures and goal orientations. In all three organizations leading managers initiated or actively supported bureaucratization reforms to enhance the effectiveness of decision-making, which led to reducing direct member control. Bureaucratization reforms also enhanced spaces for staff control, formally or informally.

Moving to how CSOs relate to central audiences not only inside but also outside their organization, *Chapter 7* deals with the second dimension used to approximate the societal responsiveness of CSOs: patterns of (in)stability of CSO identities. In line with theoretical expectations, professionalization and bureaucratization have a positive relationship with CSOs' readiness to alter central goals, while individual membership—a central association feature—supports goal commitment. These findings hold despite controlling for organizations' exposure to a range of external pressures (e.g. resource competition) that incentivize adaptation irrespective of an organization's own governance characteristics.

Chapter 8 moves to the representation yardstick, dealing with CSOs' varying propensities towards engaging in political activities and the different breadths of the political action repertoires that they cultivate. It theorizes the implications of investing in political activity as a collective, non-exclusive incentive from which non-members also profit (making it less effective to sustain member support than selective incentives restricted to members). Features of a 'voluntary association' are expected to lead to a different balance between collective (outward-orientated) and selective (inward-orientated) incentive provision than features of a 'professionalized voluntary organization'. And indeed, being orientated towards member interests and being composed of individual members—voluntary association features—have significant negative relationships with political engagement. In contrast, all characteristics associated with professionalized voluntary organizations—professionalization, bureaucratization, and state funding dependency—relate positively to political engagement.

Chapter 9 looks at how NAPA, SAS, and GPEW evolved in terms of the continuity and alteration of central goals and their political engagement pattern, both of which had positive significant relationships with core features of the 'professionalized voluntary organization' in the previous statistical analyses. Again, the findings are broadly in line with the statistical findings. As the three CSOs increasingly resembled 'professionalized voluntary organizations', managers proactively supported politicization or the broadening of political action repertoires. Importantly, this did not necessarily go at the cost of more confrontational or participatory 'outsider strategies'. While managers also supported change in CSO goals to broaden and diversify their organization's external support (financial and otherwise), they also tried to balance this endeavour with maintaining continuity to keep traditional supporters on board. Both findings again suggest that the implications for CSOs of the professionalization, bureaucratization, and state dependency might be less uniformly problematic than often argued.

Chapter 10 synthesizes the empirical findings—quantitative and qualitative—presented in this study. The two contrasting governance templates 'voluntary association' and 'professionalized voluntary association' provided useful theoretical anchors to theorize and account for CSOs' diverse contributions to democracy. Features belonging to each template—overall—generate contrasting repercussions on each of the four dimensions analysed (member activism, staff control, CSO goal reorientation, and political engagement). In other words, they push CSOs in opposite directions with regard to their likely democratic performance on each. This overall picture substantiates two fundamental claims: first, that the two organizational templates embody different 'behavioural logics', and second, that their features are of immediate relevance to how CSOs contribute to democracy.

2

The Distinct Internal Logics of Associations and Professionalized Voluntary Organizations

Chapter 1 has distinguished three normative yardsticks—intra-organizational participation, external interest representation, and societal responsiveness. From them I derived four analytical dimensions to be used as empirical benchmarks to comparatively assess the diversity of CSOs' democratic contributions. These are member activism, political engagement, organizational accountability of CSO decision-making, and stable CSO identities as foundation for meaningful CSO–constituency linkages. To be sure, neither normative yardsticks nor the related empirical benchmarks capture all aspects that might be relevant and important in terms of CSOs' democratic contributions. However, studying which CSO characteristics are associated with different forms of member participation, with a different intensity and diversity of political engagement, different levels of staff control over CSO decision-making, and different propensities towards goal reorientation and commitment will provide us with a rich and complex picture of the contradictory implications of how CSOs organize for their respective democratic contributions.

This is important not the least because how an individual CSO contributes to democracy in one respect has repercussions for how it contributes in another. It has been detailed earlier that the implications for democracy of CSOs' participatory activities such as member involvement are affected by whether CSOs engage politically in their external behaviour or not; vice versa, the likely societal responsiveness of external political engagement is affected by the nature of internal participation, whether we find member control or 'only' involvement as well as whether organizational actors remain in charge of decisions or managers take over decision-making. It is these interdependencies explored in the introduction that rationalize a multidimensional approach to study CSOs' diverse democratic contributions.

Building on the theoretical groundwork presented so far, this chapter proposes an organization-centred perspective on CSOs' democratic

Civil Society's Democratic Potential. Nicole Bolleyer, Oxford University Press. © Nicole Bolleyer (2024).
DOI: 10.1093/oso/9780198884392.003.0002

contributions that integrates two theoretical lenses prominent in interest groups, party, and non-profit research. They are particularly suitable to theorize the internal dynamics and external behaviour of membership-based CSOs: incentive-theoretical perspectives on leader–member relations and resource dependency theory. This integration allows us to conceptualize central trade-offs which membership-based CSOs have to manage that are ultimately rooted in membership organizations' own, constitutive features. These trade-offs concern tensions between what has been prominently called a 'logic of membership' and a 'logic of influence', between the twin roles of groups as locales for participation and vehicles of representation or between internal efficiency and the ability to maintain constituency linkages. They all confront CSOs with 'balancing acts'. The challenge is to account for how individual CSOs deal with them.[1] Theorizing from an organization-centred perspective their distinct handling helps to rationalize why some CSOs rather than others have little stake or interest in certain activities that tend to be considered vital to democracy from a normative perspective. It helps to identify under which conditions discrepancies between democratic potential and organizational reality are likely to be particularly pronounced.

Research has long stressed the tensions between leaders and rank-and-file members that need to be reconciled over time to keep an organization going. This chapter puts centre-stage a third group of actors that is by now important to the working of most CSOs: paid employees, especially those in leading managerial positions. They are hired by a CSO for their competences and skills to facilitate the day-to-day running of the organization and to more effectively pursue central activities. Since organizational leaders, members, and managers are characterized by different motivations (in their commitment to organizational values or the centrality they attribute to organizational maintenance, for instance), they are expected to take different positions on how to balance these trade-offs. The relative 'weight' of each group in an organization is closely tied to the way it is organized. This is why the same intra-organizational trade-off (e.g. between member control and leader autonomy; between selective and collective incentive provision) will play out differently depending on an organization's structural characteristics.

By integrating these basic assumptions, the resulting perspective allows us to theorize and, in turn, analyse whether the same CSO properties (e.g. professionalization, state funding dependency) might be conducive to one

---

[1] See, for instance, Schattschneider 1942; Wilson 1973; Schmitter and Streeck 1999; Jordan and Maloney 2007; Saurugger 2012; Kohler-Koch and Buth 2013; Lang 2013; Waardenburg and van de Bovenkamp 2014; Heylen et al. 2020.

dimension relevant to organizations' overall democratic contribution (e.g. political engagement), while being detrimental to another (e.g. member activism). Clearly, if certain activities and processes central to participation, representation, and societal responsiveness turned out to be generally difficult to reconcile on the level of the individual organization, this would have fundamental consequences for what contributions to democracy we should realistically expect from organized civil society as a whole.

This line of argument brings us back to the distinction between the *'normatively defined' democratic potential of CSOs as a class of organizations* and the *diversity of actual contributions to democracy of the variety of individual CSOs belonging to this class*. Importantly, no assumption is made about CSOs *themselves* aspiring to meet any normative expectations applied to them by academics, policymakers, or the public. CSOs in Europe and elsewhere need to first assure their own survival in increasingly difficult conditions to be able to engage in any activities at all. The aim of this study is find out which incentive structures shaping CSOs as organizations from within make it more or less likely that they will engage in activities that align with central normative expectations applied to them (whether they endorse the latter or not). This will allow us to transcend general diagnoses that organizations—due to professionalization, managerialism, and exposure to government regulation—increasingly suffer from a diminished capacity 'to fulfil their mission—to engage their publics, to empower and give voice' (Alexander and Fernandez 2021: 368–9). Engaging societal constituencies to generate voice might be some CSOs' mission—and for sure it is an important one—but CSOs that pursue different goals might also contribute to democracy in different ways. It is a contention of this study that dismissing the latter by putting the normative bar too high or specifying the normative yardsticks in too narrow a fashion might make us overlook an important part of the broader, empirical picture of how CSOs actually do in democracies.

Why Study the Discrepancies between Democratic Potential and Organizational Realities in Membership-Based Voluntary Organizations?

CSOs are defined as membership-based voluntary organizations, encompassing parties, interest groups and service-oriented organizations alike, a definition built on various conceptions in group research such as Wilson's 'voluntary association' (1973: 31), Knoke's notion of 'collective action organization' (1990: 7), and Salamon and Anheier's specification of 'non-profit organization' (1998: 216).[2] To bridge the divide between the study of groups and parties particularly, it links these concepts 'at the heart of central debates in the group and voluntary association literature' (Jordan and Maloney 2007: 30) to notions of party organization as 'voluntary associations which rely on at least a minimum of non-obligatory participation' (Panebianco 1988: 10; Wilson 1973).

Most central for the theoretical arguments developed later, membership-based voluntary organizations rely on the voluntary support of members. Whether those members are individuals or corporate actors (e.g. representatives of associations, institutions, firms) (Knoke 1990: 7)[3], they have the power to exit and their support needs to be continuously maintained. Especially in individualizing societies, the latter has become increasingly difficult, which confronts these organization with particular challenges that are not directly applicable to memberless organizations.[4] Furthermore, membership-based voluntary organizations are private, separate (though not necessarily 'autonomous'[5]) from government, self-governing, and non-profit-distributing.[6] Finally, they have a formalized infrastructure, i.e. are 'institutionalized to some meaningful extent' (Knoke 1990: 5–6; Salamon and Anheier 1998: 216; Wilson 1973: 31).[7]

This definition encompasses a wide variety of organizations to which we can—in principle—attribute democratic potential in terms of intra-organizational participation, interest representation, and societal responsiveness. This has far-fetching implications for the type of insights a study will be

[2] In Salamon and Anheier's seminal voluntary sector study, parties formed one of twelve groupings of non-profit organizations. This is little recognized (as specified in a footnote). Like religious congregations, parties were left out of the empirical analysis 'largely to keep work manageable' (1998: 217).

[3] As specified in Chapter 4, the minimum condition to speak of a member is the regular payment of fees.

[4] This is why this study does not theorize 'non-profits' (all organizations and institutions that are not profit-distributing in a legal sense) or 'organized interests' engaging in advocacy (all organizations that try to influence government action including individual actors such as local governments or firms). Neither presuppose members and, consequently, face comparable trade-offs between activities conducive to internal organizational maintenance and external goal attainment.

[5] Some seminal works refer to autonomy from the state as a defining feature of civil society (e.g. Diamond 1994). While the notion of CSO adopted here aligns with this in terms of being 'formally separate' from the state, the actual degree of autonomy (e.g. in financial terms) is treated as an empirical question as 'actually existing civil society groups are hardly completely autonomous from the state' (Uhlin 2009: 273).

[6] While a non-profit organization can be involved in for-profit activities, it cannot redistribute these profits to its members. This is *not* equivalent to a legal definition, though, as restrictions that different legal systems impose on organizations claiming non-profit status differ significantly (van der Ploeg et al. 2017).

[7] While some movement scholars argue that institutionalization or formalization as an organizational trait excludes an organization from the category of social movement organizations (SMOs), various scholars have stressed that SMOs can adopt a variety of organizational infrastructures including institutionalized, centralized, and bureaucratic structures (Knoke 1990: 19; see also McCarthy and Zald 1977; Staggenborg 1988). Hence, while movement organizations are not excluded as such, those which operate as fluid networks are because organizational trade-offs generated by tensions between self-maintenance and goal attainment do not apply to them in the same fashion as to CSOs with more formalized structures.

able to generate in contrast to earlier studies. Some definitions used previously only included specific parts of civil society—reflecting the democratic function these studies were interested in. Prominent is a focus on those voluntary organizations formed of individuals (e.g. Skocpol 2013). Other studies treat properties they deem (implicitly or explicitly) central to CSOs' role in democratic settings as defining criteria for what qualifies as CSO to start with. Examples for this are the presence of participatory structures for the involvement of members (e.g. Knoke 1990; Barakso 2004), CSO engagement in interest representation (e.g. Baroni et al. 2014), or organizations' public good orientation (e.g. Alexander and Fernandez 2021). Using the above definition of membership organization instead, all these examples of defining properties represent characteristics that CSOs might possess or not.

This is crucial, as it prevents potential drivers of or hurdles against CSOs contributing to democracy from being underexamined or left aside. To be concrete, if only associations of individuals are—from a normative point of view—assumed to provide meaningful channels for member activism and thus form the empirical focus of a study, the implications of having a predominantly individual membership for internal participatory dynamics or external advocacy activities remain inevitably outside of the picture. Similarly, if interest groups are defined as politically active organizations[8] and 'associations' or 'collective action organizations' as organizations that (at least formally) put members in charge and thus emulate democratic procedures internally (e.g. Knoke 1990; Barakso 2004), CSOs' engagement in advocacy and the provision of basic participatory channels for members are assumed from the start and 'kept constant'. Questions about the basic determinants of CSO politicization (e.g. whether or not CSOs regularly engage in advocacy) and the nature of CSO decision-making (e.g. whether or not CSOs grant members control over decisions) risk being sidelined.[9] The chosen definition tries to avoid this.

Despite the methodological advantages resulting from its broad scope, some elements of this definition demand some more justification as they do not align well with some very prominent works on similar themes. One is the inclusion of organizations composed of corporate members whose democratic potential does not seem obvious in light of traditional work on associations or citizen groups as central venues for participation (e.g. Sills 1959; 1968; Smith and Freedman 1972). As highlighted by Jordan and Maloney (2007: 195), expanding the scope beyond organizations composed of

---

[8] This is common in interest group research, see for details Chapter 8.
[9] See, for instance, Almog-Bar and Schmid (2014) on the need to treat advocacy as a possible organizational activity (hence a feature that can vary across organizations), not a defining property.

individuals reads 'oddly for those who see the interest group issue as being about mobilizing individuals for collective action'. Reflecting the normative yardstick of participation, seminal works on the participatory role of CSOs exclusively study individual membership organizations (e.g. Skocpol 2003; Barasko and Schaffner 2008). Organizations with corporate members were left to research interested in the exercise of policy influence (Grant 2000: 14; Jordan and Maloney 2007: 195), hence research concerned with representation.[10]

'Participatory benefits' enjoyed by individuals attributed to associations seem less relevant to organizations which serve as platforms for collective action between individuals who act as representatives of firms, institutions, or other associations.[11] Interaction processes between the representatives of corporate actors are likely to be more instrumental and thus less likely to meet standards of 'deliberation' which the normative literature ascribes to associations constituted by citizens (see for overviews of prominent normative and empirical arguments Fung 2003; Welzel et al. 2005; Eikenberry 2009).[12] Of course, it is still individuals who interact within organizations' organs on behalf of the corporate member as the actual 'unit of membership' (Schmitter and Streeck 1999: 63).[13] Furthermore, instrumentally oriented representatives of corporate members can also benefit from intra-organizational exchange, e.g. might learn valuable skills useful in other settings. If the organizations they operate in emulate democratic decision-making, it is unclear why positive effects ascribed to such engagement in democratic practice should not apply to them.

Returning to the study's theoretical underpinning, even if the participation yardstick was generally not applicable to corporate membership organizations, the same is clearly not the case for interest representation or the societal responsiveness as alternative normative yardsticks. Interest group research has long stressed organized interests' central role in

---

[10] That said, there is traditional interest group research with an empirical focus on individual membership organizations (e.g. Jordan et al. 2004; Dalziel 2010).

[11] Interestingly, Halpin considers 'groups of groups', i.e. groups whose members are themselves associations, as a 'derivative of the traditional group form' (Halpin 2014: 63). What remains unclear is what makes representatives of groups that interact as such within the governance organs of associations' different from representatives of institutions or firms or, alternatively, what makes them more similar to citizens interacting on their own behalf in traditional citizen groups.

[12] That said, it has been widely argued that citizens often prefer 'thin' forms of participation that have little do to with deliberative democracy either (van Deth and Maloney 2012: 2). Relatedly, whether and which types of beneficial effects are actually generated by associations composed of individuals and under which conditions has remained a matter of ongoing debate (Hooghe 2008), an issue I return to later.

[13] Indeed, the distinction between corporate and individual members as 'unit of membership' can be blurred in various types of organizations such as those representing small businesspeople, the professions, or farmers (Jordan and Maloney 2007: 194).

42 Civil Society's Democratic Potential

democratic interest representation—including organizations with individual and corporate members (and indeed organizations with no members at all). Similarly, sources of representation bias (which societal interests interest groups represent and why) have been a central concern in this field for a long time. And this concern directly relates to questions of the societal responsiveness of interest group activity (e.g. Schattschneider 1960; Schlozman 2010; Halpin 2010; 2014).

And all this leaves aside that the earlier methodological point: to examine whether 'voluntary associations' composed of individuals are more active and thus 'superior' in providing channels for or actively cultivating participation, we need to include organizations that are *not* composed of individuals as well to engage in a comparative assessment. As Jordan and Maloney forcefully argued in their seminal study on groups' participatory contributions to democracy, 'the defence of groups as participatory institutions needs to be tested rather than assumed' (2007: 25). Especially if member participation is considered more relevant and more valuable in the context of individual than corporate membership organizations, we need to examine whether organizations composed of 'ordinary' citizens rather than organizational representatives cultivate a more active membership or not.

Following a similar logic, the chosen conception of CSO recognizes that while the organizations studied here have members and are dependent on them to some extent, this dependency varies as much as the different roles that members can play in them (e.g. Evers 2014; Gauja 2015; Jordan and Maloney 1997; Schlozman et al. 2015; Skocpol 2013). This is why this study does not restrict itself to examine organizations that provide for 'formally democratic procedures' (Knoke 1990: 7). Member demands for such procedures within voluntary organizations are bound to vary (Wilson 1973: 237–9; Halpin 2006; Barasko and Schaffner 2008; Gauja 2015). Hence, which types of membership-based organizations adopt this mode of decision-making and which do not is an empirical question. To address this question, organizations included in this study 'only' have to be 'self-governing', requiring the ability to control their own activities (Salamon and Anheier 1998: 216). This criterion does not prescribe *who* within the organization—formally or de facto—does exercise such control.

To summarize, the chosen conception of membership-based voluntary organization does not require a specific type of member, a certain internal governance structure, or a specific (functional or substantive) mission. This is important to assess the diversity of democratic contributions of CSOs, their presence and absence, along the three normative yardsticks participation, representation, and responsiveness, as none of the definition's constitutive criteria closely align with either of them. In other words, the conception takes seriously that participatory contributions as well as societally responsive behaviour do not require CSOs to be political or partisan. Neither do they presuppose a public good orientation. Vice versa, external contributions to interest representation through political engagement can be generated by internally undemocratic, non-participatory, and societally unresponsive organizations.

This definition aligns closely with the *organization-centred perspective* this study builds on. To theorize the behaviour of membership-based CSOs generally, the latter integrates two theoretical lenses prominent in interest groups, party, and non-profit research: incentive-theoretical perspectives on leader–member relations and resource dependency theory. The former underlines the ongoing pressure on leaders to ensure voluntary support of members while maintaining central organizational activities through the provision of different incentive types (e.g. Clark and Wilson 1961; Olson 1965; Wilson 1973; Moe 1980). The latter, in turn, stresses the importance of resources critical to maintain an organization alongside the leadership's aspiration to maximize its autonomy in the pursuit of external organizational goals by trading against each other intra-organizational and external dependencies to various key audiences (e.g. Pfeffer and Salancik 1978; Beyers and Kerremans 2007; Nienhüser 2008). This is challenging, as members can leave at any point (Wilson 1973: 13; Hirschman 1970) and (different from firms, for instance) organizational leaders are unable to 'control' their members' behaviour directly. This has fundamental implications for how CSOs' reconcile their intra-organizational dynamics and external behaviour (Pfeffer and Salancik 1978). Organizational trade-offs rooted in this constitutive set-up are expected to impact on whether CSOs are likely to cultivate internal participation, generate societally responsive behaviour, or engage in interest representation. As this constitutive set-up is shared by parties, interest groups, and service-oriented membership organizations, they should be affected in similar ways, which will be theorized accordingly.[14]

---

[14] Of course, CSOs' primary goals are important for behaviour relevant to their contributions to democracy. Alongside the party–group distinction, many scholars have with good reason distinguished CSOs based on their predominantly political or, alternatively, social purposes. Van der Meer and van Ingen (2009: 286), for instance, distinguish leisure from interest group and activist organizations, while Alexander et al. (2012: 54) distinguish advocacy from social groups. This is why the later empirical analyses take into account organizations' central functional orientations. All statistical analyses include a variable capturing whether CSOs consider themselves as parties, interest groups, or service providers. As one would expect, they show that the party-group distinction plays a role for several (though not all) dimensions of CSOs' democratic contributions (see Chapter 10 for an overview). See, on the added value of comparisons between different organizational types from the perspective of party research, Bolleyer (forthcoming).

The Diversity of Organizational Forms and Its Consequences for CSOs' Democratic Contributions

> The quality of civil society cannot transcend the quality of its organizational forms. [...] Voluntary associations have been designated the most typical organizational form of civil society. To what extent can voluntary associations be expected to constitute the cornerstone of civil society?
>
> **(Ahrne 1996: 114)**

Which CSOs, depending on their 'organizational form', can we claim to make—overall—the greatest democratic contribution? Based on the four empirical benchmarks specified in Chapter 1 (see Table 1.2), this is the answer: a CSO with organizational features that incentivize the cultivation of high member control and involvement, regular and wide-ranging political activities, a reasonably stable commitment to central values or goals and the containment of paid staff's control over decision-making. What this study will argue, however, is that such a 'profile' is not coherently incentivized by central organizational properties commonly ascribed to 'traditional' voluntary associations. Neither is it uniformly weakened by features of professionalized CSOs frequently criticized for diminishing CSOs' democratic contributions (e.g. Skocpol 2013: 265; Kriesi and Baglioni 2003; Lang 2013; Fraussen and Halpin 2018). The theoretization of the 'voluntary association' as a 'system of governance' will underline the salience of Ahrne's question about the empirical contribution of actual 'associations' to democracy. It will reveal a fundamental tension between the portrayal of the 'voluntary association' as a central building block of a democratic civil society in a normative sense and the contradictory expectations that can be derived from its defining properties regarding the four dimensions, based on which organizations' democratic potential will be assessed later on.

Intra-Organizational Trade-Offs and the Conflicting Priorities of Leaders, Members, and Managers

Incentive-theoretical approaches and resource dependency theory have long discussed tensions arising between *leaders* (who hold status functions in a CSO) and *rank-and-file members* (who do not).[15] This study brings in a third

---

[15] Formal membership finds expression—on a minimum level—through the regular payment of fees (see for details Chapter 4 on member activism).

group of actors important in most contemporary CSOs (at least those operating beyond a local scale[16]): *managers* hired by CSOs for their competences and skills who assume responsibilities for the running of the organization or the maintenance of central activities.[17] Both organizational leaders (who are unpaid volunteers[18]) and paid professionals increasingly form part of organizations' leadership. Importantly, this notion of manager is not equivalent with any paid staff earning a living from working for a CSO but captures paid employees in leading positions (Kleidman 1994: 258). They are essential for CSO functioning and the maintenance of central activities, making their motivations and behaviour critical to how CSOs operate.

Throughout this study, I will refer to 'leaders' when speaking of organizational representatives (elected or appointed) in an organization's central leadership and of 'managers' when speaking of (unelected) paid professionals in leading organizational positions. These professionals tend to hold these positions predominantly thanks to their skills or expertise and therefore possess a degree of independence and distance from the organization they work for (e.g. Panebianco 1988; Webb and Fisher 2003; Moens 2021).[19] In empirical terms, the lines between leaders, managers and members as intra-organizational groups are not always clear-cut. Just as leaders are traditionally recruited from a CSO's membership base, being a manager is not incompatible with a prior affiliation to the organization (e.g. Webb and Fisher 2003; Karlsen and Saglie 2017; Mellquist 2022). However, the *prior* rationale for managers to hold their posts is their expertise and competence, not their organizational affiliation. Indeed, taking over such a role does not require such prior affiliation either, which tends to be different from organizational leaders. Their authority is based on claims of expertise (Lang 2013: 71; Mellquist 2022: 108) and not derived from their function as organizational representatives. Similarly, the lines are blurred between organizational leaders and volunteer staff or activists, i.e. unpaid members who take on organizational responsibilities. In decentralized or federalized CSOs, the latter

---

[16] CSOs can be completely volunteer run, in case of which paid staff are no relevant category, but as Chapters 3 and 5 will show, these organizations form a minority amongst the regionally and nationally relevant CSOs studied here.

[17] They include executive directors or paid CEOs strongly defined by managerial responsibilities but also directors of campaigning in political organizations or leading staff in charge of a CSO's overall service offer in social CSOs.

[18] Organizational leaders might be compensated for some organizational activities or costs related to their role, but unlike managers they do not raise their main income from these activities (e.g. Staggenborg 1988).

[19] This definition of manager aligns with Panebianco's notion of professionals rather than bureaucrats holding administrative roles and possessing less expertise (1988). See Moens (2021) for an insightful typology of different types of party staffers.

might hold executive functions on the regional or local level not that dissimilar to executive functions on the national level. Yet again, organizational leaders forming part of central-level organs are distinct in that they regularly make decisions relevant to the direction of the organization overall including its subunits, which is not the case for volunteer staff who might be in charge on lower levels.

Having specified the actors whose interplay is theorized, Table 2.1 denotes one intra-organizational trade-off (e.g. leader autonomy vs. member control, organizational accountability vs. expertise and efficiency in decision-making, etc.) associated with each of the four analytical dimensions capturing processes and behaviour conducive to CSOs' contribution to democracy respectively. All four trade-offs ultimately originate in membership-based CSOs' own structural set-up. Central to this, as stressed earlier, is CSOs' reliance on a voluntary membership, creating a scenario in which leaders (organizational as well as managerial) have to assure their organization's survival through sustaining voluntary support, while also seeking to maintain control over decisions to successfully pursue external activities (Wilson 1973: 30–1, 237; Moe 1980; Schmitter and Streeck 1999; Ganz 2014; Ahlquist and Levi 2014).

How each trade-off is addressed is, in the first instance, affected by the coalitions likely to form between three central groups of CSO actors—members, managers, and leaders—depending on differences and similarities in core motivations and priorities that can be attributed to each group 'as such'. Table 2.1 thus summarizes a *preliminary* step in specifying propensity of different coalitions to form in relation to each of the four trade-offs *irrespective* of the nature of the organizations these three groups operate in (see right-hand column).

Going back to Michels (1915), Wilson (1973), and Panebianco (1988), distinct orientations of *leaders, managers,* and *members* are expected to be rooted in the positions they hold in a CSO and the characteristics which allowed them to take over these roles. Accordingly, organizational leaders, members, and managers are attributed different motivations in terms of their commitment to the organization, its values, and goals. Relatedly, they are different in the centrality they attribute to organizational maintenance as an end in itself as compared to goal attainment and, tied to this, the type of resources they are oriented towards maintaining access to. On that basis we can theorize how we expect each group to—*ceteris paribus*—position itself with regard to central trade-offs confronting membership organizations and whose priorities—those of leaders and managers or those of leaders and members—tend to align accordingly.

The Internal Logics of Associations and Voluntary Organizations 47

Table 2.1 Dimensions of CSOs' Potential Democratic Contributions, Related Organizational Trade-Offs, and Orientations of Leaders, Members, and Managers

Analytical Dimension Theorized	Intra-Organizational Trade-Off Faced by CSO per Dimension	Coalitions Suggested by Basic Orientations of Three Groups of CSO Actors
Member Activism	Member Control versus Leader Autonomy in Decision-Making	- Leaders and managers prioritize autonomy - Members: no uniform preference in favour of member control
Organizational Accountability of CSO Decision-Making	Organizational Accountability of CSO Decisions versus Expertise and Efficiency in Decision-Making	- Leaders and members prioritize organizational accountability - Managers prioritize expert/efficient decisions
Stable CSO Identities	Linkages to Loyal Affiliates through Goal Commitment versus Maximization of Short-Term Support/Resources through Goal Reorientation	- Leaders and managers prioritize maximization of short-term support - Members prioritize stable linkages
Political Engagement	Provision of Selective Incentives Benefiting Members versus Collective, Non-Exclusive Incentives (e.g. advocacy)	- Members prioritize selective incentive provision - Leaders and managers prioritize incentive provision to outside audiences (including collective ones)

Members and organizational leaders share that they engage with the CSO in a voluntary capacity. They do not earn a living from their organizational involvement and are driven (at least to some extent) by organizational commitment, which should inform their ideas and preferences not only of 'what the organization is for' but also how it ought to be organized and run. Organizational leaders and managers share a joint responsibility for the day-to-day running of the organization, while also maintaining its central external activities, and tend to work closely together to reconcile the two. The shared awareness of the tensions between self-maintenance and goal attainment invites a joint concern for ensuring CSO functioning and awareness for the challenges related to this. Such a perspective is neither likely to be shared by ordinary members who might care more about their CSO's ideological purity and value commitment (even if doing so has some negative consequences) nor by paid employees in support roles who carry only little responsibility.

Compared to both members and organizational leaders, managers are more likely to have an instrumental orientation towards the organization they work for (e.g. Katz and Mair 2009). As argued by Maier and Meyer (2011: 745–6), staff's professional identity tends to be stronger than their organizational identity. Though being paid by a specific CSO, they continue to value the judgement of external peers, making these actors less dependent on the organization and its leaders, who—though being their current employers—might be only a stepping stone in an employee's career trajectory (Panebianco 1988: 229–31; Maloney 2015: 102–3).[20] Simultaneously, their incomes depend on their CSOs' performance and stakes are higher to assure the organization's ongoing performance and thus success, especially as perceived by critical outside audiences. If there are tensions between protecting the organization's core values and its performance, staff are expected to prioritize the latter. This might involve alienating CSO members who are only one of several audiences (alongside donors, the authorities, etc.) whose support (financial or otherwise) a CSO depends upon (e.g. Berkhout 2013). Meanwhile, being recruited based on skill rather than organizational commitment, managers can be expected to embrace norms of managerial efficiency (Staggenborg 1988: 596; Maier and Meyer 2011: 745–6). This suggests a greater flexibility in strategically exploiting opportunities to access institutional resources or gain support beyond CSOs' core constituencies as compared to members who might prioritize value commitment (e.g. Katz 1990; Binderkrantz 2009; Kreutzer and Jäger 2011; Karlsen and Saglie 2017). Leaders should share managerial concerns for the effective running of their organization, keen to protect their status position within their organization (Michels 1915). These—similar to paid employees' positions—are safest when the organization does well (Katz 1990: 145; LeRoux and Goerdel 2009: 518; Wilson 1973).

That said, comparing organizational leaders and managers, a 'maintenance orientation' can be expected to be more pronounced in managers (Panebianco 1988: 229–31; Schmitter and Streeck 1999). Organizational leaders—to the extent that they are themselves recruited from the CSO's membership base—can be expected to be disposed towards trying to maintain organizational accountability. This adds legitimacy to their own actions and enhances the likely compliance of followers (even if they are

---

[20] If we talk about highly qualified personnel, they also will find it easier to exit the CSO than organizational leaders (whose position is closely tied to the organization and who are at least partially driven by emotional commitment), as managers can move to another equivalent job in another organization in case of dissatisfaction with their current position.

appointed and not dependent on members re-electing them into office). It further helps sustain the voluntary commitment in members, a central driver underpinning leaders' own engagement in the particular CSO. This disposition is not necessarily shared by externally recruited managers.

Based on these differences in motivation and, relatedly, priorities when operating within an organizational context, members, organizational leaders, and managers are expected to systematically differ in what they tend to prioritize and what they more willingly compromise when having to handle the four internal trade-offs relevant to CSOs' democratic contribution. I expect that managers' and members' interests and orientations are least likely to align. At the same time, organizational leaders are expected to be more open to form coalitions 'in both directions'. Leaders usually share a non-instrumental affiliation to their CSO with members[21] but also share a functional responsibility for CSO maintenance with managers. Depending on the nature of the trade-off we deal with, one connection can be expected to override the other, and leaders to tend towards a different coalition accordingly.

As depicted in Table 2.1 (right-hand column), *ceteris paribus*, in three of four configurations the preferences and priorities of organizational leaders and managers are expected to align. A leader–manager coalition is expected when facing a trade-off between member control versus leader autonomy in decision-making affecting member control, between stable linkages versus maximization of short-term support affecting goal reorientation, and between (inwards-oriented) selective incentive provision and the provision of external collective incentives impacting investments in political engagement. Only when it comes to organizational accountability of CSO decisions versus expertise and efficiency, I expect organizational leaders to be less likely to align with managers. One reason is that leaders are unlikely per se to favour their own disempowerment by passing decision-making power on to managers.

While in the first three constellations, leaders and managers are expected to push in the same direction, members are not expected to form a 'counterweight' in each scenario. As members cannot be generally assumed to desire member control (or participation in general), they are not per se expected to push against attempts to enhance leader autonomy by downsizing member control. This is due to the diversity of CSOs' value

---

[21] In large and influential CSOs, organizational leaders might join for purely careerist reasons, but for the average (small and scarcely resourced) group or party this is unlikely to be the case.

50 Civil Society's Democratic Potential

orientations, which range from democratic and participatory to authoritarian and leadership-centred, as well as differences between ideologically driven members interested in purity of their organization's stances versus pragmatic members interested in the efficient pursuit of organizational goals (e.g. Sartori 1976; Rosenblum 1998; Halpin 2006; Jordan and Maloney 2007; Poguntke et al. 2016; Close et al. 2017; Scarrow et al. 2017). We thus cannot attribute one uniform orientation to members and should not expect a systematic relationship between the centrality of members in organizational governance generally and of member control over decision-making specifically (see on this Chapter 4). Once we consider CSOs' long-term development, we should instead expect considerable variation in how much resistance—if any—leaders and managers will face when trying to formally or informally reduce member control to enhance their own autonomy (see on this Chapter 6).

Keeping the organizational properties of CSOs constant for now, the expected coalitions with regard to each trade-off can be rationalized the following way. I start with the two trade-offs concerning how intra-organizational decision-making power is allocated (upper half of Table 2.1), member control and containment of staff control. The former trade-off centres around a 'problem of centralization' stressing a possible conflict between members and the CSOs' leadership (including organizational leaders and managers). The latter centres around the 'problem of professionalization' assuming a possible conflict between members and organizational leaders with managers. Leaders and managers of parties and groups can be expected to prioritize leader autonomy over member control to enhance their capacity to assure their organization's self-maintenance (e.g. Panebianco 1988; Schmitter and Streeck 1999). As already argued by Hirschman, 'the short-run interest of management in organizations is to increase its own freedom of movement; management will therefore strain to strip member-customers of the weapons they can wield' (1970: 124). In contrast, members and leaders can be expected to jointly prioritize organizational accountability, requiring that internal decisions remain with organizational representatives. Managers, in turn, are expected to favour expertise and efficiency in decision-making, most immediately assured when professionals themselves make the decisions. While leaders might share a concern with managers to ensure organizational functioning and enhance efficiency (and thus approve the centralization of decision-making to the detriment of member control), they are expected to be reluctant to directly pass over decision-making authority to staff.

Moving to the two trade-offs that are significant to how a CSO relates to audiences both inside and outside the organization (lower half of Table 2.1), the maximization of outside support (e.g. through fundraising) tends to require CSOs to flexibly adapt to the saliency of issues and to broaden their reach beyond core constituencies, especially in individualizing societies. This, however, might dilute the CSO's core mission that drew members into the organization in the first place. These tendencies are in tension with cultivating a stable identity and linkages to loyal members and core constituents (e.g. Jordan and Maloney 2007). Especially managers but also organizational leaders are more concerned about assuring their CSO's immediate survival. They are therefore expected to be more pragmatic than members when it comes to how to present the organization to its relevant audiences to maintain wide-ranging support. To the extent that a reframing of central issues is insufficient, they are expected to be more open to goal reorientation and to substantively alter their CSO's identity, while members attached to organizational values are likely to prioritize goal commitment.[22] Concluding with the configuration relevant to political engagement, a similar rationale applies. Again, organizational leaders and managers are expected to be more concerned with maintaining support of outside audiences (e.g. the authorities, donors) than the average rank-and-file member is. Even if political advocacy is not a core mission, they are more inclined towards investing in external political engagement as one means to signal the importance of organizational goals to a variety of external audiences. This is expected irrespective of whether policy change might benefit a wider range of people than just the CSO's members or whether members themselves care about their organizations' political engagement. *Ceteris paribus*, members are assumed to be more inwards-orientated and concerned with their own relationship and attachment to the organization. This means they are less open to compromise internal rewards for investments in external activities, should conflicts between them arise.

---

[22] Though members might be pragmatic (as indicated earlier), ideologically motivated members are more likely to actively resist attempts to redefine a CSO's central goals than pragmatic members are likely to push in its favour.

52 Civil Society's Democratic Potential

How CSOs Respond to Intra-Organizational Trade-Offs: The Different Logics of 'Voluntary Associations' and 'Professionalized Voluntary Organizations'

A fundamental assumption underpinning and thus connecting the four trade-offs that confront CSOs is that maintaining a membership-based voluntary organization requires the ongoing and mutual cooperation of all three types of actors. None of the three groups and no bilateral coalition can simply impose its preferences, at least not in the longer term.[23] Consequently, organizational actors are likely to try to find a balance between conflicting positions when handling trade-offs. This basic interdependency provides the foundation to formulate hypotheses concerning how organizational features of a CSO might shape how the same 'balancing acts' manifest themselves differently in different organizations.[24]

I argue that the distinction between 'voluntary association' and the 'professionalized voluntary organization' allows us to theorize how the tensions captured by the four trade-offs are likely to be addressed. This is because 'voluntary association' and 'professionalized voluntary organization', as two 'systems of governance', fundamentally differ in terms of who runs the organization, i.e. who ensures the latter's overall direction, control, and accountability, and in whose interest an organization is run (Cornforth 2012: 1121; see for similar notions Barakso 2004: 2; van Puyvelde et al. 2016). The defining features of each governance model (summarized in Table 2.2) systematically affect the structural position and respective 'weight' of members, organizational leaders, and managers within organizational processes. I argued earlier that certain coalitions are likely given the three groups' own generic characteristics. However, organizational features shape whether these likely coalitions can implement their priorities and how many or few compromises with the opposing group might be necessary to achieve implementation. To give one example, in a 'voluntary association' with few staff that leaves members at the centre of CSOs' governance system, leaders and managers might agree that efficiency-enhancing reforms are necessary. But if this is resisted by active members and volunteer staff, this coalition is less likely to get its way than if managers are a more prominent group of actors in the organization, as typical for 'professionalized

---

[23] One option not considered is the transformation into a de facto memberless organization. That would mean the organization as membership-based organization ceases to exist, hence, the particular tensions between self-maintenance and goal attainment as theorized in this study would not apply anymore.

[24] A range of studies have stressed the centrality of how leaders and members operate and interact (and are incentivized to operate and interact) in different organizational and political contexts. They include Ganz 2014; Lang 2013; Ahlquist and Levi 2014; Han 2014; Bentancur et al. 2019; and McAlevey 2016.

voluntary organizations'. Table 2.2 provides an overview of the central properties of each template whose internal implications can be theorized accordingly.

The distinction between 'voluntary association' and 'professionalized voluntary organization' builds on various organizational types or models proposed by earlier research. They include the 'voluntary association' and the 'voluntary agency' prominent in debates around the 'hybridization'[25] of nonprofit organizations (e.g. Billis 1991: 65; 2010: 54) or Bosso's 'professional advocacy organizations' deviating from 'classic membership groups' discussed in the interest group literature (2003: 403)—just to mention two.[26] There is overlap with organizational characteristics of what is portrayed as 'traditional' organizational form in contrast to alternative templates gaining prominence in increasingly individualized societies (that said, some parts of the debate are more concerned with CSOs' increasingly resembling public agencies,[27] while others stress their increasing similarities with for-profit organizations driven by market share[28]). In particular, the chosen

Table 2.2 Two Types of CSOs and Their Defining Characteristics

Constitutive Features of Membership-Based Voluntary Organizations	Type of Membership-Based Organizations	Core Characteristics
Voluntary membership (individual or corporate) Formal infrastructure Private (separate from government) Self-governing Non-profit-distributing	**Voluntary Association**	Governance structure Individual members Orientation towards member interests Multi-tier structure Central resources Volunteer staff Membership fees
	Professionalized Voluntary Organization	Governance structure Managerial procedures orientated towards efficiency Central resources Paid staff State funding

---

[25] The relevant strand in this literature defines hybridization as the combination of distinct governance logics within organizations (e.g. Grohs 2014).

[26] Another example that associates new organizational forms with instrumental rationales of for-profit organizations is Jordan's and Maloney's notion of the 'protest business' (1997) or what Maloney later called the 'ideal-typical professionalized interest group' (2012).

[27] For instance, the notion of 'social movement agency' describes 'hybrid' organizations that pursue social change through service delivery (Minkoff 2002: 381).

[28] See for a review on such developments Maier et al. 2016.

specification of the member-run and member-financed 'voluntary associa-tion' is in line with long-standing definitions of the concept (e.g. Sills 1959; 1968; Smith and Freedman 1972). Notions of organizational profession-alization, bureaucratization, and state dependency, in turn, are central to various prominent conceptualizations of more recent 'organizational forms' discussed in party, group, and non-profit literature. They are the central properties of the 'professionalized voluntary organization' (e.g. Panebianco 1988; Billis 1991; Katz and Mair 1995; Maloney 2012).

Given its long tradition (e.g. Smith and Freedman 1972), the label 'vol-untary association' (Billis 1991; 2010) was a rather straightforward choice, able to bridge the usual divide between membership groups that run elec-tions and those that do not (Rosenblum 2000b; Berry 1969). To find a label for the counterpart similarly applicable to parties, interest groups, and service-orientated organization was less straightforward. While the notions 'voluntary agency' (Billis 1991; 2010) or 'social movement agency' (Minkoff 2002) suggest a focus on service provision, Bosso's 'professional advocacy organization' (2003) or Maloney's ideal-typical 'professionalized interest group' (2012) are tailored to influence-seeking organizations. Panebianco's notion of 'electoral-professional party' (1988), in turn, presupposes organiza-tions' electoral participation. Similarly, core features of the 'professionalized voluntary organization' align with the cartel party model of party organi-zation, notably the importance of state funding as central income source (Katz and Mair 1995; 2009). Yet the debate around the cartel party as a model of party organization is much concerned with the empowerment of the party in public office (institutional office-holders) vis-à-vis organizational actors (in central office or on the ground) that is specific to parties as the only organizations able to take over parliamentary and governmental office. Finally, the notion of staff-driven (as compared to member-driven) group (e.g. Halpin 2014; Grömping and Halpin 2019) already suggests that orga-nizations are controlled by staff rather than members. While staff control (and, vice versa, limited member control) over decisions is associated with all three notions, not all professionalized membership organizations necessarily allow managers to assume responsibility for decision-making. What deter-mines such decision-making responsibilities and how pronounced they are is ultimately an empirical question (e.g. Heylen et al. 2020). Though clunkier than most alternative labels, the notion of 'professionalized voluntary orga-nization' seems more suitable in terms of connotation and scope. First, it stresses the professionalization of an organization as a central feature without making assumptions about its intra-organizational consequences. Second, it is neutral with regard to the core mission ascribed to range of organizations it might encompass.

On a substantive level, the parallels between organizational types developed in (widely) separate literatures echo fundamental tensions between democratic and bureaucratic governance logics respectively captured by alternative modes of organizing.[29] As Panebianco states, '[p]arties are bureaucracies requiring organizational continuity [...] and at the same time voluntary organizations which rely on at least a minimum of non-obligatory participation' which poses an organizational dilemma that membership-based voluntary organizations as complex organizations must come to terms with (1988: 6; 10). Membership organizations can manage such tensions in different ways, and the two governance templates can be considered as representations of two 'pure' solutions, with the 'traditional' association template—at least on the surface—prioritizing the 'democratic logic' and the professionalized model prioritizing the 'bureaucratic logic' (e.g. Alter 1998). Whether this will be confirmed by the later empirical analyses of how decision-making power in CSOs is actually allocated, however, remains to be seen.

Looking at the central characteristics of the 'voluntary association' and the 'professionalized voluntary organization' in Table 2.2, each template—integrating incentive-theoretical and resource dependency perspectives—is characterized with reference to central elements of its *governance structures* on the one hand and its *human and financial resources* on the other.[30]

In terms of *governance structure, voluntary associations* are traditionally defined as organizations that citizens belong to in a voluntary capacity and without pay (Sills 1968: 363; Smith and Freedman 1972: viii–ix). Accordingly, in terms of *governance structure*, voluntary associations are composed of individual members, oriented towards representing member interests, and members have a direct say over internal decisions (Billis 2010: 53–4; Paine et al. 2010; Knoke 1990). This is supported by a multi-tier structure allowing for decentralized decision-making, facilitating member mobilization and access, while enhancing the proximity between those members involved in and affected by decisions made in the organization (Lipset et al. 1956: 15; Barasko and Schaffner 2008: 194–95; Halpin 2014: 63; Skocpol et al. 1999: 492; Maloney 2012: 87). In terms of *central resources*, volunteer staff—a subset of members who are unpaid for their efforts—constitutes the

---

[29] E.g. Wilson 1973; Panebianco 1988; Knoke 1990; Alter 1998; Jordan and Maloney 2007; Halpin 2014; Maloney 2015.

[30] These two core elements echo work by Webb et al. examining whether political parties fulfil a linkage function and thereby enhance citizens' satisfaction with democracy, stressing the centrality of intra-organizational processes on the one hand and resources on the other (2019: 4). For a similar focus see Barakso 2004.

56 Civil Society's Democratic Potential

core of voluntary associations' workforce (Harris 1998: 151; Billis 2010: 54; Paine et al. 2010: 108). If voluntary associations have paid staff, such staff take on operational work but do not control any decisions (Knoke 1990: 6; Billis 2010: 59). Membership fees constitute associations' central income source (Knoke 1990: 54; Halpin 2014: 63; 67–8), consolidating the prioritization of member interests (Schmitter and Streeck 1999: 53–5).

Moving on to the alternative template of the *professionalized voluntary organization*, organizational professionalization is indicated by the growing intra-organizational reliance on professional skills and competences.[31] This reliance becomes manifest in the nature of an organizations' *governance structure* and its *human resources* (Maloney 2015: 102; Staggenborg 1988). In terms of the former, it is characterized by managerial procedures understood 'as a specific form of organizational structure' in which efficiency and effectiveness are central norms,[32] implemented through measures enhancing decision-making efficiency as well as the provision of training (Paine et al. 2010: 108). Paid staff indicate the professionalization of human resources and are often assumed to control decision-making, hence, to become central agents within this type of organization (Saurugger 2012: 72; Maloney 2015: 102; Billis 2010; Panebianco 1988). Members, instead of controlling decision-making as in traditional 'associations', are understood as a resource (Maloney 2012: 85; Halpin 2014: 69–70). This is complemented by state funding as an income source, further reducing CSOs' dependency on members (e.g. Katz and Mair 1995; Schmitter and Streeck 1999).

Conclusion

Being organized as a 'voluntary association' or a 'professionalized voluntary organization' affects who runs an organization and in whose interest an organization is run (Cornforth 2012: 1121). This fundamentally affects the respective 'weights' of leaders, managers, and members in organizational processes—three actor types with different orientations and priorities with regard to CSOs' maintenance and behaviour. Central features of these two governance templates are expected to impact on whose priorities are more likely to shape organizational processes and behaviour. This, in turn, is central to how organizational trade-offs confronting CSOs

---

[31] E.g. Panebianco 1988; Staggenborg 1988; Skocpol 2003; Hwang and Powell 2009; van Deth and Maloney 2012; Striebing 2017; Hanegraaff and Poletti 2019.

[32] Kreutzer and Jäger 2011: 638; Maier and Meyer 2011; Alexander and Fernandez 2021.

in contemporary democracies—trade-offs that shape their contributions to democracy—are likely to be resolved. This chapter has laid the theoretical groundwork to theorize how CSOs' structural characteristics feed into patterns of intra-organizational participation, interest representation, and societal responsiveness.

To be clear, the 'voluntary association' and 'professionalized voluntary organization' are not 'counter-images' whose characteristics are mutually exclusive. In line with the literature on organizational hybridization stressing the growing organizational diversity of CSOs that cut across well-established analytical categories (e.g. Minkoff 2002), there is no expectation that their central features cluster empirically. What is assumed, however, is that the features of each template incentivize the same 'behavioural logic'. This might mean longitudinally that they reinforce each other over time, which will be explored later in the case studies (see Chapters 6 and 9). From a cross-sectional perspective, it only suggests that features belonging to the same template are likely to set incentives towards resolving—in a similar fashion— organizational trade-offs impacting on CSOs' engagement in 'democracy-relevant' internal and external activities. Table 2.3 provides a first overview of the expected implications of the organizational properties associated with each template that will be developed in detail in Chapters 4–5 and Chapters 7–8.

In general terms, Table 2.3 shows how the two templates as analytical tools integrate this study by allowing us to theorize CSOs' varying performance on the four analytical dimensions used to capture different CSOs' democratic contributions. More specifically, it highlights that I expect characteristics jointly associated with the same governance model (overall) to affect the same dimension *in a similar way*. Second, I expect organizational characteristics associated with distinct templates to (overall) generate *different repercussions on each of the four dimensions* used to capture CSOs' contributions to democracy. Both underscore the importance of the multidimensional perspective on CSOs' democratic performance. If such a picture emerged from the empirical analysis conducted below, this would have broad repercussions, empirically and normatively. Let us return—as an illustration—to the CSO 'performance profile' that was associated with the most pronounced democratic contribution earlier on: high member control, low staff control, goal commitment, and a broad repertoire of political engagement. According to Table 2.3, neither organizational template should be expected to uniformly encourage or disincentivize high democratic performance in line with this profile. If so, CSOs resembling 'voluntary associations' would fall short of

58 Civil Society's Democratic Potential

Table 2.3 Two Governance Templates and Central Theoretical Expectations Regarding CSOs' Democratic Contributions

How Central Properties of Governance Template Are Expected to Shape CSO Behaviour	Implications for Dimensions Used to Capture CSOs' Democratic Contributions				
	Member Activism		Staff Control	CSO Goal Orientation	Political Engagement
	Involvement	Control			
Voluntary Association Governance structure: Individual members; Orientation towards member interests; Multi-tier structure Central resources: Volunteer staff; Membership fees	High[a]	n/a	Low	Stable	Weak
Professionalized Voluntary Organization Governance structure: Bureaucratization Central resources: Professionalization; State funding dependency	High	Low	High	Unstable	Strong

Notes: n/a indicates that no systematic relationship is expected.
[a] Individual membership is an exception amongst all other association features, as incentive-theoretical arguments suggest a negative relation with member involvement (see on this Chapter 4).

widespread normative expectations, while a trend towards 'professionalized voluntary organizations' in civil society would 'diminish democracy' less than is often claimed.

3
Methodological Choices and Data

The empirical part of this study is set up as a mixed-methods design. Hypotheses derived from the theoretical framework presented in Chapter 2 will be tested in a first step quantitatively using data from four CSO population surveys. This quantitative component is complemented by qualitative case studies.

Following state-of-the-art group research, the surveys targeted CSO actors in charge of the day-to-day running of regionally and nationally relevant groups and parties, such as chief executives, chairmen, leaders, or organizational secretaries knowledgeable about CSOs' internal operations as well as their external activities (Beyers et al. 2014: 131). The survey questionnaire was specifically designed to allow for the systematic comparison of different CSO types, i.e. partisan, advocacy, and service-oriented organizations, covering all four dimensions used to assess CSOs' varying democratic contributions. It consisted of thirty-six questions, covering a wide range of aspects related to central organizational activities, members, resources, internal processes, and external challenges. To the extent possible and suitable in light of this study's substantive interests, the survey questions were drawn from various earlier large-scale surveys such as the ones conducted by the 'Comparative Interest Group Survey Project' (Beyers et al. 2016), INTERARENA as well as 'The Organised Interest System in Australian Public Policy Project' (Halpin and Fraussen 2015).[1]

The four European countries in which surveys were conducted—Germany, Norway, Switzerland, and the UK—are most different regarding a range of important macro characteristics that existing research considers relevant for the structure, resources, and activities of different CSO types. They cover all central types of voluntary sector regimes relevant in long-lived Western democracies, which shape differently CSO professionalization, organizational finances, and organizations' relationships to government (Salamon and Anheier 1998): the UK is a liberal regime, Germany is a corporatist one, Norway is a social-democratic one, and Switzerland is considered a mix between the liberal and the social-democratic regime (Einolf 2015: 514;

---

[1] As these surveys targeted interest groups, questions were partially amended to make them equally applicable to the different CSO types covered.

Civil Society's Democratic Potential. Nicole Bolleyer, Oxford University Press. © Nicole Bolleyer (2024).
DOI: 10.1093/oso/9780198884392.003.0003

60   Civil Society's Democratic Potential

Butschi and Cattacin 1993: 367). Public resources made available to CSOs are particularly extensive in corporatist regimes. These regimes are often associated with organizational 'co-optation' by the state authorities, impacting on CSOs' political activities. Competition for policy access is considered particularly intense in pluralist systems (Zimmer and Pahl 2018). The four cases are located on opposite ends on a spectrum of generous vs. limited state funding for political parties (Germany and Norway on the generous, Switzerland and the UK on the restrictive end) (Poguntke et al. 2016). They further cover a wide spectrum of legal constraints that apply to group and party formation, operation, and dissolution. Here, Switzerland is one of the most permissive regimes and the UK one of the most constraining ones among long-lived democracies, with Norway and Germany located in between (Bolleyer 2018).

Finally, Table 3.1 classifies nineteen long-lived European and Anglo-Saxon democracies stable since the Second World War, based on country size, the federal–unitary divide, and societal heterogeneity, factors considered relevant for patterns of group formation and behaviour.[2] The four democracies selected for the survey cover four of the five empirically relevant macro configurations of these variables.[3] This suggests that this cross-national design and the variation it covers is suitable to substantiate the robustness of findings across a wider range of long-lived ('Western') democracies.

Moving from the systemic to the organizational level, to specify the population of nationally and regionally relevant membership-based CSOs active at the time the surveys were conducted, I used a bottom-up strategy based on the most inclusive sources documenting the relevant organizations in each democracy (Berkhout et al. 2018). For groups, these were the Directory of British Associations (DBA) (UK), the *Enhetsregisteret* (The Central Co-ordinating Register of Legal Entities) (Norway), the German *Taschenbuch des öffentlichen Lebens—Deutschland 2016*, and the Swiss Publicus (*Schweizer Jahrbuch des öffentlichen Lebens 2016*). This strategy ensured the inclusion of the full spectrum of politically and socially oriented membership-based organizations, ranging from classical interest groups—e.g. economic associations (e.g. Baroni et al. 2014)—to service-oriented associations and

---

[2] Sociocultural fractionalization as a proxy for societal heterogeneity is based on 1985/2000 data by Patsiurko et al. (2012); the federal-unitary distinction is based on Biela et al. (2013); the distinction big vs small states based on average population size (1990–2014) UN World Population Prospect 2015.

[3] The only category that is not covered is that of small, federal states that are societally homogeneous, which is—unlike all the other empirically relevant categories—only represented by one case, Austria. Austria is considered by the literature as only 'quasi-federal' given its very weak regional governments (Biela et al. 2013). While Norway is constitutionally unitary, it has directly elected regional governments with limited competences not dissimilar to Austria. Leaving the latter out is unlikely to significantly affect the representativeness of the findings.

Table 3.1 Macro Characteristics of Long-Lived Democracies and Case Selection for Surveys

	Societal Structure	Big State	Small State
Federal	*Sociocultural Fractionalization* **below** *OECD Mean*	**Germany,** United States, Canada, Australia	Austria
	Sociocultural Fractionalization **above** *OECD Mean*	n/a	**Switzerland,** Belgium
Unitary	*Sociocultural Fractionalization* **below** *OECD Mean*	**UK,** Italy, France	**Norway,** Finland, Iceland, Denmark, Sweden, New Zealand, The Netherlands, Luxembourg, Ireland
	Sociocultural Fractionalization **above** *OECD Mean*	n/a	n/a

inwards-oriented hobby or self-help groups (e.g. Salamon 1994). This strategy was emulated for parties, with the aim to include all party organizations participating in elections, parties' defining characteristic (e.g. Sartori 1976), which avoided a bias towards covering predominantly parties with privileged institutional access. Electorally active political parties were identified based on the respective party registers: in the UK, the Register of Political Parties of The Electoral Commission; in Switzerland, the *Parteienregister*; in Norway, the *Partiregisteret*; and in Germany, the *Liste der Zugelassenen Parteien und Wahlbewerber*. From these lists, parties were included that nominated candidates at the last national election in the respective country prior to the survey. Groups and parties included in the survey had an active website at the time the survey was launched (indicating that they were in operation at the time). Based on the websites, up-to-date email contacts of those in charge of the day-to-day running of the organization were collected (e.g. chief executives, chairperson, leaders, organizational secretaries), which then were invited to participate in the online surveys. The four country surveys were launched between April and October 2016.

The response rates were the following: in the UK 21 per cent, in Norway 28 per cent, in Germany 30 per cent, and in Switzerland 41 per cent. The resulting dataset covers 828 organizations in the UK, 351 in Norway, 1420 in Germany, and 666 in Switzerland. Its composition is widely representative regarding the distribution of parties and groups. So are the CSO-type-specific country samples in terms of core organizational

62 Civil Society's Democratic Potential

characteristics. More specifically, the distribution of groups and parties in the sample is broadly representative of the overall population of organizations. The percentage of groups in the population is 98.6 per cent, and in the dataset, it is 97.2 per cent; the percentage of parties in the population is 1.3 per cent; in the dataset 2.8 per cent. Furthermore, the group survey data has a representative response rate in terms of policy fields for each country sample based on the R-indicator (Schouten et al. 2009), which are the following: 0.94 for the UK, 0.87 for Norway, 0.92 for Germany, and 0.92 for Switzerland (the closer to 1, the more representative the sample). Similarly, the party survey data is broadly representative in terms of the proportion of parliamentary and extra-parliamentary parties as well as in ideological coverage. The proportion of parliamentary parties in the sample is 26 per cent; in the population it is 20.7 per cent. Meanwhile, all main party families constituting the four party systems are covered in the country samples.

As survey data is typically characterized by a high number of missing values, I have used multiple imputation techniques following King et al. (2001) via the Amelia package in R (King et al. 2001; Honaker et al. 2011) in all statistical analyses presented in Chapters 4–5 and 7–8. Doing so decreases the risk of losing valuable information or of having a selection bias (King et al. 2001: 49–50). Meanwhile, this increases the number of observations to 3265 across all models. As model choices differ depending on the nature of the dependent variable, those are detailed and justified in Chapters 4–5 and 7–8, presenting the individual statistical analyses.[4] To make central findings more accessible, effect sizes will be reported as marginal effects when discussing them, i.e. as the estimated change in the respective dependent variables undertaken by a typical organization associated with a unit change in the covariates.

Complementing the analyses of survey data, this study relies on an extensive range of primary materials (predominantly documents)[5] to conduct qualitative case studies. They trace the long-term trajectories of three CSOs operating in the UK—one political party, one service-oriented organization, and one interest group (details on the rationale for choosing the specific organizations are presented below). Complemented by existing secondary studies, primary material analysed included organizational statutes, financial and annual reports to relevant regulators (e.g. Company House, the Electoral Commission, the Charity Commission of England and Wales),

---

[4] Diagnostic tests indicate that multicollinearity is not a problem in any of the analyses. Replication material for the findings presented in Tables 4.2, 5.1, 7.2 and 8.1 are available via www.oup.co.uk/companion/Bolleyer.

[5] Chapters 6 and 9 provide more information on the sources used and how they were analysed. Documentation on the primary sources used for each case study is provided in the Online Appendix made available www.oup.co.uk/companion/Bolleyer.

organizational publications such as newsletters and press releases, and public lectures or interviews with key organizational actors (past and present). These documentary sources were complemented by semi-structured interviews with organizational representatives such as current and former leaders, managers, and members to assess intra-organizational dynamics that were difficult to trace based on documentary evidence alone. In 2017, nine initial interviews were conducted across the three CSOs, followed by ten interviews in 2022[6] to cover more recent developments and to fill remaining gaps and ambiguities that emerged when systematically integrating the variety of different sources compiled earlier.[7]

Triangulating these qualitative sources allowed me to cover the three organizations' whole lifespans up to summer 2022, covering a range of aspects. These include organizational changes and internal reforms impacting on the allocation of decision-making power, changes in (functional and substantive) goal orientation and in political engagement patterns as related organizations' professionalization and bureaucratization, as well as shifts in organizational finances.[8] Relatedly, even though the quantitative measures for CSO professionalization, bureaucratization, and state funding dependency are not strongly correlated (see for details the following section), the case studies are able to show how the features of the 'professionalized voluntary organization' such as professionalization and bureaucratization can support each other over time.

Linking the qualitative component back to the framework presented in Chapter 2, the case studies will allow us to capture not only the interactions but also interconnections between members, organizational leaders, and managers as 'three faces of membership organizations'[9] that Chapter 2 associated with distinct motivations and priorities. Their interplay will be examined in the context of the long-term evolution of three CSOs that started out resembling traditional associations and increasingly transformed

---

[6] All interviews were recorded and anonymized. An anonymized list of interviews is provided in the Online Appendix made available via www.oup.co.uk/companion/Bolleyer. For all data collection efforts (qualitative and qualitative), ethical approval was acquired by the respective bodies at the University of Exeter and the LMU Munich.

[7] The team of the by now completed ERC project STATORG conducted extensive document analyses not only in the UK but also in Germany, Norway, Ireland, Italy, the Netherlands, and Spain as well as over 110 interviews in Norway, Italy, the Netherlands, and the UK which are presented elsewhere (Bolleyer and Correa 2020a; 2020b; 2022a; 2022b; Bolleyer et al. 2020; Bolleyer 2021a; 2021b; Ivanovska Hadjievska 2018; Ivanovska Hadjievska and Stavenes 2020; Stavenes and Ivanovska Hadjievska 2021). Further information on the CIVILSPACE project can be found here: https://cps-lmu.org/civilspace.html.

[8] More detail on central operationalizations based on the qualitative data will be provided in Chapters 6 and 9.

[9] This metaphor is borrowed from Katz and Mair's prominent distinction between three faces of party organization (1993).

into professionalized voluntary organizations. This, in turn, allows for an assessment of how moving an organization away from the one governance template towards the other tends to affect these CSOs' performance on the four dimensions: member activism, staff control, goal reorientation, and political engagement.

Measures Used in the Quantitative Analyses

The Dependent Variables: How to Measure CSOs' Diverse Contributions to Democracy

In the statistical analyses presented in Chapters 4–5 and 7–8, individual CSOs' democratic contributions in terms of participation, representation, and societal responsiveness are captured using the following indicators, all constructed based on the survey data described earlier.

Starting with measures for CSO contributions to participation, *member activism* is conceptualized through two concepts, as explained in Chapter 2—*Member Control* and *Member Involvement*. This dimension of CSOs' democratic contribution is therefore captured empirically through two separate measures. To measure *Member Control* over decision-making I use an index that is based on three indicators from a survey question in which participants had to indicate how their organizations primarily make decisions in different areas. The index has been constructed by adding up (with equal weight) the following dimensions, which have been selected as they align closely with notions of intra-organization democracy: 'Appointing board members or the executive', 'Appointing the chairperson or the leader', and 'Changing the statutory rules or the constitution'. They are particularly indicative of who controls the power structure of an organization. They concern the selection of leaders who—leaving aside very small organizations able to prevent the formation of any internal elite—are in charge of the running of the organization, including its strategic priorities. They also concern the alteration of those rules that define basic rights and obligations of intra-organizational actors, including members and leaders, and hence the distribution of power within the organization. Each component indicator has been coded as 1 when decisions in an organization were taken by consensus or by voting among members (indicating members' *direct* control over decisions in the respective domains) and 0 when decisions were made otherwise (i.e. by the board, by the chairperson, by senior staff). The index has values that range from 0 to 3, indicating different degrees of member control (0 means members don't have direct control over core areas of decision-making and 3 means members have the maximum level of control).[10] The measure for *Member Involvement* as the second form of member activism studied in Chapter 4 is based on a survey question (a five-point Likert scale) asking participants how involved their members are in their organization, 1 being not at all involved and 5 extremely involved.[11]

Moving to the societal responsiveness of CSO behaviour as the second normative yardstick underpinning my framework, *organizational accountability of CSO decision-making (or the lack thereof)* can serve as one empirical proxy of meaningful constituency linkages (see for details Chapter 2). Consequently, the analysis in Chapter 5 considers the extent to which domains of decision-making are controlled by senior managers as a third group of actors (and potential decision-makers) actively involved in CSO governance, alongside members and organizational leaders. *Staff Control* is measured based on the same survey item as *Member Control* but considers all domains relevant to organizational governance in terms of organizational maintenance and mission attainment, including technical, administrative, and political domains which staff might become involved in (Cornforth and Edwards 1998: 2; Ben-Ner and Ren 2010; Barbieri et al. 2013).

Unlike the measure of *Member Control*, which aimed to capture whether or not members have control over areas essential for the distribution of power in a CSO, *Staff Control* is interested in the pervasiveness of paid staff in organizational life more broadly. Senior staff's ability to make its own decisions might take hold in technical or administrative areas that are perceived to be 'low-key'. Such a shift still demarcates a break with accountability structures that require actors affiliated to the CSO in a more than instrumental fashion to be in charge, and can be expected to impact on an organization's culture. Consequently, an index is constructed based on nine indicators derived from the question that asked participants how their organization primarily makes

---

[10] While Member Control serves as one of the two dependent variables in the analyses on member activism presented in Chapter 4, it is—as an important feature of CSO governance—also included in the analyses of *CSO Goal Reorientation* and *CSO Political Engagement as an independent variable* (Chapters 7 and 8). This was feasible as all CSOs participating in the survey were asked—after having indicated how their organizations primarily make decisions in different areas *currently*—whether this has changed in the last five years and if so, how decisions were made *beforehand*. This allowed for the construction of an equivalent measure of *Past Member Control*. Its inclusion was not possible in the analysis of drivers of *Staff Control* (Chapter 5) as the measure for *Staff Control* and for *Member Control* are partially based on the same survey items.

[11] To enhance the robustness of the findings, a measure for *Increased Member Involvement* is—as Past Member Control—added to the remaining analyses as an independent variable. Based on a separate item that asked CSOs whether the degree of member involvement changed in the last five years and, if so, how, a dummy variable was constructed coding 1 CSOs which indicated an increase in involvement and 0 CSOs which did not.

decisions considering the following domains: budget, hiring staff, appointing board members/executives, appointing the chairperson/leader, selecting electoral candidates, admitting new members, expelling members, changing the organization's statutes or constitution, and establishing the organization's policy/programmatic positions.[12] Each of those indicators is coded as 1 when participants indicated that decisions in the respective area are primarily made by 'employed senior staff', and 0 otherwise. The values of the nine items are then added up, leading to an index on staff control ranging from 0 to 9 (0 indicates that staff exercised no control in any domain and 9 indicates that staff exercised control across all governance domains). The index assigns each decision-making area equal weight. Of course, staff control over decision-making might be perceived as more sensitive in some areas than in others. Still, the full range of decision-making domains should be taken into consideration in order to assess in an encompassing fashion the relative scope of decision-making power that staff acquire within individual membership-based organizations formally 'owned' by members (Billis 2010), which is normatively contentious as such (see, for more details on this, Chapter 5).

With regard to the measures capturing the nature of intra-organizational decision-making (member and staff control) as well as involvement introduced so far, it is important to note that the literatures on parties, groups, and professional discretion have long highlighted discrepancies between formal rules and the actual practices (e.g. Panebianco 1988; Barasko and Schaffner 2008; Wallander and Molander 2014). The relevant survey items therefore asked about the *actual* nature of decision-making and actual levels of member involvement in organizational processes, not about formal rules that might be used by members or not. This is equally crucial for *Member Control* and *Staff Control*, which are constructed based on the same survey question. While, on the one hand, members might possess formal powers they rarely use, on the other hand, formal rules and procedures generally tend to assign decision-making competences to organizational representatives, not to paid employees—be this due to normative considerations or legal constraints (Salamon and Flaherty 1997; van der Ploeg et al. 2017). Hence, neither the formal allocation of decision-making power to members nor the absence of such formal allocation to managers necessarily reflects accurately how decision-making power is allocated between members, organizational leaders, and managers. And this was considered in the design of the measures.

---

[12] This question is based on an item used in the Comparative Interest Group Survey Project (Beyers et al. 2016).

As a second indication of the societal responsiveness of CSO behaviour alongside *Staff Control*, I explore *whether CSO identities are likely to provide a foundation for meaningful constituency linkages*. This is done by assessing the drivers of *CSO Goal Reorientation* (as opposed to CSO commitment to central goals). This variable is measured using a dummy variable based on the following question: 'It is fairly common for organizations to make changes in order to make their survival prospects. Has your organization undertaken any of the following strategies in the last five years?' CSOs which answered with a 'yes' regarding the item 'We have changed the mission or programme of our organization' were coded 1 (indicating goal reorientation); those that answered 'no' were coded 0 (indicating goal commitment).[13]

Moving to the last normative yardstick, i.e. whether CSOs operate as *vehicles of interest representation,* this is assessed considering CSOs' *political engagement.* Whether CSOs are engaged in the aggregation and articulation of 'politically relevant' interests central to interest representation (Salisbury 1984: 64) is captured through two closely connected variables, one measuring *CSO Politicization*, another measuring a CSO's *Political Action Repertoire.* They are based on the following survey item: 'The table below lists a range of activities organizations can engage in to exercise political influence. Please indicate which activities your organization engages in nowadays'. For each option, organizations were asked to indicate whether they engage in the respective activity never, rarely, sometimes, often, or very often.[14] The activities listed were the following:

- Contact reporters, write letters to the editor, issue press releases
- Paid advertisements in media outlets
- Arrange debates/hold press conferences
- Encourage members and others to contact decision-makers
- Participate in public consultations
- Contact government officials (e.g. ministers, members of parliament, civil servants)
- Publish analyses and research reports
- Legal direct action (e.g. authorized strikes) and public demonstrations
- Civil disobedience and illegal direct action
- Electoral and/or referenda campaigns
- Donations to political parties
- Cooperation with specific interest or advocacy group(s)
- Cooperation with a political party/parties

---

[13] Additional items were offered to survey participants referring to less significant changes such as of strategy and tactic (see on this Chapter 7).

[14] The survey item was based on the Comparative Interest Group Survey by Beyers et al. 2016.

In line with the conceptualization of interest representation in interest group research as well as studies on non-profit organizations' political activities (e.g. Chaves et al. 2004; Kimberlin 2010) (see also Chapter 2), the thirteen activities deliberately cover a wide spectrum including political and partisan activities, conventional and unconventional forms of political participation, activities directed towards government institutions, as well as those targeting the public. I consider a CSO as politically active—i.e. as *politicized*—if it engages in one or more of these thirteen activities *either often* or *very often*. In contrast to *occasional* or *rare* engagement, this indicates the prioritization of political activity. If resources are regularly invested in the latter, this usually happens at the cost of other activities, i.e. CSOs are forced to engage in trade-off decisions, making choices between conflicting priorities central to this study's theoretical framework. *Political Activity Repertoire* captures the intensity and diversity of such engagement based on the number of political activities an organization engages in often or very often, captured through an additive index ranging from 0 to 13 (see for details on the conceptual underpinning Chapter 1).

Central Explanatory Variables: CSOs' Governance Characteristics

The crucial explanatory variables in all statistical analyses discussed in Chapter 4–5 and 7–8 are the CSO characteristics constitutive for the two governance templates integrating this study (see Chapter 2, Table 2.2 for an overview). Their central characteristics are measured through the following indicators, respectively. The three defining features of a *Professionalized Voluntary Organization* are: *Bureaucratization* central to its governance structure and *Professionalization* and *State Funding* as its core resources. To measure *Bureaucratization* I capture the increasing entrenchment of managerial procedures using an index which is based on two items from a question asking what types of changes an organization made in the past five years to enhance its survival prospects. An organization was coded 2 when it 'reinforce[d] investments in managerial competences/skills of the organization' *and* 'streamlined decision-making processes to enhance efficiency', 1 when it implemented only one of these changes, and 0 if none. To capture *Professionalization*, i.e. the professionalization of the human resources sustaining a CSO, I measure its reliance on paid personnel (e.g. Farrell and Webb 2002; Halpin and Thomas 2012). The survey asks for the total number of paid full-time staff. As this variable has a right-skewed distribution,

I include the logarithmic version suitable to deal with heavy skewed data (Ansolabehere et al. 2002; Healy and Malhotra 2009). And finally, to measure organizations' reliance on *State Funding*, I use a survey question that asks organizations about the relevance of different types of financial support for an organization's budget over the last five years (Jordan and Maloney 1997; Beyers et al. 2016).[15] I have constructed an index capturing CSO state funding dependency by adding up two items capturing the relative relevance of public funding from national government and from other levels of government respectively. Capturing subnational funding was important to avoid a bias, considering also regionally focused CSOs and including both unitary and federal political systems. In each case, I distinguished those organizations for whom these sources of income were 'important' or 'very important' (coded 1) from those for whom they are not (coded 0). The index ranges from 2 (high dependency) to 0 (low dependency). This operationalization is in line with resource dependency theory (e.g. Nienhüser 2008), as it aims at distinguishing whether the respective income source is likely to be strategically important or not, and hence can be expected to have behavioural repercussions.

Moving to the *Voluntary Association* template, its five central features were measured in the following fashion: first, *Member Interest Orientation* is captured through a dummy variable that takes the value 1 if the organization indicates that 'it pursues goals that primarily benefit the members' and 0 if not. Second, whether an organization has a *Multi-tier Structure* is captured through a dummy variable based on a question in which organizations indicated whether they are composed of more than one organizational tier (coded 1, 0 otherwise). Third, with regard to central resources, the number of *Volunteer Staff* was (as *Professionalization*) based on a question asking an organization about its different types of personnel, including how many volunteers work for the organization. Given its right-skewed distribution, I again use the logarithmic version in our analysis. Fourth, to measure organizations' reliance on *Membership Fees*, I use (as for *State Funding*) a survey item about the relevance of membership fees for an organization's budget over the last five years. Again, I capture in line with resource dependency theory whether this income source is strategically important to an organization or not by distinguishing those organizations for whom membership fees were an 'important' or 'very important' source of income (coded 1) from those for whom it was not (coded 0). Fifth, the nature of an organization's composition—*Individual Membership*—is captured based on a survey item

---

[15] This mediates problems of reverse causation as CSOs' *past* financial situation is covered.

asking about the type of members that constitutes an organization. It takes the value 1 if the membership is 'predominantly composed of individual citizens' and 0 otherwise.

Control Variables Central to the Functioning of CSOs Generally

To assure the robustness of the findings, a range of control variables is included in all models presented in this study. They capture features that, based on earlier research, can be expected to affect how CSOs as membership organizations—given their constitutive set-up—operate in general, rather than being of particular relevance to individual analytical dimensions distinguished by the framework.

CSO Type is a central one of those factors. Its importance has been discussed in detail earlier and its impacts will be explicitly theorized in several analyses. It captures organizations' functional orientation, based on a question in which organizations classified themselves as either a political party, an interest group, or a service-oriented organization. This avoids mischaracterizations as specifying the type of group can be particularly challenging since CSOs can possess characteristics of both interest group and service-oriented organizations (Binderkrantz 2009: 662). Based on this question, two dummies are included in the later analyses: *Interest Group* and *Service-Oriented Organization*, with *Political Party* as a reference category, expecting the distinction between group and party to be more pronounced than between the two group types. Three variables are added that capture the nature of organizations' membership base and their relations to members constitutive for CSOs, as defined in this study (see, for details, Chapter 2), given their basic dependency on voluntary member support: *Membership Instability* and *Membership Size*. *Membership Instability* exposes CSOs to the exit of organizational members (e.g. Hirschman 1970; Wilson 1973). To capture this pressure, I used a question in which CSOs were asked about the importance of various challenges for the maintenance of their organization. CSOs were coded 1 when they indicated the challenge of 'retaining and recruiting members' as important or very important and 0 otherwise. *Membership Size* is widely considered an important factor shaping how organizations operate internally and externally, indicating CSOs' relative strength and resource availability crucial for self-maintenance and goal attainment alike (e.g. Jordan and Maloney 2007; Scarrow et al. 2017). As the variable has a right-skewed distribution, I again use the logarithmic version in all the models. In addition, I control for organizational *Age*, an important proxy for organizational consolidation and resilience important to internal organizational dynamics and external behaviour (e.g. Panebianco 1988).[16] To account for country differences, all models include three country dummies, with *Norway* as reference category (a social democratic welfare state, in which CSOs operate in a permissive legal environment, both *enhancing* the autonomy of the CSO sector as compared to the *UK, Germany*, and *Switzerland*).

Control Variables Relevant to Specific Dimensions of CSOs' Democratic Contribution

Beyond the controls impacting on the overall nature of CSO functioning, additional variables were included depending on the specific dimension studied, if earlier research suggested that individual factors might be particularly relevant. Competition for and CSOs' dependency on (often volatile) donor support is a frequently discussed concern, especially in group and non-profit research, which has been said to contribute to the central role of professionals in CSOs, the propensity of CSOs to strategically change their mission, and the nature of their advocacy engagement (e.g. Bosso 1995; Maloney 2012; 2015; Lang 2013; Suarez 2010a). The analyses on *Staff Control, Goal Reorientation*, and *Political Engagement* (Chapters 5, 7–8) therefore include a variable capturing CSOs' *Donor Dependency*. As with the index to capture CSO dependency on *State Funding*, two items—one on donations and gifts from individuals and one on those from donors other than individuals—were combined into an additive index, respectively distinguishing those organizations for whom each source of income was important or very important over the last five years (coded 1) from those for whom it was not (coded 0). The index, ranging from 0 to 2, hence captures CSOs' growing dependence on income from donations. It is a prominent argument that *Marketization* of the voluntary sector has enhanced the centrality of paid professionals within CSO governance (e.g. Eikenberry and Kluver 2004). The analysis of drivers of *Staff Control* in Chapter 5 therefore considers CSOs' past dependence on sales and services. As with the other funding measures, the variable distinguishes CSOs for whom 'income generating activities including service/sales to members, savings/investments etc.' were 'important' or 'very important' as an income source over the last five years (coded 1) from those for whom

---

[16] The average age of political parties is thirty-five years while the average age of interest groups and service-oriented organizations is fifty-two and fifty-seven.

72   Civil Society's Democratic Potential

they were not (coded 0). Relatedly, market pressures generated on the population level as well as those directly perceived by individual CSOs have long been central explanatory variables in studies of group behaviour (e.g. Gray and Lowery 1995; Baumgartner and Leech 1998; 2001; Halpin and Thomas 2012). I capture this aspect through two variables. First, *Competition Density* (to use the terminology common in group research) captures the number of groups or parties a CSO competes with in its 'substantive' area or 'hunting ground'. For groups, the latter is defined by the policy field a CSO specializes in; for parties, it finds expression in their ideological orientation, which can be captured by the party family they belong to (e.g. Baumgartner and Leech 2001; Mair and Mudde 1998). The more organizations are present in an 'area' or 'niche' and the more CSOs thus substantively resemble each other, the more intense issue- or ideologically-based competition in that area or niche (e.g. Gray and Lowery 1995; Fisker 2015; Meguid 2008). Which substantive niche a CSO belonged to was coded manually and, depending on CSO type, based on the distinction between nine policy fields (in the case of groups) and nine party families (in the case of parties).[17] The groups' policy orientation was established based on their websites, main activities, goals, and manifestos. For parties, 'family membership' data was taken from the Chapel Hill Expert Survey 1999–2014 (Polk et al. 2017), or for those parties that were not included, information was taken from party manifestos. I include the logarithmic version suitable to deal with skewed data. Second, in line with earlier studies, I included *Resource Competition* as a measure of direct competitive pressure, as perceived by the individual CSO. This variable captures whether organizations are exposed to competition from similar organizations for key resources such as members, funds, or government contracts (coded 1), or not (coded 0). As both measures capture externally generated pressures, they were included in the analyses of *CSO Goal Reorientation* and *Political Engagement* (Chapters 7 and 8), the two dimensions to which CSOs' relations to external audiences—for whose support CSOs compete with substantively similar organizations—is likely to be relevant.[18]

CSOs often struggle to maintain the attention of the public and the media, which has strong repercussions for their substantive profiles and the core

---

[17] The categories used to code groups were: Economy; Social policy; Health; Recreational activities; Education and culture; Politics; Environment; Religion; and other (Jentges et al. 2013); for political parties: Radical right, Religious; Conservatives and Christian Democrats; Liberal; Social Democrats; Greens; Far left; Regionalists; and Single-issue (Polk et al. 2017).

[18] Since I expect the relationship between *Competition Density* and *Goal Reorientation* as well as *Political Engagement* to be non-linear, I used the logarithm of the former in the respective analyses.

issues they focus on to maintain their support base as well as the support of other critical audiences. This challenge to maintain issue attention can be expected to be particularly relevant for patterns of *CSO Goal Reorientation* (see for details Chapter 7). To measure such *Visibility Challenge*, i.e. the difficulties perceived by CSOs to maintain the visibility and thus saliency of their core issues, I created an index ranging from 0 to 2, based on two items from a question in which organizations indicated the importance of several challenges for the maintenance of their organization (Hanegraaff and Poletti 2019: 132–3). The index is based on the items asking about 'Changes in public opinion about the issues important for your organization' and to 'Access to the media' as potential challenges. A CSO was coded 1 for each item when they identified the challenge as either 'important' or 'very important'; 0 if not. Two further variables expected to be particularly relevant for the adaptability of CSO goals were added to this analysis (see for a detailed rationale Chapter 7): first, the variable *Aggregation Challenge*, a dummy variable coded 1 when a CSO identified 'individualization/growing societal diversity' as an 'important' or 'very important' challenge for its maintenance and 0 if not; second, the variable *Member Control over Policy* capturing member control over the organization's policies.[19]

CSO Diversity and Why the Voluntary Association and the Professionalized Voluntary Organization Are Not Treated As Counter-Images

This section takes a brief look at central resource variables associated with the two governance templates (both human and financial), disaggregated by type of CSO. Service-oriented organizations have the largest average staffing size in terms of paid staff, i.e. their level of professionalization; a central marker of the 'professionalized voluntary organization', is on average, higher than that of parties and interest groups. The average number of paid staff is 489 in service-orientated organization as compared to about fourteen in parties and interest groups. In terms of professionalization, interest groups resemble parties more than service-oriented groups. Contrasting this with the number of volunteer staff, a core resource of voluntary associations, the two group types more closely resemble each other. Parties rely less on the support of

---

[19] Details on the survey items and descriptive statistics are provided in the Online Appendix available on www.oup.co.uk/companion/Bolleyer.

volunteers, having 309 volunteers involved in organizational work on average, as compared to interest groups and service-oriented organizations, with 1367 and 1167 volunteer staff on average.

The membership sizes of service-oriented organizations are on average biggest (though the standard deviation indicates a large variation in terms of size); for interest groups they are smallest. The distributions of membership sizes in service-oriented organizations and interest groups are more skewed, i.e. there are many more organizations with small membership sizes than large sizes. Interestingly, membership sizes (indicating the size of a CSO's recruitment pool) do not visibly feed into differences in volunteer staff (i.e. unpaid members involved in the running of and working for the organization): the correlation between the two variables is positive but weak. More specifically, despite having more than twice as many members than interest groups on average, parties report only 309 volunteer staff on average, more than two-thirds less than interest groups. Service-orientated CSOs on average tend to rely relatively more on both paid and volunteer staff, while parties rely less on both (though both have relatively similar average membership sizes). Indeed, we find a positive correlation between the number of paid and volunteer staff, not a negative one. In short, central features associated with the 'professionalized voluntary organization' and 'association' are not necessarily in tension with each other. This is a critical issue for how this study is set up, which I return to below.

Table 3.2 shows that financial contributions of members are—for most organizations, irrespective of type—an important or very important income source. Even though interest groups have on average smaller memberships than both parties and service-oriented organizations, this income source is on average slightly more important to them. State funding is important or very important for many fewer organizations than are membership fees. Worries around excessive financial dependency on the state are predominantly a concern regarding a minority of privileged organizations. Though a higher proportion of parties (mean score 0.30) indicate state funding as important/very important as compared to interest groups and service-oriented organizations (mean score 0.20 and 0.26), the overall patterns are nevertheless remarkably similar across CSO types. The biggest difference is seen with regard to income from sales and services. This income source plays a bigger role amongst service-oriented organizations, which aligns with earlier research that stresses the growing importance of marketization pressures in the non-profit sector (e.g. Eikenberry and Kluver 2004).

As most CSOs are small, it is unsurprising that membership fees are more important than state funding to keep organizations going. This is underlined

Table 3.2 The Relative Importance of Different Income Sources by Type of Organization

Organizational Type	Membership Fees	State Funding	Private Donations	Sales and Services
Parties	0.77	0.30	0.36	0.12
Interest Groups	0.87	0.20	0.17	0.29
Service-Oriented Organizations	0.74	0.26	0.17	0.49

Note: Importance of membership fees, state funding, private donations, and sales and services are standardized with a range between zero and one for ease of comparison.

by the fact that donations are on average much less relevant to CSOs than membership fees. Also, this income source is more easily attracted by bigger, influential players with a higher public profile. Though intuitive, the pattern displayed in Table 3.2 is interesting in light of ongoing debates around whether members as a resource have become less important in light of an often highlighted, increasing dependency of the civil society sector on the state.[20] Clearly, the above figures do not allow ruling out prominent arguments that organizations able to access state funding care less about members or that organizations able to rely on paid professionals consider volunteer staff as less crucial. Yet the descriptive data does suggest that—at least in Germany, Norway, Switzerland, and the UK—voluntary members (as financial contributors and contributors of organizational work) still play an important role for CSOs.

On a more general level, this short illustration of CSOs' central organizational characteristics further indicates that the dividing line between interest groups, service providers, and parties—usually considered distinct classes of organizations—is not very clear-cut. In some respects, interest groups and service providers—on average—more closely resemble each other, and contrast with parties (e.g. reliance on volunteer staff). In other respects, the politically orientated organizations, parties, and interest groups appear, on average, more similar and contrast with service-oriented groups (e.g. professionalization). With regard to some properties, we find little difference across all three groups (e.g. dependence on membership fees). Consequently, none of the two governance templates 'voluntary association' and 'professional

---

[20] E.g. Mair 1994; Katz and Mair 1995; Jordan and Maloney 1997; Chaves and Galaskiewicz 2004; Billis 2010; Larsson 2011; Bloodgood and Tremblay-Boire 2017.

76 Civil Society's Democratic Potential

voluntary organization' clearly aligns with one of the CSO types. The different implications of both templates' constitutive features can therefore be sensibly examined across membership organizations generally.

Relatedly, it is important to stress that the two governance templates are not to be understood as 'counter-images' in an empirical sense. This means their central characteristics are neither mutually exclusive, nor do each template's central characteristics cluster,[21] which brings us back to the diversity of organizational forms that CSOs adopt in contemporary democracies. In fact, there are no strong correlations between any of the eight characteristics defining the two templates (see Chapter 2, Table 2.2). While *Professionalization, Bureaucratization,* and *State funding dependency* are positively correlated with each other, these correlations are all below 0.1. At the same time, all three are positively correlated with at least two of five characteristics of typical voluntary associations. Indeed, the strongest positive correlation between all eight defining characteristics (0.318) we find between *Professionalization* and *Volunteer staff,* which cuts across templates.[22] Vice versa, two of the association features—*Multi-tier structure* and *Volunteer staff*—have positive correlations with all three features of the 'professionalized voluntary organization', while being negatively correlated with at least one association feature. Overall, features associated with each template are not empirically connected to an extent that would justify the construction of two summary measures based on the two sets of characteristics to capture the extent to which CSOs correspond to each template.

Most problematically, the construction of such summary measures would treat as an assumption what ought to be empirically tested. I have argued in Chapter 2 that the two governance templates are useful analytical tools as they allow me to formulate systematic expectations about how the organizational features associated with each of them feed differently into CSO behaviour. This is because each template supports a distinct behavioural logic. To put this claim to the test requires empirical analyses that treat these eight variables as separate independent variables. Only then we can establish whether significant variables associated with the *same* template have *similar* implications for CSOs' democratic contributions and whether significant variables associated with *distinct* templates indeed have *opposite*

---

[21] See for a correlation table the Online Appendix made available via www.oup.co.uk/companion/Bolleyer

[22] The same goes for the strongest negative correlation which is between dependency on *State Funding* and *Membership Fees.* Though this is across templates, this correlation is only weak (−0.257).

implications. This leaves aside that a construction of summary measures would mean a considerable loss of information. Notably, it would prevent us from finding out which organizational characteristics of each template specifically matter for different dimensions of CSOs' democratic contribution, associations that then can be explored directly in the case studies.

The Advantages of a Mixed-Methods Design

Statistical analyses that are able to cover a wide range of CSOs, including groups and parties, and are able to consider a wide range of explanatory and control variables, are crucial to identify broader patterns between CSO characteristics and their implications for membership activism, staff control, CSO goal reorientation, and political engagement. At the same time, these analyses have inevitable limitations: they cannot give us insights into developments over time and thus how a CSO's increasing transformation from 'association' to 'professionalized voluntary organization' impacts on each of the four dimensions used to capture CSOs' democratic contributions. For instance, cross-sectional analyses are susceptible to reverse causality, and cannot capture the connection between changing levels of professionalization and evolving patterns of member activism that follow the latter. Similarly, the statistical analyses of patterns of member involvement and control provide us with only limited insight into what members actually do in different types of membership organizations and how this plays out in terms of process. How and by whom is member control curtailed in increasingly professionalized organizations? How exactly do association features such as reliance on volunteer staff and multi-tier structures create a barrier against staff control? Qualitative case studies can bring both over-time dynamics and organizational agency into the picture.

The qualitative case studies presented in this book compare the long-term trajectories of three CSOs, from their foundations several decades ago to summer 2022 (when I finished the qualitative data collection). They are designed to capture the evolving internal dynamics and relations between rank-and-file members, organizational leaders, and managers as 'three faces of membership organizations' in CSOs that increasingly resemble 'professionalized voluntary organizations'. These case studies are tightly integrated with the quantitative analyses preceding them. Essentially, the qualitative Chapters 6 and 9 focus on the most central findings of the quantitative assessments presented beforehand, i.e. the theorized variables significantly associated with patterns of member activism and staff control, and patterns of goal reorientation and political engagement, respectively.

The Selection of Three UK CSOs for In-Depth Study

Each CSO studied in depth was deliberately selected as representative of one of the three CSO types covered in this study. Analysing a party organization, an interest group, and a service-oriented organization allows us to explore the extent to which similar dynamics are at play in membership-based CSOs with very different functional orientations. This, in turn, helps us to substantiate the broader conceptual argument that these types of organizations can indeed be suitably theorized and analysed by the same overarching analytical framework (e.g. Wilson 1973; Fraussen and Halpin 2018; Bolleyer 2018; 2021a Bolleyer and Correa 2020a; 2022a).

The chosen case studies are the Green Party of England and Wales (GPEW), the interest group Surfers Against Sewage (SAS), and the National Activity Providers Association[23] (NAPA), a service-oriented organization. The GPEW was formed in 1973, is composed of individual members, and has traditionally focused on environmental issues. Formed in 1990, the SAS is an interest group composed of (predominantly) individuals, and is dedicated to the protection of marine life and the coastline. NAPA, formed in 1997, works in the health and care sector, and organizes professionals who provide services in care settings. Unlike the other two organizations, NAPA has a mixed membership, including individuals and corporate members such as care homes, with a variety of membership strands for activity staff but also service users and their families.

All three organizations operate in the UK, which, compared to other long-lived democracies, provides for a highly constraining legal environment for both groups and parties. They are subject to complex regulatory regimes that allocate only few, narrowly tailored benefits (Bolleyer 2018). Consequently, compared to more permissive contexts, incentives for CSOs to professionalize are strong (Ivanovska Hadjievska 2018; Ivanovska Hadjievska and Staveness 2020). In such a legal environment, the effects of CSO professionalization and bureaucratization should show with particular clarity, both in their potentially positive and negative implications for CSOs' 'democratic performance'. At the same time, UK company law, UK party law and English

---

[23] Until 2014 the organization's name was: 'National Association for Providers of Activities for Older People'.

charity law—which regulate the legal forms that CSOs tend to operate in[24]—are 'neutral' in one important respect. They neither require nor prevent formal member control over CSO decisions or otherwise interfere much in the basic set-up of CSOs' internal governance structures (van de Ploeg at al 2017; Bolleyer et al. 2020). More so than the legal regimes of the other three survey countries, the UK legal framework allows groups and parties to determine how they want to organize themselves internally.[25] This ensures that the internal allocation of decision-making power reflects the interplay between organizational leaders, managers, and members.

Moving to one central t similarity between the three organizations that merits discussion, none of them has developed into a large organization (neither in terms of membership size nor budget). This is noteworthy as although small CSOs constitute the majority of membership-based organizations in all three organizational subgroups—parties, interest groups, and service-providers—studies of organizational governance have tended to focus on large, affluent, and heavily professionalized groups (Fraussen and Halpin 2018: 30; Bolleyer 2013a). To explore the implications of CSOs' growing reliance on paid staff, processes of bureaucratization, and changing financial dependencies, three organizations are examined, which—within their 'reference group'—have remained small or been small organizations for most of their histories. These cases allowed me to capture the evolving balance between early associational features and a growing resemblance with the template of the 'professionalized voluntary organization' from these CSOs' formation until data collection was completed (summer 2022). As none of the organizations ever became a large player, they can be expected to display developmental dynamics more relevant to a wider range of organizations in the civil society sector than 'pathologies' commonly associated with large mass organizations.

Considering the three CSOs' substantive and functional orientations, I contrast two political organizations with a focus on environmental issues (GPEW, SAS) with a service-oriented organization in the area of social care (NAPA). This covers two very distinct policy areas, one of which is traditionally associated with a strong orientation towards advocacy and tendencies towards politicization (e.g. Dalton et al. 2003). In the other, an orientation towards service delivery and the cultivation of close voluntary–state

---

[24] These were traditionally company by limited guarantee and charity and, since 2006, the form of charitable incorporated organization (CIO).

[25] The most striking contrast to this is the intense, legal regulation of political parties in Germany. Though this is much less pronounced in the other two countries, in Germany, Norway, and Switzerland the legal forms usually taken by groups provide for a stronger position of members in the organization than the legal framework in the UK (Bolleyer 2018).

relationships are more common (e.g. Mosley 2010). The different dispositions prevalent in these two policy fields should have implications for various dimensions relevant to CSOs' potential democratic contribution: the decline of member control should be more contested, while political engagement more incentivized in the more politicized environmental field than in social care. Staff control should be more prevalent in the latter, since a focus on service delivery tends to enhance the importance of paid staff providing relevant expertise. At the same time, it is insightful to pair a party (the GPEW) and a group (SAS) both operating in the environmental field to tease out potential differences related to their different primary functions. Research on Green parties suggests that, in these very ideologically motivated organizations, a downsizing of member control and a weakening of organizational accountability relationships should be strongly resisted (e.g. Faucher 1999). Research on environmental groups, in contrast, has pointed towards these CSOs' transformation into 'protest businesses' (Jordan and Maloney 1997; Bosso 1995). The crucial question is whether—despite these differences—we still find similar tendencies in all three in line with the quantitative findings.

Having presented the broader rationale for the selection of case studies, it is important to highlight again that this study focuses on electorally active political parties, most of which have no or only limited access to government institutions. These parties mostly remain extra-parliamentary organizations throughout their existence. This is the case for the GPEW, although the Green Party family has been—alongside the new (populist or radical) right—one of the most successful new party families across advanced democracies (e.g. Meguid 2008; Bolleyer 2013a). Unlike other Green parties in Europe, the GPEW has remained a marginal player in UK politics. In a comparative study from 2008 including fifteen Green parties that emerged in advanced democracies since the 1960s, the GPEW was the least established and showed the weakest development towards a traditional election-orientated party organization (Frankland et al. 2008: 269). This judgement also held when comparing the party to the Scottish Greens, which formed their own organization fifteen years later than the GPEW (Birch 2009: 67). Parliamentary representation of the GPEW has remained weak throughout its history. Only twenty-five years after being formed, in 1999, the GPEW gained access to the European Parliament—an institutional presence that ended in January 2020 with the UK's departure from the European Union. Only in 2010 (more than three decades after being formed) it won one single seat in the House of Commons. Attempts to broaden its representative base on the national level since then have failed. This is relevant as within party organizations with a lasting and significant parliamentary presence public office-holders—the 'party in public office'—tends to become a central force, often dominating the extra-parliamentary leadership in central office as well as the party's membership base (Katz and Mair 1995; 2009). Such 'party in public office' composed of professional politicians as a central and possibly dominant group of actors within major parties does not exist in the groups. As the GPEW has not developed such tendencies, the interplay between members, managers, and organizational leaders (very few of whom have managed to enter public office) as the three central groups of internal actors has remained central to its internal power dynamics, which assures its comparability to the two groups.

Conclusion

This chapter detailed the methodological and empirical foundations for this study, including the underlying logic of the chosen mixed-methods design. It specified the different data sources used and presented the operationalizations of central concepts—notably those of the characteristics associated with the 'voluntary association' and of 'professionalized voluntary organization', the two governance templates that integrate this study. Based on these measures, the chapter briefly illustrated the organizational diversity of CSOs constituting civil society in the four European democracies studied, a diversity cutting across widely used distinctions between parties and groups. This not only substantiates the study of membership organizations more broadly, it also rationalizes the theoretically grounded decision to separately assess the implications of the two templates' central features for CSOs' democratic contributions rather than constructing summary measures. Only then can we actually test whether each template's features actually embody the same behavioural logic. If this claim is valid, the features associated with the same template should push CSOs in similar directions on each of the four dimensions that capture CSOs' democratic contributions. Characteristics belonging to different templates should have the opposite implications.

The following 'analysis part' of the study consists of six chapters jointly implementing the theoretical framework detailed in Chapter 2. It is organized along each of the four dimensions capturing CSOs' diverse democratic contributions presented in Chapter 1, both quantitatively and qualitatively. The next three chapters (Chapters 4–6) are focused on CSOs' internal processes and concerned with patterns of member activism and staff control. They are followed by another three chapters (Chapters 7–9) concerned with their outside relations, namely patterns of goal reorientation and political engagement.

4

The Distinct Roles of Members in Civil Society Organizations

Trading Member Control against Leader Autonomy

Which membership-based CSOs constitutive for organized civil society—be they party organizations, interest groups, or service-oriented organizations—keep their members active, which forms of activism do they cultivate, and why? As discussed earlier, there is a long—though by no means uncontested—tradition that considers the active participation of members in organizational life as a central contribution of CSOs to democracy. At the same time, empirical research has shown that the roles members actually play in CSOs differ widely. Those roles can have very different repercussions for intra-organizational dynamics and the prevalent power relations within CSOs, which, in turn, impact on CSOs' participatory contributions to democracy. Essentially, this chapter uses the analytical distinction between the 'voluntary association' and 'professionalized voluntary organization' developed in Chapter 2 to theorize patterns of member activism, distinguishing two forms thereof—member control and member involvement.

Approaching CSOs as 'systems of organizational governance' instead of collectives of individuals (e.g. Wilson 1973; Cornforth 2012; Han 2014) highlights that member control and involvement as two forms of activism have different intra-organizational consequences. 'Member involvement' in organizational work and activities is best understood as an organizational resource—or what Katz called a valuable source of help (1990: 152). It can be directed by a CSO's leadership towards activities conducive to organizational functioning, maintenance, and goal attainment and thus is compatible with a wide variety of governance structures, democratic or not. 'Member control' denoting members' direct say over internal decisions—akin to established notions of 'intra-organizational' or 'intra-party democracy'—allows

---

Civil Society's Democratic Potential. Nicole Bolleyer, Oxford University Press. © Nicole Bolleyer (2024).
DOI: 10.1093/oso/9780198884392.003.0004

members to hold organizational leaders accountable (e.g. Halpin 2006; Scarrow 2005; Binderkrantz 2009; Cross and Katz 2013; Gauja 2017).[1]

Starting from here, the roles that members can play in CSOs – different forms of activism they might engage in - are theorized from the perspective of a CSO's leadership, i.e. the actors in charge of the day-to-day running of the organization including organizational representatives and managers.[2] In line with the overarching framework of this study presented in Chapter 2, this organization-centred perspective puts centre stage the efforts of leaders and managers to maintain an organization in increasingly volatile environments in which member support can be less and less taken for granted. It further recognizes that member activism is rarely self-sustaining but needs to be cultivated and invested in (Andrews et al. 2010: 1192; Scarrow 1996; Han 2014; Betancur et al. 2019).

To keep members actively involved requires resources that organizations may or may not have, or which they might prefer to invest elsewhere. The crucial question here is under which conditions a CSO's leadership considers the cultivation of such involvement worthwhile as a means to support organizational self-maintenance or goal attainment. In other words, though involvement is conceptualized as an organizational resource that can be directed by a CSO's leadership into the 'right areas', this does not necessarily mean that for each CSO the benefits of such involvement outweigh the costs of cultivating it. Especially in CSOs with a large mass membership, the costs of cultivating member involvement might outweigh its benefits.[3] Under such conditions, the core benefit of sustaining a passive rather than active membership lies in the latter's financial contribution and the societal legitimacy the organization is able to claim on its basis (e.g. Bosso 2003; Jordan and Maloney 2007).

---

[1] Existing distinctions of different patterns of member activism proposed in party research cut across this distinction. For instance Demker et al. (2019) distinguish in a recent study more internally oriented 'party workers', members who attend meetings, influence policies, and hold office—hence are involved and exercise influence—from more electorally oriented 'party ambassadors' focused on involvement activities directed at voters to convince them to vote for the party and to discuss party policies with non-members. While informative, these distinctions are not suitable for this study as they are not applicable to CSOs other than parties.

[2] To approach member participation from the perspective of members themselves (with a focus on individual-level characteristics) is an important tradition. The organization-centred perspective used here in line with the overall theoretical framework thus constitutes only one pillar for developing an encompassing perspective on intra-organizational participatory dynamics in future research, as member activism is shaped both by individual-level characteristics (affecting which incentives specific members are after and what they expect from their CSO) and the opportunity structures created by organizational leaders aiming towards mobilizing, recruiting, and sustaining a particular type of membership (e.g. Wilson 1973; Katz and Mair 1995; Schmitter and Streeck 1999; Skocpol 2003; Jordan and Maloney 2007).

[3] This is one reason why all statistical analyses control for membership size.

84   Civil Society's Democratic Potential

Meanwhile, if members are passive, they are unlikely to use formal channels to exercise control, should those be available. The exercise of member control over decisions conflicts with leaders' and managers' attempts to protect their own room for manoeuvre if such a right is actively used (e.g. Hirschman 1970; Webb 1994; Maloney 2009; van Deth and Maloney 2012; Evers 2014; Heylen et al. 2020). Though the idea of members being in charge of decision-making is closely associated with traditional notions of the 'voluntary association' (e.g. Knoke 1990), as highlighted earlier, it is far from clear whether associations as 'organizational form' are indeed prone to cultivate an 'empowered' (rather than 'only' involved) membership. Members themselves might not be interested in exercising control and prefer to enjoy organizational services or solidary activities. Nor do they necessarily need control over decisions to keep leaders in line, as members always have the power to exit if they are unhappy, a constraint which organizational leaders are well aware of (e.g. Wilson 1973; Jordan and Maloney 2007; Barasko and Schaffner 2008).

A Governance Perspective on Member Activism in Civil Society Organizations

Members are individuals, organizations, and institutions that join a CSO by accepting its mission and core values, usually in return for certain organizational benefits (e.g. information, influence, social activities, services etc.) (Staggenborg 1988: 586). Member activism is defined as the range of activities through which members participate within CSOs. Active membership contrasts with passive membership[4] that is restricted to the regular payment of fees—the central formal act distinguishing members from followers or supporters.[5] Reflecting the fact that members can be perceived as liability or asset by an organization's leadership,[6] 'being active' in a membership-based CSO can be understood in different ways.

Members exercise control when they have a direct say over core areas of organizational decision-making such as the allocation of core posts or the change of central constitutional rules that define the authority structure of

---

[4] 'Activism' is an encompassing concept that overlaps in meaning with those of 'participation' or 'engagement'. As a wide variety of uses of these concepts coexist in the various literatures discussed, I opt—in terms of my own terminology—for (forms of) member *activism* as 'counterpart' to *passive* membership.

[5] Duverger 1964: 90–116; Katz 1990: 152; Jordan and Maloney 1997: 187; 2007: 156; van Haute and Gauja 2015: 1.

[6] Katz 1990: 143–5; Scarrow 1996: 15–19; Maloney 2012: 92–4; Hustinx 2014: 104.

the organization. Members are involved in an organization when they engage in organizational work[7] or provide information and feedback to the organization by expressing opinions or attending meetings.[8] In this scenario, members cannot impose their preferences on organizational representatives and managers that make up an organization's leadership. Still, the latter cannot ignore members altogether when facing a membership that is 'only' involved, as it profits from such involvement. Unhappy members might become passive and withdraw their support or, in the worst case, exit. Compared to member control, when facing an involved membership, CSO leaders and managers have considerable leeway as to how to consider member preferences that can, but need not, be expressed through involvement activities. Such leeway is enhanced when most or all members are passive.

The governance templates 'voluntary association' and 'professionalized voluntary organization' provide the central analytical building blocks to theorize which CSOs might be inclined to cultivate member involvement and grant member control and which might not. These hypotheses are complemented by theoretical expectations about how *CSO type*—the difference between political party and (interest or service-orientated) group—are expected to shape patterns of member activism.

Hypotheses on Member Activism in Professionalized Voluntary Organizations

To recap, bureaucratization as a central governance feature of a 'professionalized voluntary organization' denotes organizational structures in which efficiency and effectiveness are central norms (Kreutzer and Jäger 2011: 638). They become manifest in measures enhancing decision-making efficiency as well as training of those running a CSO (Paine et al. 2010: 108). This feature is qualitatively distinct from organizational professionalization, denoting an increasing reliance on paid staff as a central resource (e.g. Farrell and Webb 2000). That said, with regard to the role of members in organizational life, the two phenomena have similar implications. Managers favour—in terms of 'organizational structure preferences'—procedures that ensure continuity in

---

[7] Typical examples are activities that are often subsumed under the notion of 'volunteering'. They include supporting fundraising activities, participating in recruitment activities, mobilizing support for petitions, contacting politicians, or canvassing ahead of elections (e.g. Scarrow 1994; Pestoff et al. 2012; Hustinx 2014).

[8] Passive members would be neither involved nor exercise control. In contrast, volunteer staff (members who contribute to the running of the organization but unlike staff do not earn their living from this work (Staggenborg 1988: 586)) would be, by definition, involved.

86 Civil Society's Democratic Potential

the performance of maintenance tasks. 'Organizing' is a career to them, which is why they can be expected to push for reforms that encourage effective and efficient goal attainment enhanced by bureaucratization (Panebianco 1988: 231–2; Staggenborg 1988: 594–5; 597; Maier and Meyer 2011). This concern for the effective running of their organization is likely to be shared by organizational leaders in charge, closely working with staff on a day-to-day basis (Katz 1990: 145; LeRoux and Goerdel 2009: 518; Wilson 1973).

Moving to the central trade-off that CSOs face on the participation dimension, both professionalization and bureaucratization favour leader autonomy over member control. On the level of actors, this is most clear-cut when managers—actors not driven by a voluntary commitment—take over decision-making themselves (see also Chapter 5). However, tensions between bureaucratization or professionalization on the one hand and member control on the other can already be expected when managers remain in support and advisory roles. Leaders of professionalized organizations (reliant on an increasing number of staff) become less dependent on members to sustain organizational activities and pursue organizational goals. Meanwhile, they can be expected to take seriously managerial concerns about CSO maintenance and about the limited predictability and insufficient expertise underpinning decision-making by members.

This is paralleled on the structural level when CSO procedures become increasingly bureaucratized: membership-based decision-making can be cumbersome and difficult to predict, while managerial procedures aim at streamlining decision-making to enhance efficiency. Enhancing efficiency and moving especially technical matters (requiring specialist knowledge) outside of democratic fora can help to better 'manage' such governance processes, including the bypassing of member input that might conflict with the priorities of an organization's leadership. Simultaneously, the training of volunteer staff to enhance a CSO's skills basis and a standardization of such procedures across the organization help to align member preferences and activities with the priorities of leaders and managers, which can facilitate a steering of organizational processes by these leaders and managers.[9] Taking these arguments together, we should expect a negative association between professionalization and bureaucratization as organizational features and member control.

Moving to member involvement, some research in movement studies has long argued that organizational professionalization (often closely associated

---

[9] E.g. Schmitter and Streeck 1999; Mair et al. 2004; Poguntke and Webb 2005; Nienhüser 2008; Maloney 2009; Billis 2010; Barakso and Schaffner 2008; Paine et al. 2010.

with bureaucratization) can inhibit or, alternatively, facilitate volunteerism (e.g. Staggenborg 1988; Holland 2004). To understand the consequences of professionalization, distinguishing different forms of voluntarism of members was considered essential (Kleidman 1994: 257–8). Building on this important insight, theoretical expectations regarding the implications of bureaucratization and professionalization for member involvement are very different than those for member control. From the perspective of leaders and managers, member involvement can enhance organizational functioning to the extent that it can be steered into strategically desirable areas. Hence, conflicts between members' contributions to organizational life and the leadership's goals and strategies can be mediated, if not avoided (e.g. Nienhüser 2008). CSOs with more paid staff (whether in support or managerial roles) and bureaucratized CSOs with more efficient operating procedures can be expected to be conducive to the promotion of member involvement through generating more efficient structures for member and volunteer management (e.g. Maloney and Rossteutscher 2005; Paine et al. 2010). Since it is directed towards areas that are useful to ensure organizational functioning, including self-maintenance and goal attainment, member involvement does not affect the leadership's control over decision-making. Hence, in contrast to the trade-off related to member control, no comparable trade-off arises restricting leading actors' room for manoeuvre. Furthermore, an involved membership projects the image of a participatory organizational culture conducive to the organization's external legitimacy (e.g. Bosso 2003; Jordan and Maloney 2007; Scarrow 2015). In contrast with claims that professionalized and bureaucratized organizations can be expected to prefer a passive membership (e.g. Skocpol 2013), I expect a positive relationship with member involvement.

Moving to dependency on state funding, both resource dependence theory and the relevant specialist literatures on parties, groups, and non-profits have long argued that the types of income sources that membership organizations rely on (e.g. state vs. non-state) shape how a CSO's leadership relates to its members (e.g. Walker 1983; Katz 1990; Katz and Mair 1995; Froelich 2005). Having the opportunity to access state funds, which tend to be more reliable sources of income than member contributions in increasingly individualized societies (e.g. Skocpol 2003; Fraussen 2014), an organization's leadership is expected to trade the reduction of uncertainty granted by such funds against a reduction of external control that dependence on the latter implies (e.g. Pfeffer and Salancik 1978). When accessing state funds, leaders' and managers' accountability is expected to shift away from their societal base—which members form part of—towards the state, in order to ensure ongoing access to this resource (e.g. Katz 1990; Katz and Mair 1995; Froelich 2005; Fraussen 2014; Bolleyer 2021a). In sum, state funding dependency implies both a lower pressure on and a weaker inclination of the leadership to give members a say (even if this is actively demanded, which is not necessarily the case), as a CSO is increasingly able to sustain itself with fewer member contributions—financially and otherwise (Katz 1990: 146; Katz and Mair 1995; 2009; Bosso 1995; 2003). This suggests a negative relationship between state funding dependency and member control.

The implications of state funding dependency for member involvement are less clear-cut. State funding dependency makes members' contribution to organizational work in some areas less helpful. This is because this particular income source increases the importance of managerial and administrative tasks, e.g. reporting related to the receipt of state funding or state-sponsored service provision (Froelich 2005: 260; Bloodgood and Tremblay-Boire 2017: 404–5). As these tasks are more difficult to delegate to 'amateurs', state funding decreases organizational incentives to actively involve an organization's broader membership in these areas.

At the same time, the notion of the 'professionalized voluntary organization' as governance template suggests that the availability of state funding and the professionalization of human resources often go hand in hand (Maloney 2015: 105; Katz and Mair 2009; Billis 2010; Karlsen and Saglie 2017). Usually, once state funding access has been achieved, paid staff are either already in place (often instrumental to successfully applying for funds) or can be hired to deal with more technical tasks. While creating costs of its own, member involvement can be usefully redirected into useful areas, as state funding (similar to professionalization) enhances a CSO's capacity to engage in proactive 'volunteer management'. Member involvement, then, has the advantage of contributing to organizational maintenance or goal attainment—functionally and symbolically—while keeping the organization updated on the concerns of more committed and active members willing to engage with their organization.

Finally, recent comparative research on the professionalization of parties and groups as triggered by their exposure to legal regulation that is associated with access to state resources has shown that smaller organizations with few or no staff systematically recruit volunteers with specialist skills (Ivanovska Hadjievska 2018; Ivanovska Hadjievska and Staveness 2020). Such targeted recruitment to ensure a form of 'volunteer professionalization' is more likely to be successful if members are involved rather than passive. Jointly, these lines of argument suggest that for the average CSO—instead of making the cultivation of member involvement less worthwhile—dependence on state funding should create incentives towards, not against the cultivation of member involvement.

To sum up, we can formulate the following overall hypothesis on patterns of member activism in professionalized voluntary organization:

H1 (*Professionalized Voluntary Organization–Member Activism Hypothesis*): In CSOs with features of a 'professionalized voluntary organization', members will have less control over decision-making but will be more involved than in CSOs without such features.

Hypotheses on Member Involvement in Voluntary Associations

The 'voluntary association' is traditionally considered central to a democratic civil society—a participatory vehicle in which citizens jointly pursue shared goals, be those goals political or social, self-interested or public-spirited (see for a detailed discussion Jordan and Maloney 2007). This literature often treats member control over core decisions as a defining feature of an association rather than a 'variable' (e.g. Knoke 1990; but see Barakso and Schaffner 2008). At the same time, the empirical connections between organizations being member-serving, member-run and member-financed on the one hand and 'intra-organizational democracy' on the other have remained a contested theme (e.g. Halpin 2006; Jordan and Maloney 1997; 2007). Linking association features to member control makes the assumption that organizational members generally aim for active participation in internal decision-making and, relatedly, demand their organization to cultivate such processes. This is problematic from several angles, as previously mentioned. Both the group and party literature emphasize the vast diversity of value orientations and ideological dispositions cultivated by CSOs in pluralist societies, which range from democratic and participatory to authoritarian and leadership-centred (e.g. Sartori 1976; Rosenblum 1998; Poguntke et al. 2016; Close et al. 2017; Scarrow et al. 2017). As organizations tend to recruit a membership base supporting their own core values (e.g. Duverger 1964; Wilson 1973), being a member as such does therefore not mean embracing democratic, participatory norms. Consequently, structural features contributing to the centrality of members and their interests within a CSO should not be expected to shape member control specifically, neither positively nor negatively. This is underlined by a growing body of research that stresses that more and more citizens in individualizing societies positively prefer 'thin' or 'low cost' participation, as long as the organization efficiently pursues its political goals or delivers member services effectively (e.g. Jordan and Maloney 2007; van Deth and Maloney 2012; Halpin 2014).

In contrast, being a 'voluntary association' is expected to positively feed into member involvement. First, central activities of organizations whose core mission is oriented towards member interests (rather than broader constituencies transcending the latter—be those citizens or voters) are likely to be more inwards-orientated and more directed towards the maintenance of close connections with members. Cultivating the latter's involvement in organizational life is one means to achieve this. Involvement activities further help to keep whoever runs the organization in touch with members' concerns, whether the latter prefer democratic, bottom-up, or top-down decision-making.

Second, a multi-tier structure facilitates the generation of and makes more valuable the involvement of members around joint activities. This is the case, as lower-level branches tend to be more homogeneous internally and the proximity between those involved in such activities is enhanced (Barakso and Schaffner 2008: 194–5; Skocpol et al. 1999: 492; Maloney 2012: 87). In multilevel settings, solidary incentives and a collective identity are more easily and effectively cultivated through involvement activities than in unitary structures.

Third, the more an organization is resourced by its members—in terms of volunteer staff holding managerial roles or membership fees contributing to a CSO's budget—the stronger its incentives to foster involvement. This is because involvement is a means to strengthen organizational ties of those members willing to contribute to organizational life beyond paying their fees, while stabilizing the regular financial contributions of passive members who do not (Witko 2015: 123; Paine et al. 2010). In sum, when conceptualizing member involvement as organizational resource, the following hypotheses can be formulated:

> **H2.1** (*Member Governance–Involvement Hypothesis*): In CSOs oriented towards member interests and in those with multi-tier structures, members will be more involved than in those CSOs without such features.
>
> **H2.2** (*Member Resources–Involvement Hypothesis*): The more a CSO relies on member resources (financially or in terms of volunteer staff), the more involved its members will be.

Different from the template of the 'voluntary professionalized organization' whose three core features generate the same basic expectations about member involvement (H1), being composed of individual as compared to corporate members (e.g. firms, institutions, or associations) is expected to follow a different logic from the other association features when it comes to member involvement. At odds with normative perceptions of citizen groups as central participatory venues, incentive-theoretical arguments suggest a negative relationship between CSOs having an individual membership and member involvement. This expectation is linked to the earlier observation that, while involvement as a resource can be valuable to organizations generally (whether they have individual or corporate members), it needs to be actively cultivated by a CSO's leadership, which generates costs of its own.

Essentially, involvement is expected to be more easily stimulated and maintained by CSOs with a corporate membership than those with an individual one (costs factored in by CSO leaders and managers when deciding to invest in involvement activities or not). This is because the range of incentives that individual members might be responsive to is more diverse (i.e. demand is more heterogeneous) than in the case of corporate members (Offe and Wiesenthal 1980: 81–2). While material selective incentives exclusively available to members should be equally relevant for organizational maintenance irrespective of a CSO's composition, this is not the case for solidary incentives (non-material selective incentives). Different from individual members, members who are representatives of organizations or institutions are unlikely to care much for activities that strengthen feelings of group solidarity (Clark and Wilson 1961: 134–5; Schmitter and Streeck 1999: 14–15; Salisbury 1969; Bolleyer and Weiler 2018). Furthermore, in CSOs with a corporate membership, a range of demands is already dealt with by the corporate members as central units, hence, beneath the level of the CSO, limiting the diversity of demands the latter has to deal with (Offe and Wiesenthal 1980: 81–5). Facing a more uniformly instrumental behavioural rationale of (more homogeneous) corporate representatives should make it easier for a CSO's leadership to develop an effective strategy to maintain their involvement. This is supported by the observation that interests of corporate members tend to be specialized and less diffuse than those of individual membership groups (Berkhout 2013: 235–6). Finally, as compared to the average individual member, a corporate representative (who forms part of the organization in a professional capacity) is likely to be well equipped to get involved in terms of skills and resources (which takes time and effort). They should be more responsive to CSO initiatives to get involved, if those initiatives present themselves as means for pursuing his or her organization's or institution's interest within the CSO (Schmitter and Streeck 1999: 63–4).[10] Taking those arguments together forms the rationale for the following hypothesis:

> **H2.3** (*Membership Composition–Involvement Hypothesis*): In CSOs composed of individual members, members will be less involved than in CSOs composed of corporate members.

Expected Impacts of CSO Type on Patterns of Member Activism

While I expect the features of the two governance templates to be central for patterns of member activism, this does not mean that CSOs' functional orientation is irrelevant for CSOs' varying participatory contributions to democracy. CSO Type—whether an organization is a party or group—can be expected to matter in two ways. First, research suggests that the distinction between parties and groups feeds into distinct expectations of relevant audiences—inside and outside the organization—towards whether or not a CSO ought to grant members control. Second, the extent to which member involvement qualifies not just as resource but as a 'critical' resource for an organization's ability to maintain central activities (Pfeffer and Salancik 1978: 86) can be expected to vary with what CSOs mainly do (Beyers and Kerremans 2007).

Unlike groups (whether advocacy- or service-orientated), political parties recruit political personnel that participate in elections which might enable the latter to enter parliament, take over government, and implement policies (Sartori 1976). Consequently, parties play a more institutionally predefined role in democratic representation than groups. As a consequence of this special status, they can be expected to face stronger normative pressures to replicate democratic standards within their organizations, reinforced by citizens' increasing 'reluctance to choose among pre-packaged party-platforms' (Kittilson and Scarrow 2003: 59; Allern 2010: 93–4). Being 'special players' in democratic regimes, parties' responsiveness to such normative expectations is important to enhance their legitimacy, which is a central resource in the political process (Allern 2010: 93–4; Walker and McCarthy 2010). A range of parties have therefore embraced an agenda of internal democratization, expanding membership rights (especially in the selection of leaders) through internal reform. This included parties that are—ideologically speaking— in

---

[10] Note that all these arguments are expected to apply irrespective of the CSO's size, i.e. the number of members in an organization.

principle more inclined towards centralization (e.g. Kittilson and Scarrow 2003; Cross and Blais 2012; Gauja 2017). Following this strand of research, we might therefore expect parties to grant their members more direct control over decision-making than groups.[11] Group engagement in the political process is expected to be much more varied, as are the ways groups relate to members (e.g. Rosenblum 1998; Hasenfeld and Gidron 2005; Halpin 2006; 2014).

Regarding leaders' incentives to cultivate member involvement, the distinction between groups and parties can be expected to have similar implications. However, the rationale suggesting such difference follows a 'material' rather than 'normative' logic. In principle, all organizations composed of members profit from involved members 'as a resource', if the latter help them to sustain themselves and to accomplish organizational goals, simply because (unlike professional staff) these members do not need to be paid. More specifically, parties profit from their members' mobilization to win elections since member involvement in canvassing is an important endeavour, especially as winning elections is increasingly a matter of successfully mobilizing parties' own support base (e.g. Enos and Hersh 2015; Panagopoulos 2016). Interest groups profit from mobilizing members to support organizational efforts to set the public agenda or influence policymakers (e.g. Halpin 2010). This is the case for interest groups engaging in campaigns targeting the wider public whose endeavours gain legitimacy if their membership base actively participates. It also holds for sectional interest groups that profit from grass-roots lobbying if their particular members contact politicians and policymakers to underline their demands' importance (e.g. Holyoke 2013a; 2014). Service-oriented organizations, in turn, can profit from members' support in the provision of services or the raising of funds (e.g. Kreutzer and Jäger 2011; Jordan 2012).

What is likely to differ between parties and the two group types is the extent to which member involvement is a *critical* resource to ensure the organizations' most central activities (e.g. Pfeffer and Salancik 1978). If the electoral success of political parties, at least to some extent, still relies on active members (e.g. involved in canvassing) as argued by party research, parties face strong incentives to build up and maintain their membership base, and thus to invest in ongoing party activities accordingly. Similar incentives exist for

---

[11] The cartel party literature has theorized that elites might give rank-and-file members more *formal* say as they can be more easily manipulated than mid-level activists, leading to a de facto empowerment of the same elites, rather than real member control (Katz and Mair 1995). As the approach presented here theorizes and measures (as detailed in Chapter 3) *actual* control/involvement of members, not the mere presence of members' *formal* decision-making rights, the analyses below cannot say anything about the discrepancy between formal rules and organizational practices.

94 Civil Society's Democratic Potential

groups. Here too, a membership that is not just occasionally involved in organizational activities can be more easily mobilized to contribute to the organization when necessary or useful. However, parties run elections whose regularity is institutionally prescribed. Furthermore, for parties, an involved membership is particularly useful as a pool of committed members willing to stand for office. This is a demanding form of involvement with little benefit for the candidates, as in most cases there is no realistic chance of winning a seat. Interest groups and service-oriented organizations face comparatively fewer incentives to continuously engage in membership-focused activities and can be more selective regarding when and how they involve their membership (Holyoke 2013b; Evers 2014; Hustinx 2014). For these reasons I expect higher levels of involvement in the average party than the average group.

A Quantitative Analysis of Member Activism in Civil Society Organizations

Table 4.1 summarizes the hypotheses derived from the two governance templates. In essence, features of the 'professionalized voluntary organization' are expected to relate to the two forms of activism in opposite ways. Though expectations are overall less coherent, association features also suggest different implications for each form, partially at odds with prominent claims in more normative work. On the one hand, association features are expected to be 'neutral' towards *member control*. On the other, they are expected to incentivize *member involvement*, with individual membership forming an exception by generating countervailing expectations.

Overall, the theoretical expectations summarized here rest on the assumption that the two forms of activism are qualitatively different phenomena, which is why they ought to be theorized and analysed separately. Empirical

Table 4.1 Theoretically Expected Patterns of Member Control and Involvement

	Expected Effect on Member Activism	
	Member Control	Member Involvement
Features associated with 'Professionalized Voluntary Organization' (H1)	Negative	Positive
Features associated with 'Voluntary Association' (H2.1/2)	n/a	Positive (except for individual membership)

Note: +/− = positive/negative association with control/involvement; n/a = no systematic relationship expected analysis of both the data and the relationship between the two forms of member activism (see Chapter 3 for details on the measurements) substantiates this claim. To give concrete examples: among organizations that grant their members the greatest level of control, only 17 per cent also show the highest level of involvement, with 12 per cent indicating their members to be not at all or only slightly involved. Vice versa, around 47 per cent of the organizations that do not grant any control to their members still have very or extremely involved members.

Table 4.2 shows the results of the statistical analyses. Model 1 has member control; Model 2 member involvement as dependent variable. To assess the impact of the independent variables, both of which are ordinal variables (see Chapter 3 for details on measurement choices), I used heterogeneous choice models. These are most suitable because they account for differences in the degree of residual variation across CSOs and solve the problem of the violation of the proportional odds assumption, allowing not only for ordinal dependent variables but also a more flexible specification of the variance equation (Williams 2009: 532, 548; 2010: 556).

Overall, the findings show that—in line with theoretical expectations— organizational features linked to the 'professionalized voluntary organization' are associated with lower member control and higher involvement, while none of the 'voluntary association features' have robust effects on control. In contrast, the latter are with one exception (individual membership) positively related to involvement, as is the majority of features of the 'professionalized voluntary organization'. The findings emphasize a tension between member involvement and control within professionalized organizations. At the same time, they underline that member involvement is compatible with and can be useful to CSO leaders in very different organizational settings.

The findings highlight the fundamental implications of professionalization for intra-organizational dynamics when it comes to the status of members in organizational life. In line with H1, the statistical analyses also stress its complex repercussions for member control and involvement. Indeed, reliance on paid staff is the only theorized organizational trait displayed in Table 4.2 that shows significant and robust associations with both forms of activism. It relates to member control and involvement in opposite ways. The negative relationship with control displays the trade-off between leader autonomy and the empowerment of members in CSO decision-making theorized in Chapter 2. Essentially, the more staff-driven organizations are, the less control members tend to have over core areas of decision-making. More concretely, each additional member of staff an organization relies on

96 Civil Society's Democratic Potential

Table 4.2 Heterogeneous Choice Models for Member Control and Member Involvement (With Multiple Imputations)

Main Effects	Model 1: DV = Member Control		Model 2: DV = Member Involvement	
	Coefficient	SE	Coefficient	SE
Features of Professionalized Voluntary Organization				
Bureaucratization	−0.04	(0.03)	0.17***	(0.04)
Professionalization (log)	−0.17***	(0.03)	0.06*	(0.03)
State Funding	−0.06	(0.04)	−0.07	(0.05)
Features of Voluntary Association				
Individual Membership	0.02	(0.05)	−0.70***	(0.09)
Member Interest Orientation	−0.04	(0.05)	0.35***	(0.08)
Multi-Tier Structure	0.05	(0.06)	0.31***	(0.07)
Volunteer Staff (log)	0.02	(0.02)	0.16***	0.02
Membership Fees	0.02	(0.08)	0.15	(0.09)
CSO Type				
Interest Group (ref: parties)	−0.13	(0.16)	−1.23***	(0.21)
Service-Oriented Organization (ref: parties)	−0.27	(0.16)	−1.31***	(0.21)
Controls Relevant to CSO Behaviour Generally				
Membership Instability	−0.00	(0.06)	−0.08	(0.07)
Membership Size (log)	−0.04**	(0.01)	−0.11***	(0.02)
Organizational Age (log)	0.10**	(0.03)	−0.03	(0.04)
UK (ref: Norway)	−0.46***	(0.11)	0.42***	(0.12)
Germany (ref: Norway)	0.44**	(0.14)	1.16***	(0.13)
Switzerland (ref: Norway)	0.41**	(0.15)	0.77***	(0.12)
Variance Equation				
Multi-Tier Structure	0.28***	(0.06)	—	—
UK	−0.65***	(0.12)	−0.01	(0.06)
Germany	−0.49***	(0.12)	−0.14*	(0.06)
Switzerland	−0.04	(0.13)	−0.14*	(0.07)
Volunteer Staff (log)	—	—	−0.02*	(0.01)
Membership Fees	−0.20*	(0.08)	—	—
/cut1	−1.24***	(0.22)	−4.54***	(0.36)
/cut2	−0.88***	(0.20)	−2.35***	(0.28)
/cut3	−0.24	(0.20)	−0.55*	(0.25)
/cut4	—	—	1.14***	(0.25)
N	3265		3265	

Note: Standard errors in parentheses * p<0.05, ** p<0.01, *** p<0.001

makes it 2.65 per cent less likely that an organization shows high level of member control, while each additional member of staff makes it 0.72 per cent and 0.28 per cent more likely that members are very or extremely involved respectively. In line with earlier research, this suggests that organizational leaders who can rely on staff can gain autonomy from members and expand their control over the organization, thereby restricting the decision-making power of members (Jordan and Maloney 2007: 113–19; Kreutzer and Jäger 2011). In contrast, the member involvement model shows a positive significant relationship between organizational reliance on paid staff and member involvement. This echoes the broader claim that member involvement is suitably conceptualized as a resource which is positively affected by factors enhancing organizational capacity such as CSO professionalization (e.g. Staggenborg 1988; Maloney and Rossteutscher 2005).

The bureaucratization of organizational structures is positively associated with involvement (as is professionalization), supporting a more efficient member and volunteer management (Paine et al. 2010). One unit change in the index capturing bureaucratization makes it 3.23 per cent and 2.16 per cent more likely for a CSO to have very involved or extremely involved members respectively. Against expectations, it has no implications for the power allocation within the organizations by disincentivizing member control. Consequently, amongst the three constitutive features of the 'professionalized voluntary organization', it is professionalization which is particularly pervasive with regard to member activism. This echoes earlier research that has put a particular emphasis on the professionalization of human resources for intra-organizational dynamics (e.g. Billis 2010; Panebianco 1988). At the same time, the positive association between bureaucratization and involvement demonstrates the value added of separating out these two aspects that are often treated as closely intertwined or two components of the same overall concept (e.g. Staggenborg 1988; Hanegraff and Poletti 2019). This claim will be further substantiated by Chapter 5 on the drivers of staff control over decision-making.

Moving to the second resource central to 'professionalized voluntary organizations' alongside professionalization, dependency on state funding does not have a significant relationship with member control in the model presented in Table 4.2. Consequently, prominent arguments in party and group research that link CSO dependency on state funds to a disempowered membership (e.g. Walker 1983; Katz and Mair 1995; Bosso 1995; 2003) are not supported. This is interesting in light of Heylen et al.'s recent results

(2020: 1236) which show a significant negative influence of state funding on member influence on politically active CSOs' public policy positions. This effect, however, only holds for organizations whose budget is less than 50 per cent state-funded, which suggests that the repercussions of state funding dependency present themselves as more complex than traditionally assumed. The qualitative case studies in Chapter 6 will offer a possible take on such contradictions, suggesting that state funding dependency might predominantly have an indirect effect on member control through professionalization. The qualitative findings show that access to state funding can function as an important catalyst for the growth of human resources, enabling CSOs to hire more staff. Staff, in turn, support reforms curtailing member control over decision-making later on. State funding is more likely to have such intra-organizational repercussions in terms of triggering reforms in earlier periods when the organization has not yet fully professionalized or bureaucratized and not yet achieved a very high level of state funding access. This might rationalize why the negative relationship found by Heylen et al. does—slightly counter-intuitively—not concern those CSOs which are predominantly or fully state-financed (i.e. in which state funding dependency is most pronounced).

With regard to association features, the overall findings substantiate research sceptical of organizational members' desire for active participation and 'democratic control' (e.g. Halpin 2006; Jordan and Maloney 2007). Not only does dependence on membership fees show no significant effect. Member control has no significant robust relationship with any of the association features. Structurally resembling a 'voluntary association' seems not to generate a barrier against the centralization of decision-making. In contrast, organizations oriented towards member interests, with a multi-tier structure, and those more reliant on volunteer staff have more involved members, fully substantiating H2.1 and partially H2.2. More specifically, organizations orientated towards member interests are 4.44 per cent and 2.31 per cent more likely to have very and extremely involved members than those orientated towards broader constituency interests. Multi-tiered organizations are 7.22 per cent and 4.43 per cent more likely to have very and extremely involved members than those with a unitary structure. Finally, each additional volunteer an organization can rely on makes it 0.59 per cent and 0.21 per cent that members are very or extremely involved respectively. In CSOs sharing those properties, member involvement appears to be more worthwhile as a means to stabilize ties to members and is *ceteris paribus* easier to cultivate. This, in turn, creates incentives for CSOs to make the necessary resource investments to keep their members involved.

While these findings are broadly in line with earlier works which have stressed the relevance of these features for member activism (e.g. Skocpol 1999; Halpin 2006; Barakso and Schaffner 2008; Paine et al. 2010), not all features of the 'voluntary association' point in the same direction. In line with incentive-theoretical arguments underpinning this study (e.g. Schmitter and Streeck 1999; Berkhout 2013), CSOs predominantly composed of individuals are less likely to have involved members than those composed of corporate members, substantiating H2.3. Being a CSO composed of individuals as compared to corporate actors makes it 15.21 per cent and 8.97 per cent less likely that the CSO has very or extremely involved members. This suggests that the more instrumental behavioural rationale of corporate representatives make it easier for CSO leaders to develop an effective strategy to maintain such members' involvement than when facing more heterogeneous demands of individual members (Berkhout 2013: 235–6; Offe and Wiesenthal 1980). Taking a normative angle, this can be considered paradoxical as—implicitly or explicitly—an active membership is often considered as less beneficial—or less relevant—for democracy if CSO members are corporate representatives, not individual citizens. This is why studies interested in CSOs' participatory contributions tend to exclude CSOs with (predominantly) corporate members (e.g. Skocpol 2013; Jordan and Maloney 2007) (see Chapter 2 on this).

Finally, CSO type is relevant for member involvement by shaping the relative importance of assuring continuous member engagement. I find a significant relationship between the type of organization and the level of member involvement, indicating party members on average to be more involved than members of the two group types. The pressures related to regular electoral participation makes mobilization of party grass roots on a continuous basis—who contribute to campaign, fundraising, or stand for office—more critical for parties. This generates stronger incentives for parties to involve their members continuously than for groups which enjoy more flexibility and thus control over the frequency and timing of those activities that can benefit from member involvement (Holyoke 2013b).

In contrast, I find no support for the expectation that parties as such —given their central role in democratic regimes—face particularly strong normative pressure to replicate democratic standards within their own organization. While a range of parties across the ideological spectrum have actively embraced an agenda of internal democratization (e.g. Kittilson and Scarrow 2003; Gauja 2017), normative expectations towards internal democratization are more likely to be a concern of major parties with institutional access and thus high visibility (which studies of intra-party reform focus on).

Unlike those major players, most minor parties (which form the majority of electorally active parties covered in this study) represent only small sections of the electorate and receive only very little or no media attention. This, in turn, suggests very little public knowledge about their internal functioning. Such conditions make it unlikely that CSOs grant more member control than they are ideologically inclined to. Alternatively, normative pressure to emulate 'state democracy' intra-organizationally might only unfold once parties are actually operating within state institutions (e.g. Bolleyer et al 2020), which again is not the case for most parties.

These findings hold despite controlling for a range of other variables that earlier research identified as relevant to CSOs' internal dynamics. As was to be expected, the results show a negative relationship between membership size and both types of activism. The negative association with member control echoes a long tradition of arguments about larger organizations tending towards oligarchical structures and centralization (Michels 1915). Each additional member makes it 0.03 per cent less likely that an organization grants high member control. The negative association with involvement suggests— even though involvement as a resource can be useful in very diverse organizational settings—that in the context of mass organizations, the benefits of involvement might be outweighed by its costs (Jordan and Maloney 2007: 163–5; 1997). Interestingly, older organizations tend to grant significantly more control to their members, which challenges research associating higher institutionalization (that tends to increase with age) with centralizing tendencies (e.g. Panebianco 1988). Indeed, each additional year makes it 0.03 more likely that a CSO grants high member control. This finding suggests that an organization's institutionalization might provide a more suitable context for members to exercise actual control than still 'immature' and structurally 'fluid' organizations. Empirically, this reading aligns with experiences made by some new party organizations, especially those that underwent significant growth early in their development (Bolleyer 2013a). On a conceptual level, it echoes the notion of the 'tyranny of structurelessness'—much discussed in the movement literature. This notion highlights unintended, corrosive effects within younger, informal structures that can allow for high levels of inequality (Freeman 1974). Relatedly, movement entrepreneurs, having formed an organization, might try to stay in control and exploit their privileged position to do so (Staggenborg 1988), therefore supporting a downsizing (or containment) of member control despite holding democratic credentials. Such a tendency we will come across later in the qualitative analyses.

Conclusion

The question of which CSOs cultivate member involvement and control—two qualitatively distinct forms of member activism—is a fundamental one in light of prominent claims about the participatory contribution of organized civil society to democracy and, indeed, the decline thereof. As detailed in Chapter 2, member activism has been linked to both political and social benefits to democracy, both on the individual and system level, whether organizations' primary mission is partisan, political, or social (e.g. Dekker 2009; Maloney 2009; Hustinx et al. 2010; van Haute and Gauja 2015). Consequently, answers to the question about the organizational drivers of member activism have important implications for the conditions under which CSOs are likely to be beneficial for democracy in terms of the legitimacy as well as the resilience of democratic governance.

Analytically, the findings clearly stress the importance and usefulness of distinguishing the two types of member activism—control and involvement—on the one hand and the two systems of organizational governance—'voluntary association' and 'professionalized voluntary organization'—on the other. The findings also suggest that the integration of incentive-theoretical arguments on leader–member relations with resource dependency theory provided a useful foundation to formulate hypotheses on how central characteristics of the 'voluntary association' and the 'professionalized voluntary organization' relate to the two forms of member activism respectively. Essentially, features of the 'professionalized voluntary organization' tend to be associated with lower member control and higher involvement. Most voluntary association features are positively related to involvement, but none had a significant relationship with control.

Unlike member control, member involvement conceptualized as organizational resource has no direct implications for the intra-organizational allocation of power. Indeed, the majority of core characteristics of both templates—bureaucratization and professionalization on the one hand and a multi-tier structure, volunteer staff, and orientation towards member interests on the other—all had positive significant coefficients. The only factor contradicting this overall pattern is individual membership, which showed a significant negative relationship with member involvement. This is at odds with normative perceptions of citizen groups as central venues for participation, which are often considered superior in their contributions to democracy as compared to organizations pursuing corporate or institutional interests (e.g. Warren 2001; Eliasoph 2013). In contrast, incentive-theoretical arguments central to this study have long suggested such a negative relationship, highlighting the relative costs that CSO leaders are confronted by when trying to cultivate the involvement of individuals. These costs are higher than in CSOs composed of—on average—more instrumental, more skilled, and better resourced corporate representatives, often pursuing more narrowly defined interests (e.g. Offe and Wiesenthal 1980; Schmitter and Streeck 1999; Berkhout 2013). From the perspective of these works, higher average levels of member involvement in CSOs composed of corporate members are less of a surprise.[12]

Importantly, the analysis has shown that member involvement can flourish in diverse organizational settings. This is the important even though this involvement is sometimes associated with notions of only 'thin participation' (e.g. Jordan 2012; Skocpol 2003; Maloney 2009), and it is debated whether involvement akin to 'volunteering' is really conducive to 'political activism' (e.g. Eliasoph 2013). As was emphasized earlier on, its contributions to democracy through social benefits should not to be underestimated (Hustinx et al. 2010: 417–18; 422). Neither should its contribution to CSO maintenance, which directly benefits democracy when CSOs are politically active (see Chapter 1 for details).

Of course, if involvement is conducive to organizational self-maintenance generally, it can be used as a 'resource' by all sorts of organizations that coexist in pluralist societies, including authoritarian and extremist ones (Rosenblum 1998; Fung 2003). This brings us back to the basic assumption underpinning this study that most CSOs are *not* to be directed against democracy or its core values (e.g. not to cultivate intra-group solidarity to undermine the democratic regime or to repress other parts of society) (see Chapter 1 on this). This is a reasonable assumption to make examining membership-based CSOs in long consolidated, stable European democracies. Nevertheless, the study of member involvement and its drivers has immediate relevance for the resilience of 'bad' or 'uncivil' society (see for an overview Bob 2011),[13] hence for the performance of CSOs whose effects on democracy— as a regime or in terms of its culture—can be problematic.[14]

Returning to classical works on civic associations, the findings of this chapter interestingly suggest that, when it comes to member control, the 'voluntary association' falls short of normative expectations traditionally

---

[12] Note that this effect holds despite controlling for organizational size.

[13] This is less the case for member control, to the extent that CSOs hostile to democracy and its constitutive values are less likely to adopt democratic procedures within their organization.

[14] On the ongoing debate around democratic self-defence, i.e. on whether and, if so, how democratic states ought to fight non-democratic groups and parties, see, for a recent overview, Malkopoulou and Kirshner 2021.

associated with it (Smith and Freedman 1972). None of the features associated with the 'voluntary association' template has a significant relationship with member control—the notion of activism closely associated with the democratic accountability of decision-making (e.g. Maloney 2009; Cross and Katz 2013). Structurally resembling a 'voluntary association' seems not to generate a barrier against centralization of decision-making or—vice versa— positively relate to member control over decision-making. The normative expectation that citizens who join organizations have an interest in active participation is difficult to uphold. Considering the plurality of value orientations that associations represent in increasingly individualized, modern societies, this finding was to be expected and supports more recent empirical studies on the participatory contribution of and citizen expectations towards interest or party organizations (e.g. Jordan and Maloney 2007; van Deth and Maloney 2012; Cross and Katz 2013; Close et al. 2017). Furthermore, it has important normative repercussions, since, strictly speaking, the centralization of decision-making power to a small leadership is not equivalent to oligarchy if it is not objected to by members (Leach 2005: 331), a scenario we will be able to explore later on in the case studies (Chapter 6).

While the features of the two governance templates have an impact across different organizational types, also significant is whether organizations are a party or group. On average, party members tend to be more involved than group members, indicating that the nature of an organization's primary activity affects how critical the generation of member involvement as an organizational resource is to sustain their central activities (e.g. Pfeffer and Salancik 1978; Beyers and Kerremans 2007).[15] The externally imposed regularity of elections provides an institutional incentive for parties to cultivate involvement more continuously than groups, which also will be stressed by the case study of the GPEW in Chapter 6. The latter will highlight the role of one form of involvement uniquely important to party organizations: members' willingness to stand for elections—especially when there is little hope for success. Being central to parties' primary mission of electoral participation, the pressure to recruit candidates provides a powerful incentive—not relevant to groups—to build and maintain an involved membership base as recruitment pool.

The finding that party members, on average, tend to be more involved than group members has important implications for organized civil

---

[15] Note that this does not mean that there are more parties with an active membership than groups, given group populations are much bigger (see Chapter 3).

society'spotential to function as a venue for participation in an age where parties are unpopular and the centrality of parties as organizations for democracy is frequently questioned (e.g. Katz 1990; Dalton and Weldon 2005). While being a party per se does not create incentives to be internally more democratic than groups, higher involvement levels in parties qualify concerns around parties becoming outdated venues for participation that might be displaced by alternative—more issue-specific—types of organizations.[16] This gains further weight when considering that involvement in parties—unlike involvement in service-oriented organizations—by definition supports the pursuit of political goals and contributes to interest representation. This leaves aside suggestions in earlier research that beneficial effects of associational membership on political participation are more pronounced in CSOs with political goals, which are central to parties by definition (see Chapter 1).

Whether members directly control internal decisions or not, their involvement in parties has consequences for democracy. This finding suggests that, despite organizational landscapes in contemporary democracies diversifying to offer citizens an ever-growing choice of venues to express their opinions and pursue their interests individually or collectively, political parties remain a central venue for member mobilization and engagement in increasingly individualized democracies that cannot easily be replaced. Despite many parties' increasingly close relations with state institutions and their declining popularity amongst citizens (e.g. Katz and Mair 1995; 2009; Dalton and Weldon 2005; Biezen and Kopecký 2017; Whiteley 2011), they remain important venues for member activism. This is echoed by research that indicates that both mainstream and new parties try to create new participatory structures that can reinvent and diversify party–constituency linkages both online and offline (e.g. Hazan and Rahat 2010; Gauja 2015; 2017; Scarrow 2015; Gerbaudo 2019; Barberà et al. 2021).

To conclude with the most interesting finding 'cutting across' groups and parties, professionalization relates to member control negatively and to member involvement positively. It underscores the centrality of organizations' increasing reliance on paid staff as a feature fundamentally shaping organized civil society in a democracy though in more ambivalent and complex ways than often expected (e.g. Skocpol 2013; Rogers 2005). Interestingly, despite a significant literature on the growth of professional advocacy organizations that are memberless by choice (e.g. Walker et al. 2011; Schlozman et al. 2015),

---

[16] See on this discussion, for instance, Lawson and Merkl 1988; Daalder 2007; Norris 2002; Thomassen and van Ham 2014; Ignazi 2021.

the empirical findings do not suggest that organizational professionalization invites a transformation from membership-based into memberless organizations or even a passive membership. On the contrary, the positive association between professionalization and member involvement suggests that professionalized CSOs can better exploit members as a resource (e.g. Maloney and Rossteutscher 2005; Paine et al. 2010). This enhances—if only in functional terms—members' value to the organization. Hence, despite its negative association with member control as central indication of 'intra-organizational democracy', a uniformly negative evaluation of the observed trend towards organizational professionalization in civil society is problematic. It does not do justice to the fact that professionalization can help to strengthen ties between organizations and their members. This will become even clearer in Chapter 6, when we will qualitatively explore how and through which mechanisms enhanced CSO professionalization affects both forms of member activism over time.

5
When Managers Take Over
Drivers of Staff Control in Civil Society Organizations

Prominent literatures in politics and sociology—whether they focus on parties, interest groups, or non-profits—have long stressed the fundamental implications of professionalization and bureaucratization not only for how organizations are *managed* but how they are *governed*.[1] Going back to Michels' iron law of oligarchy (1915) much of the party and group literature has focused on the 'problem of centralization', as concerned with the extent to which an organization's leadership is in charge of decision-making with little accountability towards its members, the central theme of Chapter 4. However, in light of the increasing professionalization of interest groups, parties, and non-profit organizations, the question of 'who controls decisions' is no longer fully addressed by considering the 'classical question' of whether and when members are 'disempowered' and decisions become detached from the 'grass roots'. This long-dominant perspective on organizational governance has been challenged, notably by Saurugger, who argued that nowadays the 'counter-hypothesis' to associations' contribution to political socialization and democratic efficiency 'refers to staff domination of groups' (2012: 71; see on this, with a focus on parties Panebianco 1988; with a focus on NGOs, Lang 2013). This chapter theorizes and examines to what extent central traits of the 'professionalized voluntary organization' allow for managers to take control of CSO decision-making, a process at the risk of displacing both rank-and-file members and organizational leaders. Its analytical counterpart—the 'voluntary association'—serves as a foundation to theorize and examine the organizational conditions under which such tendencies might be contained.

The professionalization and bureaucratization of CSOs have been associated with the growing decision-making power and autonomy of paid employees in the running of CSOs for a while. Though using different

---

[1] E.g. Panebianco 1988; Katz and Mair 1995, 2009; Jordan and Maloney 2007; Suarez 2010a; Reid 1999; Miller-Millesen 2003; Skocpol 2003; Beyers et al. 2008; Salamon and Lessans-Geller 2008; Saurugger 2008; Maloney 2009; van Deth and Maloney 2012; Klüver and Saurugger 2013; Schlozman et al. 2015.

Civil Society's Democratic Potential. Nicole Bolleyer, Oxford University Press. © Nicole Bolleyer (2024).
DOI: 10.1093/oso/9780198884392.003.0005

terminologies, studies on parties and groups have equally highlighted a fundamental trade-off that membership organizations face between a growing demand for expertise in and for the efficiency of CSO decision-making and the maintenance of meaningful accountability relationships with societal constituencies.[2] Staff control over decisions brings to the fore this trade-off, reflected in contradictory evaluations in current research of the growing importance of managers in organizational life. Staff control over CSOs is considered beneficial from a 'statist' or 'public agencies perspective', as it contributes to the efficient delivery of public services and the meeting of contractual or legal requirements.[3] From a 'societal perspective', in contrast, it is problematized, as the concentration of managerial and governance functions in the hands of managers risks undermining organizational accountability relationships.[4]

It is the latter perspective that makes the study of staff control relevant to an overall assessment of CSOs' contributions to democracy. As detailed in Chapter 1, the presence and level of staff control provides insights into the relative propensity of CSOs to make decisions responsive to societal demands, in contrast to instrumental decision-making predominantly directed towards assuring organizational survival.[5] To establish meaningful linkages, the ability of organizational representatives to define organizational ends is crucial, especially when policy initiatives increasingly try to connect societal and state actors in processes of policy formulation, implementation, and service-provision (e.g. Waardenburg and van de Bovenkamp 2014; Fyall 2017). That staff control over (as opposed to mere influence on) decisions might reduce this ability has growing practical importance, as policymakers present the involvement of CSOs in, particularly, service provision, as a means to invigorate governments' ties to citizens and boost civic activism (e.g. Bovaird 2007; Brandsen et al. 2014). If CSO professionalization and bureaucratization—which state authorities usually welcome and incentivize by offering opportunities for collaboration—diminish CSOs' ability to exercise 'societal voice' in favour of the 'voice' of its staff, the claimed democratic benefits of such government initiatives are put into question.

Unlike public agencies or firms (composed of paid staff), in which the presence of staff exercising decision-making control is a matter of course,

---

[2] A corresponding trade-off has been formulated with regard to parties as employers who to try to reconcile a growing need for competence and skills amongst their staff and those staff's loyalty to organizational values (e.g. Webb and Fisher 2003; Moens 2021).

[3] E.g. Smith and Lipsky 1993; Frumkin 2002; O'Regan and Oster 2005; Salgado 2010.

[4] E.g. Jordan and Maloney 1997; O'Regan and Oster 2005; King 2017.

[5] E.g. Panebianco 1988; Katz and Mair 1995; Jordan and Maloney 1997; O'Regan and Oster 2005; Lang 2013; King 2017.

in CSOs, managers (as agents) are formally accountable to members and organizational leaders (as principals). While delegating certain tasks to staff is bound to be the norm, it is organizational representatives who ought to define organizational ends, not only normatively but also legally speaking (Edwards and Cornforth 2003; Hopt and von Hippel 2010; Chatelain-Ponroy et al. 2015). The main legal forms adopted by CSOs in civil and common law regimes (e.g. association, charitable company) allocate central governing responsibilities to volunteer actors (van der Ploeg et al. 2017; Hopt and von Hippel 2010), which sits uneasily with a de facto take-over of decision-making by paid employees (Hoye and Cuskelly 2003: 70).

As compared to other organizations or institutional structures, CSOs are 'least likely settings' for staff control to emerge. Examining drivers of staff control within CSOs thus constitutes a 'hard test' for the often-claimed pervasiveness of professionalization and bureaucratization in organizational governance and their negative implications for democratic accountability structures. While often assumed, there is no conclusive evidence that processes of professionalization and bureaucratization are 'automatically' translated into staff control. Heylen et al. (2020: 1226) recently showed that we find professionalized interest groups with an active, powerful membership base as well as those with a passive and powerless one (see also Bentancur et al. 2019). And while Chapter 4 indicated that professionalization negatively impacts on member control, the analysis equally showed that this is not equivalent to members being passive and unimportant. Neither are staff, once present, automatically in charge, thereby displacing organizational representatives.

Of the surveyed CSOs with paid staff, only 31 per cent allow managers to control any decisions rather than 'merely' exercising influence which we can take as a given once staff are around. This substantiates the theoretical expectation presented in Chapter 2 that organizational actors—members and leaders—show a basic scepticism towards shifting decision-making authority to paid employees. The distinction between the 'professionalized voluntary organization' and 'voluntary association' will provide the foundation for theorizing why staff control only materializes in some CSOs reliant on paid staff but not in others. This will rationalize why some CSOs resolve the cross-pressures between operating in a more efficient and expertise-based manner and maintaining organizational accountability structures in favour of the former, while others prioritize the latter. In line with the overall framework presented in Chapter 2, association features are expected to constitute a barrier against managers becoming decision-makers 'in their own right'. Features of the 'voluntary professionalized organization'—prioritizing expertise and efficiency—ought to facilitate this transformation.

A Governance Perspective on Staff Control in Civil Society Organizations

It is widely accepted in the party, group, and non-profit literature that the growing presence of paid professionals within membership organizations implies their growing importance in organizational governance. Similarly, it is little contested that membership organizations in contemporary democracies face increasing pressure to professionalize as well as bureaucratize, to enhance efficiency as well as expertise. Such pressures not only impact on the substance but also the structural nature of organizational decision-making (Panebianco 1988: 231–2; Webb and Kolodny 2006: 339; Jordan and Maloney 2007; Moens 2022). Nevertheless, not all CSOs with paid employees allow their staff to control actual decisions, i.e. to define organizational ends in central areas of governance. Many restrict their staff to the implementation of goals as defined by organizational actors instead. Clearly, the disconnect from organizational actors implied by staff control makes the latter contentious, more so than mere influence that most staff are likely to have by channelling advice or expertise into governance processes (Golensky 1993; Saidel and Harlan 1998; Wallander and Molander 2014).

Hypotheses on Staff Control in Professionalized Voluntary Organizations

Paid professionals recruited for their skills are bound to consider expertise and efficiency in decision-making as essential, more so than both organizational leaders and members who joined an organization based on their voluntary commitment to a certain cause. This expectation towards professionalization aligns with bureaucratization as a type of organizational structure in which efficiency and effectiveness are central norms. Once established, it favours further efficiency-enhancing reforms as well as the provision of training to reinforce skills in a CSO's professional and volunteer base (e.g. Kreutzer and Jäger 2011; Paine et al. 2010). Accordingly, both organizational features of the 'professionalized voluntary organization' should work in favour of staff control, to the detriment of organizational accountability.

Despite the two phenomena's affinity, there is a long tradition in public administration research—going back to Weber's conception of bureaucracy—that stresses the tensions between managerial control and professional discretion (Toren 1976: 36; Nass 1986; Pollitt 1990: 440; Ferlie and

Geraghty 2007: 425–6; O'Reilly and Reed 2011: 1083). The latter distinction is relevant here as it suggests differentiated expectations regarding the implications of professionalization and bureaucratization for staff control. In essence, while both are expected to make it easier for managers to assume control of decision-making, the former is expected to be less pervasive than the latter.

Looking at professionalization more closely, as the prevalence of employees with professional expertise increases, governing bodies will be more prone to take advantage of their knowledge base and grant them control over decisions (Ben-Ner and Ren 2010: 615–16; Nesbit et al. 2012: 13; Meyer and Maier 2015). This renders the presence of staff control more likely, based on the assumption that managers prefer to control decisions directly in areas they consider themselves to be competent (and more competent than amateurs). However, as staff control in specific domains is established, this is unlikely to 'spill over' into areas that can still be straightforwardly handled by members and organizational leaders without comparable technical skills or knowledge. This is not only due to possible resistance of organizational actors—especially leaders—keen to maintain a say over these areas but also as managers themselves are unlikely to be keen on such 'expansion'. The latter acquire control over decisions based on their specialized professional judgement (Toren 1976: 37; Ahlbäck Öberg and Bringselius 2015: 502; Shepherd 2018). Consequently, while being keen to gain control over their 'own' specialist areas, professionals are expected to be reluctant to venture into domains in which their expertise is less relevant (Heclo 1978; Wilensky 1964: 145; Ferlie and Geraghty 2007: 425–6; O'Reilly and Reed 2011: 1085–7). Given professionals' orientation towards achieving recognition by external peers operating in the same fields (Barberis 2013: 340; Ahlbäck Öberg and Bringselius 2015: 503), their interest in the general operation of the organization will be relatively limited. If this is the case, it is unlikely that professionalization enhances the scope of staff control.

A similarly restricted effect is expected from CSO dependence on state funding as the second central resource of a 'professionalized voluntary organization'. Access to those funds invites the adoption of governing mechanisms typical for the public sector to enable CSOs to cope with complex requirements in the areas of financial management, reporting, and performance evaluations (e.g. Frumkin and Kim 2002; Salgado 2010). Hence, organizations with higher state funding dependence have greater need for administrative and project-specific staff hired exclusively to 'solicit, manage, and report on the use of government grants and contracts' (Frumkin and Kim 2002: 3–4; Smith and Lipsky 1993). Organizations that are dependent on contracts can be particularly exposed to competitive quasi-market pressures when competing for contracts. Once they have won contracts, CSOs become subject to demanding accountability requirements that require reliance on professionals (Saidel and Harlan 1998; Smith 2010). Within specific domains, state funding dependency incentivizes paid employees to take on more proactive roles. But again, as such control is based on technical, specialist knowledge, it does not provide the foundation (from the perspective of organizational actors) or the motivation (from the perspective of managers) to expand such control to wider areas of decision-making. We thus can summarize the following expectation about the implications of professionalization and state funding for patterns of staff control:

H1.1 (*Professionalization/State Funding–Staff Control Hypothesis*): The more professionalized and the more dependent on state funding a CSO is, the more likely *the presence of staff control.*

In contrast to the two core resources of the 'professionalized voluntary organization', bureaucratization is a governance principle. It becomes manifest in a specific form of organizational structure assuring organizational control, coordination, and the overall integration of an organization's components. It is concerned with the efficient and effective operation of the organization as a whole (Kreutzer and Jäger 2011: 638; Toren 1976: 36; Ward 2011: 205; Barberis 2013: 331). It pushes organizations towards hierarchical structures in which senior staff access information from different organizational departments, which, in turn, should bolster their control over decisions (Harlan and Saidel 1994; Heimovics et al. 1995: 246; Miller-Millesen 2003). Unlike professionalization, bureaucratization rests on generic, generally applicable principles—notably efficiency and effectiveness (Hood 1991: 8)—motivating and allowing managers to systematically embed themselves in organizations and colonize new domains (Hwang and Powell 2009: 269; Shepherd 2018: 1671). Streamlining operations in accordance with corporate governance principles, senior managers are expected to push CSOs to expand and alter existing accountability systems that do not align with these principles (Ward 2011: 210–11; Meyer and Maier 2015: 45, 48). Unlike professionalization and state funding dependency, bureaucratization is therefore expected not only to make the presence of staff control more likely but also to expand its scope, to the detriment of organizational accountability structures.

H1.2 (*Bureaucratization–Staff Control Hypothesis*): The more bureaucratized a CSO is, the more likely *staff control is present and the broader its scope.*

Hypotheses on Staff Control in Voluntary Associations

As detailed in Chapter 2, leaders and members are generally expected to be sceptical towards granting staff control. But under which conditions is this scepticism likely to lead to its actual containment? Echoing fundamental challenges of principal–agent control (Maggetti and Papadopoulos 2018: 175–6), the principals in membership-based CSOs—organizational leaders or members—might remain passive towards managers due to information asymmetry, preference heterogeneity, and the general inability or unwillingness to act collectively. Whatever the specific reasons for such passivity, the more inactive the membership base and their representatives who formally 'own' an organization are, the bigger the decision-making vacuum likely to emerge. This vacuum is likely to be filled by managers who end up making decisions—be they technical, strategic, or substantive (e.g. Cnaan 1991; Billis 2010; Clarence et al. 2005). Some staff control might even emerge when individual leaders are proactive. Leaders, themselves volunteer actors, have only limited capacities and might be unable to deal with all areas of organizational governance themselves. Facing a passive membership (and hence few volunteer staff to support them) might make a division of labour all the more attractive, with managers in charge of technical and leaders in charge of substantive matters.

Considering these scenarios, the crucial question, then, is under which structural conditions members or leaders have sufficient 'voluntary capacity' that enables them to maintain core organizational activities on a continuous basis (Cairns et al. 2005: 872), *without* relying on paid staff. Association features are expected to counter pressures towards efficient and expert decision-making by managers at the cost of organizational accountability structures for two basic reasons. First, they are expected to enhance CSOs' voluntary capacity. Second, in voluntary associations those actors remain central to the running of the organization who are less willing to see traditional accountability structures compromised.

Staff control is most ambiguous from the perspective of members. Not because members necessarily want to keep decision-making power for themselves. But they are keen to see their own interests considered in CSO governance. While managers are unlikely to ignore members altogether, they can be expected to consider their interests alongside the interests of other key audiences, such as the CSOs' wider societal constituencies, donors, or institutional funders (e.g. Berkhout 2013). Depending on the subject matter concerned, managers might be pressed to weigh against each other long-term and short-term costs and benefits of prioritizing one audience's interests over the other, should those conflict. Based on such an assessment, staff can be expected to regularly trade member interests against those of other audiences considered equally or more important to organizational maintenance and performance. Generally, given their more instrumental outlook (see Chapter 2), they can be expected to do so more willingly than organizational leaders sharing a voluntary affiliation with members.

In line with this logic, the consideration of member interests and, with this, the reluctance to grant staff control should be more pronounced in member-serving organizations than public-serving organizations that represent wider and more diverse constituencies. Similarly, more pragmatic and instrumental corporate members can be expected to grant staff greater leeway to pursue CSO goals, and in doing so to prioritize effectiveness and efficiency. This contrasts with more value-oriented individual members, which suggests a negative relationship between individual membership and staff control. Also multi-tier structures are expected to disincentivize staff control. They provide a more favourable environment for member mobilization and enhance the ability to overcome collective action problems. Members in multi-tier CSOs should thus be more able to constrain actors in 'central office'—including senior managers—than members operating in unitary structures (Barasko and Schaffner 2008: 194–5; Halpin 2014).

Moving to an association's core resources, in CSOs strongly reliant on volunteer staff (i.e. unpaid members holding administrative and managerial roles), the room for managers to take over decision-making should be more curtailed, thereby delimiting staff control, than in CSOs that do not. This is not only the case because volunteers can be expected to guard control over domains they are themselves active in and thus can be expected to care about. Reliance on volunteer staff—essentially active members—gives member interests more structural weight in the organization as a whole. Similarly, reliance on membership fees should make it more difficult to ignore the voice of active members, who are likely to care about the direction their CSO is taking and about decision-making to remain in the hands of members directly or representatives accountable to them. In short, the relationship between the dependence on membership fees and staff control should also be negative.

To conclude this section with two broader issues, it is important to note that the theoretical rationales just presented are consistent with those underpinning the earlier expectation that association features should be unrelated to member control, as members do not necessarily hold pluralist or democratic values. The assumption here is that members are committed to central organizational values and interests (whether these values are democratic or authoritarian), as otherwise they would not have joined the particular organization (e.g. Hooghe and Kölln 2020). It can be expected that those members prefer for those values and interests (whether they endorse democratic bottom-up or top-down decision-making) to be central considerations in CSO decision-making. This, in turn, is more likely if organizational actors sharing such attachments are in charge, compared to managers competitively recruited for their skills. Hence, CSOs 'built around' members and their preferences as embodied by the 'voluntary association' provide a barrier against staff control, irrespective of whether these characteristics invite member control. Relatedly, as association features have implications for the overall power relations and priorities within CSOs—rather than suggesting effects in particular domains (as is the case with professionalization and state funding) – they can be expected to impact on both the presence and scope of staff control.

We thus can formulate the following hypothesis:

> **H2** (*Association Features–Staff Control Hypothesis*): In CSOs with voluntary association features, staff control is *less likely to be present and will be narrower in its scope* than in CSOs without such features.

A Quantitative Analysis of Staff Control in Civil Society Organizations

As detailed in Chapter 3, staff control is measured through an index capturing the presence of staff control across nine domains that are central to organizational governance, including technical areas (e.g. budget) and administrative areas (e.g. membership admissions) as well as political ones (e.g. change of organizational statutes). We find staff control in only 31 per cent of those organizations reliant on paid staff. This discrepancy underlines that the definition of organizational ends by managers is not a 'default outcome' in CSOs with paid staff, challenging previous research that stressed the centrality of managers in the organizational governance of staff-reliant CSOs (Heimovics and Herman 1990; Wood 1992; Hoye and Cuskelly 2003). Similar to Chapter 4, which showed that being composed of members does not mean that members exercise decision-making control, being reliant on paid staff does not suggest a straightforward empowerment of managers as decision-makers either. Clearly, among CSOs with staff, the majority keep decision-making power in the hands of organizational actors. The transition to hiring paid staff (and not being completely volunteer-run anymore) is thus less of a 'transformative event' than sometimes portrayed in the literature (e.g. Billis 2010).

To test the hypotheses developed above, I estimated a zero-inflated Poisson model (Hu et al. 2011). Several reasons render this modelling choice particularly appropriate. First, zero-inflated models are able to accommodate both an abundance of zeros and a skewed distribution of non-zero values in the dependent variable. Second, the two-part structure of zero-inflated models is appealing because it reflects the logic underlying the hypotheses. The zero-inflated Poisson model is a mixture consisting of a degenerate distribution at zero and a Poisson distribution. Zeros may arise from both the point mass and the count component. The zero-inflated model thus explicitly partitions zeros into two types: (i) 'structural' and (ii) 'sampling' or 'chance' (Hu et al. 2011). Such treatment of null values is well suited for this analysis, since organizations that do not have any paid staff cannot exhibit staff control (i.e. these are 'structural' zeros), while other CSOs that hire paid workers do not allow them to control decision-making ('chance' zeros),[6] as illustrated earlier.

Table 5.1 presents the findings. It displays the expected change in *the probability of staff control being present* (Zero Model, column 1) and *in the number of areas controlled by staff* (Count Model, column 2) associated with a unit change in each predictor, holding all other variables constant. To start with two broader observations, the overall findings provide support for the theoretically expected *opposite* implications for staff control of association features as compared to features of the 'professionalized voluntary organization'. Essentially, all association features that display a significant relationship with the presence or the scope of staff control relate to it *negatively*. In contrast, features of the 'professionalized voluntary organization' that have significant and robust effects relate to staff control *positively* (note that the 'zero model' of the zero-inflated model gives the propensity for staff control *not* to be present (i.e. counter-intuitively signs of coefficients are 'in reverse' in column 1 as compared to column 2)). Consequently, the distinction between the two governance templates is empirically relevant to staff control, shaping patterns of organizational accountability of decision-making: the features of the two templates push CSOs in opposite directions, with association features supporting accountability to organizational actors and features of the 'professionalized voluntary organization' weakening it. Indeed, the overall relevance of the distinction between the two templates is more pronounced for staff control than in the case of member control studied in Chapter 4

---

[6] By contrast, hurdle models—which are also able to accommodate zero-inflation and right-skewed counts—assume that all zeros are 'structural', an assumption that is inadequate in this setting.

116 Civil Society's Democratic Potential

Table 5.1 Zero-Inflated Count Regressions with Poisson Distribution (With Multiple Imputations)

	Zero Model		Count Model	
	DV = Presence of Staff Control		DV = Scope of Staff Control	
	Coefficient	SE	Coefficient	SE
(Intercept)	4.39***	(1.11)	−0.63	(0.37)
Features of Professionalized Voluntary Organization				
Bureaucratization	−0.17	(0.16)	0.16**	(0.05)
Professionalization (log)	−2.15***	(0.23)	0.05	0.03
State Funding	−0.41	(0.22)	−0.01	(0.06)
Features of Voluntary Association				
Individual Membership	0.18	(0.38)	0.02	(0.10)
Member Interest Orientation	0.08	(0.33)	0.02	(0.10)
Multi-Tier Structure	0.07	(0.28)	−0.23**	(0.09)
Volunteer Staff (log)	0.27**	(0.10)	−0.05*	(0.02)
Membership Fees	0.57	(0.42)	−0.08	(0.10)
CSO Type				
Interest Group (ref: parties)	−0.08	(0.93)	0.05	(0.28)
Service-Oriented Organization (ref: parties)	−0.10	(0.96)	0.16	(0.28)
Controls Relevant to CSO Behaviour Generally				
Membership Instability	−0.81*	(0.32)	−0.09	(0.11)
Membership Size (log)	−0.09	(0.10)	0.09***	0.02
Organizational Age (log)	−0.29	(0.15)	−0.11*	(0.05)
UK (ref: Norway)	−0.37	(0.44)	0.35*	(0.16)
Germany (ref: Norway)	−0.90*	(0.46)	−0.34*	(0.16)
Switzerland (ref: Norway)	−0.99*	(0.48)	−0.24	(0.16)
Increased Member Involvement	0.07	(0.27)	−0.09	(0.08)
Dimension-Specific Controls				
Donor Dependency	0.05	(0.23)	0.01	(0.07)
Resource Competition	−0.12	(0.26)	0.15	(0.09)
Marketization	−0.48	(0.29)	0.11	(0.08)
Log(theta)	—	—	2.29***	(0.50)
N	3265		3265	

Note: Standard errors in parentheses * $p<0.05$, ** $p<0.01$, *** $p<0.001$.

(which was negatively related to features of the 'professionalized voluntary organization', with association features remaining 'neutral').

Furthermore, only one variable—volunteer staff—shows a significant relationship with both the presence and the scope of staff control, and its effect in the count model is not robust across different specifications. While the directions of effects are generally in line with the hypotheses, we neither find the expected pervasiveness (i.e. impacts on both presence and scope of staff control) of bureaucratization (H1.2) nor of association features generally (H2). At the same time, the fact that the theorized variables tend to shape either one or the other aspect of staff control highlights the suitability of a two-part model. It separates out factors that allow staff control to take hold in an organization from factors that allow staff control (once established as a mode of decision-making) to permeate into a wider range of domains.

Having a closer look at the individual findings, in line with H1, professionalization is positively and significantly related with the presence of staff control (column 1). In contrast, it is not relevant to its scope (column 2). This estimate is consistent with theoretical expectations yet contradicts prominent views about the pervasiveness of the presence of full-time employees (as compared to volunteer staff) on the broader governance culture of organizations (e.g. Harris 1989; Heimovics and Herman 1990; Hoye and Cuskelly 2003). Instead, the differentiated implications of CSO professionalization lend credence to classical arguments suggesting that professional control—as it is based on exclusive knowledge—is likely to remain confined to particular domains in which specific types of expertise are relevant (Wilensky 1964; Toren 1976; Ferlie and Geraghty 2007). They explain why this factor does not provide the foundation for an expansion of staff control to wider areas of decision-making. Heavy reliance on paid staff does not necessarily stifle the voice of members and volunteers, nor does it necessarily undermine the overall representativeness of organizations, as sometimes suggested (Skocpol 2013; Frumkin 2002; Jordan and Maloney 2007).

While state funding does not have a significant effect here, the latter case studies indicate that indirect state funding (e.g. tax benefits through charitable status) and direct state funding can impact on the role that staff play in an organization. Both incentivize the granting of staff control, as organizational leaders tend to leave the handling of related budgetary matters and reporting to paid staff, who de facto make the necessary decisions that tend to be—in line with legal requirements—formally approved by leaders.[7]

Bureaucratization, the central governance feature of the 'professionalized voluntary organization', has no significant relationship with the presence of staff control. It does, however, positively relate to its scope. As noted before,

---

[7] As indicated earlier, such transfers should not be equated with 'centralization' as far as they do not move the responsibility for domains "upwards" away from members but "sideways" from organizationally accountable to non-accountable actors operating jointly on central level.

bureaucratization rests on generic, generally applicable principles—e.g. efficiency and effectiveness—that allow managers to systematically embed themselves in organizations and colonize new domains (Hwang and Powell 2009; Shepherd 2018). The establishment of a centralized hierarchy within organizations, a core characteristic of managerial culture (Hall 1968; Willis 1978) helps to reinforce the decision-making power of managers. The analysis provides some empirical evidence that bureaucratization can facilitate staff control to expand into wider domains, which might hamper the societal representativeness of membership-based voluntary organizations by detaching decision-making from organizational actors (Wilderom and Miner 1991; Milligan and Fyfe 2005).

Yet for this to happen, staff control as a mode of decision-making needs to have previously taken hold in an organizational setting. This becomes the more likely the more professionalized a CSO becomes, as indicated by a growing presence of paid staff in the organization. In other words, for bureaucratization to facilitate that staff control can expand into further domains, managers need to have established themselves as decision-makers in the first place, which becomes more likely the more numerous they are. As detailed in Chapter 3, bureaucratization is captured empirically through 'reinforce[d] investments in managerial competences/skills of the organization' and 'streamlined decision-making processes to enhance efficiency'. Chapter 2, in turn, argued that managers tend to favour—in terms of 'organizational structure preferences'—procedures able to assure continuity in the performance of maintenance tasks as well as reforms enhancing effective and efficient goal attainment (Staggenborg 1988: 594–5, 597; Maier and Meyer 2011). If so, professional staff can be expected to favour bureaucratization not just in specific domains but generally and thus to push to enhance towards bureaucratization (e.g. thorough efficiency-enhancing reforms), as they gain more prominence in an organization.

In this sense, professionalization and bureaucratization appear as qualitatively different but complementary phenomena when it comes to staff control. Increasing professionalization enhances the chances of managers being able to take decisions in their area of expertise (supporting the presence of staff control). Bureaucratization as a governance principle—likely to be promoted by managers—facilitates such decision-making practices to be spread to further domains (enhancing the scope of staff control). Indeed, this interpretation will be substantiated by the case studies presented in Chapter 6. They will show how managers initiate bureaucratization reforms that downsize member control over decision-making (rationalized as enhancing more efficient internal processes). Such downsizing of member control tended to most immediately benefit the organizational leaders and did not simply empower managers. Yet once (unpaid) organizational leaders had to handle an increasing range of responsibilities as a consequence, passing over more technical areas to specialist staff (with whom leaders work closely) became more attractive to them as a way to make their own workload more manageable.

Moving to the association template, as already highlighted, all significant features affect staff control in the theoretically expected direction. They help to contain staff control by either making its presence less likely or curtailing its scope (H2). Volunteer staff and multi-tier structures have a significant and robust negative effect on staff control respectively. That multi-tier structures correlate negatively with the scope of staff control is consistent with earlier research linking decentralized organizational infrastructures to a strengthened capacity for collective action and member influence in governance processes (Milligan and Fyfe 2005; Barakso and Schaffner 2008; Albareda 2018; Heylen et al. 2020). Hence, in multi-tier structures, organizational actors tend to be more able to provide a counterweight against transfers of decision-making power to managers. This is different from keeping rank-and-file members directly in charge, as highlighted by the analysis in Chapter 4 (which did not find a significant relationship between multi-tier structures and member control).

Chapter 6 will suggest that the critical aspect is the importance of volunteer staff as a subset of a CSO's wider membership to organizational maintenance. If we find a division of labour and mutual dependency between the subnational branches (which tend to be volunteer-run) and the central organization (where paid staff tends to be concentrated) the tasks or domains dealt with on the subnational level by default remain in the hands of organizational actors. This creates an effective barrier against the expansion of staff control, which would require the centralization of decision-making at the managerial level. The centrality of member mobilization for keeping staff control at bay—which is supported by multi-tier structures—is underlined by the opposite influence of a growing membership size which supports the expansion of staff control. This finding echoes a long tradition of research on Michel's 'iron law of oligarchy' (1915) that associates large membership organizations with leadership dominance thanks to leaders' superior knowledge and skills (though the role of paid employees tends not to be systematically theorized in the early work, but see Panebianco 1988).

Volunteer staff, in turn, has a negative and statistically significant effect on both the presence and the scope of staff control, though the latter does not hold in all model specifications. Focusing on the robust effect in the zero model (column 1), the negative effect of the number of volunteer staff on the probability for staff control to be present—the core human resource of 'voluntary associations—mirrors the positive effect on its presence of professionalization captured by the number of paid staff—the core "human resource" of "professionalized voluntary organizations". Indeed, qualitative studies tracing organizations' long-term evolution have shown that CSOs often start out (when having only modest financial means) by hiring some (part-time) administrator unlikely to take over any substantive decisions, while volunteers continue to hold central posts in the organization. Once the paid workforce grows, managerial roles with leadership functions are taken on by (more qualified) paid professionals (e.g. Ivanovska Hadjievska 2018). Given the nature of their roles and, relatedly, higher levels of qualification, they are more likely to shape decision-making processes proactively in their areas of responsibility.

This interpretation of the negative association between volunteer staff and the presence of staff control neatly aligns with another significant effect—the positive impact of membership instability on staff control, one of the control variables. In CSOs that perceive member retainment and recruitment as a challenge for their maintenance (i.e. they perceive their base as unstable), the likelihood that staff control decisions increases. This is somewhat counter-intuitive. One might have expected that if members are not happy with the CSO and leave, or societal supporters are unwilling to join, a CSO attempts to counteract this by establishing closer ties to members and constituencies. One strategy to achieve this could be to enhance organizational accountability to members, which directly clashes with staff controlling decisions. Thus, the positive relationship between membership instability and staff control suggests a different rationale. As the strength of a CSO's membership base—as expressed through the strong involvement of volunteers in the organization—makes staff control less likely (see Table 5.1), the perceived weakness and lack of reliability of a CSO's support base make it easier for staff to take over. The case studies in Chapter 6 suggest the following dynamic. Domains strongly affected by professionalization in both groups and parties and hence strongly shaped by managerial initiatives were member admissions and volunteer management. To prevent or counter member decline, CSOs did not enhance accountability to members and supporters as potential decision-makers (a role that only some members are likely to be interested in), i.e. member control. Instead, they altered and diversified their strategies to attach different member and supporter groups to the organization through member involvement, while providing targeted support for members taking over responsibility in the organization, endeavours fully compatible with and benefitting from staff control.

Conclusion

The growing professionalization, bureaucratization, and state dependency of groups and parties are contested phenomena sitting at the heart of conflicting demands confronting CSOs in contemporary democracies. They face pressures towards more efficient and expert decision-making, while still maintaining meaningful linkages with societal constituencies. Staff control—allowing senior managers to take decisions directly—is one answer to this trade-off. This answer risks weakening the organizational accountability of CSO decision-making and, with this, CSOs' societal responsiveness and their ability to engage in democratic representation driven by societal demands (e.g. Smith and Lipsky 1993; Frumkin 2002; Skocpol 2013; Karlsen and Saglie 2017). In line with the theoretical framework of this study, association features and features of the professionalized voluntary organization push membership-based CSOs in opposite directions when facing this trade-off. Association features favour responsiveness towards organizational actors and thus helped contain staff control. Features of the professionalized voluntary organization give more weight to efficiency and expertise, which favours the emergence of staff control.

In membership-based CSOs, even if they are professionalized and bureaucratized, staff control is not inevitable. This is so when members take on managerial roles and collective action is enabled by multi-tier structures, both association features. This supports earlier qualitative evidence suggesting that staff control emerges and is likely to be perpetuated in organizations where voluntary organs do not assert themselves in relation to staff (Harris 1989: 330). The relevance of the two association features further qualify prominent claims regarding the declining importance of CSO members as a consequence of civil society professionalization (e.g. Skocpol 2003; Schlozman et al. 2015). Chapter 4 has indicated that association features do not incentivize member control over decision-making. But how members and volunteers operate in an organization is still important for the distribution of decision-making power in CSOs, although in a different way than traditional work leads us to expect. Association features might not curtail centralization in a classical sense. Instead, they affect how prominent a role managers are able to play in organizations and thus whether the accountability of decision-making to organizational actors is likely to remain intact.

Considering the implication of the central features of the 'professionalized voluntary organization', it is most interesting how exactly the—very intuitive—positive relationships with staff control manifest themselves exactly. Public administration and public management research have long highlighted the distinct repercussions of professional discretion as compared to managerial control for the distribution of decision-making power in organizations (e.g. Salvatore and Numerato 2018; du Gay and Pedersen 2020). The findings of this chapter underscore classical works on the differences between professionalization and bureaucratization (e.g. Toren 1976; Pollitt 1990; Ferlie and Geraghty 2007; O'Reilly and Reed 2011). They suggest that CSO professionalization makes staff control more likely, without inviting its expansion across governance domains. It is bureaucratization, a structural principle, that relates to the scope of staff control positively. Professionalization is thus compatible with the setting of key priorities in areas in which expert knowledge is less relevant by governing bodies that represent members and constituencies (Kikulis et al. 1995; Anheier 2000; Miller-Millesen 2003; Grohs 2014; Bentancur et al. 2019; Heylen et al. 2020). Put in more normative terms, professionalized CSOs do not automatically become 'staff-controlled' organizations that marginalize the voice of members and volunteer leaders, as implied by some earlier research (Frumkin 2002; Skocpol 2003; Jordan and Maloney 2007).

So what are the broader repercussions of this for our understanding of CSOs' contributions to democracy? As laid out in Chapter 2, from a normative point of view, member control ought to enhance CSOs' democratic contribution, while staff control ought to weaken it. The picture resulting from existing empirical research on the matter remains mixed. Some researchers suggest that increased staff control discourages volunteer and member engagement in decision-making and marginalizes the role of organizational (volunteer) leaders (e.g. Harris 1989; Murray et al. 1992; Paine et al. 2010), echoing widespread normative concerns discussed earlier. Other scholars, by contrast, argue that CSOs with developed managerial practices around organizing membership and volunteer engagement can strengthen both member recruitment and intra-organizational participation (Netting et al. 2004; Maloney and Rossteutscher 2005; Nesbit et al. 2017). They imply more complex repercussions of CSO professionalization and bureaucratization for democracy-relevant CSO practices and activities. Such controversies highlight the importance of illuminating the processes that connect central CSO characteristics and their long-term consequences for CSO governance in terms of both staff control and member control.

This is relevant beyond normative debates, as governments in advanced democracies have lamented the increasing detachment of their citizens from the state. Their policies—in part designed to tighten links between the authorities and society—tend to invite a growing entanglement between the two spheres, an entanglement which tends to favour CSO professionalization and bureaucratization, i.e. supports CSOs' transformation from 'voluntary association' to 'professionalized voluntary organization'. If participatory benefits and societal responsiveness are our central concerns, the findings in Chapters 4 and 5 jointly suggest that central features of the 'professionalized voluntary organization' might have somewhat problematic implications for how decision-making power is allocated in organizations and, related to this, for the nature of CSO–member and CSO–constituency relations. At the same time, several of these features had positive implications for member involvement. Hence, taken together, the findings so far not only highlight opposite implications of professionalization for different forms of member activism, but also the potentially complementary role of professionalization and bureaucratization in establishing managers as a third group of decision-makers alongside members and organizational leaders. Both aspects deserve more in-depth exploration. This is what the case studies in Chapter 6 will do.

6

From Voluntary Association to Professionalized Voluntary Organization

The Evolution of Member Activism and Staff Control in Civil Society Organizations

Organizational governance concerns all decisions taken within CSOs directed towards organizational maintenance and goal attainment, two purposes fundamental to organizational survival that at times can be difficult to reconcile (Cornforth and Edwards 1998: 2; Ben-Ner and Ren 2010; Barberis 2013; Bolleyer and Correa 2020a). As Chapters 4 and 5 indicated, both rank-and-file members and managers can be central decision-makers in CSOs. They tend to set different priorities if conflicts emerge between the two: members in favour of mission attainment; managers in favour of self-maintenance. Their respective weight in governance processes is shaped by the extent to which a CSO is either characterized by association features or by features of the professionalized voluntary organization.

Member control and staff control are central to the internal distribution of power in CSOs and thereby fundamentally shape organizational goals and behaviour. Member control is present when members themselves make decisions in central areas of governance. It is absent either when (unpaid) organizational leaders (be those elected by members or appointed by governance organs) or paid staff take final decisions. These scenarios capture two alternative indications of 'centralization'. While member control and staff control are inversely related, the absence of member control does not necessarily indicate the presence of staff control. As shown in Chapter 5, organizational leaders might remain in charge and refrain from delegating decision-making to managers.

Before we qualitatively explore these two intertwined yet separate phenomena and their interplay, it makes sense to briefly take stock of the statistical findings that set the stage for our three case studies. The professionalization

Civil Society's Democratic Potential. Nicole Bolleyer, Oxford University Press. © Nicole Bolleyer (2024).
DOI: 10.1093/oso/9780198884392.003.0006

of human resources—allowing for a more prominent role of managers—was the only theorized variable with a robust effect on member control which (as theoretically expected) was negative. In contrast, member control has no significant robust relationship with any defining feature of the association template. Structurally resembling a 'voluntary association' seems not to generate a barrier against centralization by strengthening members as decision-makers. Meanwhile, professionalization and bureaucratization at the heart of the 'professionalized voluntary organization' have significant positive relationships with staff control over decision-making. The latter is negatively associated with whether an organization can rely on volunteer staff and has multiple tiers facilitating member mobilization—both association features. Association features essentially capture an organization's 'voluntary capacity', the extent to which unpaid members or volunteers—in leadership or support functions—enable an organization to perform core activities on a continuous basis (Cairns et al. 2005: 872). Taken together, the statistical findings imply that whether managers can become decision-makers in their own right is not only linked to how numerous paid staff are and whether or not procedures are increasingly bureaucratized. It also depends on whether staff operate in organizational settings in which members and volunteers actively contribute to the actual running of an organization.

Tying this overview to the theoretical framework, it is the negative relationship between CSO professionalization and member control that most clearly reveals the trade-off between the cultivation of participatory activities and leaders' and managers' desire to enhance their autonomy. For the trade-off between organizational accountability of decision-making (in tension with staff control) and the growing demands for efficient and expertise-based decision-making (favouring staff control), we found both professionalization and bureaucratization working in favour of staff control, while reliance on volunteer staff and multi-tier structures worked against it. Both sets of features are likely to interact as an organization evolves and changes its structure in the longer term and to examine their interactions a qualitative exploration is paramount.

The three CSOs chosen for in-depth analysis are the National Activity Providers Association (NAPA), a service-oriented organization; the interest group Surfers Against Sewage (SAS); and the Green Party of England and Wales (GPEW). While also considering the consequences of bureaucratization reforms and state funding access, the case studies will particularly focus on the implications of the process of professionalization which—according to the statistical findings—should affect the evolution of both types of member activism as well as staff control. All three CSOs underwent such processes from their formation onwards as a central marker of their development, moving away from the association template towards the professionalized voluntary organization.

On a more general level, the qualitative case studies will allow us to explore the evolving interplay of members, organizational leaders, and managers as three sets of actors driving intra-organizational dynamics. They will allow us to see how member control is reduced, through formal reform or informally. We can explore how shifts from volunteer-run processes to managerial decision-making occur in specific domains. Relatedly, we can identify the mechanisms through which volunteer staff active both centrally and subnationally might counter staff control. This last example leads us back to a fundamental issue alluded to earlier. To gain a deeper understanding of the changing functioning of CSOs that increasingly resemble 'professionalized voluntary organizations', we need to know how central 'independent variables' in the statistical models affect each other over time. This concerns features of the 'professionalized voluntary organization' that become more pronounced over time, notably professionalization and bureaucratization. It also concerns 'association features' that continue to shape organizational life, notably the reliance on volunteer staff and the presence of multi-tier structures.

The interplay of the latter 'pair' is particularly informative to understand how problematic tendencies such as the expansion of staff control associated with professionalization are mediated when it comes to the allocation of decision-making power. Leaving large, resource-rich CSOs aside, organizational layers below the national level that constitute multi-tier structures within CSOs tend to professionalize more slowly, if at all. Even in increasingly professionalized CSOs, these layers tend to remain volunteer-run. This means that the dependency on volunteers for the maintenance of organizational activities is particularly pronounced on the subnational level. If so, the role that regional and local units play in a CSO overall will impact on the extent to which reliance on volunteer staff will shape a CSO's internal power allocation.

In this respect, two basic types of multi-tier structures that CSOs might adopt can be usefully distinguished. Subnational units—regional and/or local—can have formally assigned governing functions in a CSO, i.e. own rights and competences granted through organizational statutes. On that basis, certain powers might be exercised regionally or locally with little national interference. Member control is formally 'anchored' in a CSO's decentralized decision-making structure. This is reinforced if subnational representatives form part of the CSO's central governing apparatus and participate in organization-wide decision-making (e.g. Bolleyer 2012). When regional units have such a strong structural status, the running of regional activities and units by volunteer staff can be expected to be particularly forceful in terms of containing staff control by essentially preventing a vertical centralization of power from subnational to national level, i.e. by containing decision-making power within subnational organizational units. If so, a shift of decision-making power from organizational actors (leaders or members) to managers is also prevented, as—compared to the national level—paid staff are likely to play only a very limited, if any, role. The national organization might have the upper hand in regional–national negotiations or conflicts over the reallocation of competences if it has superior access to resources. But the formal centralization of competences that are actively used and claimed by regional or local actors will nevertheless be difficult, thereby providing a powerful counterweight to staff control.

This scenario is, however, only one possibility and, particularly in groups, less common. Many CSOs build multi-tier structures without regional or local units forming part of their formal governance apparatus. They are set up for functional reasons, i.e. directed towards maintaining organizational activities locally or strengthening the CSO's support base that can be cultivated more easily on a smaller, local or regional, scale. Subnational units have no formally assigned competences or rights (and indeed are not mentioned in a CSO's formal statutes). They still might provide the foundation for (regionally active) members and volunteers to gain influence on decision-making informally, thereby curtailing the influence of leaders and managers. Two aspects (that are often interconnected) are likely to be relevant for whether this is likely to emerge. Multi-tier structures can be created through the top-down formation of subnational units by the national headquarters linking up members who happen to be based in different regions. Alternatively, they can be created bottom-up through territorial expansion through the successive mobilization of pre-existing local groups and by integrating pre-existing constituencies concerned about similar issues central to a CSO's mission (e.g. Panebianco 1988; Han 2014). The lines between these two formative dynamics are blurred as the presence of supporters interested in engaging in regionally or locally focused activities are central to both processes. However, the process is easier to control in the top-down than bottom-up scenario. Organization-building from below taps into pre-existing local or regional groups mobilized around already salient issues that have their own identity. On that basis, structures can be built more easily, but are also more difficult to steer (let alone abolish) than regional groups that are centrally created. Such units, by default, are more likely to provide a counterweight to central actors than those created by the latter.

A related question is what the central organization wants from the lower tier. It is an important difference whether the latter does work considered important for organizational maintenance or for achieving central goals or whether, alternatively, they predominantly function as communication channels for gathering information and knowledge about local members and their needs. The latter is less likely to be a foundation for a division of labour across territorial tiers that constitutes a mutual dependency. Such dependency is likely to enable regional voices to influence national decisions informally because their cooperation is strategically important to the central leadership, whether they have any formal rights to give input or not. The three case studies to follow display different patterns of organization-building, with important implications for intra-organizational dynamics and decision-making.

Intra-Organizational Dynamics and Decision-Making Power in a Service-Oriented, a Political, and a Partisan Organization

The National Activity Providers Association (NAPA)

The National Activity Providers Association (NAPA, formerly the National Association for Providers of Activities for Older People) is a charitable company.[1] It works in the health and social sector and currently (as of 2022) has about 3200 members. It is service-orientated and predominantly dedicated to providing information, training, and support to activity, management, care, and support staff in care settings such as older people's homes. For instance, while providing training to care home staff (which alongside membership fees generates the organization's main income[2]), NAPA has always operated a helpline for activity providers granting practical and emotional support. Beyond these service-oriented activities, it by now also actively engages in standard-setting to achieve appropriate practices in the provision of activities for people in care (on its evolving mission see Chapter 9).

---

[1] This means it is incorporated as company by limited guarantee (reporting to Companies House) while also having charitable status (reporting to the Charities Commission of England and Wales).

[2] Only in some periods could the organization rely on third party funding by foundations or the state (see below). How its core goals and activities evolved since its formation will be analysed in detail in Chapter 9.

Over the course of its development, NAPA underwent a steady professionalization process benefiting from funding from a range of public and private sources. Having been formed in 1997, it hired its first director of training already one year later. This was made possible by a grant of £10,000 from the Tudor Trust. This director developed a programme of training courses for those working as activity organizers with older people, which has remained a central organizational activity until today. In 2001, by when the organization had grown to about 360 members, it obtained funding from the Growing with Age Project from the National Lottery Community Fund and a national project manager was appointed. The organization also received grant funding through the Kensington and Chelsea and Westminster Health Authority and funding for an administrator by grant aid from the Carnegie UK Trust. Importantly, in 2002, NAPA received grants from Lloyds TSB Foundation to cover the costs of employing an interim (i.e. temporary) chief executive officer, while Help the Aged helped to cover administrative costs. In 2002, the Esmee Fairbairn Foundation further agreed to fund the services of a project worker (Ivanovska Hadjievska 2018: 126).

Overall, between 2001 and 2003, the organization's membership had more than doubled and part-time staff increased from one to four. Though at this point administrative work (e.g. membership administration, newsletter editing) was still done by unpaid volunteers and trustees, in this period the CSO moved from an amateur-run towards becoming a more professionally run organization. This intensified when in 2004 NAPA received a grant from the Big Lottery Fund and a three-year grant from the Department of Health, which enabled the organization to hire its first permanent member of staff. Since 2005, NAPA has had permanent staff, including a strategic director and a communications director. Its level of professionalization in terms of number of paid staff has been relatively stable. Between 2004 and 2010, the organization maintained four staff, which over the last years stabilized at five.

Considering the link between staff developments within this (predominantly) service-oriented organization and types of *member involvement* encouraged in NAPA, in the early years the organization aspired to form a regional infrastructure to enhance member activism 'on the ground'. In 1999, the year NAPA hired its first employee and acquired a headquarters (HQ) in Central London, regional development was declared an 'important next step for NAPA' and the appointment of a regional development officer a top priority. This development was at least in part bottom-up, as regional groups in Yorkshire and the Midlands had reached out to people in Scotland and Northern Ireland who were interested in links with the organization. By 2001,

NAPA had ten regional groups to which the HQ sent its newsletters, which, back then, featured a section with 'Regional Updates'.

Regional groups held their own AGMs and relied on their own finances, while national trustees put in place 'Guidelines how to support the development of satellite groups'. Furthermore, an honorary coordinator of regional groups had been put in place, who in 2001 organized the first meeting of regional groups to enable NAPA to 'grow' its own leaders. Their representatives were expected to attend national board (i.e. executive) meetings at least twice a year. Regional groups had no formal role in organizational decision-making. However, regional group leaders were co-opted into the NAPA board—'to bring the regions into the heart of NAPA management' as part of its regional development.[3] This ensured the representation of regional perspectives in the organization's central governance organ and thus the organization's vertical integration. By 2003 (when the organization's staff capacity had been further enhanced), NAPA's staff met with regional groups to map out members' needs in the regions and to tailor its training approach to those needs. With funding from the Esmee Fairbairn Foundation received in 2002, NAPA financed a project directed towards consolidating its regional structure to improve access to education and training of members affiliated to NAPA in different localities. This process was supported by a dedicated project officer. From 2003 until 2005, this officer dealt with the training and support needs of regional groups.

Although the development of a regional infrastructure for activity providers has remained a priority for the organization until today, NAPA trustees decided in 2009 to disband its regional organizations as an intermediary structure. Not only could the CSO 'no longer offer enough support from the centre either financially or in staff time', as was indicated on its website,[4] but the lack of proactive coordination by a dedicated member of staff after external funding had run out (which the CSO could not afford to fully replace) created problems 'on the ground'. Some local groups became inactive. More problematically, others started to pursue their own priorities, and the central organization found it increasingly difficult to ensure the proper use of funds on the local level. In essence, the national organization worried about its ability to bring local activities in line with its goals and core message. On that basis, the CSO's managerial leadership advised the trustees that closing down the local groups was the best course of action. Later attempts towards strengthening the CSO's regional connections (at some

---

[3] NAPA Spring 2001 Volume 4 Issue 3, p. 2.
[4] https://napa-activities.co.uk/about-us, accessed 28.10.2022.

stage, individual trustees were assigned responsibility for specific regional areas) proved unsuccessful as well.

Instead, since the late 2000s, the organization started to focus on direct modes of communication with its member and its broader support base, a shift already indicated by the hiring of a (part-time) communications director in 2005, the same year that the development worker dedicated to supporting regional groups finished his work. The types of member involvement cultivated by NAPA changed accordingly. Between 2005 and 2015 (the year it reached its maximum number of staff), the organization grew from 400 to nearly 3000 members and the NAPA newsletter changed from a 'photocopied black and white newsletter' put together by volunteers into a proper magazine. In these newsletters, members' suggestions and feedback are regularly published in a section called 'How you see NAPA', which is complemented by an online forum on NAPA's website to provide an opportunity for people to interact and get in touch with the organization. NAPA has a closed Facebook group with more than 600 members, along with an open page, and members are regularly asked for feedback through their membership renewal forms.

The growth and consolidation of staff support contributed to a growing diversification of strategies to maintain ties to different types of individual and corporate members alongside efforts to broaden the organization's support base. While NAPA has long organized annual conferences and training events, which are well attended by members, from 2015 it also held a leaders' dinner, bringing together major care providers to exchange ideas. In 2016, the organization established a new policy to measure the impact of the organization's work for members and users and a dedicated project and communications officer enhanced NAPA's social media profile on Facebook, Twitter, and Pinterest. By then, NAPA News was sent to 3000 recipients each week. This orientation towards the use of new social media as well as a stronger emphasis on online training was further reinforced by the Covid pandemic.

In sum, the service orientation of the organization shaped the nature of involvement activities that staff cultivated. These activities are tailored towards gathering information about the services that the organization provides to members and how to provide such services more effectively. This is done through a combination of events encouraging face-to-face exchanges and various tools for online communication and feedback. As an interviewee indicated, these mechanisms establish an important linkage. While NAPA's approach caters towards members' needs, it prevents the detachment of NAPA's leadership from NAPA's 'membership base'.

132 Civil Society's Democratic Potential

While selective incentives such as discounts for training consultancies and audits are important to keep members attached to NAPA, members have historically not just been 'service-users' (or been considered by NAPA as such). For once, the organization always had an activity provider as trustee on the board, providing the 'voice of the grassroots'. Furthermore, NAPA members could exercise *member control* for most of the organization's history. Since its incorporation in 1997, NAPA's constitution granted its fee-paying members a range of formal voting rights (Ivanovska Hadjievska 2018: 125–6; 130), which means we found *member control* in a range of important domains. At NAPA's annual conferences, the CSO held annual general meetings (AGMs) at which fee-paying members could select the organization's trustees and participate in decision-making over NAPA's programmatic priorities: 'the wider membership was involved in constitutional requirements of the AGM e.g. proposing and seconding decisions including our strategic and spending plans and approving the annual report and budget'.[5] However, though members were formally granted the power to shape these areas, members who attended the annual conference were not very interested in actively using their rights. Only a small section of individual members was involved in decision-making through voting since 2002. In this period the number of part-time staff had increased from one to three, suggesting—at the least— that staff keen to create and diversify channels for member involvement had no similar interest in encouraging member participation in decision-making. The rationale for this is simple: as members have limited time and resources, from a managerial perspective, if they are to invest them in the organization, involvement is preferable to control. This became evident in 2014, when the organization's chief executive initiated a major review of NAPA policies and procedures when preparing an application for accreditation by Skills for Care, a government regulator.

This review process was actively supported by the chair of the board who shaped the substantive aspects of the reform process, which involved extensive consultation of trustees about the CSO's policies to generate the necessary support to get the reform approved. Management, in turn, designed the structural components of the reform, which significantly altered the internal operations of the CSO. The review had direct implications for formal member control, as it included an examination of its membership's voting rights. This examination concluded that the organization's constitution does not provide for decision-making rights of ordinary members and that—legally speaking—the trustees are the only 'members' of

[5] NAPA email correspondence, 13.09.2018

the CSO, by then a charitable company. While up to then trustees had been selected by fee-paying members at the AGM, the trustees adopted a resolution to formally amend NAPA's constitution. This amendment explicitly defined the serving trustees as 'members with voting rights'. All other members (e.g. care homes, individuals, organizations that choose to uphold the values of NAPA) became 'subscribing members' without any voting rights, a development that aligned with involvement activities designed by NAPA staff around members as 'users' rather than 'participants' described earlier.

An interviewee describes the initiative as the result of a longer professionalization process:

> [O]ne part of the professionalization that took a long time to achieve is recognizing the issue of members' rights and voting rights. [...] in 2014 [...] [NAPA] realized that wasn't an appropriate process, that technically those people were subscribers, not members and that the constitution has not given them any kind of format previously to have voting rights [...] which is why [NAPA] then reviewed the memorandum of understanding and the trustees decided to change that in 2014, so the voting rights sat with them as members and everybody else was an associate or a subscriber if you like, who received services, but did not have the right to decide and vote on services.[6]

In effect, NAPA's leadership—following a managerial initiative—brought in line the organization's formal rules with existing practice, as members—though actively providing input on the nature of services provided by NAPA through the involvement channels set up by staff—had made little use of their decision-making rights prior to the reform. Already in 2004 (following an initial increase in staff numbers), the minimum attendance quorum for AGMs had been reduced to only ten members. In 2014, the same number of members passed the resolution that made trustees the only members of the organization and abolished fee-paying members' formal rights. This again underlines members' limited interest in exercising control as well as in protecting their formal channels to do so. Accordingly, the removal of members' participatory rights granted since the organization's foundation had no detectable intra-organizational costs. In 2015, the organization reported an increase in its membership of 6 per cent to 2980. Hence, there is no indication that the 2014 reform made the organization—overall—less attractive

---

[6] Interview, NAPA, 30.05.2017.

to its members.[7] Neither did it make members less willing to engage with the organization: attendance at the NAPA conference in 2015 was 130, in contrast to seventy-five in 2013.

This does not mean there was no resistance against the reforms. But it did not come from members. While the executive director and the chair of the board worked closely together to ensure the implementation of the reform, as already indicated, there was scepticism from some trustees on the one hand and some staff members on the other. One component of the reform was to bureaucratize the organization to enhance the efficiency of CSO procedures, applying similar types of mechanisms to both volunteer leaders and paid staff. This involved a more formalized recruitment process for trustees and changes to the operation of the board, which was opposed by a minority of trustees (see below). It also meant that staff responsibilities were more clearly specified, including performance targets, which was not welcomed by more established members of staff.

That procedural reform elements were designed by the managerial leadership displays a clear link between NAPA's more professionalized human resources and the formal reduction of member control as well as the CSO's bureaucratization. The timing of the reform adds an interesting nuance: it took place after NAPA had experienced a significant drop of income as a consequence of the economic crisis in 2013. At that time, a range of members could not afford the organization's services or even the membership fees anymore. Hence, the reform followed a decrease in financial and staff capacity, which was another reason for management to review NAPA's 'way of working' to make the organization more resilient and efficient.[8] Protecting members' rights within the organization was not considered a means to achieve such resilience, ensuring that both staff and the board worked more efficiently (in essence bureaucratization) was.

NAPA's evolution illustrates—in line with theoretical expectations—how the professionalization of human resources contributed to an enhancement of member involvement and how managers were instrumental in the formal reduction of member control. One might be tempted to interpret the latter development as indication that NAPA was never a 'real' membership organization in the first place: given the blurred boundary between 'member' and 'user' in this service-oriented organization, it might seem

---

[7] Obviously, aggregate figures do not capture to what extent member exits were compensated for by new recruits. However, the increase still suggests that the organization's membership base has not suffered after 2014.

[8] Another indication thereof was the revision of the membership renewal process, to send out renewal notices at the beginning of the year rather than on a monthly basis, to facilitate the management of the annual budget.

'natural' that members did not care about having a say in decision-making. It is therefore important to stress that NAPA clearly meets the criteria of a membership-based voluntary organization, as it is composed of members with the power to leave the organization (Wilson 1973; Jordan and Maloney 2007).[9] This threat of a potential exit has been important to the organization's internal dynamics throughout its history. Meanwhile, NAPA members are responsive to the organization's involvement activities, which reflect considerable effort by NAPA staff to elicit feedback and find out what members want to keep them in the organization. The latter's endeavours to retain and recruit members were particularly pronounced in the period after the economic crisis, during which reliance on paid staff became more pronounced.

Relatedly, one important reason for caring about member retainment and recruitment was NAPA's ongoing dependence on membership fees as a central source of income that the CSO was keen to sustain. Membership fees (alongside training, consultancy and audit work tailored to their member and supporter base) remain NAPA's main sources of income until today. In contrast, the organization's ability to attract outside support such as state funding—though it was an important enabling factor for its professionalization in the 2000s—has been more mixed. Consequently, the abolishment of member control was no straightforward matter, in light of NAPA's structure and principal income sources.[10]

Moving to the dimension of *staff control*, up to 2005—when CSO staff were linked to particular projects—managers had a limited capacity to establish a counterweight to volunteer leaders within intra-organizational decision-making. Nevertheless, the first signs that operational matters would be moved from control by organizational leaders to staff members could be seen as early as 2003, when the number of part-time staff increased from one to four, and again in 2005, once NAPA had permanent staff in place. In both years, NAPA changed Article 49 of its Articles of Association to grant staff increasing authority to operate the organization's bank accounts, which

---

[9] This leaves aside that NAPA from relatively early on pursued political goals alongside its service agenda (see Chapter 9).

[10] The statistical analysis in Chapter 4 did not find a significant relationship between the importance of membership fees and higher involvement levels. This suggests that involvement activities might not—depending on the nature of the organizational setting—be perceived as suitable means to maintain or enhance members' and supporters' financial contributions. However, one important qualification needs to be kept in mind: all three case studies looked at here are—within their reference category (party, interest group, or service-oriented organization)—relatively small organizations for whom the cultivation of involvement is likely to be less costly and more effective than for larger mass-based organizations (for whom membership fees apply, hence maintaining a passive membership might be the priority). That the statistical analysis in Chapter 4 found a significant negative association between membership size and both types of member activism substantiates this reading.

beforehand had been a prerogative of the trustees alone. Once a small but stable permanent staff base was established, we see more proactive attempts by the managerial leadership to actively push for efficiency-enhancing reforms and thus the CSO's bureaucratization, including tighter control of how local members could influence the organization; the abolishment of regional groups in 2009 was one example of this. Similarly, the 2014 reform reduced member control and enhanced staff control, through structural reforms that explicitly established a clearer division of labour between organizational and managerial leadership. This increased the autonomy of staff in the day-to-day running of the organization, while focusing the board's attention on long-term oriented strategic planning and monitoring. Domains such as hiring staff—which the chair of the board had participated in beforehand—as well as financial matters were handled more autonomously by staff after the reform. At the same time, the chair of the board continued to ensure the formal approval of decisions by the trustees and tried to maintain a 'healthy tension' between granting management sufficient autonomy to run the organization operationally and financially and assuring that trustees meet their legal responsibilities.

Importantly, the fact that managers became more able to take substantive decisions as the CSO professionalized and bureaucratized did not mean that the trustees as organizational leaders became less active. In between formal board meetings, it is the staff team which is proactive in approaching trustees when they need input or advice. Yet the board has remained in charge of ensuring that the CSO does not deviate too much from its core mission. Indeed, the 2014 reform—while enhancing spaces for staff control—deliberately increased the ability of these organizational leaders to provide a counterweight to managers. Allowing staff to operate more independently, especially in financial, legal, and administrative matters, in itself reduced the trustees' workload, increasing their capacity to focus on substantive issues. Since the CSO's professionalization in 2005, recruitment of trustees had become more strategic, in order to enhance the board's expertise regarding business and commercial matters. This, in turn, enabled trustees to more proactively challenge initiatives by paid management. The 2014 reform aimed at creating a more active board. This involved establishing a more formalized recruitment process for trustees, which more closely resembles that for the hiring of staff: criteria for new trustees were clearly specified in advance and candidates were formally interviewed by the chair and director. This led some trustees to resign and be replaced by more proactive board members. Relatedly, the board (echoing performance targets set for paid staff) started to engage in more formal target-setting for its own quarterly meetings. Taking this development further, around the time of the reform, board members also initiated the creation of an expert panel of volunteers, which includes experts on substantive issues such as dementia as well as legal experts. This panel serves as a source of outside advice used both by trustees and by staff. Benefiting from this, trustees were subsequently more proactive in asking questions and challenging the decisions of the board.

To understand why institutionalizing a stronger division of labour between managerial and organizational leaders was possible, it is important to take into account in a final step that the boundaries between organizational and paid actors have been blurred throughout NAPA's history. This constellation might have helped to generate the necessary trust amongst trustees to allow staff to operate more independently. NAPA's first employee (a training post created in 1998) was taken over by one of its trustees, who resigned from the latter role in 2000, following advice from the Charity Commission. Also, its first executive director and permanent member of staff (2005–2019) had been an active NAPA member for one and a half years prior and already worked for the organization on a voluntary basis when applying for the post. She is active as a NAPA ambassador until today, i.e. stayed on as a volunteer. Similarly, the current director who started in post in 2019 was recruited through a competitive process, but had been an activity provider herself in the past and affiliated to NAPA. Indeed, the majority of the candidates interviewed for that post had such a pre-existing affiliation. While this is less the case for staff in support roles, the CSO has, thus far, managed to combine organizational commitment and competence when recruiting people into leading positions.

We find similar tendencies in the case of trustees, i.e. organizational leaders. Since the CSO's professionalization, there has been a systematic and proactive effort to strengthen the board by incorporating different types of expertise. As a consequence, NAPA membership was not a formal requirement for taking on a leadership role from relatively early on. Nevertheless, trustees who were proactively recruited from the leadership's networks often happened to be members or having worked for one of its corporate members (as was the case with the last two chairs of the board). This ensured that trustees share the organization's philosophy and values, which the organization was unable to guarantee with regard to the regional groups that were abolished in the late 2000s. Taking the two elements together, as both managers and the members of the CSO's central governance organs tended to have a prior affiliation with the organization, differences in priorities or motivations of these groups were likely to be limited from the start, irrespective of shared affinities that might result from their respective roles in the organization.

Surfers Against Sewage (SAS)

SAS was formed in 1990 by a group of twenty surfers in Cornwall concerned about sewage disposal as a CSO dedicated to the protection of marine life. Over the course of its history, SAS underwent significant organizational growth. By the end of its first year, it had 1000 members, which has increased to about 12,500 members today. Unlike NAPA (whose professionalization was marked by membership increases until it stabilized at its current size), professionalization in SAS was unsteady. SAS grew from two staff in 1991 to eight staff in 1994 (Ivanovska Hadjievska 2018: 131). By 2008, the full-time staff was down to three. In that year a new chief executive took over and SAS again grew rapidly in a short period of time: this time from three members of staff in 2008 to nine in 2011. By 2017, it had fifteen staff, which had grown to twice that size in 2022.

When asked about key milestones in SAS's organizational development, the centrality of staffing was identified by various interviewees. An early member stressed its importance when SAS was formed in the early 1990s:

> The moment you do that [employing a member of staff] everything changes, because you go from purely voluntarily to it being someone's day-to-day responsibility and their job. And the moment we did that transition, we could feel that change, [be]cause suddenly there is someone there at the end of the telephone, there is someone who will answer, nowadays answer emails, but then answered letters and things. There is someone who could go to the Houses of Parliament [...].[11]

Other interviewees identified the renewed and more intense professionalization in the late 2000s as a central turning point in SAS's evolution. At that time, the organization faced the threat of closure, which required SAS to 'professionalize dramatically' and 'reinvent' itself. In 2008, when the number of staff had declined to three, and the trustees considered closing the organization. In the end, the organization put in place a new chief executive instead, a charity professional, who had been active in SAS from a young age and initiated an overhaul of the way the CSO operated. As in NAPA, the internal implications of these developments were complex. The increases in staff size positively influenced member involvement and negatively influenced member control, substantiating the statistical findings detailed in Chapter 4. At the same time, member involvement was enhanced by the formation and

---

[11] Interview, SAS, 26.05.2017.

successive expansion of a multi-tier structure maintained by volunteer staff. This helped to contain staff control and to keep staff accountable to the organization's volunteer base, in line with earlier findings.

Taking a closer look at processes of organization-building, during its first accelerated professionalization in the 1990s, SAS started to establish a network of regional representatives. They were essentially volunteers who took a leading role in local campaigns, recruitment, and management of volunteers, as well as educational activities, fundraising, and other SAS projects in their local area. Hence, the notion of 'regional representatives' existed—informally—from the start. The intention of growing the organization through the formation of regional groups was already made explicit in the second SAS newsletter published in 1990. As pointed out in SAS's first chairman's report:

> we will be looking to set up regional SAS Action Groups. To date much of the work we have been able to do has been limited to a relatively small section of the coast-line. The reason for this is simple. It's the bit we know. Regional action groups will cover your local problems. SAS will support regional action groups with informa-tion, advice, merchandise, fundraising etc. *We believe that this is the way for the SAS to evolve and attain its goals over a larger area. Local groups tackling local issues with national SAS support* [italics added].[12]

Already at the first AGM in 1990, the organization had the aim to cover wider areas nationwide which rationalized the need for hiring staff. Starting out with a natural focus on the Cornish region, SAS successively expanded its reach by connecting pre-existing but 'disparate groups of surfers' across the UK coastline. To ensure the CSO's integration alongside its territorial expansion, SAS's executive committee successively coopted members into the executive to expand into new regions. At the first Annual General Meeting (AGM) in 1990 'spreading nationally' was identified as 'one of our trickiest problems'.[13] Over time, regional representatives not only multiplied but trans-formed, from key local people constituting SAS's link to its members into 'organizational positions' or 'roles' that were increasingly 'managed' as SAS professionalized. They were central to a multi-tier structure that was increas-ingly formalized when the organization started its renewed growth in the late 2000s, directed towards consolidating a fluid and heterogeneous mem-bership base (Wheaton 2007: 291). Starting out with less than a handful of

---

[12] Pipeline news, 1990, 2, p. 4.
[13] Pipeline news, 1990, 2, p. 7.

140   Civil Society's Democratic Potential

representatives in Cornwall in the early 1990s, SAS currently has 213 trained representatives across the UK.

The executive director currently running the organization was not only an SAS member since the early 1990s but a regional representative. Since he took over the organization in 2008, efforts to both institutionalize and professionalize SAS's regional structures intensified. These efforts became visible in several ways; firstly in the nature of staff specialization. In 2011, specific staff in the organization's management team were dealing with beach-cleaning projects and volunteers, but by 2014, further growth in staff numbers allowed for one staff member to be dedicated to regional representatives and volunteer management specifically. This, in turn, reflects a close connection between enhanced member involvement and the formation of SAS's regional structures. Secondly, it showed in the creation of the 'regional representatives programme' that was established in the same year. This formalization meant the provision of training for not only prospective reps (who need to formally apply with a CV and motivation letter) but also for current ones. Annual group training sessions bring together regional reps across the country, which allows for the sharing of good practice. Of the 205 reps who were active in SAS by the end of 2019, 188 received training during the year. Thirdly, this formalization process involved the allocation of financial resources to regional representatives, which allowed them to broaden and diversify their activities beyond beach cleans—still a central activity. This included the development of educational material to work with local schools and raise public awareness regarding environmental issues.[14]

These more recent measures at an infrastructure level, directed towards bureaucratizing the 'regional representative tier', ensure that the volunteers who assume this role have the skills to effectively recruit local and other sympathizers for SAS projects such as campaigns, and to implement projects successfully.[15] They also provide support for regional reps to travel to other regions to support local activities elsewhere. The by now significant investment of financial resources in the regional reps programme (£135,636 in 2019, the year before the pandemic) indicates particularly clearly the ongoing importance of volunteers and members to SAS's maintenance.[16] Overall, the institutionalization of SAS's regional structures underlines how, until today, volunteer staff and volunteering are central to SAS's operations.

---

[14] In 2014 the organization also made investments in a new membership system, including an electronic direct debit system and a membership welcome booklet.

[15] Examples would be the coordination of grass-roots lobbying of MPs through sending in centrally drafted letters that reps tailor to local circumstances.

[16] Relatedly, in 2019, SAS presented the organization of over 2210 events and working with over 90,500 volunteers as central achievements, signaling the organization's capacity as well as its legitimacy.

From Voluntary Association to Professionalized Voluntary Organization 141

Relatedly, we see an intensification and diversification of member involvement strategies cultivated by staff. SAS's management regularly communicates through their newsletter to encourage members to get in touch with regional representatives and get involved in their campaigns, fundraising activities, and other local events. For instance, members are active as volunteers during beach-cleaning initiatives organized by regional coordinators as well as in reporting cases of pollution in their areas, as part of SAS campaigns.[17] An interviewee put it the following way:

> Everyone participates in their own way. Some people want to give us money but not time. Some people wanna give us time but not money. Other people want to contribute their professional skills to us. Other people want to do a beach clean or an education talk. Some people just wanna put a sticker in their car window and nothing else, but they're all valuable to us and they're all important and we welcome every piece of support that we receive.[18]

The organization's reliance on staff does not mean that member involvement and volunteers are less valuable; instead, the professionalization of human resources within SAS has underpinned a growing and more systematic involvement of those willing to provide (different forms of) support. The increasingly numerous and specialized staff direct volunteers towards activities useful to the maintenance of the organization and the implementation of core activities. This was paralleled by a process in which volunteer staff who took on organizational tasks and coordinating roles on the regional and local levels were more systematically recruited, supported, and trained to enhance their effectiveness in the running of the organization. In other words, as the organization professionalized its human resource base through the hiring of professionals, volunteers were increasingly trained to operate like professionals as well.

The awareness that expert knowledge is an important asset to the organization existed from the very start. The 'WANTED section' of the very first Pipeline newsletter included a call for new members able to bring in expertise ('With the help of Doctors, Solicitors, Microbiologists, etc. we will be that much stronger').[19] Initial SAS members included doctors who were involved in programme development with regard to monitoring sea pollution. Meanwhile, the SAS's executive committee tried to complement its expertise by the

---

[17] The POW (Protect our Waves) campaign, for instance, was dedicated to the protection of surf spots from unacceptable levels of environmental impact.

[18] Interview, SAS, 16.06.2017b.

[19] Pipeline news, 1991, 1, p.2.

142 Civil Society's Democratic Potential

addition of external advisors and strategic coalitions with CSOs with related interests and specialisms. To this day, honorary consultants form part of the SAS team.

The ability to increasingly rely on paid staff and the latter's increasingly proactive role in the running of the organization meant that the drawing of expertise into the organization through the training of skilled volunteers became more systematic and more formalized, underpinned by a bureaucratization of volunteer recruitment. This process took place not only in the context of SAS's regional expansion and organization-building described earlier. It also affected its organizational leaders in SAS's central governance organ, the board of trustees.[20] As indicated by Ivanovska Hadjevska's study of the recruitment of volunteers with expertise in CSOs' governance organs, SAS has shown signs of 'board professionalization' through skilled volunteers early on, a tendency intensifying in the late 2000s when the organization could rely on a growing number of paid staff (2018: 189–90). While this could involve the recruitment of people external to the organization to ensure marketing skills or knowledge on financial matters within the executive, board members were generally expected to be SAS members and if they were not, expected to join. Where possible, 'organic leaders' from within SAS were recruited into (unpaid) leadership positions (Ivanovska Hadjevska 2018: 190).[21] That said, especially since becoming a charity in 2012—an organization with a broader remit than the SAS of the 1990s (see Chapter 9)—the emphasis on recruiting trustees with expertise relevant to organizational maintenance such as legal and business skills became more pronounced.

By now, new trustees are actively recruited by staff from the networks around SAS leadership (paid and volunteer). A pre-existing formal affiliation to SAS as organization does not play a role anymore. Present and former trustees include environmental lawyers, business managers, journalists, PR consultants, and marine biologists. SAS receives services from these trustees and their businesses, including legal advice and advertising services. Overall, reflecting the higher profile of the CSO, recruitment on the board has become more outward oriented and instrumental than in earlier periods. Prominent or influential figures are drawn into the organization as trustees with whom SAS has collaborated or from whom it has received support, rather than co-opting long-term supporters or regional representatives into the board, prioritizing organizational loyalty and commitment. Reports to

[20] This was initially the CSO's executive; after SAS's incorporation as company by limited guarantee it became the board of directors, and in 2012—when becoming a charity—the board of trustees.

[21] For instance, one member of the board of directors (1995–2000) had been a member since 1990 and later on, in 2016, took on the role of regional representative.

the charity commission available since 2012 document the financial benefits SAS received from trustees. They show that the value of those transactions has been significant, including donations of services worth over £150,000. For instance, the managing director of M&C Saatchi, one trustee, provided significant advertising services pro bono in a range of years. Another trustee provided repeated consultancy work on data protection regulation (GDPR). The managing director of the Iceland Foods Group became a trustee in 2018 and then chair in 2021, following several years of joint campaign work against plastic pollution by the company and SAS. This also involved significant donations from the business to SAS.

How did those developments affect the distribution of decision-making power in SAS in terms of member control on the one hand and staff control on the other hand? Essentially, the organization centralized its governing structures twice since it was formed, each time decreasing the possibility of direct member control over decisions as a consequence. These processes coincided with the growing influence of paid staff on the running of the organization which created spaces for staff control.

The evidence with regard to the formal reduction of direct member control is clear-cut. This development took place despite the fact that SAS founders aimed for a participatory organization. Initially, members were encouraged to take part in intra-organizational decision-making and to put themselves forward for election to the executive committee. Reliance on paid staff had just peaked for the first time, when in 1994 the organization—following the advice of an accountant—was legally incorporated as a company by limited guarantee. This change was aimed at legally protecting its founding members (who engaged in government-critical activities) as well as to be able to engage in trading activities, as sales of merchandise were a central income source. Incorporation was linked to the adoption of the organization's first formalized governing structure. This structure consisted of a two-tier membership system, in which the formerly direct voting rights of the fee-paying members (B-members) at the annual meeting were changed to the right to vote for delegates (A-members). These A-members were in charge of proposing candidates for and selecting the board of directors. This structure was chosen in the context of a rapidly growing membership: SAS had 12,500 members by 1994, compared to about 7000 only a year earlier (Wheaton 2007: 269) and 1000 members in 1991.

Over eight staff were in place to support this reform that ensured efficient decision-making in a much-grown organization and thereby contributed to the CSO's bureaucratization. The reform was also motivated by concerns of founding leaders that members—if they continued having a direct say—might initiate drastic changes to the identity and running of 'their' organization. A two-tier structure in which the founding leaders themselves would take over the role of delegates served as 'structural protection' to prevent that. As one interviewee explained: 'It was realizing that it can all be taken away if we did not put that structure in place.'[22] This illustrates founders' desire to stay in control of the CSO by downsizing direct member control, irrespective of initial participatory credentials (see on this dynamic Staggenborg 1988: 594).

By the late 2000s, when the organization's staff size again started to grow rapidly, members were already little involved in determining SAS's programmatic priorities. Predominantly, members of the board rather than fee-paying members participated at AGMs. Several interviewees (including members) underline that, when members still had formal rights, they did not attend AGMs. Neither were they involved in electing members of the board or decision-making over SAS goals and policies. Hence, by that time, the organization was, in practice, already governed by organizational leaders and managers. This situation provided the background for members' formal rights to attend the AGM and participate in intra-organizational decisions to be formally removed in 2012. This happened when SAS became a charity and again reformed its governing structures, now in accordance with the Companies Act 2006.

Importantly, there are no legal requirements in English charity law to grant (or not to grant) formal voting rights to members, i.e. placing the trustees fully in charge was only one possible option. Consequently, the SAS's registration with the Charity Commission—a process very much driven by leading management—was used as an opportunity to amend the CSO's governing structures in that way. Under the new Articles of Association (2012), the formal members are now the trustees of the charity (Article 20) (i.e. the members of the board) and 'The number of Trustees must always be the same as the number of Members' (Article 20.1). Consequently, with this reform, trustees were the only members with formal voting rights entitled to attend the AGM, whereas the broader fee-paying membership lost those rights.

From a managerial perspective, membership growth had made direct voting procedures unmanageable and less formal 'voice mechanisms' preferable. As with NAPA, there is no evidence of any intra-organizational resistance from members against this change. Indeed, SAS's income has tripled between 2012 and 2018, with income from membership subscriptions increasing each

---

[22] Interviews, SAS, 26.05.2017; 17.06.2022.

year, from £110,775 in 2012 to £155,302 in 2015, and more than doubling to £406,627 in 2020. As membership fees as form of 'unconstrained revenue' can be used freely (Weisbrod 1997), member recruitment and retainment have been central to the organization's financial strategy, both before and after the reform. This makes it unlikely that the leadership would initiate any reform that risks significant member exit.[23] SAS's evolution suggests that member control as a form of activism was perceived by both organizational leaders and managers as cumbersome and possibly disruptive. Members, in turn, had little interest in control but valued involvement, which was actively cultivated by a growing and increasingly specialized SAS staff.

But was this centralization of decision-making (and, relatedly, the reduction of member control and enhanced bureaucratization of SAS procedures), fuelled by SAS's professionalization, also accompanied by the expansion of staff control over decision-making? And vice versa, to what extent was the enhanced reliance on volunteer staff on the regional level and the increased formalization of the latter over the years instrumental to maintaining accountability and responsiveness of central decision-making to SAS's organizational base, as the statistical analysis in Chapter 5 suggests?

The picture revealed by SAS's long-term evolution is complex, as in the course of the organization's professionalization, volunteer staff and organizational leaders themselves have become more skilled through more systematic recruitment. This allowed for a broader range of SAS activities to be implemented through its volunteer base—as desired by SAS leaders. It also meant that—as volunteer actors' ability to assume responsibility for tasks independently was enhanced—management's dependence on volunteer actors intensified accordingly. This was reinforced by SAS engaging in nationwide activities that require coordination across localities and regions. Hence, one unintended side effect of formalizing (volunteer-run) regional structures was that the formal decline in influence of SAS's broader membership was partially compensated for by a greater informal 'voice' of active members handling regional operations. Informal vertical channels helped to maintain the organizational accountability of central decision-making. As suggested by a long-term member, the cultivation of the active involvement of volunteers in terms of organizational work granted this group of people more say, thereby making SAS 'more participatory'.

---

[23] Relatedly, it is interesting to note that already a few years before the reform, in 2008, staff had started to use the term 'supporter' rather than 'member' in the SAS newsletter, signaling a changing approach towards its 'support base' embraced by a new chief executive who took charge of the organization that year (Ivanovska Hadjievska 2018: 171). This is echoed by interviewees stressing the importance of social media as a tool to broaden and mobilize SAS's support base.

> If you wanted to grow, if you wanted to succeed, if you wanted to get your mes-
> sage out further, you have to become more inclusive. You can't do all that with
> just a small group of staff or anything else, you have to increase the networks and
> by increasing the networks and letting go and *letting other people do more, you
> obviously have to listen more as well* [italics added].[24]

While broadening its support base by cultivating what in the literature has been labelled 'low-cost participation', especially through social media (e.g. Jordan and Maloney 2007; Kaur and Verma 2016), SAS simultaneously developed 'different layers of members' interested in different forms of involvement. One of these layers was the regional representatives, who provide more valuable organizational support, which, however, had a price. It granted 'reps' more weight in the organization than SAS's wider (more passive) support base, via a vertical two-way process between regional representatives and central staff. Regional representatives are contacted through a separate email list or through individual emails to provide feedback on changes to the organizations' substantive priorities such as its lobbying activities, the regional implications of national plans, or how project funding ought to be allocated across regions, input that feeds into central decision-making. Such vertical linkage prevents detachment but it needs to be stressed that this is not equivalent to control over decisions as exercised by SAS's managerial and organizational leadership. As highlighted by an interviewee, regional representatives are asked to:

> comment on the direction of the organization. Obviously not in the same way that
> a board of directors or trustees would act, not in that way, so almost a policy direc-
> tion is kind of being set by the board and the staff and they were communicating
> that direction and what they needed their regional reps to do [...] but equally there
> was an opportunity for the reps then to comment on that and give their feedback
> [...] the staff were very good at setting direction and this was the kind of thing they
> wanted reps to do, but equally allowing the reps to have their own specialty [...] I
> think it [is] an illustration of how they are open to people and listening and allowing
> people to influence their decisions.[25]

Meanwhile, a formalized recruitment and training of volunteers is likely to have changed the relationship between managers and members taking on formal, organizational roles. One likely repercussion is a growing proximity

---

[24] Interview, SAS, 16.06.2017b.
[25] Interview, SAS, 16.06.2017b.

between volunteer and paid staff in terms of work mode, priorities, and orientations, facilitating the central steering of volunteers.

At the same time, several staff in central managerial roles themselves have been recruited from SAS's membership base, which is likely to facilitate any 'assimilation tendencies' between the two groups of actors. The organization's first paid director ran SAS for nearly ten years and was a founding member. He moved from running the organization as part of the SAS executive committee (being a volunteer leader) into taking over the day-to-day running of SAS as a paid employee. This means in the early phase that leaders and managers formed part of the same circle of friends. SAS's current campaigns director, an environmental scientist, has led SAS's political activities since 2003 and has been an SAS member from his teenage years onwards. The campaigns director heading the organization from 2002 to 2008 (when a separate post of executive director was created) has been involved with SAS since its early days. As mentioned earlier, today's executive director, who has been in charge for fourteen years, and has a professional background in the non-profit sector, started out as an SAS member in the early 1990s and was a regional representative in the 1990s. In essence, key figures in SAS's management team tend not only to remain in post for long periods—several of them have themselves been long-term affiliates before taking over paid leadership roles. While this is unrepresentative for SAS's staff base today, it still illustrates a linkage between SAS's management and its activist base.

Examining the evolution of *staff involvement in decision-making*, SAS's first director worked closely with the SAS executive committee of which he—as co-founder—had been a leading member. He proposed the budget as well as programmes, which then needed clearance from the executive. Many initiatives were developed jointly through close collaboration between the director and the executive's chair. This close collaboration remained unaffected by the first accelerated professionalization the CSO underwent in the first half of the 1990s, which allowed the director to delegate tasks to staff that were formerly dealt with by him alone.

By now SAS is organized in departments covering a range of external domains (e.g. campaigning, fundraising, merchandising) as well as internal ones (e.g. finance, regional representatives/volunteer management, and membership). Managers, thanks to their increasing specialization, could become more proactive in a wider range of domains. Whether this is described more as 'staff control' over decisions or more as 'staff influence' varies with the roles held by interviewees. From the perspective of long-term members and volunteers, the central management team including the current executive director have become more dominant in the day-to-day running of

148　Civil Society's Democratic Potential

the organization. Relatedly, SAS's direction is perceived as 'very much led by staff'—especially since the last accelerated professionalization in the late 2000s—as compared to the role of (many fewer) staff in earlier periods, suggesting tendencies towards staff control. This is presented not as a problem but as necessity for SAS's success—to make sure 'that the organization follows the right path [...] they are the keepers, they are the people looking after the image and the name'.[26] In particular, staff support for political campaigns has been enhanced significantly, a domain in which the role of staff is perceived as particularly prominent (see also Chapter 9).

The portrayal by staff is more ambivalent. While in practice staff and trustees are jointly in charge of the organization's governance, they stressed that it has always been and still is the board which makes the decisions. This of course reflects the legal requirements of charity law, which SAS must comply with. SAS board members have met regularly since the 1990s, and the ability to recruit high-profile figures as trustees has de facto strengthened paid management. Today's trustees are people with demanding careers and often a high public profile. Their situation and motivation are very different from, for instance, regional representatives active in their localities who became trustees back in the 1990s. Today's trustees have only little time and are, from a managerial perspective, no different from 'any other volunteer'. They make variable contributions in line with their interests and expertise. But they cannot and should not be involved in the day-to-day running of the organization.

Today's trustees attend quarterly board meetings and are invited by staff to participate in committees (which in the last few years started to be formed around particular projects). Their recruitment has become more selective, and they are increasingly drawn from management's professional networks. Once in post, managers proactively draw on their expertise and knowledge. As the current campaign manager put it: '*We can pull on these people* [the trustees] *when we need some input*, making sure that what we are saying is absolutely factually correct [italics added]'.[27] All this suggests a proactive role of SAS management and a reactive role of trustees as 'organizational leaders'. At the same time, the management team has gained increasing autonomy in performing 'executive functions' and dealing with technical and legal matters. This corresponds to the notion of staff control, an interpretation that aligns with the perspectives of activists and volunteer staff interviewed. Overall, the picture emerges

---

[26] Interview, SAS, 16.06.2017b.
[27] Andy Cummins, SAS Campaigns Director, Lecture on 'The Evolution of Surfers against Sewage', 2012, https://vimeo.com/2,108,158, accessed 17.07.2021.

that, thanks to a growing capacity and specialization, management has increasingly become the driving force behind SAS's activities, which transcends the implementation of organizational goals predefined by leaders or members.

To conclude this case study, SAS professionalization went hand in hand with the enhancement of member involvement and the bureaucratization of CSO structures. Member control was downsized, while spaces for staff control emerged. To what extent these two manifestations of organizational centralization—reduced member control and enhanced staff control—are normatively problematic is hard to judge. Paradoxically, trustees seem nowadays to be less 'organic leaders' recruited from within the organization than leading managers, though the latter scenario (staff being recruited 'from within') by now has become 'atypical' as well. Management presents itself as mindful of SAS's values and highlights the need to generate the necessary support, especially from volunteer staff, for implementing changes considered necessary or beneficial to the CSO's performance. Echoing the trade-off between efficient and expertise-based decision-making and organizational accountability conceptualized in Chapter 2, SAS's professionalization is considered a necessary and valuable development. It is also a challenge whose intra-organizational repercussions need to be dealt with carefully. When asked about the need to grow to more effectively implement SAS's goals, the current executive director indicated in a public lecture in 2016 that, while growth in staff would be beneficial because it enhances capacity, it should not go too far. It still needs to allow for the integration of the managerial team within the wider organization.[28] That said, by summer 2022, SAS's staff size had doubled compared to 2016, with the intention to hire more people in the following year.

The Green Party of England and Wales (GPEW)

GPEW was formed in 1973 as 'People'. Its founders were deliberately *not* trying to create a political party but a 'green movement', an organization that initially did not have a formal constitution.[29] A year after participating in the 1974 national election, however, after being referred to by the media consistently as a 'political party', the organization renamed itself into 'Ecology Party'. In 1985, it changed its name again to the 'Green Party' to give it a

---

[28] The Exeter Lectures: Hugo Tagholm, Chief Executive, SAS, May 2016.
[29] Prior to the 1998 Registration of Political Parties Act it was not necessary to be a formal political party to run elections under a group name (rather than as 'Independent').

less 'scientific', 'sterile' and 'middle-class' name. In 1993 the party split along territorial lines, leading to the formation of separate Scottish and Northern Irish Green parties, triggering its (to date) last renaming into the Green Party of England and Wales (GPEW) (McCulloch 1988: 191; Carter 2008: 224; Birch 2009: 54).

Exploration of the party's long-term evolution will reveal a fundament divide within its organization. Some parts of the organization aim for enhanced effectiveness through centralization to engage more effectively and successfully in elections. Other parts aim for the maintenance of intra-party democracy through extensive member control that is more strongly directed towards societal activism. Both this chapter on member activism and decision-making and Chapter 9 (on goal reorientation and political engagement) will show how shifts towards professionalization over the last five decades repeatedly benefited the 'centralizers', yet without the latter having been able to establish a lasting dominance.

Tying this case study to the statistical results, GPEW's formally enshrined multi-tier structure and extensive reliance on volunteer staff should not only be positively associated with member involvement but also help to contain staff control. As these association features are particularly pronounced, GPEW is a 'likely case' to substantiate the related theoretical expectations. In contrast, if professionalization is indeed a central driver of the allocation of decision-making power in membership organizations generally, we should find some indications of reduced member control and enhanced staff control also in GPEW. Since the party formally embodies its commitment to intra-organizational democracy in its set-up and has members strongly attached to this notion, it is therefore a 'hard case' with regard to the theoretical expectations linked to CSO professionalization.

As in the case of SAS, the GPEW's long-term trajectory in terms of staffing was uneven, reflecting dramatic increases and losses in its membership base (Rüdig and Lowe 1986; Birch 2009; Dennison 2017). At the same time, contrary to SAS, professionalization took off slowly. Only in 1981, eight years after being formed, the Green Party rented offices for the first time, started paying its general secretary (who had started to work unpaid after the 1979 elections), and hired a part-time administrative assistant to allow the secretary to focus more on publicity and policy matters. During the 1979 election, the completely amateur-run party had managed to field more than fifty candidates (numerically more than 10 per cent of its membership at the time). This allowed it to access free broadcasting time and thus attract considerable public attention (Rüdig and Lowe 1986: 267; 274), a success which led to a significant growth of the party from 600 members in 1978 to almost

From Voluntary Association to Professionalized Voluntary Organization   151

6000 members after the 1979 election.[30] This made the hiring of staff possible but also necessary as volunteers responsible for the influx of members found it difficult to cope with the resulting administrative problems (McCulloch 1992: 426).

Staff numbers remained modest throughout the 1990s and 2000s, with the organization essentially remaining amateur-run except for a few staff based in London (Evans 1993; Dennison 2017). During the early 1990s, the party employed six full-time staff, but by 1993 (four years after the Scottish Greens, followed by the Northern Irish Greens, had created their own organization (Birch 2009: 54)) there were only two full time and one part-time staff left (Evans 1993: 329). During this period, the party was threatened by bankruptcy and close to collapse (Rüdig and Lowe 1986: 266; Burchell 2000: 145). By 2006 the central party was still operating with three staff but by 2008 staff numbers had recovered to over six. At that time, support staff of the party's elected representatives (MEPs and London Assembly) were still more numerous. However, the latter's staff support changed relatively little over the years and took a hit with the UK's departure from the European Union. Staff numbers in the central party organization, in contrast, started to significantly grow from 2008 onwards. It repeatedly doubled its number of staff in the period after: from 12.5 to 25.8 between 2013 and 2014, increasing to 54.7 in 2019, and peaking at 77.7 in 2021. This had important implications for the allocation of decision-making power, both in terms of member and staff control.

As already mentioned, the GPEW has always had a formally decentralized structure with important competences—notably the selection of electoral candidates—assigned to its local party branches. These branches have their own constitutions, granting them a strong formal status in the overall organization. Though interviews indicate that in some areas the hiring of part-time staff to support the regions was feasible and some party officers aspire to have their 'own staff', local and regional dependence on volunteer staff remains the dominant picture until today (Thompson and Pearson 2021). This is the case despite the fact that decisions ought to be taken below the central party level, if at all possible.

The prominence of this 'subsidiarity principle' is due to the GPEW's long-term genesis out of highly autonomous local parties. A layer that was able to integrate the organization as a whole formed only slowly and against considerable resistance from below (McCulloch 1983; 1992). For the GPEW, the subsidiarity principle is a constitutive norm closely tied to the party's early

---

[30] Up to 1979, in its first six years of life, the party had only gained 500 members (McCulloch 1983: 3).

mission 'to create a self-reliant, community based way of life' (McCulloch 1983: 4). This understanding expresses itself organizationally in its allocation of decision-making power and organizational finances until today. As highlighted in its current statutes, 'The general practice of the Party shall be to encourage the greatest possible autonomy of each Local Party in its pursuit of the Object of the Party' (Constitution of the Green Party after Autumn Conference 2021, Art. 5 i), a provision that existed in a similar form from the very start (McCulloch 1983). Party subscriptions are collected by the national party but divided up between local, regional, and central party (Art. 4. iii)) with the different layers being in full control over their respective budgets. That said, should the central organization want to raise membership fees, it needs approval from a party conference composed of local members, which imposes a powerful constraint on the central party to manage income levels.

The strong position of local party units also shapes central party structures. Regional representatives have always taken—through membership in the National (later Regional) Council—part in national decision-making. Alongside considerable local autonomy, this 'federated structure' that ensures strong regional representation in central organs has remained a constitutive feature. This is the case despite various attempts (some successful, some not) to shift towards more centralized governance structures over the course of the party's development.

An assessment of the evolution of member activism reveals that the party's enhanced professionalization supported member involvement, but contributed to a reduction of direct member control over decision-making. Regarding member involvement, one reason why the GPEW's first remarkable electoral success in 1989—it won 14.9 per cent of the vote at the European election—could not be capitalized on was the inability of the party infrastructure to capture potential members (Dennison 2017: 14). While its membership rose significantly at this point, the party lost more than half its members between the end of 1990 and mid-1992, having struggled with high turnover throughout its existence (Rüdig and Lowe 1986: 267). Recurrent exposure to membership instability highlighted the challenge to and importance of translating 'one-off electoral support' into lasting rather than just temporary organizational affiliations. The party eventually recognized that reliable support needed to be 'properly managed'.

One means to do so was the systematic cultivation of member involvement.[31] Between 2011 and 2015, the party not only ran successful European

---

[31] The post-1989 experience clearly highlighted the need for reform, as 75 per cent of members and former members participating in a panel survey in 1990/91 indicated a 'lack of proper leadership' as their reason for leaving (Birch 2009: 68).

From Voluntary Association to Professionalized Voluntary Organization **153**

and local elections and saw its number of staff double, its staff also reformed the party's membership system. According to members of the party's executive, this reform made possible what was called the 'Green Surge' (Dennison 2017: 44; 68), a process during which the party's membership base broadened from 14,000 in early 2014 to a remarkable 60,000 by the time of the 2015 general election[32] (Dennison 2017: 3–5). Beforehand, of the 13,000 reported Green members, only 8500 supported the party financially—because fees were left outstanding (Dennison 2017: 44). Hence, despite having built up a significant base, the party as an organization was unable to use its membership as a resource to boost its financial capacity. The reform of its membership system changed this: after the 'Green Surge' in 2014/15 the party could report an annual membership income of £1,058,749, compared to £237,208 in 2013. The reform also established an infrastructure that 'graduated' the process of becoming a member: it started with uninformed members of the public, attempting to mobilize them as supporters, then to motivate the latter to volunteer and then to encourage volunteers to become fee-paying members (Dennison 2017: 44–5). Hence, from 2014/15 onwards, not only were membership fees systematically collected, but the newly devised recruitment process aimed at motivating involvement (in itself beneficial to the party) as a means to strengthen supporters' commitment and then to translate such commitment into a longer-term affiliation in terms of formal membership and active contributions to campaigning.

Such affiliation brought not only financial but also other resource-related benefits by mobilizing potential and current members to volunteer for the party. Already prior to 2014/15, staff had encouraged member involvement in organizational activities such as canvassing and campaigning. Volunteers were invited to support staff responsible for external communications and PR, a process that, for instance, led to the updating of over 140 local party websites. Other strategies to enhance involvement of the party supporters that were initiated and supported by professional staff (such as the new directors for national campaigns and for fundraising and operations) included guidance for local volunteers to run digital campaigns, the setting up of a website that allowed people to sign up as volunteers, and a phone bank for inquiries from the public (Dennison 2017: 44; 78).

Traditionally, the party had struggled with low levels of member activism (Rüdig and Lowe 1986: 268; Burchell 2002: 121; McCulloch 1983; 1992). This remained a challenge after the surge in 2014/15, as 'most of these

---

[32] At this election, the party won its best ever result in terms of national vote share—3.8 per cent—which more than tripled (though it again only won one seat).

members [...] didn't actually intend to be active.'[33] Nevertheless, widening its pool of members 'quantitatively' was one foundation to more effectively cultivate one demanding form of involvement specifically relevant to political parties: the ability to recruit candidates for elections. Doing so is not only an important condition to enhance a party's vote share but is central to its visibility.[34] As suggested in Chapter 4, the participation in elections at regular intervals provides particularly strong incentives for parties to generate ongoing involvement. Earlier studies on the evolution of new (usually minor) parties across the political spectrum have stressed the importance as well as difficulty of building a sufficiently large recruitment pool for electoral candidates (Bolleyer 2013a). Compared to other member activities beneficial to a party organization, this form of involvement not only requires from members a public commitment to the party but—if pursued seriously—considerable time and effort—in the context of the British First Past the Post system—without any realistic chance of success. A party officer on the local level put it the following way:

> the main function of the local party is to put forward candidates locally [...]. We do this even though we, generally speaking, won't have any chance of being elected, but the idea is to have candidates nationwide so that people can see we are a national party [and ...] there is an active campaign. None of them are simply a matter of having names on the ballot paper. They'll be encouraged to go and canvass for the campaign wherever it is.[35]

Though the GPEW could not fully maintain the 60,000 members recorded in 2015,[36] it is indicative that following the expansion of its organizational base, the party could place more candidates at national elections than ever before: 573 in 2015 as compared to 310 in 2010. This was not simply driven by the party's bigger 'recruitment pool' but also by professional support given to local parties in charge of not only candidate recruitment but also fundraising. Such support was essential to shield the party from the fear of losing numerous election deposits (Dennison 2017: 44; 75; 79–80). The lack of careerist incentives to potential candidates might be a reason why, in most cases, minor electorally active parties face particularly strong incentives to actively cultivate involvement through organizational means. Doing so boosts their

[33] Interview, Green Party, 13.06.2017.
[34] In 2010, only 57 per cent of existing party members voted Green, also a result of the limited ability of the party to nominate candidates; by 2015 it was 83 per cent (Dennison 2017: 75).
[35] Interview, Green Party, 13.06.2017.
[36] Most recent figures from 2021 indicate a membership of 54,306 members. Electoral Commission Report and Financial Statements Green Party (Central Office) 2021, p. 3.

ability to provide solidarity or ideological incentives to those who might be willing to stand without any chances of winning.[37]

For sure, GPEW's professionalization also led to tasks being delegated to specialist staff, both temporary and long-term. Examples are social media activists that the party hired in the run-up to the 2015 election as part of their new communication strategy. New regional campaign coordinators freed up central office from certain responsibilities, and regional funds were directed to key constituency campaigns implemented by amateur-run local parties (Dennison 2017: 44–5). This went hand in hand with systematic attempts to provide training to local activists and significant increases of financial 'local party support', which since 2010 has more than doubled in consecutive years. While local parties in the GPEW fiercely guard their autonomy to select their own candidates, run their own campaigns, and formulate policies tailored to their local contexts, the downsides of this in terms of effective electoral coordination are recognized (see also Chapter 9).

Consequently, central investments and support by staff as well as the party executive for subnational campaigns that came with the party's professionalization were overall evaluated positively by local party activists. They included skill shares and training sessions for local parties, as well as support for the creation of new local parties to broaden GPEW's reach across the country. These ongoing efforts were accompanied by the creation of new posts of regional managers in 2016, one dedicated to elections, the other to local training and capacity-building. As the party did increasingly well at local elections, it started to provide guidance to those interested in becoming local councillors. Meanwhile, the central organization provides a step-by-step guide to its members on how to produce higher quality motions at the party's conference by formalizing the process from initiative to submission. Because it was unable to curtail member rights to put forward party policies at conference (a right fiercely guarded by activist members), the central organization tried to steer the process of developing and enhance the quality of member initiatives instead.

In essence, the professionalization of human resources in the GPEW did not mean that member and volunteer contributions were deprioritized or less valuable as a consequence. Neither did staff only enhance the organization's ability to collect financial contributions, which would have suggested

---

[37] This is not to dismiss the important literature around cartel party organizations which—as major parties in their system—can afford to neglect extra-parliamentary structures thanks to party elites' ability to access financial resources through public office and significant party funding, as well as to attract— thanks to their superior access to public office—outside candidates if necessary (e.g. Katz and Mair 1995; 2009). Minor parties, by contrast, tend not to enjoy these privileges—especially in the UK, where state funding is generally scarce.

a general preference for a passive, 'only' fee-paying membership. Changes to broaden its base were paralleled by structural reforms and strategies led by management that aimed at better exploiting the various contributions of members and supporters.

As in the two groups, growing investments in member activism directed towards expanding and diversifying involvement activities did not to the same extent apply to member control over decision-making. This was the case although the GPEW (different from the two groups) is explicitly committed to intra-party democracy as a fundamental structural principle. Essentially, with the party's growth, the GPEW's governance structures have been increasingly perceived as problematic by organizational actors—yet for opposing reasons: as increasingly dysfunctional and inefficient by some; as ensuring insufficient horizontal integration and local member control over central decision-making by others.

Focusing on the evolution of direct member control, in recent times, the adoption of a traditional leadership structure consisting of a leader and deputy leader in 2007 was a notable change and major success of the 'electoralist wing' of the party.[38] It replaced a system of two 'principal speakers', which has been an issue of contention since the 1980s (McCulloch 1992: 435). Motions towards adopting a 'leader' had been a regular feature at conferences for years but did not receive sufficient support by members, being perceived as establishing a formal hierarchy between leaders and followers.[39] The eventual success of this reform was closely tied to the party's enhanced professionalization from the mid-2000s onwards, with the central party—including leaders and managers—pushing for a reorientation towards electoral politics.

Although the party has maintained the new leadership structure adopted in 2007, other reforms were less successful. The organization of the party conference, the organization's central decision-making body, has been a long-standing issue of contention, which is still the case today. Unable to settle on a solution acceptable to the party at large, its operating principles were reversed repeatedly. Since 1979, two annual party member conferences have been held, one for policy development, one as AGM for electing office-holders, whose format was altered repeatedly. The electoral success of the 1989 European election enabled the party to hire six full-time staff, which

---

[38] https://www.greenparty.org.uk/files/reports/2007/CreatingaLeaderandDeputyLeaderorCo-Leaders-Final.pdf, accessed 03.03.2023. Shaughnessy, M., 12 March 2015, 'Britain: A short history of the Green Left current within the Green party', http://links.org.au/node/4335, accessed 10.03.2022.

[39] https://web.archive.org/web/20,081,202,113,444; http://www.newstatesman.com/200,703,260,059, accessed 03.03.2023.

enhanced the central leadership's capacity to put forward reform initiatives. The 'Green 2000' reform (passed in 1990) not only created a national executive (GPEx) that was directly elected by members, it also moved conference voting rights from rank-and-file members to member delegates, i.e. a shift away from direct member control over central party decisions. By the end of the decade in 1999, however, the provision of a delegate conference was reversed. The party re-established direct member control by again allowing all paid-up members to not only attend but also vote in conferences. This reversal had followed a period of crisis during which the number of central staff had been reduced to less than three and the organization had been threatened by bankruptcy (Burchell 2000; 2002). This reversal was followed by a hybrid model. As long as the membership was below 10,000, the conference ought to be composed of members with direct voting rights. If the membership size grew above this threshold, it ought to be run as a delegate conference. This provision became practically relevant from 2010 when the party started to grow significantly. Subsequently, the threshold was raised from 10,000 to 25,000 (see Art 10i of the 2012 and 2016 constitutions), only to go back to the initial model: By 2021, Art. 10i again indicated that 'all paid up members of the Green Party shall be eligible to attend and vote at Conference' (2021 constitution).

The repeated failure to formally curtail direct member control is rooted in 'a strong movement in the party not to have a delegate system', which is viewed by many activists as the attempt of 'the leaders and people at the centre [...] to make policy decisions without going through the full conference process'.[40] Voting rights are not the only aspect related to the party conference that leaders and managers tried to change to enhance efficiency but were unable to implement. The 'Holistic Review' reform,[41] a major reform attempt starting in 2017, aspired to reduce the number of annual conferences from two to one. This would have lowered the capacity of the conference to determine party policy. Even with two conferences, ten to twenty motions (that participants are entitled to initiate) cannot be heard. According to critics, this could have doubled under the new regime.

After a promising start, the implementation of the more controversial measures proposed by the 'Holistic Review' (especially those that require constitutional change) look unlikely. The reform process itself as well as the initiatives following its failure are telling with respect to the conflicting concerns of leaders, managers, and members, conflicts that are likely to shape

---

[40] Interview, Green Party, 26.06.2017.
[41] https://www.greenparty.org.uk/holistic-review/for-statement.html, accessed 08.08.2021.

the evolution of this party in the longer term. More specifically, the reform process is indicative of the negative connection between professionalization and member control and the positive connection between bureaucratization and staff control.

To put the 'Holistic Review' in context, this process was predated by the 'Governance Review Working Group' set up in 2013 which had a very different agenda. It aimed to strengthen the accountability of central decision-making to local members. Accordingly, it could be freely joined by interested members and eventually produced a new constitution. This new constitution—which according to critics concerned itself 'more with representation than effective governance'—was debated in the Autumn Conference 2017 but did not receive enough votes to pass. Instead, a motion was endorsed to start a 'holistic review of how [the party] organises and operates'.[42] The previous year, the management coordinator of the party executive (GPEx) had already started to review how to improve the way the executive worked, as well as the working relationship between the leadership and senior staff. This, for instance, included a discussion of training opportunities for both paid managers and volunteer leaders in the executive enhancing the party's bureaucratization.

In 2017, the 'Holistic Review Commission' was created on the initiative of central office staff. Its members were selected by the central executive GPEx and the regional council (GPRC) for their skills and experience. This was done through a formal interview process, which was criticized as elitist and detached from the broader membership, compared to the reform deliberations that took place earlier on. Relatedly, while the earlier 'Governance Review' was focused on member participation, the 'Holistic Review Report' was focused on effective governance. Echoing earlier concerns raised by GPEx, it aimed to 'reduce the pressure on members taking on political and organizational responsibilities'[43] in the running of the party in between conferences. The twenty-member GPRC composed of regional volunteers operated (unlike the party executive) without any staff support and was considered by some as 'stretched to breaking point' by 'the significantly greater demands of a much larger party'.[44] Complementing the 'Holistic Review' reform, GPEW was meant to change legal form and become a company by limited guarantee. Still today, members of the executive—running an unincorporated association—are personally liable, both legally and financially.

---

[42] https://leftfootforward.org/2019/01/new-reforms-threaten-the-green-partys-internal-democracy/, accessed 08.08.2021.
[43] https://www.greenparty.org.uk/holistic-review/for-statement.html, accessed 08.08.2021.
[44] https://greenworld.org.uk/article/all-change-party-fit-21st-century, accessed 09.08.2021.

Looking at central measures envisaged, in terms of GPEW's basic governance structure, the new constitution proposed in the Holistic Review report would have replaced GPEx and GPRC by three organs to operate alongside only one annual party conference as the party's main governing body: first, a forty-five-member 'Council' consisting of representatives of the regions; second, a small, outward-facing 'Political Executive' including a significant number of professional politicians (e.g. the party leaders, MPs, MEPs) and a minority of directly elected members. Importantly, both organs ought to have the power of interim policy decisions without conference ratification. Third, the reform proposed a board whose members—except for the chair and treasurer—ought to be appointed by the Council without direct member input. This new body was envisaged to take over staff-related matters and the party's legal and financial responsibilities (e.g. accounts, electoral expenses, staff management). In these areas, GPEx was perceived as struggling to provide sufficient oversight. Unsurprisingly, this restructuring of central organs—especially the creation of a (predominantly appointed) board—received heavy criticism as a centralizing move that would detach decisions, such as key strategic financial decisions, from direct member control.[45]

The reform whose implementation would have required constitutional changes was accepted by the Autumn Conference in 2018 and received over 70 per cent support in the necessary member referendum (overall turnout was only 16 per cent but was over the necessary 15 per cent quorum).[46] Then, at the Spring Conference 2019, the Memorandum and Articles of the Association for the new company by limited guarantee were approved. The latter had been drawn up, alongside the new constitution, by a lawyer under the guidance of a transition team formed in early 2019 to implement the new structures. Up to this point, the reform's implementation looked as if it was well under way.

In essence, had the Holistic Review reform—as envisaged in 2019—been implemented, it would have reduced the overall scope for direct member control. In some technical areas (e.g. financial and legal issues) it would have freed decision-making from the direct accountability to representatives

---

[45] A similar critique concerned the replacement of constitutionally enshrined and elected standing order committees by time-limited task-and-finish groups set up ad hoc by the new Council and disbanded when tasks are finished. The proposal left unresolved the critical question of who would decide the substantive remit of these groups. Between conferences, the three new organs ought to be in charge.

[46] http://bright-green.org/2019/01/06/new-year-new-structures-and-new-policies-green-news-round-up-week-1/, accessed 08.08.2021. Electoral Commission Report and Financial Statements Green Party (Central Office) 2018, p. 6.

elected by members. The board, proposed as a new central organ, embodied most clearly a bureaucratic logic prioritizing expertise and efficiency over democratic accountability, a tendency that characterized the overall reform attempt. Importantly, to have most board members appointed and recruited through an interview process was a deliberate choice and not a reflection of legal constraints or formal necessities resulting from GPEW's decision to incorporate. To curtail the control of members over decisions was more likely to be driven by the desire to guarantee the necessary competence on the board. This might or might not be ensured through member elections, whose outcomes are less predictable. As indicated by the 'Holistic Review Report', the proposed reform formed a response to new demands in terms of legal and financial expertise in 'areas such as electoral law, human resources and risk management' resulting from the party's growing size.[47] Accordingly, the recommendation that the board should not be elected was justified by the argument that the necessary expert skills required of board members might be in tension with qualified candidates' readiness to publicly stand for elections. If so, this might prevent the party from recruiting the best people for managerial roles. This, of course, echoes long-standing debates around fundamental tensions between democracy and bureaucracy as alternative modes of governance (Alter 1998). Here the framing in the party's report, implicitly suggesting a tension between a proactive participation in democratic processes and managerial skills and competences:

> We want to encourage the members who prefer to quietly get on with the job and serve the party, particularly for the board. There are many members who would not put themselves forward for election, but would be happy to serve on the board if chosen. These are often the members who have exactly the kind of skills we need for the management of the organization.[48]

Overall, both the process and substance of the reform proposal was shaped by the organization's increasing professionalization, prioritizing the enhancement of efficiency, competences, and skills not only procedurally but also regarding its human resource base (paid and unpaid). Such measures favour the organizations' bureaucratization, directly tapping into the ongoing conflict between those who want the GPEW to operate like a conventional party—'professional' and 'exclusive'—and those prioritizing

---

[47] Report of the Holistic Review Commission—A New Recipe for Success, p. 9. https://my.greenparty. org.uk/sites/my.greenparty.org.uk/files/HRReportAsAmendedFully.pdf, accessed 08.08.2021.
[48] Report of the Holistic Review Commission—A New Recipe for Success, p. 9. https://my.greenparty. org.uk/sites/my.greenparty.org.uk/files/HRReportAsAmendedFully.pdf, accessed 08.08.2021.

bottom-up participation.[49] In the GPEW as a political party, the professionalization process driving such initiatives did not only involve the hiring of more numerous and more specialized staff in the central organization. It was marked by a growing number of (initially unpaid) volunteer leaders in central leadership organs who became public office-holders and thus (paid) career politicians themselves. These developments suggest an assimilation of managers and organizational leaders as decision-makers within the party's central leadership, a fact that could also be observed (albeit through different mechanisms) in SAS and NAPA.

That in 2018 the initial reform had been approved by over 70 per cent of members, while only 16 per cent of members participated, did not suggest that the reform was widely considered problematic or contentious (either by those members who attended the conference or the wider membership which did not bother to participate).[50] However, by summer 2022 the situation had changed. As the spring conference in 2020 was cancelled due to the Covid-19 pandemic, the implementation of the reform and the incorporation process were delayed. A special conference to approve the new constitution's specific regulations eventually took place in May 2021. However, as attendance was not sufficient to reach the necessary quorum of 15 per cent of members,[51] the new constitution approved in 2018 could not be implemented. While the party's annual report to the Electoral Commission for 2019 (issued in summer 2020) had indicated that implementation was still planned for the beginning of 2022, the report for the year 2020 (issued in summer 2021) had become vague in terms of the reform's prospects: '[t]he Extraordinary Conference in May 2021 failed to agree a proposed constitution to take to the members and this issue remains ongoing'.[52]

Reporting of the most recent party conference in spring 2022 and speeches by party leaders at the event did not indicate that organizational reform was a central theme. Neither did it feature in recent party communications to members. Indeed, some interviewees indicated that, as of summer 2022— four years after its formal approval—few people are left who are enthusiastic about the reform. The sense had become prevalent that a big enough minority of members opposing the envisaged constitutional changes had mobilized, sufficient to block the reform if it were put on the agenda again.

---

[49] https://leftfootforward.org/2019/01/new-reforms-threaten-the-green-partys-internal-democracy/, accessed 08.08.2021.

[50] Fifteen per cent was required for the decision to be quorate.

[51] Between 2009 and 2016, conferences were attended by 800–1000 members on average (Stavenes and Ivanovska Hadjievska 2021: 10). More recent reports suggest attendance 'in the hundreds' https://women-uniting.co.uk/2022/02/13/green-party-democracy/, accessed 23.07.2022.

[52] Electoral Commission Report and Financial Statements Green Party (Central Office) 2021, p. 6.

162 Civil Society's Democratic Potential

This, however, does not mean that all the reform's central issues are off the table. Though the 2021 special conference was not quorate, GPRC still has the authority to try to implement the constitutional reform, and aspirations remain to realize central elements successively rather than trying to implement one large reform package. Consequently, a new GPRC working group, the 'Party Structure Working Group', engaged in various consultations in 2021 and 2022 and developed a series of conference motions. To improve the operation and interplay of the party's governance organs remains a central endeavour. One current proposal envisages the reorganizing of the Standing Orders Committee by establishing an internal division of labour to reduce the workload of people involved in it. Furthermore, while the idea of a smaller political executive and an unelected board proposed in the initial 'Holistic Review Report' is gone, now the goal is to divide responsibilities more clearly between the two existing governance bodies, GPRC (the regional council) and GPEx (the national executive), to separate out more clearly managerial from political issues. GPRC ought to become the main body dealing with political strategy, which would suggest a transition away from acting as a regional body. GPEx ought to focus on organizational matters instead such as staffing activities and working with the key GPEx subcommittees on issues such as policy development. To achieve this, the size of the executive ought to be reduced, with only the chair and treasurer being individually elected to their specific roles plus seven ordinary members voted into the executive in one vote. The individual portfolios of the latter would be decided by the executive itself once it has been formed, depending on the respective skills and competences of members elected on it.[53] Party leaders—currently GPEx members—ought to become part of the GPRC as the political voice and the strategy body of the party instead.

Alongside enhancing the efficiency of internal processes by establishing a clearer division of labour, also legal incorporation is still on the table, which would mean a push towards further bureaucratization as well as opening spaces for staff control. By autumn 2021, Art. 1 of the 'Constitution of the Green Party after Autumn Conference 2021' contained three new clauses that will be added to the constitution 'when commencement date for them is agreed'. If adopted, these clauses will change the legal form of the party to company by limited guarantee, while preventing the Articles and Memorandum of the company from affecting any constitutional terms or provisions (2021 Constitution Art 1. v)–vi)). Although the necessity to

---

[53] Currently a variety of different GPEx roles are voted on separately, with only a few candidates applying for each.

protect organizational leaders from personal liability was widely supported, there is resistance by some to its implications. Notably, in the new legal structure, local parties would cease to be separate legal entities. The role of central managers, i.e. personnel 'with the skills appropriate ensuring that the company complies with all financial, legal and electoral regulations'[54] is bound to be strengthened by this.

Which of the remaining proposals (some of which will again involve constitutional change requiring a two-thirds majority) will receive sufficient member support or will be modified during the conference process is difficult to predict. The drawn-out nature of reform attempts over the last decade is a clear manifestation of the unresolved conflict between electoralists (in favour of professionalization to win elections and gain institutional access) and decentralists (in favour of social activism and grass-root control) that is unlikely to go away. This became visible in the recent consultations of the 'Party Structure Working Group'. When discussing five reform scenarios suggesting different degrees of centralization of the respective party governance structures, two favoured options emerged, which represented nearly the opposite ends of the spectrum. One envisaged an even more member-orientated and decentralized structure than was currently in place (the most decentralized option); the other was a more centralized and incorporated model (the second most centralized option).

We have clearly seen that opposition against the formal reduction of member control is a recurrent theme. But so are attempts to enhance efficiency, competences, and skills of decision-making that favour staff control. In line with the latter, the 'Holistic Review' proposed various measures related to resource allocation and procedural matters (which do not require constitutional change and thus received less attention). They included a further professionalization of the party's member and volunteer management, which staff started to develop when managing the 'Big Surge' a few years earlier. More concretely, the report suggested that training and skill-sharing 'should be for members at different stages of their involvement in the party, from first joining, to first volunteering, through to becoming active in the party or defending a seat'.[55] It also proposed a more formalized handling of its volunteer base (to be developed as a potential recruitment pool for electoral candidates). Relatedly, volunteers ought to be predominantly guided by professionals instead of other volunteers, who might be unable to ensure the necessary continuity of support. Those measures present themselves

---

[54] https://greenworld.org.uk/article/all-change-party-fit-21st-century, accessed 08.08.2021.
[55] Report of the Holistic Review Commission—A New Recipe for Success, p. 15; https://my.greenparty.org.uk/sites/my.greenparty.org.uk/files/HRReportAsAmendedFully.pdf, accessed 08.08.2021.

as natural continuations of changes analysed earlier enhancing member involvement that were adopted in the course of GPEW's accelerated professionalization throughout the 2010s. Related ideas recurred in its 'Political Strategy to 2030' adopted at the 2021 spring conference, which plans to grow staff numbers and to improve staff management. Reference is made to more support for the coordination between staff groups dedicated to local and national party activities and the standardization of recruitment and employment practices to enhance efficiency in how the organization is run.

The recurrent efforts to bureaucratize the handling of members and staff by those in charge of the organization finally raise the question whether or not informal shifts towards greater centralization as well as spaces for staff control could take place, circumventing the formal hurdles coming with official reform attempts. Indeed, already from 2010, the perceived costs of member participation started to expose a central divide within the party of whether decisions should be made centrally by professional staff or by the party's membership (Dennison 2017: 45; 48). And there are indications that this divide manifested itself in an informal reduction of member control and, relatedly, the creation of spaces for staff control. The following instances suggest such informal developments, which especially concerned the domains of budgetary planning, campaigning, and election strategy.

In the run-up to the 2015 general election the new directors for national campaigns and for fundraising and operations effectively circumvented the annual Green Party Executive elections, perceived as 'cumbersome' and 'disruptive' to election planning. Streamlining decision-making processes to enhance efficiency, they drew up a two-year spending plan that moved day-to-day budgetary planning away from directly elected organs. This meant 'a conscious transfer of decision-making power on long-term budgetary and strategic issues to professional staff in order to override the "destabilizing" annual GPEx elections' (Dennison 2017: 48). Leeway to do that was provided by the fact that, while the constitution formally requires GPEx to provide a report on central party finances at the party conference, the executive is not required to change the national budget in response to members' input (2021 Constitution, Art 7, xvi). Hence, though member scrutiny of the central party budget could be very intense and critical, this domain was not subject to direct member control to start with. At the same time, it was widely accepted that the finance coordinator ought to be an accountant, hence, that the handling of the central budget requires specialist knowledge. This seemingly bureaucratic move shifted the balance towards expanding the possibilities for staff control in strategically important domains in which the benefits of professional expertise were particularly pronounced and considered essential for the party to enhance its electoral performance. The new national campaigns director also adopted a centralized approach to electoral campaigning which involved the development of the party's strategy outside conference and without member input by bringing together central office staff, organizational leaders, and public representatives. Furthermore, he created a new layer of regional campaigners who provided canvassers with standardized scripts, thereby restricting the autonomy of local branches, clashing with the Greens' fundamental commitment to decentralized power and subsidiarity which created considerable friction in some constituencies (Dennison 2017: 45–9; see on this also Chapter 9).

Returning to the broader arguments put forward in this study, GPEW has been confronted with the trade-off between member participation and leader autonomy as well as the trade-off between organizational accountability and the need to ensure efficient, professional decision-making as theorized in Chapter 2. Clearly, these trade-offs contributed less to formal changes favouring leader autonomy and staff control than in the two groups NAPA and SAS. Still, the growing number of paid staff in central office has de facto insulated the national executive from the party's volunteer base, which is in line with earlier research on party organization generally and Green parties specifically.[56] From a leadership perspective, a more prominent role for managers and weaker presence of activists enhanced the strategic abilities of the party. From the perspective of activists, this invited a disconnect between local and central level and, relatedly, growing difficulties of the regional council to hold the central executive to account.

Overall, the long-term development of the GPEW demonstrates that even in an organization strongly committed to intra-organizational democracy and subsidiarity, professionalization not only helped to enhance and diversify member involvement but also supported a weakening of member control. Some reforms prior to 2010 enhanced centralization formally. Examples are the creation of a national executive and the move to a single leader model, both of which met strong resistance. The downsizing of member control since the party's accelerated professionalization from 2010 happened informally and benefited managers rather than organizational leaders. These developments were less pronounced in GPEW than in NAPA and SAS but all the more telling, as in the latter two CSOs, members only lost something they had little interest in—power over decision-making. In GPEW, the reforms could take place despite strongly held notions in favour of democratic

---

[56] E.g. Panebianco 1988; Katz 1990; Katz and Mair 1995; 2009; Burchell 2000; 2002; Bolleyer 2013a; 2013b.

(or at least democratically accountable) governance and against centralized and bureaucratized governance.

From the perspective of the central leadership, staff control over certain key areas (e.g. budgeting, election planning, party strategy, technical and legal matters) was increasingly perceived as necessary to ensure the functioning of the party. For staff to do their jobs effectively (be it organizing national campaigns or line-managing a growing number of support staff), they should not be micromanaged (in the worst case by several GPEx members giving contradictory instructions) or even much constrained by GPEx. Concerns about leaders' qualifications are exacerbated by the fact that positions in GPEx and the regional council are not necessarily contested and elected members of national organs cannot be assumed to know much about staff management or legal matters. Neither are their individual 'projects' and priorities necessarily in line with broader goals of the party.

This last point brings us back to a fundamental issue also emerging in the cases of NAPA and SAS, that of whether organizational leaders are necessarily more likely to be committed to CSO goals than managers. Similarly, in GPEW, members and leading managers are not mutually exclusive groups. That the party's first full-time general secretary started to be paid in 1981, only after being in post for two years (McCulloch 1992: 426) is an illustration of how organizational leadership roles became paid positions. Until today, it is not unusual that paid positions are given to people who worked for the organization in a volunteer capacity first, on the local or regional level or within national organs such as GPEx. One leading manager overseeing the 2017 national election (and major proponent of the party's professionalization) started out as a local activist and remained a party member after leaving his post. Though connections between staff and the party's membership base appear weaker today than in mid- to late 2010 (there were well over seventy staff in 2021), the lines between volunteer and paid staff remain blurred.

As the party has too little parliamentary success to attract members for careerist reasons, those who transit from active volunteer to staff are likely to be ideologically committed. From the perspective of leaders, this can create problems for the organization when people used to following their own political convictions are asked to follow instructions by others. Vice versa, leading managers who were former activists associated with a particular current in the party could find that their initiatives were interpreted as attempts to pursue a particular political agenda rather than just doing their job.

Despite these downsides, there are active attempts in GPEW to link staff's professional skill and expertise with commitment—hence to moderate the trade-off between organizational accountability and the need for efficient and expertise-based decision-making. This concerns especially office-holders' support staff. A recent study of professionalization processes in the GPEW reports that the party has developed an internship programme for activists to work in Green politicians' offices to build up a 'talent pool' within the party, to avoid having to make a choice when hiring staff between loyal party member and candidates with the necessary skills. Furthermore, the GPEW tries to link professionalization and commitment through the obligations it places on its staff, on the one hand, and its public office-holders (another group of professionals), on the other. Paid staff cannot be members of another party and must endorse the Green Party's values, hence meeting the same minimum requirements as members joining the party. MPs, in turn, are expected to contribute parts of their salaries to the party budget (Thompson and Pearson 2021: 945–7). This practice is common in many left-wing parties across Europe (e.g. Bolleyer and Trumm 2014). It ensures that those people who seek to make a career out of their membership remain committed to their organization and to demonstrate this by returning some of the financial benefits resulting from this career to their organization.

Conclusion

This chapter showed that in all three case studies the organizations' primary goals shaped the nature of involvement activities such that growing staff numbers with more and more specialized portfolios started to mobilize with increasing efficiency. In NAPA, a service-orientated organization, member involvement is directed towards the gathering of information and feedback from members (a central pool of service users) on the services and support provided by the CSO, for which it has set up various communication channels and events to connect to different constituencies. In SAS and GPEW, involvement activities are more diverse. In both organizations, campaign and fundraising activities are central endeavours and members are actively involved in them. In GPEW, electioneering and candidate recruitment play an important role. Despite these differences, the relationship between CSO professionalization and a diversifying and more systematic use of members 'as organizational resource' was broadly visible.

The different nature of involvement activities further indicated that SAS and GPEW had more interest in members doing actual 'work' relevant to organizational maintenance and goal attainment than NAPA. These differences align nicely with the distinction between 'organizing' and 'mobilizing' proposed by Han (2014), two ways in which CSOs can relate to their members. 'Organizing' as the more centralized approach focuses on encouraging discrete, transactional encounters with a wide range of people, as cultivated by NAPA. 'Mobilizing' refers to a more decentralized approach focused on developing relationships that encourage autonomous collective action, as cultivated by SAS and GPEW.

This difference became structurally manifest in the evolution, internal role and position of subnational units. As professionalization supported member involvement in all three CSOs, it initially supported subnational organization-building in all three. A subnational infrastructure generally helps to expand and stabilize still immature organizations' growing but still fluid membership base. NAPA, however, only followed this path until the mid-2000s. In this initial period, it tried to grow the number of regional groups and to strengthen and integrate them structurally within the overall organization. These attempts benefited from the CSO's growing reliance on paid staff and external funding dedicated to this purpose. However, after grant funding ran out, the CSO disbanded its regional groups in 2009. From then on, it diversified its communication channels online and offline and focused on forms of member involvement directed towards soliciting feedback on services from different user and supporter groups. Relatedly, it developed a political profile, getting involved in standard-setting in the health and care sector, a dimension explored later on (see Chapter 9).

In contrast to NAPA, local and regional groups or branches in SAS and GPEW have continued to make significant contributions to maintaining central organizational activities. Over time, they became recipients of targeted training and material resources from the central organization. This was supported by a growing number of professional staff—as part of efficiency-enhancing structural changes successively increasing these CSOs' internal bureaucratization. SAS groups have, unlike GPEW's local parties, no formal role in organizational decision-making. Nevertheless, SAS volunteers taking on vital roles on the regional level are de facto consulted and informally feed into central decision-making. This also had implications for staff control. As regional actors can influence decisions through informal channels, central decision-makers—especially management—have remained vertically integrated. The case of SAS, in particular, reveals how the bureaucratization of volunteer recruitment and training constitutes one mechanism through which regional actors can be enabled to counterbalance staff control. It illustrates how member involvement and volunteering can be the foundation to gain influence in decision-making processes, even when the CSO does not formally grant member control.

The latter qualification is important, as in all three CSOs, the attitude of managers towards member control was ambivalent at best. Managers initiated or actively supported bureaucratization reforms that enhanced efficiency and expertise but also tended to support a centralization of decision-making away from rank-and-file members. In the two (non-party) groups, management actively contributed to the abolishment of formal member rights. Also, in GPEW, we find a link between professionalization and centralizing reforms (both successful and unsuccessful). Furthermore, we found informal tendencies to insulate strategically important domains such as budget and election planning from democratic, volunteer-run organs. Meanwhile, in all three CSOs, as the presence of managers intensified, organizational structures and procedures in domains such as member and volunteer management were bureaucratized. This tended to consolidate the influence of organizational leaders and managers in their efforts to align the work of volunteers and activists with central priorities.

All three case studies indicated that CSO professionalization and bureaucratization had not only significant repercussions for the downsizing of member control, but also contributed to the emergence of staff control. This became visible in strategically important or technical domains in which professional knowledge and expertise are particularly valuable. That such tendencies materialized, formally or informally, in highly participatory and service-providing CSOs alike suggests their relevance for membership organizations generally.

Finally, the case studies generated some broader implications for the theoretical framework of this study. As detailed in Chapter 2, organizational leaders as organizational affiliates were expected to be sceptical towards the emergence of staff control, not only because they are organizational affiliates but also because granting it might reduce their own power. However, by exploring the reduction of member control and the enhancement of staff control that emerged in the context of reform processes, we could see why leaders might accept staff empowerment, not despite but because it reduces their own say. Shifting power away from members to organizational leaders enhances the latter's remit. This means more power but also more responsibilities, which leaders as volunteer actors might find difficult to cope with. Under such circumstances, leaders might welcome a division of labour in which staff take over more technical areas, as this reduces their own workload, which, in turn, enables them to focus their energy on—in their eyes—more critical, substantive issues.

Furthermore, the qualitative findings have implications for the conceptualization of members, leaders, and managers as three distinct groups of actors, as well as the basic assumption that staff control risks the societal detachment of CSO behaviour. All three organizations had until recently or still have leading managers in charge who have been members or affiliates before moving into paid positions. In all three organizations, especially in earlier phases of their existence, we saw efforts to recruit skilled people with prior organizational attachments. Although such aspirations became less pronounced as all three CSOs increasingly prioritize expertise over organizational loyalty, to empirically and normatively evaluate the evolving relationships between managers, organizational leaders, and members, the recruitment of CSO staff needs does need close consideration, a theme I will revisit in the concluding chapter of this study.

7

CSO Goal Reorientation in Individualizing Societies

Between Commitment and Change

Maintaining linkages with societal constituencies is central to the contributions that membership organizations are likely to make to a healthy democracy. They are indicative of the responsive nature of CSO activities—be those activities partisan or advocacy- or service-oriented. The second part of the empirical analysis encompassing Chapters 7-9 is not predominantly concerned with the intra-organizational distribution of power between members, leaders, and managers. Instead, it deals with how CSOs present themselves to central audiences—both inside and outside their organizations—and handle conflicting demands between these audiences.

Specifically, this chapter deals with the reorientation of CSO goals at the heart of organizations' identity, i.e. the propensity to change what is central, enduring, and distinctive about an organization from the perspective of members and followers (e.g. Albert and Whetten 1985; Gioia et al. 2013; Moufahim et al. 2015; Werner 2020). While terminologies differ across the subdisciplines that study interest groups, parties, or non-profit organizations, it is relatively undisputed that whether or not membership organizations alter central goals, their mission or programmatic identities have important implications for how a CSO relates to its members and to its external audiences (e.g. Gioia et al. 2013; Karthikeyan et al. 2016). CSOs' basic goal orientations make them recognizable to key audiences such as members, supporters, funders, and voters (Halpin 2014: 46; Karthikeyan et al. 2016). They serve as an organizational compass and help to direct organizational behaviour towards a particular cause, thereby signalling what the organization's priorities and intended impacts are (Minkoff and Powell 2006: 592; Fraussen 2014: 409; Frumkin 2002; Meguid 2008; Rangan 2004). CSOs' central substantive goals are crucial to the societal anchoring of an organization as they signal commitment and responsiveness to the interests and needs of certain constituencies. This is the case not only when members and affiliates are representative of a

Civil Society's Democratic Potential. Nicole Bolleyer, Oxford University Press. © Nicole Bolleyer (2024).
DOI: 10.1093/oso/9780198884392.003.0007

CSO's target constituency but also when members and societal constituencies diverge, as is often the case in political parties and public interest groups (e.g. Halpin 2006; Mair 2002).

Amongst the various 'layers' constituting organizations, the goals defining a CSO's identity are expected to be less malleable than the strategies or tactics an organization might employ for goal attainment (Hannan and Freeman 1984: 153–4; 156; Halpin and Daugbjerg 2015; Karthikeyan et al. 2016). Changing them is likely to be significant for how a CSO relates to core audiences both inside and outside its organization and is likely to alter the nature of accountability relationships with its traditional constituencies (Minkoff and Powell 2006: 594; Gioia et al. 2013). When a CSO frequently changes its core goals, the cultivation of stable linkages to constituencies becomes more difficult and the societal responsiveness of organizational activities less likely. Frequent reorientations are more likely to express a strategic attempt to appeal to new, wider, or more diverse audiences than responsiveness to changing demands of the CSO's traditional constituencies, as those are likely to change only slowly. Especially in increasingly volatile environments, meaningful linkages do require both parties and groups to present a 'reasonably clear identity' as well as a 'reasonably predictable posture' to signal reliability (Wilson 1973: 312; Halpin 2014: 45; 107; Hannan and Freeman 1984: 153–4; Moufahim et al. 2015: 93; 104). To the extent that CSO goal reorientation alters aspects 'global to the group's personality' (Halpin 2014: 46, 107–9), it risks alienating core supporters.

For a CSO's leadership, these repercussions create constraints, reducing leaders' and managers' ability to redefine target constituencies, though they are, in principle, more open to instrumentally change CSO goals than members prone to defend causes central to their identification with the organization (Moufahim et al. 2015: 93–4). This difference between members, leaders, and managers is likely to matter for how CSOs balance the need to cultivate commitment with the maximization of outside support. This remains the case, even though membership-based organizations in principle face considerable incentives towards maintaining a recognizable identity. Given the organizational structuring of many CSOs, such an identity demonstrating fidelity to (social or political) goals is of existential importance, since it was commitment to these goals that allowed them to mobilize voluntary support, resources, and legitimacy, i.e. to generate collective action, in the first place (Hannan and Freeman 1984: 152; Frumkin and Andre-Clark 2000; Wilson 1973). Consequently, fundamental organizational incentives incline towards cultivating lasting commitments to long-term goals, given that these goals serve as a central mechanism of organizational reproduction (Halpin and Daugbjerg 2015: 36).

For members who are not in charge of running an organization and overseeing its decision-making (i.e. whose affiliations are predominantly non-instrumental), the commitment to central goals (that finds expression in a stable, distinct identity) signals a reliability and accountability of organizational behaviour (e.g. Albert and Whetten 1985; Gioia et al. 2013; Moufahim et al. 2015). While all CSOs are somewhat dependent on continued membership support (e.g. Wilson 1973), they differ in how pronounced the benefits of goal commitment are to their maintenance. These relative benefits are shaped by how strongly a CSO relies on purposive and solidary incentives whose provision is supported by stable value attachments. Such reliance, in turn, varies with how CSOs are organized. As argued earlier, individual members central to the association template are expected to be particularly receptive to those incentives, which would make goal reorientation more costly to organizations which rely heavily on their members. This contrasts with professionalized voluntary organizations that are more reliant on staff to maintain their activities, in whose governance leaders, supported by managers, play a more prominent role. For them, the benefits of goal reorientation might outweigh its costs.

Concerns around mission drift and goal displacement as processes preventing CSOs from pursuing their original mission have been pronounced in group and non-profit research (e.g.Scott 1967; Warner and Havens 1968; Froelich 2005; Jones 2007; Minkoff and Powell 2006). Meanwhile, arguments around the crucial need to maintain a particular ideological or programmatic identity distinct from one's competitors have been prominent in party research, especially in studies of minor, niche, or challenger parties (e.g.Lucardie 2000; Meguid 2008; Herzog 1987; Karthikeyan et al. 2016; de Vries and Hobolt 2020). Such parties characterized by a focus on a relatively narrow set of issues or policies constitute the vast majority of electorally active (mostly small) party organizations studied here. They are most comparable to interest groups and service-orientated organizations that tend to restrict their activities to particular sectors or policy domains.

'Mission change' in groups and 'programmatic change' in parties can thus be considered as equivalent expressions of CSO goal reorientation. They are comparable as significant alterations of these organizations' identities, substantiated by research on so-called niche and challenger parties. Seminal works consider the prioritization of, strong commitment to, and limited willingness to deviate from a narrowly defined issue profile as central to these parties' electoral appeal and long-term viability

(Adams et al. 2006; Meguid 2008; de Vries and Hobolt 2020). This contrasts with the pressure to take positions on a wide range of issues that major mainstream parties operating in parliamentary and governmental institutions are faced with. In their case, the presence or absence of any programmatic change as such is not necessarily an indication of whether the organization altered its central goals recognizable to followers or other outside audiences.[1]

It is thus important to stress that 83 per cent of parties included in the dataset qualify as niche, single-issue, or minor parties (Meguid 2008; Herzog 1987, Bolleyer and Correa 2020b). Furthermore, advocacy organizations, service-orientated groups, and political parties participating in the survey were asked whether they changed their mission or programme in the last five years (the measure for CSO goal reorientation used in the later analysis), with only 22.5 per cent answering in the affirmative across all CSOs.[2] The distributions among self-identified parties, interest groups, and service-oriented CSOs are remarkably similar: 21.5 per cent of parties, 22 per cent of interest groups, and 24 per cent of service providers engaged in such change. Consequently, all three CSO types tend towards stability, as only between about a quarter and a third of organizations engaged in such change. The chosen measure is therefore unlikely to capture the mere tweaking of a CSO's profile, and this applies to all three CSO types covered.[3]

In individualizing European societies in which group affiliations are in decline (e.g. van Biezen et al. 2012), the question of whether to persist with or adapt central goal orientations confronts CSO with a trade-off. The maximization of external support in the short or medium term (e.g. for fundraising purposes, attracting government funds, or maximizing vote shares) requires CSOs to be flexible and strategically react to the changing saliency of issues or altered government priorities. This creates incentives to adapt their profile accordingly. In this scenario, societal or institutional pressures counteract the cultivation of long-term commitments as foundation for meaningful ties between CSOs and society. CSOs risk becoming caught between mission fidelity and survival pressure (Minkoff and Powell 2006: 592) or, as Rangan (2004) called it, 'mission stickiness' and 'market

---

[1] A large, sophisticated literature deals with programmatic changes of parties based on the analyses of party manifestos or expert data, assessing the strategic adaptation of party policy positions and their drivers on major axes of competition. These studies, however, tend to focus on the parties operating within parliamentary institutions and do not encompass electorally active parties generally.

[2] In contrast, changes in tactics and service offers that CSOs were asked about alongside mission change were engaged in by 33 per cent and 48 per cent of CSOs respectively.

[3] The figure for parties is also remarkable, as parties are bound to have prepared for some elections in the period the survey question referred to and most parties modify their programme somewhat ahead of elections. The low figure thus reinforces the interpretation that the item captured major modifications.

stretchiness'. The same tension also features prominently in party research. This literature considers 'catch-all strategies' to maximize vote support as potentially detrimental to the maintenance and cultivation of a loyal support base (e.g. Kirchheimer 1965). Parties which too readily adapt their profile risk 'brand dilution', to mention only one prominent concept in party research, highlighting the value of continuity in order to remain recognizable to one's support base (Lupu 2017).

Of course, organizations are likely to be exposed to differing degrees of external pressure toward goal reorientation. The gist of the central argument of this chapter is that CSOs—depending on the roles that members, leaders, and managers play within them—respond to similar levels and types of exposure differently. This brings us back to the distinction between more outward-orientated 'voluntary professionalized organizations' and more inward-orientated 'voluntary associations'. Building on the broader rationale outlined up to now, the following section theorizes the links between the features of the two governance templates and CSOs' propensity towards goal reorientation or commitment. Organization-centred arguments are then complemented by a consideration of CSO exposure to different types of external pressures and how such pressures can be expected to incentivize goal reorientation.

A Governance Perspective on CSO Goal Commitment and Reorientation

Voluntary Associations and Professionalized Voluntary Organizations: Hypotheses on Responsive Goal Commitment versus Instrumental Goal Reorientation

A central trade-off that membership-based CSOs face in individualizing societies is constituted by the need to maintain a stable organizational base, while facing pressures to maximize (increasingly volatile) support from various external audiences (whose preferences are not necessarily in line with each other either). This confronts CSOs with conflicting pressures towards goal commitment on one hand and flexible goal reorientation on the other. Members, leaders, and managers are expected to position themselves differently with regard to what the 'right balance' between these pressures might be. Members are expected to prioritize commitment to CSO goals as they express those values that drew them into an organization in the first place. In contrast, leaders and organizational managers—being more concerned with

176 Civil Society's Democratic Potential

organizational maintenance and survival—tend to be keen to enhance their organization's ability to effectively tap into available resources, if necessary, by changing central organizational goals.

The distinction between 'voluntary association' and 'professional voluntary organization' provides the foundation to theorize how CSOs manage this important tension fundamental to CSOs' propensity to establish societal linkages and to engage in behaviour responsive to constituencies. Depending on which template CSOs resemble, they should tend towards goal commitment or reorientation. Voluntary association features—putting members and their interests centre stage—are expected to disincentivize the alteration of substantial goals. In contrast, CSOs resembling professionalized voluntary organizations and thus granting managers a more central role are expected to prioritize the maximization of outside support, to the detriment of central goals and values. These different rationales can be summarized in two hypotheses.

> **H1** (*Professionalized Voluntary Organization-Goal Reorientation Hypothesis*): Features of the 'professionalized voluntary organization' incentivize goal reorientation.
>
> **H2** (*Association–Goal Commitment Hypothesis*): Features of the 'voluntary association' incentivize goal commitment.

Starting with the mechanisms underpinning H1, the prioritizing of concerns related to process (e.g. efficiency, expertise) rather than substantive goals (Hood 1991: 8; Hwang and Powell 2009: 269; Shepherd 2018: 1671) would indicate that bureaucratization as typical for 'professionalized voluntary organizations' should facilitate the modification of basic goals, if doing so promises to enhance and diversify access to income streams that are crucial for organizational survival. A similar rationale applies to the template's central resources. Professionalization implies the presence of staff who can (at the least) exercise intra-organizational influence by providing advice to organizational leaders on what course of action an organization ought to take. Organizational leaders responsible for CSO maintenance tend to work more closely with managers than with (more numerous and potentially more remote) rank-and-file members and volunteer staff. Consequently, they can be expected to be receptive to managers' advice and might willing leave certain domains to them altogether. As detailed in Chapter 2, managers' organizational identity can be expected to be relatively weak, as they might soon enough change position and leave the organization (Maier and Meyer 2011: 745–6). At the same time, the stakes for managers to ensure the organization's performance are higher than for organizational leaders and members whose livelihoods do not depend on the CSO. They can be expected to be particularly ready to strategically adapt organizational goals to enhance its short- and medium-term performance (e.g. in terms of raising donations and securing state funding) (Maloney 2012: 108–12; Lang 2013).

Moving to finances, if state funding as a central income source consists of block grants, recipient CSOs might have wide discretion over how to use it. Yet this is increasingly less the case, as state funds are increasingly earmarked and made available for specific purposes that reflect current government priorities. This situation can incentivize organizations to alter their goals accordingly to gain or maintain access as government priorities change (Froelich 2005; Chaves and Galaskiewicz 2004; Bennett and Savani 2011). More generally, as organizations can rely more on state funding (however provided), they do become less dependent on contributions from members, making commitment to the latter's concerns less of a constraint for its leaders (Mair 1994; Katz and Mair 1995; van Biezen 2005). Both rationales suggest that state funding dependency should facilitate goal reorientation.

In sum, all three central characteristics of the professionalized voluntary organization are expected to incentivize instrumentally driven (rather than value-oriented) behaviour, prioritizing short-term performance over long-term commitments. This should, in turn, make goal reorientation more likely.

Moving to H2, features of the 'voluntary association' are expected to invite opposite tendencies, hence, to incentivize the long-term commitment to organizational goals instead. This is expected given the centrality of specifically individual members to a CSO's governance structure and the pronounced dependence on member resources in terms of fees and volunteer staff. CSOs' central goals allow those who support the organization—internally and externally—to orientate their commitment to a shared purpose (e.g. Gioia et al. 2013; Moufahim et al. 2015). This rationale should be particularly relevant for organizational members who, unlike mere supporters, pay regular fees and enter a commitment by joining their organization, and even more so to volunteer staff, i.e. members willing to assume responsibility in the running of the organization. Consequently, the reliance on voluntary staff should reduce CSOs' propensity towards goal reorientation, as should a CSO's orientation towards member interests (rather than wider societal constituencies). To the extent that active members and volunteers find it easier to collectively organize and forcefully articulate their collective interests when operating in multi-tier structures, the latter should also contribute to CSOs' disinclination towards goal reorientation. Similarly, member interests ought to gain weight in CSO decisions when membership fees are an important income source. Finally, considering the implications of CSO composition, compared to the average individual member, a corporate member (who represents another organization or institution in a professional capacity) is likely to give more weight to their CSO's external recognition enhancing his or her ability to pursue their own organization's or institution's interests in the context of the CSO. As detailed in Chapter 2, for them the CSO is more likely a means to an end, whose basic orientations might have to be modified if circumstances change (e.g. initial goals become unpopular or unrealistic). In contrast, individual members are more likely to be emotionally invested in their organization. They can be expected to be less open towards resolving trade-offs between value commitments and the pragmatic maximization of outside support to the detriment of the former. CSOs composed of individual members are thus expected to be less inclined to strategically alter substantive goals that are central to their members' identification with and commitment to the organization.

Bringing in Market and Constituency Pressures: External Sources of Instrumental and Responsive Goal Reorientation

Alongside CSOs' governance characteristics expected to shape CSO goal orientations, I now consider two sets of external pressures that might enhance CSOs' readiness to adapt central goals. The first set encompasses *market pressures* to which CSOs are exposed as part of a group system in which organizations compete with each other. This set of factors aligns with the behavioural logic attributed to the professionalized voluntary organization template, as these pressures can be expected to incentivize instrumentally driven goal reorientation directed towards the maintenance of or access to core resources essential to ensure organizational survival. CSO exposure to market pressures encompasses three factors which have been shown to affect especially interest group behaviour in a variety of ways: *resource competition* (direct competition between similar organizations for key resources); *competition density* (exposure to a high number of competitors in the substantively defined field or sector that a CSO operates in); and a *visibility challenge* (the struggle to maintain public and media attention for core values essential for issue saliency). CSOs confronted with these pressures (or higher levels thereof) can be expected to adapt their goals more readily than those which are not.

The second set of pressures refers to *constituency pressures* relevant to the ability of CSOs to maintain their support base, which emphasize that responsiveness to constituents can be expressed through not only goal commitment but also goal reorientation. This is the case if goal reorientation is a reaction to changes in organizations' societal base and aims to re-establish and consolidate societal linkages. If affiliates' and supporters' expectations towards a CSO have changed or diversified, this puts pressure on a CSO to adapt its goals to align with the interest and priorities of its traditional supporters. If such a rationale holds, CSOs exposed to an increasingly diverse or unstable support or membership base should engage in goal reorientation more readily than CSOs which are not. This is why the later analysis includes alongside *membership instability* (which forms part of all analyses in this study, see Chapter 3) also a proxy for CSOs' exposure to *aggregation challenges* resulting from CSOs' struggle with societal individualization or growing societal diversity.

Table 7.1 summarizes how market and constituency pressures and the patterns of goal reorientation expected from them align with the behavioural rationales underlying the two governance templates.

Table 7.1 suggests that CSOs resembling voluntary associations are—more so than professionalized voluntary organizations—confronted with a dilemma in individualizing societies. In individualizing societies, it becomes more difficult to keep members and supporters happy, i.e. many CSOs are confronted with the growing diversity and instability of their support base. When trying to be responsive to core constituencies, CSOs are likely to face a conflict between, on the one hand, sticking with central goals to maintain the loyalty of a smaller group of active members contributing to the organization (e.g. as volunteer staff), and on the other, adapting to changing demands of their wider (mostly passive) support base that might provide important material resources and enhance a CSO's wider legitimacy. As highlighted

Table 7.1 CSO Goal Reorientation and Commitment: Drivers and Their Behavioural Rationales

	Rationale Underpinning CSO Behaviour	
Nature of Drivers	Instrumental	Responsive
Governance Features	Professionalized Voluntary Organization → **Goal Reorientation**	Voluntary Association → **Goal Commitment**
External Pressures	Market Pressures → **Goal Reorientation**	Constituency Pressures → **Goal Reorientation**

by Table 7.1 (right-hand column, shaded), when it comes to building and maintaining societal linkages, associations operating in individualizing societies are likely to be exposed to countervailing pressures from inside and outside their organization. While association features structurally favour goal commitment (upper right-hand quadrant), responsiveness to changing constituency interests disincentivizes it (lower right-hand quadrant). This tension will be more difficult to handle, the more diverse and unstable the support base becomes and the more central—in relative terms—a CSO's membership is to its survival.

Professionalized voluntary organizations do not face comparable tensions (Table 7.1, middle column). Given their own internal characteristics, they are expected to tend towards instrumentally adapting their goals anyhow, while being less likely to cater to members' or supporters' interests as a central endeavour, as associations do. If so, they should find it easier to cope with a diverse and volatile support base. Just as they are less dependent on committed members (e.g. those who work as volunteer staff), they are also less constrained by them (this is reflected by changes in many CSOs that essentially replace formal membership by a 'looser' supporter status, e.g. Bosso 2003; Scarrow 2015). Accordingly, their support base is more malleable and can be adapted more flexibly. While a basic constituency linkage might remain in place, this does not equate to the cultivation of stable ties to society, especially if organizational goals are broadened or blurred.

Meanwhile, growing 'market pressures'—i.e. exposure to competition for key resources—not only follow an instrumental logic resembling professionalized voluntary organizations' own internal logic, they are themselves considered central drivers of CSO professionalization, i.e. of organizations' transformation from associations into professionalized voluntary organizations (e.g. Skocpol 2013). Indeed, the tension between goal commitment and reorientation that associations might be exposed to in individualizing societies could—in the long run—support their transformation into professionalized voluntary organizations (whose internal logic is more in line with external demands).

The below analysis of the four sets of factors depicted in Table 7.1 will help us to explore to what extent CSOs resembling voluntary associations are likely to be affected by such a tension between their own 'in-built' demands for goal commitment and external pressures towards adaptation and change. If this was the case, association features and constituency pressures should have countervailing effects on CSOs' propensity towards goal reorientation—the former making it less, the latter making it more likely.

A Quantitative Analysis of CSO Goal Reorientation and Commitment

Given the binary nature of the dependent variable capturing the presence or absence of CSO goal reorientation, I ran a logistic regression to assess which factors increase or decrease the propensity of an organization to change central goals. As mentioned above, only 22.5 per cent of CSOs studied undertook such change in the last five years (coded 1), a considerable majority did not (coded 0), with the distributions being quite similar across parties and groups. The central explanatory variables are the three characteristics of the professionalized voluntary organization and the five variables associated with the voluntary association. To capture market pressures and constituency pressures, the model further includes measures for resource competition, competition density, and visibility challenge on the one hand and membership instability and aggregation challenge on the other. Alongside standard controls (e.g. country, organizational age), a number of additional variables are added to the model given the nature of the dependent variable. It can be debated whether donor dependency creates incentives for a CSO to stick to a certain brand to stay recognizable to central donors or whether it should enhance CSOs' readiness to adapt to maximize its donor support at any given time. The answer to this question is likely to vary with the number and nature of central donors that individual CSOs are supported by. Yet because the group and non-profit literature emphasizes the strategic importance of this income source, especially to CSO leaders and managers, it is included. Second, I added past member control over policy, i.e. whether members had direct control over the organization's policy or programmatic positions in the past five years, which can be expected to matter for CSO goal reorientation that captures changes in CSOs' mission or programme (see for details on the respective operationalizations Chapter 3).

Table 7.2 shows the findings that broadly confirm theoretical expectations. The characteristics of the two governance templates not only push CSO decision-making in opposite directions (Chapters 4–6) but also their propensity to alter central goals. Professionalized voluntary organizations are clearly more prepared to adapt their substantive focus. All three of their characteristics—professionalization, bureaucratization, and dependency on state funding—have significant positive associations with goal reorientation. With each additional member of staff in the average organization, the probability to reorient goals increases by 0.5 per cent. One unit change in the index measuring bureaucratization makes it 9 per cent more likely that an organization changes central goals. One unit change in the index capturing

182 Civil Society's Democratic Potential

Table 7.2 Logistic Regression on Drivers of CSO Goal Reorientation (With Multiple Imputations)

	DV = CSO Goal Reorientation	
Intercept	Coefficient	SE
Main Effects	−1.74***	(0.41)
Features of Professionalized Voluntary Organization		
Bureaucratization	0.48***	(0.06)
Professionalization (log)	0.10*	(0.04)
State Funding	0.15*	(0.07)
Features of Voluntary Associations		
Individual Membership	−0.34**	(0.11)
Member Interest Orientation	0.15	(0.13)
Multi-Tier Structure	0.00	(0.11)
Volunteer Staff (log)	−0.04	(0.03)
Membership Fees	−0.24	(0.14)
CSO Type		
Interest Group (ref: parties)	0.36	(0.37)
Service-Oriented Organization (ref: parties)	0.24	(0.38)
Controls Relevant to CSO Behaviour Generally		
Membership Instability	0.10	(0.13)
Membership Size (log)	0.02	(0.03)
Organizational Age (log)	−0.04	(0.06)
UK (ref: Norway)	−0.23	(0.19)
Germany (ref: Norway)	−0.24	(0.18)
Switzerland (ref: Norway)	0.23	(0.18)
Increased Member Involvement	0.53***	(0.10)
Past Member Control	−0.05	(0.05)
Dimension-specific Controls		
Donor Dependency	−0.07	(0.10)
Resource Competition	0.27**	(0.10)
Competition Density (log)	−0.06	(0.05)
Visibility Challenge	0.15*	(0.06)
Aggregation Challenge	0.17	(0.11)
Member Control over Policy	−0.18	(0.11)
N	3265	

Note: Standard errors in parentheses * $p<0.05$, ** $p<0.01$, *** $p<0.001$.

state funding dependency makes this 2.75 per cent more likely. As detailed earlier, CSO goal reorientations (rather than the choice of tactics or services through which those goals are pursued or implemented) are central to CSOs' identities. They define 'what CSOs are for', and their continuity signals the CSOs' commitment to the interests and needs of certain constituencies (Halpin 2014: 46; Frumkin 2002; Moufahim et al. 2015). Goal reorientation as driven by characteristics of the professionalized voluntary organization can be associated with an instrumental rationale instead. This aligns with the portrayal of staff-run CSOs financed by the state in the literature on parties, groups, and non-profits alike. The findings suggest that these organizations are particularly inclined to strategically adapt their substantive goals to maximize outside support. They can afford this as members and volunteers actively contributing to organizational work (actors predominantly motivated by an emotional or ideological attachment) become less relevant for organizational maintenance and goal attainment (e.g. Katz and Mair 1995; Maloney 2009; Lang 2013).

Moving to responsive goal commitment expected to be invited by association features, the one factor that is negatively and significantly associated with goal reorientation is being composed of individual (rather than corporate) members. Organizations composed of individuals (as compared to corporate members) are 6.28 per cent less likely to change central goals, holding other variables constant. This suggests that individual members are more strongly orientated towards purposive and solidary incentives whose provision is supported by goal commitment.

Closely aligned with the instrumental rationale associated with professionalized voluntary organizations are CSO responses to market pressures which were expected to facilitate goal reorientation as well. Unlike competition density in a CSO's substantive field or niche (which is not significant), resource competition (CSOs' exposure to similar organizations competing for key resources such as members or funds) has a significant and robust positive effect on goal reorientation, stressing this factor's relevance in line with earlier research (e.g. Halpin and Thomas 2012). Visibility challenge, the perceived difficulty to maintain saliency and media attention regarding a CSO's core issues, has a significant positive relationship with CSO goal reorientation. This aligns with earlier research indicating such pressures' impact on group and party behaviour alike (e.g. Dalton et al. 2011; Binderkrantz et al. 2015; Hanegraaff and Poletti 2019; Guo and Saxton 2020). That said, this relationship is not robust across all model specifications. To explore this further, future research should aim for distinguishing the conditions under which declining issue saliency and attention merely stimulate a change in CSOs' communication strategies and in the framing of central issues from those conditions that invite the more fundamental and less frequent change of CSO goals examined here.[4]

---

[4] As indicated earlier, as compared to 22.5 per cent of CSOs that reoriented substantive goals, 33 per cent changed tactics and 48 per cent changed their service offer.

184 Civil Society's Democratic Potential

The distinction between changes in 'substance' as opposed to changes in 'message' or 'emphasis'—of the goals themselves or of the way goals are packaged and communicated—is also relevant in light of the following 'non-finding'. Unlike market pressures, aggregation challenge and membership instability as constituency pressures (that are perceived by CSOs themselves as challenges to their maintenance) seem not to matter for CSOs' propensity towards substantive goal reorientation. This is at odds with a literature high-lighting that groups and parties increasingly struggle with a growing diversity of constituencies' interests and the growing instability of societal support. As organizations' constituencies become more diverse and less reliable as contributors of material or non-material organizational support, maintain-ing stable societal ties and, relatedly, surviving becomes more difficult. Such pressures have been shown to influence the orientation and behaviour of partisan, political, and service-oriented CSOs alike (e.g. Biezen et al. 2012; Bolleyer and Correa 2020a). Yet similar to the challenge to maintain visibility in the public domain, constituency pressures might motivate CSOs to mod-ify the presentation of central goals to make their messages more effective or appealing to different supporter groups and audiences, or, alternatively, make their presentation (in 'catch-all fashion') vaguer, rather than to change their substance.

Conclusion

This chapter argued that insights into the propensity to change central goals and the factors that drive such propensity grant insights into how CSOs relate to their constituencies and the behavioural rationales underlying CSO behaviour more broadly. While members central to the association template were expected to prioritize goal commitment, managers and organizational leaders more prominent in professionalized voluntary organizations were assumed to be more open to strategic change, if such change makes the organization more appealing to outside audiences. Whose preferences win out has important repercussions for whether CSOs are likely to cultivate a stable societal anchoring and sustain meaningful linkages to constituencies.

As in the earlier analyses, the findings underline the distinctive behavioural rationales associated with the two governance templates at the centre of this study. To summarize the main patterns, reliance on individual members, an association feature, invited goal commitment. In contrast, the defining features of the 'professionalized voluntary organization' all supported goal reorientation, implying that the instrumental rationale suggested by this governance template is particularly forceful. Also conducive to such change is increased member involvement, which - unlike member control – functions as an organizational resource that can be steered by leaders and managers in line with their priorities (see Chapter 4).

Considering the range of drivers of goal reorientation as identified by the analysis—intra-organizational and external— jointly does support interpretations that associate an instrumental rationale with such change. This rationale goes beyond the 'in-built' logic of the 'professionalized voluntary organization' since it also concerns CSOs' response mode to external pressures. Returning to Table 7.1, all factors (internal or external to CSOs) with significant, positive associations with goal reorientation were conceptualized as favouring an instrumental behavioural rationale underpinning CSO behaviour.

Overall, external pressures—whether market or constituency pressures— seem to play a less important role than one might have expected, in light of what we know about CSOs in individualizing societies. As previously mentioned, the only significant variable in those two categories (Table 7.1) that is robust across specifications is resource competition (CSOs' direct exposure to competition from similar CSOs). It invites goal reorientation as theoretically expected. Of course, as discussed earlier, the other pressures in that category might incentivize change, just less fundamental change than considered here (e.g. change in communication strategies or the framing of issues). However, the overall finding that intra-organizational factors seem to matter more might also be linked to the particular nature of governance features. Unlike external pressures, the internal features of the 'professionalized voluntary organization' capture CSOs' general willingness—i.e. an inherent disposition—to make substantive changes to what the organization stands for, while individual membership as feature of the 'voluntary association' captures a general disinclination against this. These two rationales—in turn—find reflection in the opposite relationships between governance features and patterns of goal reorientation. This, in turn, also suggests that experiencing membership instability or challenges of interest aggregation—which in individualizing societies are likely to confront many CSOs resembling either template—might invite quite different responses from CSOs, depending on how they are organized. If so, the exposure to these external pressures as such might be unlikely to generate coherent effects on patterns of goal reorientation if responses to these pressures are mediated by CSOs' own set-up.

This brings us back to the distinction in Table 7.1 between incentives towards goal reorientation through market and constituency pressures and

CSOs' own, in-built tendencies towards or against goal reorientation as shaped by their internal logics that express distinct interplays between members, organizational leaders, and managers. The analysis seems to suggest that the pervasiveness of such inherent structural logics affect CSOs' varying readiness to change what they stand for, irrespective of the pressures that CSOs themselves consider as immediate challenges to their survival. This, in turn, has implications regarding the broader question raised above whether voluntary associations are—more so than professionalized voluntary organizations—increasingly torn between societal responsiveness (driven by constituencies that might push for change) and their internal responsiveness towards long-term members favouring goal commitment (as supported by its own structural set-up). The empirical analysis presented in this chapter does not support this, as only individual membership has a negative effect on goal reorientations, while factors associated with 'responsive change' were insignificant. Again, the findings suggest that organizational features shape CSO responses to external pressures in particular ways which makes these features crucial for CSOs' democratic 'performance', a picture that will be further substantiated by Chapter 8 on CSOs' political engagement and the qualitative explorations in Chapter 9.

8

CSOs' Political Engagement

Between the Logic of Membership and the Logic
of Influence

Although individualization increasingly weakens group affiliations in European democracies (e.g. van Deth and Maloney 2012), groups and parties still play a crucial role in contemporary democracy by mobilizing, aggregating, and channelling collective interests into the democratic process (e.g. Beyers et al. 2008; Saurugger 2008; 2012; Schlozman et al. 2015; Grömping and Halpin 2019). At the same time, 'civil society' and 'political society' remain distinct phenomena. That is to say that not all CSOs are politically active, even if we define 'political engagement' broadly—transcending classical lobbying to include awareness raising, protest, the provision of expertise, or the financial support of central political actors (e.g. Chaves et al. 2004; Beyers et al. 2008; Cinalli and Giugni 2014) as done in this study.

In the following, a CSO is considered as politically active (i.e. politicized) if it engages in at least one type of political activity in a sustained fashion. This is important from a theoretical perspective because, in contrast to occasional or rare engagement, it indicates the prioritization of political activity. When resources are regularly invested in the latter, this usually goes at the cost of other activities that might be equally or even more crucial to ensure organizational maintenance. The question of whether or not to make such investments confronts CSOs with a trade-off that—depending on the organization—might be resolved in favour or against political engagement (e.g. Olson 1965). An affirmative answer cannot be taken for granted. Only 67 per cent of CSOs surveyed qualify as politicized, 33 per cent do not. This leads to the following two questions. First, which types of CSOs are politicized, as indicated by sustained political engagement, and why? And second, if CSOs are politicized, how wide-ranging are their political action repertoires defined by the diversity of political activities regularly engaged in?

As argued in Chapter 2, active engagement in interest representation does not necessarily ensure that an organization establishes an effective linkage between society and the state (Beyers et al. 2008: 1117) in line with the

Civil Society's Democratic Potential. Nicole Bolleyer, Oxford University Press. © Nicole Bolleyer (2024).
DOI: 10.1093/oso/9780198884392.003.0008

classical 'transmission belt scenario'. Nevertheless, such activities are a *necessary precondition* for such a connection to materialize (Albareda 2018: 1219). Whoever they mobilize or whatever interests CSOs focus on, organizations that do not engage in *any* regular political activity are less likely to give 'voice' to societal demands or collective interests than those that do. This gains further weight as a wide-ranging action repertoire is central to the likely success of such activities (Binderkrantz 2008: 177–8; Halpin and Fraussen 2017). Echoing Schmitter and Streeck's seminal distinction between a 'logic of membership' and a 'logic of influence' (1999), this chapter will argue that CSOs resembling 'professionalized voluntary organizations' 'perform better' than those resembling 'voluntary associations' when it comes to their external engagement in political activities. They are more likely to be politicized and their political action repertoires tend to be wider.

Before theorizing the implication of the two governance templates for CSOs' political engagement, a preliminary question presents itself when considering the broader context of this study. Which membership organizations regularly engage in interest representation activities and, if so, how and why, seem to be questions fundamental to the study of democratic representation and, with that, the quality of the democratic process. So why has this question not been exhaustively addressed by the literatures on parties, on interest groups, and on non-profits already? There is some insightful research around the theme that tackles the above questions more directly in non-profit research. But neither party nor group research dealing with 'by definition' political organizations have paid much attention to it, as both strands tend to consider it—for slightly different reasons—a 'non-question' whose answer is 'too obvious' or at least a secondary concern.

Since participating in elections is widely considered a defining feature of political parties (Sartori 1976) and this is clearly a political activity, it is sensible to assume that parties are—by definition—'politicized'. Party scholars do not need to ask the question about whether parties are politically active as their subject of study itself already embodies an affirmative answer. That said, the literature on minor parties in particular has highlighted discrepancies between the intention to nominate candidates for elections and its actual implementation by organizations that consider themselves political parties. This literature hence recognizes that organizational goals might for various reasons not become manifest behaviourally. Some organizations might form and intend to run in elections and try to nominate candidates or to register as a political party. However, they might not manage to overcome formal barriers to do so, i.e. already fail at the threshold of recognition, as they are, for instance, unable to nominate a sufficient number of candidates necessary to get on the ballot (Pedersen 1982; Bischoff 2006; Bolleyer 2018). That said, the survey data shows that less than 5 per cent (4.6) of parties do not engage in any of the thirteen political activities considered regularly. Essentially, nearly all engage in some activity relevant to interest representation in a sustained fashion. As assumed by most party research, organizations that consider themselves as parties can be reasonably assumed to be politically active.

In contrast, the study of what drives the breadth of party organizations' political action repertoires as compared to those of groups cannot be dismissed as easily. Interestingly, when focusing on the type of political activity reflecting parties' *raison d'être*, electoral participation, only 66 per cent of parties in the survey regularly get involved in electoral and/or referenda campaigns to exercise political influence. This clearly contrasts with the over 95 per cent of parties that qualify as politicized when considering the full range of activity types. This discrepancy suggests that a significant minority of parties predominantly engages in sustained political activity unrelated to election campaigns. Whether or not political parties use different channels or strategies to reach audiences in different (societal or institutional) spheres is important for the diversity of access points into politics that these organizations are able to provide to citizens. This is easily neglected when studying electorally (more) successful players as well as the activities of party representatives within parliament and government, which party scholarship traditionally tends to focus on (Bolleyer forthcoming).

Recognizing this, recent literatures have started to look into how and when parties become politically active in other arenas, e.g. by sponsoring protest activities (e.g. Borbáth and Hutter 2021) or by using new digital tools and social media to enhance the salience of issues inside and outside the institutional arena (e.g. Barberà et al. 2021). Yet these strands of research tend to focus on particular types of political activity or channels. Consequently, asking what incentivizes CSOs including parties to engage in a wider (or narrower) range of political activities to start with provides a valuable addition. This is also the case as nearly half of the parties surveyed engage in more than three types of political activity regularly, 66 per cent in more than two. Hence, despite struggling with scarce resources and despite being widely perceived as 'electoral vehicles', most party organizations tend to regularly pursue several strategies of influence-seeking simultaneously.

Relatedly, we know little about how parties' political action repertoires compare to other politicized membership organizations. This is a problematic caveat, as parties' role as central vehicles of representation has undergone extensive critique for some time (Chapter 1). This occurred without much systematic evidence on whether non-partisan CSOs perform any 'better' when it comes to interest representation, which is a central activity for parties and groups alike. As compared to 49 per cent of parties which engage in more than three political activities regularly, only 25.5 per cent of interest groups and 19 per cent of service-orientated organizations do so. If this picture is confirmed in the quantitative analysis, i.e. the average party were to engage in a broader range of political activities than the average group, they would offer citizens a wider range of channels to engage with politics. If so, their increasingly questioned status as '*primus inter pares*' in organized civil society (Rosenblum 2000a; 2000b) could be defended in terms of the contribution to interest representation. Alongside parties' tendency to cultivate higher levels of member involvement (Chapter 4) this would suggest that, with regard to both the yardstick of participation and representation, the vitality of political parties has particular relevance for civil society's overall democratic contribution. (This leaves aside ex ante any possible contributions through their governing roles from within public institutions, i.e. those channels unavailable to other CSO types not considered in this study.)

Moving to the two group types, the question about drivers of CSO political engagement is theoretically and empirically important, irrespective of whether advocacy is an organization's primary goal or 'only' a secondary activity. Yet as interest group populations are commonly defined by politically active organizations (e.g. Baroni et al. 2014), cross-national comparative group research has tended to focus on the nature of advocacy strategies and behaviour (e.g. Beyers 2004; Binderkrantz 2008; Dür and Mateo 2013; Hanegraaff et al. 2016; Berkhout et al. 2017; Dür 2018). In contrast to party research, there has been a considerable interest in explaining the nature and range of political activities or influence strategies that interest groups might employ. Whether 'organizations enter the political fray' has received less attention (Schlozman 2010: 5; Halpin 2014; but see Bolleyer and Weiler 2018; Bolleyer and Correa 2022b).[1]

This relative side-stepping of group politicization is not only striking considering the number of interest groups that do not qualify as politicized. The survey data reveals surprisingly little difference between (self-declared) interest and service-oriented organizations in this respect. Amongst interest groups, 32 per cent are not politically active on a regular basis in any way, while amongst service-oriented organizations, 38 per cent qualify as not

---

[1] Similarly, we know little about the conditions conducive for 'supportive organizations'—service-oriented 'halfway houses' associated with social movements (Kriesi 1996: 152–4)—to be politically active in their own right. This suggests similar caveats exist in neighbouring fields as well.

politicized. As already pointed out, interest group research tends to assume that interest organizations are politically active, therefore leaving aside organizations that are not. Similarly, studies on 'political organizations' tend to include parties, interest groups, and social movements but leave out predominantly service-oriented organizations (e.g. Wilson 1973; Fraussen and Halpin 2018). The survey data implies that—at least in the four democracies covered—membership-based voluntary organizations that consider themselves as interest groups tend to be less politically active than often assumed. The majority of CSOs whose core mission is service-related engage in politics regularly, i.e. engage in politics more often than assumed. These distributions, yet again, underline prominent arguments in the literature on organizational hybridization. In this strand of the literature, prominent voices have long highlighted the increasingly blurred boundaries between different parts of the group sector, due to an increasing number of CSOs pursuing a mixture of political and 'non-political' goals (e.g. Minkoff 2002; Hasenfeld and Gidron 2005).

The non-profit literature has most explicitly done justice to this, and for some time recognized that organizations can engage in political activities 'as a secondary activity supporting a mission of direct service' (Kimberlin 2010: 165; Cairns et al. 2010; Berry and Arons 2003). In this field we do find a literature dealing with the question of which service-oriented organizations, *despite* their primary mission, engage in advocacy and how they do so, and which do not (e.g. Child and Grønbjerg 2007; LeRoux and Goerdel 2009). Limitations—as perceived from the perspective of this study's core interests—do not result from not asking the question but from the prevalent theoretical angle and empirical focus of existing studies. Theoretically speaking, non-profit scholars tend to focus on service providers. Similar to interest group research concentrating on 'advocacy organizations', they tend to assume the drivers for advocacy to be qualitatively different depending on CSOs' primary mission (Almog-Bar and Schmid 2014: 28) thus tailoring theories to the latter. Relatedly, they are less concerned with intra-organizational dynamics, as 'having members' is not often a feature used to define 'non-profit organization'. Instead, and here the theoretical angle feeds into empirical focus, we find the frequent use of legal categories to specify the organizations analysed.[2] As a consequence, this subfield is still dominated by single-country studies, especially on the US. Cross-national studies, especially those exploring the implications of different country settings on CSO political engagement, have

---

[2] E.g. many studies focus on organizations with 501(c)(3) status in the US irrespective of any organizational properties.

remained rare (see for a recent meta-analysis Lu 2018b; but see Bolleyer and Correa 2022b).

Essentially, despite a wealth of interesting research relevant to the broader theme, we find both little theorization and comparative analysis of the organizational trade-offs and dilemmas that membership-based CSOs (including those with social, political, or partisan missions) are generally confronted with when trying to engage in interest representation activities (Schlozman 2010: 5; Almog-Bar and Schmid 2014: 27; Child and Grønbjerg 2007). In an attempt to address the resulting caveats, this chapter will use the distinction between 'voluntary association' and 'professionalized voluntary organization' as a conceptual anchor to formulate contrasting hypotheses about CSO politicization and organizations' political action repertoires. This is followed by expectations about differences between parties and groups.

A Governance Perspective on CSO Political Engagement

I conceptualize CSO engagement in interest representation activities in two stages. Whether a CSO can be considered as 'politicized' is indicated by its regular recourse to (whatever form of) political activity that transfers issues from the private to the public sphere (Salisbury 1984: 64–5; Kriesi 1996: 157; Cinalli and Giugni 2014: 85). A CSO's political action repertoire, in turn, denotes the range of political activities it regularly engages in (Binderkrantz 2005: 694; Kriesi et al. 2007). While politicization addresses whether a CSO exercises 'voice' to start with, the range of political activities indicates the diversity of channels for political engagement it makes available to members and followers.

Each aspect further points to a different reasons why we should find (or not find) CSO engagement in political activities, politicization being foremost concerned with the motivation to make the relevant investments, a CSOs' political action repertoire being most strongly concerned with organizational capacity. When a CSO is politicized, this grants insights into its basic priorities, into 'what and who it is for' (Halpin 2014: 46). This is the case whether political engagement is a primary or secondary function, as will be illustrated in Chapter 9 which assesses the evolution of CSOs' functional goal orientation. There is a 'resource threshold' to achieve politicization as sustained engagement in at least one activity, but it is relatively modest and has become more so with the growing availability of online tools. Once a CSO pursues political goals (Zamponi and Bosi 2018) and this becomes manifest in its outside behaviour, the range of methods chosen to achieve these goals—the breadth of its political action repertoire—are likely to be strongly resource-driven, less a matter of not wanting to. This is not because they want to provide multiple connections to the political sphere as an end in itself, though this enhances their democratic contribution from an outside perspective. It is because combining a diversity of strategies across different arenas generally enhances CSOs' chances of exercising influence (Binderkrantz 2005: 694; Binderkrantz 2008: 177–8; Halpin and Fraussen 2017). As Andrews and Edwards point out, 'resources crucial to the initiation or continuation of advocacy are unevenly distributed' (2004: 489) and most organizations struggle with a scarcity of resources (e.g. Gray and Lowery 1996; Salamon and Lessans-Geller 2008). Hence, while using several channels rather than just one tends to be desirable to politicized CSOs, they cannot necessarily afford it. Even though politicization and political action repertoires are closely linked empirically, they suggest that when theorizing the two governance templates' implications for political engagement patterns, we need to consider two aspects: first, how the respective CSO features might enhance or weaken the motivations to invest resources in political activities compared to other activities; and second, how they might shape organizational capacity, thereby enabling or preventing CSOs from engaging in a range of political activities at the same time.

Moving to the central substantive arguments, party and group research have long argued that membership-based CSOs—irrespective of their primary mission—need to balance (often conflicting) inwards-oriented and outwards-oriented goals and activities (e.g. Olson 1965; Panebianco 1988; Schmitter and Streeck 1999; Foley and Edwards 2002; Ahlquist and Levi 2014). This tension is rooted in two major challenges that membership-based voluntary organizations in general need to cope with, which I will use as the foundation to theorize CSO political engagement: first, the *ongoing need to sustain the support of voluntary members* (Wilson 1973) and second, *the nature of political advocacy as collective, non-exclusive incentives* from which non-members also profit (by definition less effective to sustain member support than selective incentives) (Olson 1965: 51; 132). Linking these two challenges faced by membership-based organizations, I formulate hypotheses on how the organizational characteristics of the 'voluntary association' and the 'professionalized voluntary organization' respectively shape the *balance between collective and selective incentive provision within membership-based CSOs*. The recognition that political activity constitutes a collective, non-exclusive incentive (Olson 1965: 51; 132; Moe 1980: 6) is crucial, especially, when theorizing the behaviour of organizational leaders and managers in charge of the day-to-day running of an organization. It is their responsibility to maintain voluntary organizations through different strategies of incentive provision to members who are able to leave the organization at any point (e.g. Wilson 1973; Barasko and Schaffner 2007).

It is a classical argument that investments in political activities confront leaders and managers with a free-rider problem. Even if 'policy change' can be achieved and an organization can effectively claim credit for it, membership of the organization is no prerequisite for benefiting from this achievement. Non-members with similar interests can equally enjoy its advantages. This problem of non-exclusivity makes selective incentives (material or solidary) restricted to members *ceteris paribus* more effective to ensure organizational maintenance (Olson 1965: 51; 132; Clark and Wilson 1961).

This suggests that especially when (*ceteris paribus* more inward-orientated) members are at the heart of an organization's governance system and give direction to organizational activities (Cornforth 2012: 1121), while resources are limited (as is usually the case), investments in political engagement (a form of collective good provision) becomes less likely (see, for a similar rationale, Ahlquist and Levi 2014). Contrary to the 'professionalized voluntary organization', the 'voluntary association' run by individual members and volunteers should disincentivize engagement in interest representation activities accordingly. The contrast between the two templates will be developed in detail in the following.

Hypotheses on the Political Engagement of Voluntary Associations and Professionalized Voluntary Organizations

Starting with the 'professionalized voluntary organization', both professionalization and bureaucratization enhance CSOs' overall capacity to engage in a range of activities simultaneously—including political ones—and, with this, their ability to deal with conflicting internal and external demands (Maloney and Rossteutscher 2005: 97–8; Hwang and Powell 2009; van Deth and Maloney 2012). This suggests a positive effect of these features on organizations' political action repertoire, to the extent that those running a CSO consider such activities as worthwhile to invest in to start with.

In terms of CSOs' propensity towards politicization, as the reliance on paid staff and bureaucratization increases, the centrality of member interests and the latter's weight in intra-organizational processes should decrease. Hence, an orientation towards selective incentive provision should become weaker, compared to the strategic considerations of organizational leaders and managers also considering external audiences such as the authorities or donors.

As argued earlier, orientations and behaviour towards maintaining external resources, outside support, and broader societal legitimacy are particularly likely when those in charge of a CSO have strong concerns about organizational survival. This tendency is especially associated with managers (Schmid et al. 2008: 585; Mosley 2011: 441; Staggenborg 1988), which has direct repercussions for CSOs' politicization. Even in CSOs that are predominantly service-orientated, some forms of political activity are likely to be conducive to such endeavours, even when advocacy is pursued only as a secondary goal. Media campaigns to maintain the salience of core issues as part of organizations' fundraising strategy or the lobbying of political elites to maintain state funding are two prominent examples of activities relevant to advocacy- and service-oriented CSOs alike.

Relatedly, both organizational leaders and managers are expected to care strongly about maintaining state funding, often a more reliable income source than, for instance, donations (Billis 2010: 60; Fraussen 2014: 406; Lu 2018a: 205–6; Bosso 2003). While some have associated state funding dependence with restrictions on organizations' political activities (e.g. Bloodgood and Tremblay-Boire 2017), others have highlighted that state resources are capacity-enhancing and thus benefit political activity (see for a recent overview Lu 2018a). More specifically, state funding access creates direct incentives to lobby for more funding (Salamon and Lessans-Geller 2008: 13–14; Chaves et al. 2004). Meanwhile, access to state funding facilitates regular contact with state officials and thereby increases the chances that political advocacy efforts will be successful (LeRoux and Goerdel 2009: 517–18). Overall, state funding reliance can be thus expected to make both investments in organizational politicization and broader political action repertoires more likely.

In line with Schmitter's and Streeck's (1999: 53–5) classical argument that CSOs' enhanced autonomy from members (as embodied by the features of the 'professionalized voluntary organization') facilitates their influence-seeking, we can formulate the following hypothesis:

H1 (*Professionalized Voluntary Organization–Political Engagement Hypothesis*): CSOs with the features of a professionalized voluntary organization are more likely to be politicized and their political action repertoires are broader than organizations without such features.

Features of voluntary associations are expected to incentivize opposite patterns. Starting with individual membership, group research has long emphasized that differences in membership composition are likely to affect the tactics that groups employ to pursue their goals (e.g. Gray and Lowery 1995; Foley and Edwards 2002). While we can expect selective material incentives exclusively available to members (e.g. access to specific resources or benefits excluded from non-members) to be equally relevant to sustain membership irrespective of the type of member, this is not the case for solidary incentives. They can be assumed to be an important driver for at least some individual members in groups. These are members who predominantly enjoy group life, rather than being interested in selective material incentives (e.g. access to member services[3]) or collective incentives (e.g. the implementation of the organization's political agenda) (Clark and Wilson 1961: 134–5). Members that are organizations or institutions themselves are unlikely to care much for activities that strengthen group solidarity. Thus, selective solidary incentives are unlikely to be useful investments for leaders to prevent corporate members from free riding (Schmitter and Streeck 1999: 14–15). Consequently, organizations composed of individual members (unlike corporate membership organizations) face pressure to sustain member support, not only through the provision of selective material incentives, but also through (selective) solidary incentives. They face more diverse (and more costly) demands for intra-organizational selective incentives from members, which reduces resources available for externally oriented political activities (Bolleyer and Weiler 2018: 1633–4). Being composed of individual members thus has implications for CSOs' organizational capacities that ought to negatively impact on CSOs' political action repertoires. Meanwhile, we also can expect inclinations towards politicization to differ with a CSOs' membership structure. *Ceteris paribus*, more instrumentally driven corporate members (individuals representing their organization's, institution's, or association's interests within a CSO) are likely to consider a CSO's external political engagement to attract the attention and support of outside audiences more worthwhile to start with than the average individual member more concerned with his or her involvement in organizational life. This is the case as they are more likely to consider CSOs' outside recognition by key audiences as strategically important, not only to sustain the CSO but also to achieve central goals, an external recognition that political activities can help to generate and strengthen.

---

[3] Note that this notion of member services (used in relation to CSOs providing selective incentives) is unrelated to the CSO type of 'service-orientated organization' as defined by an organization's primary goal. Indeed, many service-orientated organizations provide services to wider constituencies, not to members only.

Furthermore, groups can pursue the interests of their members—as typical for 'member-serving' voluntary associations (Billis 2010: 54)—or the interests of wider societal constituencies transcending their membership—'public-serving' organizations (Harris 1998: 149). Linking this distinction to Olson's 'by-product theory' (1965), I expect political engagement as one form of collective good provision to be less likely and less wide-ranging in more inwards-oriented, member-serving organizations. This is because the latter are more strongly incentivized to invest in activities exclusively benefiting members, who may be (but cannot be assumed to be) interested in political activities (Jordan and Maloney 2007: 25; 33). This contrasts with public-serving organizations (in which membership base and constituencies/beneficiaries diverge), an orientation which makes investments in collective incentives from which external actors can also profit more worthwhile. This suggests that, if member support can indeed be more effectively maintained through selective incentives than through (non-exclusive) political activities (Olson 1965; Jordan and Maloney 2007), the more central member interests are to the definition of organizational priorities, the stronger the pressure to prioritize selective incentives. Relatedly, when central managerial roles in an organization are held by volunteer staff (Harris 1998: 151; Billis 2010: 54; Paine et al. 2010: 108; Knoke 1990), and hence member interests shape the day-to-day running of an organization, this should feed into its involvement in various internally and externally oriented activities. Manpower in terms of volunteers can be crucial to help an organization (especially those with limited financial resources) to simultaneously sustain a broader range of activities, including political ones, especially if paid staff focus on service provision. However, if members are indeed more responsive to selective incentives, and given that volunteers tend to be a subset of members, the centrality of volunteer staff in organizational governance should disincentivize political activities in favour of other activities in terms of motivation, despite the availability of volunteers in principle enhancing organizational capacity. Moving to the implications of multi-tier structures, as argued earlier, they facilitate member mobilization and collective action. This allows active members to voice their preferences more effectively, which in turn—*ceteris paribus*—should favour selective over collective incentive provision. Similarly, dependence on membership fees as a central financial resource is expected to consolidate the prioritization of member interests ('the logic of membership') and thus to be detrimental to investments in political activities ('the logic of influence')

198 Civil Society's Democratic Potential

(Schmitter and Streeck 1999: 53–5).[4] On that basis we can formulate the following hypothesis, in contrast to H1:

> **H2** (*Association–Political Engagement Hypothesis*): CSOs with association features are less likely to be politicized and their political action repertoires are narrower than organizations without such features.

Expected Impacts of CSO Type on Political Engagement

Among the four dimensions jointly capturing CSOs' democratic contributions, patterns of political engagement—more so than any of the other dimensions—are likely to be affected by CSOs' functional orientation, i.e. differences in CSO type. This is the case as the decision to engage politically is closely tied to whether or not a CSO considers the pursuit of political goals as part of its identity (Zamponi and Bosi 2018). It has been argued earlier that political parties can be expected to be politicized in terms of regular political engagement, given that running elections is widely considered their defining feature (e.g. Sartori 1976). Different from groups, engagement in some partisan (by definition political) activity such as electoral participation is central to parties' identity and thus less likely to be a 'by-product' that can only be produced if selective incentive provision is also ensured, as Olson famously theorized for economic organizations (1965). This, however, does not mean that parties' interest representation activities are exclusively focused on electoral engagement. The expectation towards a broader political action repertoire than the one adopted by groups is tied to the broader set of roles attributed to parties in a democracy that cut across various domains, both societal and institutional (see Chapter 1). Responding to this diversity of roles, the average party can be expected to be engaged in a broader range of political activities than the average group, activities that help to establish channels between citizens and the political sphere well beyond the electoral arena.

---

[4] This does not assume that all CSO members are by definition not politically interested or solely focused on selective incentives but that, if we keep everything else constant (e.g. the CSO's mission which might be political and hence reflect members wanting their organization to pursue political goals), the dynamic implied by the centrality of members in organizational governance (especially individual members) as such is expected to disincentivize political engagement.

A Quantitative Analysis of Political Engagement of Civil Society Organizations

As indicated earlier, 33 per cent of CSOs that participated in the survey are not politicized to start with. Those CSOs which are politicized engage in up to eleven political activities in a sustained fashion (see for details on the operationalizations Chapter 3). I ran two models, one with politicization as dependent variable, the other with political action repertoires as dependent variable.[5] Given the nature of these two dependent variables, the model on politicization uses logistic regression (M1), the political action repertoire model uses a zero-inflated negative binomial regression (M2).[6] Table 8.1 presents the results of the two models alongside each other.[7]

Most importantly, in line with the overall framework of this study, the significant effects of features of the 'voluntary association' relate to both politicization and political action repertoire negatively, while features of the 'professionalized voluntary organization' relate to both positively. Indeed, all three constitutive features of the latter have a positive association with CSO political engagement, whereas the majority of association features works the opposite way. These differences again suggest that the features of the two governance templates invite different behavioural logics.

Most variables that have significant effects are relevant to both CSO politicization and the breadth of their political action repertoires, reflecting the close link between the two. This is the case for professionalization and bureaucratization, which are positively associated with both dependent variables, in line with H1. In particular, each additional member of staff makes it 2.9 per cent more likely that a CSO is politicized. Similarly, a one unit increase in the index capturing bureaucratization makes this

---

[5] To assure the robustness of the findings, the analyses consider (alongside the standard controls) measures for direct competition, resource competition, and competition density in the CSO's niche, as well as dependency on donations, which, based on earlier research, can be expected to impact on CSO political behaviour (see for details Chapter 3).

[6] This is a suitable choice as I am dealing with count data with excess zeros (a lot of CSOs are not politicized), overdispersion and a skewed positive count (most politicized CSOs engage in only few political activities regularly) (Zeileis et al 2008).

[7] An alternative to two separate analyses would have been a zero-inflated count data regression model with Poisson distribution composed of two distinct parts: first, a 'zero model' that operates as a binary logistic regression modelling politicization (the dependent variable) as binary outcome (non-zero versus zero), and second, a 'count model' that uses a truncated Poisson distribution to model the range of political activities regularly engaged in, considering the values that are non-zeros (Hu et al 2011: 367–9). In light of test statistics not indicating the two-part model to be superior and given that theoretical expectations with regard to the two interlinked dependent variables *Politicization* and *Political Action Repertoire* are the same with regard to all theorized variables, two separate models are presented. The results using the alternative specification are essentially the same.

200 Civil Society's Democratic Potential

Table 8.1 Drivers of CSO Politicization and Their Political Action Repertoires (With Multiple Imputations)

	Model 1 DV = CSO Politicization		Model 2 DV = Political Action Repertoire	
	Coefficient	SE	Coefficient	SE
(Intercept) Main Effects	2.49***	(0.55)	1.01***	(0.15)
Features of Professionalized Voluntary Organization				
Bureaucratization	0.33***	(0.06)	0.18***	(0.03)
Professionalization (log)	0.43***	(0.05)	0.21***	(0.02)
State Funding	0.14*	(0.07)	0.05	(0.03)
Features of Voluntary Association				
Individual Membership	−0.68***	(0.11)	−0.39***	(0.05)
Member Interest Orientation	−0.49***	(0.11)	−0.23***	(0.05)
Multi-Tier Structure	0.12	(0.10)	0.08	(0.04)
Volunteer Staff (log)	−0.03	(0.03)	−0.03*	(0.01)
Membership Fees	0.20	(0.13)	0.10	(0.06)
CSO Type				
Interest Group (ref: parties)	−2.44***	(0.57)	−0.70***	(0.13)
Service-Oriented Organization (ref: parties)	−3.01***	(0.57)	−1.09***	(0.14)
Controls Relevant to CSO Behaviour Generally				
Membership Instability	0.35**	(0.11)	0.18***	(0.05)
Membership Size (log)	0.04	(0.03)	0.03*	(0.01)
Organizational Age (log)	−0.18**	(0.06)	−0.11***	(0.02)
UK (ref: Norway)	−0.18	(0.17)	−0.06	(0.08)
Germany (ref: Norway)	0.15	(0.16)	0.05	(0.07)
Switzerland (ref: Norway)	−0.16	(0.16)	−0.02	(0.07)
Increased Member Involvement	0.25**	(0.10)	0.14***	(0.04)
Past Member Control	0.00	(0.04)	−0.02	(0.02)
Dimension-Specific Controls				
Donor Dependency	−0.05	(0.08)	0.05	(0.04)
Resource Competition	0.21*	(0.09)	0.13**	(0.04)
Competition Density (log)	0.10*	(0.05)	0.05*	(0.02)
N	3265		3265	

Note: Standard errors in parentheses * p<0.05, ** p<0.01, *** p<0.001.

5.55 per cent more likely. These findings not only highlight the centrality of the overall capacity of the human resources available to CSOs to engage in a wider range of activities but also that of enhanced efficiency, effectiveness, and competences in CSO structures (Ward 2011 210–11; Meyer and Maier 2015: 45; 48; Binderkrantz et al. 2015: 95–6). Reliance on professional personnel and reformed governance principles created incentives towards reconciling internal and external demands rather than prioritizing members, which makes investments in outward-facing political engagement more likely.

Individual membership and member interest orientation, in turn, are negatively associated with both dependent variables, in line with H2, underlining research that emphasizes the dynamics generated by different types of members (e.g. Gray and Lowery 1995; Foley and Edwards 2002) as well as the importance of CSOs' different orientations towards members, compared to wider constituencies they might serve (e.g. Halpin 2006). More specifically, being composed of individuals instead of corporate actors makes it 12.16 per cent less likely that a CSO is politicized. Member-orientated organizations are 10.34 per cent less likely to be politicized than public-oriented CSOs. Both findings suggest that association features make CSOs more inwards-orientated, focusing on selective incentives, less likely to become politically engaged, and if they do so, to use a variety of channels. Importantly, these findings challenge a long-standing and influential tradition that perceives associations of individual citizens as cornerstones of a democratic civil society (e.g. Warren 2001; Fung 2003; Skocpol 2013; Jordan and Maloney 2007; Hoch 2008).

Only two of the theorized independent variables have significant and robust effects with regard to only one of the two aspects of CSOs' political engagement, each belonging to one of the governance templates respectively. Both are resource variables and shape political engagement in opposite ways. State funding increases CSOs' propensity to politicize, i.e. to engage in at least one activity regularly (Model 1, Table 8.1), challenging claims that associate the dependence of CSOs on state funding with de-politicization (e.g. Choudry and Kapoor 2013; Bloodgood and Tremblay-Boire 2017). More specifically, one unit increase in the index capturing state funding dependency makes politicization of the average CSO 3.84 per cent more likely. Interestingly, state funding dependency is not associated with a wider range of strategies, i.e. has no significant effect regarding CSOs' political action repertoires (Model 2, Table 8.1). Though enhancing organizational capacity, it might incentivize shifting additional resources into particular types of political activities only, such as lobbying the authorities for more funding (Salamon and Lessans-Geller 2008: 13–14; Chaves et al. 2004), thereby disincentivizing diversification. Vice versa, reliance on volunteer staff is associated with a narrower political action repertoire specifically, even though it suggests that organizations can in principle rely on more support for a wider range of activities. This supports H2 stressing the factor's motivational rather than its capacity implications. If, on average, particularly individual members are likely to care more about selective incentives than their CSOs' contribution to collective goods, their prominence in the running of organizations should be unfavourable to CSOs' political engagement. This is what the findings suggest, though being reliant on volunteers seems not to affect the propensity towards politicization.

Moving to CSO type, despite controlling for a wide range of organizational properties, political parties are on average more likely to be politicized and engage in a broader range of political activities than the average interest groups and the average service-oriented organizations, respectively. With regard to politicization, especially when comparing parties and service-oriented organizations, this is not surprising. Different to the latter type of organization, the self-understanding as a party would suggest that organizations at least regularly engage in some election-related activities (though as mentioned earlier, the data shows that a significant minority of the 95% politically active parties is not focused on election-related matters). Similarly, for the average party to engage in politics is less likely to be a mere 'by-product' than for the average interest group as group survival can be more strongly reliant on the provision of member services than political activism (Olson 1965).

The significant difference between parties and the two group types in terms of political action repertoires—with the repertoire of parties being on average systematically broader—is more interesting. This becomes clear when we go back to the political activities that CSOs were asked about in the survey. In line with the broader theoretical perspective adopted by this study, the relevant survey question only included activities relevant to all three CSO types (see Chapter 3 for details). In particular, no political activities that required institutional access, such as parliamentary seats or ministerial posts relevant to parties alone, were considered, since the inclusion of those types of activities would have risked 'biasing' the results in favour of parties, at least some of which would have had a wider range of (realistic) options. Only one activity—electoral and/or referenda campaigns—can be considered as particularly aligned with what parties 'are'. Indeed, some activity types such as donations to political parties can be expected to be more relevant to groups, as parties usually do not give financial support to their competitors. The difference that was found between parties and groups is therefore unlikely to be driven by the choice of measure.

That parties engage in a wider range of political activities than other CSOs gains further relevance when considering that political parties tend to be (predominantly) composed of individuals, hence they tend to possess—more frequently than groups—one central 'association feature' that is negatively associated with political engagement. Parties therefore provide individual citizens with a wider range of opportunities for participating in political activities relevant to interest representation than other CSO types, even though being composed of individual citizens in itself tends to create incentives in the opposite direction.

Depending on the literature one starts out from, this finding is not necessarily intuitive, since important strands of research portray parties as preoccupied with elections, as state-centred and -dependent, and increasingly detached from society (e.g. Mair 1994; Katz and Mair 1995; 2009; Biezen 2004). They provide a prominent critique of parties' declining ability and willingness to provide meaningful linkages between society and the state. For sure, this literature is concerned with mainstream parties that dominate governing institutions in democratic regimes and benefit from state funding much more than the average electorally active party analysed here (see Chapter 3). Still, perceiving parties as predominantly vote- or policy-seeking (rather than office-seeking) would still have rationalized a narrower (institutionally focused) repertoire rather than a broader one. Besides, the analysis controls for factors such as membership size and importance of state funding for a CSO's budget and thereby considers the variation between major, privileged organizations and minor, marginal ones.

If one adopts a societal rather than an institutional perspective instead, one might have expected that the average electorally active (minor) party that operates outside public institutions throughout its existence might be difficult to distinguish from the average interest group (indeed, a few organizations included in the survey as a political party, based on their presence on an electoral register, self-identified as interest groups). But if so, the difference between parties and groups should not have mattered, especially as the analysis considers a wide range of organizational properties and resource variables that are important drivers of political engagement. All in all, the findings do suggest that the average party provides citizens with a wider range of channels to connect with the political sphere than the average group, which signals their central role as 'vehicles for representation'.

A number of control variables considered relevant to CSO behaviour generally have significant effects on CSO political engagement patterns, which substantiates the robustness of the main findings. In line with earlier work, external competitive pressures matter. Both resource competition and competition density, CSOs' direct and indirect exposure to competition by other CSOs, increase the propensity for CSO politicization and for a broader political action repertoire, hence, making investments in political activism more worthwhile. Being exposed to market pressures, political engagement might serve as a way to signal an organization's broader relevance to external audiences, which not only include a CSO's support base from which members are recruited but also state authorities or donors whose support for the organization is affected by the latter's political relevance and the perceived legitimacy of its issues in the public domain. Another organizational property with a significant positive effect in both models is increased member involvement over the last five years, again aligning with the notion of member involvement as a resource (Chapter 4). While enhancing organizational capacity and positively affecting organizations' ability to engage in a wider range of activities, including political ones, it does not align with the logic attributed to the 'voluntary association' (expected to deprioritize political engagement). This is because, unlike member control, involvement can be directed by leaders and managers towards areas they consider useful rather than channelling member preferences into organizational processes and behaviours. Membership size (as a proxy for a growing organizational capacity) positively impacts on CSOs' political action repertoires but does not support politicization (i.e. whether investments in regular political activities are considered worthwhile in the first place). Similarly, exposure to membership instability tends to be linked to broader political action repertoires (but not politicization, this effect in Table 8.1 is not robust across different specifications). This can be read as an attempt to keep different types of members in the organization or to attract supporters more widely by diversifying the range of influence strategies to highlight the importance of organizational issues across different arenas. Finally, age is negatively associated with political engagement. This aligns with classical arguments indicating a stronger orientation towards selective incentive provision and a growing inwards-orientation as CSOs mature and institutionalize (e.g. Panebianco 1988).

Conclusion

This chapter has theorized how the different ways that CSOs organize affect their interest representation activities vital to the contribution that CSOs can make to democracy. This last of the four large-N analyses presented in this study again suggests that the two templates 'voluntary association' and 'professionalized voluntary organization' embody distinct logics whose constitutive characteristics tend to push CSOs in opposite directions. Different from the three dimensions already analysed, CSOs resembling a 'professionalized voluntary organization' fare better in terms of their 'democratic performance' than those resembling associations. They make it more likely that CSOs politicize and exercise voice, while enhancing the diversity of channels that CSOs are likely to use to engage in interest representation. While professionalization and bureaucratization positively relate to both, state funding dependency is positively associated with politicization. This contrasts with these properties' implications for the other dimensions. They suggested that features of the 'professionalized voluntary organization'—notably professionalization—make member control less and staff control over decision-making more likely, while incentivizing CSOs to adapt their core goals—a tendency inviting the detachment of CSOs from societal constituencies. While association features are not relevant for member control, they help to contain staff control and invite goal commitment conducive to stable societal connections. The findings of this chapter show that member interest orientation, individual membership, and reliance on volunteer staff—three of five features of the 'voluntary association'—disincentivize political engagement as a necessary precondition for politically relevant linkages between society and state to materialize (Albareda 2018: 1219).

While again underlining the usefulness of analytically distinguishing voluntary associations from professionalized voluntary organizations, CSO politicization and organizations' political action repertoires are also affected by an organization's primary goal—i.e. by whether or not they are political parties. In particular, the positive association with the breadth of political action repertoires implies that political parties, on average, provide individual citizens with a wider range of opportunities for participating in activities relevant to interest representation—activities that transcend the electoral arena—than the two group types. This is especially noteworthy as, unlike groups, parties are usually composed of individual citizens—an association feature which in itself disincentivizes political engagement. Considering the results of all statistical analyses conducted alongside each other, CSO type had significant effects in half of the models run (member involvement, politicization, political action repertoire), while being insignificant with regard to the other half (member control, staff control, goal reorientation). Given that the sample of parties (though broadly representative) was small (see Chapter 3), it is the significant findings that deserve particular attention. They suggest that party status, compared to group status, indeed seems to contribute in a positive fashion to CSOs functioning both as venues for participation and as vehicle for representation.

Returning to the broader picture and where we go from here, as argued earlier, goal commitment is considered conducive to stable linkages between

CSOs and societal constituencies. Political engagement—carrying organizational interests into the public domain—is central to transform 'civil society' into 'political society'. The classical transmission belt presupposes linkages and voice. Yet theorizing the interplay of members, organizational leaders, and managers provided the foundation to rationalize why we can expect the same CSO characteristics associated with the voluntary association and the professionalized voluntary organization respectively to push CSOs to strengthen one, yet weaken the other. Individual members at the heart of associations were expected to prioritize goal commitment and the cultivation thereof. Solidary incentives can help with that, thereby reducing resources available for outside activities, such as political ones. Managers and organizational leaders central to the professionalized voluntary organization were considered to be more flexible, even when reforms might alter the goals at the heart of their organizations' identity, as long as the latter make the organization more appealing or legitimate to relevant outside audiences. Engagement in political activities, in turn, might be one strategy towards achieving the latter. It can enhance a CSO's societal legitimacy and emphasize the salience of core issues towards funders, state authorities, or the wider public, whose support is perceived to be as crucial as that of members. Considering these interconnections, a CSO's decision to expand its mission from only service goals towards political goals unites the two dimensions of goal reorientation and political engagement (assuming that goal reorientation leads to actual behavioural change, hence, a CSO starts engaging in political activities accordingly). Building on this observation, Chapter 9 will explore the two dimensions in conjunction and explore their connections longitudinally, as NAPA, SAS, and GPEW increasingly move from voluntary association to professionalized voluntary organizations.

9
From Voluntary Association to Professionalized Voluntary Organization

CSO Goal Reorientation and the Evolution of Political Engagement

The statistical analyses presented up to now suggest that CSOs resembling 'professionalized voluntary organizations' adapt their goals more readily, are more likely to be politically active on a regular basis, and use a broader range of strategies directed towards exercising political influence regularly than CSOs without these characteristics. As with Chapter 6, this chapter is particularly focused on the implications of those CSO characteristics belonging to the two templates that, according to the statistical analyses in Chapters 7 and 8, had repercussions for both goal reorientation and political engagement.

All three features central to the professionalized voluntary organization—professionalization, bureaucratization, and state funding dependency—have significant and robust associations with both goal reorientation and political engagement in theoretically expected directions. This means they push CSOs in opposite directions with regard to their overall democratic 'performance'. They make it less likely that CSOs cultivate stable constituency linkages, while making them more likely and effective in providing 'voice' in the political process to those constituencies they claim to speak for, a tension highlighted in earlier research on NGOization (e.g. Lang 2013). In other words, these features are beneficial with regard to effective engagement in representation as a process, but not necessarily with regard to the content of representation activities, insofar as one expects the latter to be shaped by societal demands as defined by members and supporters. Rather than articulating 'authentic' societal demands, 'voice' as exercised by professionalized CSOs might be the result of strategic manoeuvring (e.g. Maloney 2012). This, in turn, highlights a discrepancy between assumed representation activities and democratic representation discussed in detail in Chapter 2 (e.g. Beyers et al 2008; Houtzager and Gurza Lavalle 2009).

Civil Society's Democratic Potential. Nicole Bolleyer, Oxford University Press. © Nicole Bolleyer (2024).
DOI: 10.1093/oso/9780198884392.003.0009

This chapter again analyses the evolution of the NAPA, SAS, and GPEW, all of which increasingly resembled the professionalized voluntary organization template. This showed most clearly in terms of professionalization and bureaucratization. All three increasingly relied on paid staff and reformed their procedures along the way to enhance efficiency and their organization's competence base, hence bureaucratized structurally. In the course of this process, ordinary members became less powerful and managers more so—formally or informally. A decline of member control was generally rationalized in terms of ensuring efficiency in the context of growing organizations. The emergence of spaces for staff control was justified in terms of an increasing need for professional competences and skills.

All three CSOs could access direct state funding at different points of their development, which proved to be an important catalyst for hiring more staff, thereby enhancing professionalization. That said, none of the three organizations ever became highly dependent on state funding, a scenario problematized in various literatures (e.g. Katz and Mair 1995; Weisbrod 1997; Salgado 2010; Bloodgood and Tremblay-Boire 2017). The GPEW has had the most continuous and reliable access to state resources in the recent period by virtue of having achieved a certain presence in parliamentary institutions (regional, national, and until 2021 EU). This is the case, even though in the UK state funding for political parties is scarce and mainly linked to public office-holders such as in the form of so-called 'Short Money' provided to opposition parties with parliamentary representation. Yet, thanks to considerable organizational growth from the late 2000s onwards, the relative contribution of membership fees to the party's budget has grown at the same time, meaning private funding as well has gained more importance as the CSO professionalized (Thompson and Pearson 2021). NAPA and SAS received state funding intermittently for specific projects but never became strongly reliant on such support either. Private income sources, especially membership fees, have remained important to all three CSOs until today. This means that in terms of their finances the three CSOs' transformations into 'professionalized voluntary organization' was both less consistent and less pronounced than it was in terms of their professionalization and bureaucratization.

Returning once more to the statistical findings, the one 'association feature' identified as relevant for both goal reorientation and political engagement is being composed of individual as compared to corporate members. In line with theoretical expectations, CSOs composed of individual members show higher levels of goal commitment but, at the same time, are less likely to be politically active than CSOs composed of corporate members. Of the three case studies, only NAPA transitioned from an individual membership towards cultivating a predominantly corporate base, which is why this feature is specifically discussed in the context of this case study.

By mediating limitations inherent in the analysis of cross-sectional data more generally (see Chapter 3), the case studies help to do justice to the wealth of literature dealing with interest groups', non-profits', and NGOs' political activities and influence strategies on the one hand, as well as to research dealing with processes of organizational goal displacement and mission drift on the other. Both literatures provide valid arguments to consider the conclusions drawn from the quantitative analyses in Chapters 7 and 8 as insufficiently nuanced.

Starting with political engagement, one might argue that, although the diversity of CSOs' political activities is important for organizations' democratic contribution, so is the nature of the political activities that groups try to exercise political influence with (e.g. Maloney et al 1994; Beyers 2004; Binderkrantz 2008; Dür and Mateo 2013; Lang 2013; Hanegraaff et al 2016; Berkhout et al 2017; Dür 2018). One prominent line of argument in group and non-profit research is not so much concerned with depoliticization (finding expression in the narrowing or even shutting down of regular political engagement). Instead, it suggests that professionalization as well as dependency on state funding invites a reorientation towards less confrontational political activity. Especially state funding might positively incentivize specific types of political activity such as conventional lobbying, while disincentivizing unconventional, extra-institutional strategies such as public protest, which risk upsetting existing working relations with public authorities and funders (e.g. Berry and Arons 2003; Suarez 2010a; Toepler 2010; Lu 2015; Dür and Mateo 2016; Stavenes and Ivanovska Hadjievska 2021). Such shifts do not necessarily show in the range of political activities studied in Chapter 8. Indeed, the range might increase as CSOs diversify their insider strategies while dropping the most confrontational outsider strategies along the way. If this were the case, the analysis in Chapter 8 would make us overlook an important consequence of CSOs' transformation into professionalized voluntary organizations in terms of interest representation.

A similar argument can be made with regard to the analysis of CSOs' propensity towards goal reorientation and commitment in Chapter 7, which tells us something important about the adaptability of CSO identities. However, it does not capture processes of organizational transformation that can occur rapidly in response to sudden crises as well as incrementally over many decades (Halpin 2014; Halpin and Daugbjerg 2015). How these processes are shaped by the interactions between members, leaders, and managers is important because these interactions are essential to judge whether or not change is the result of leaders' or managers' detached strategic manoeuvring. If so, related tendencies might lead not only to the diversion of resources and activities from CSOs' actual mission but also the modification, transformation, or subversion of organizational objectives to satisfy external audiences—as suggested by notions such as mission drift and goal displacement (Scott 1967: 160; Warner and Havens 1968: 541; Froelich 2005: 250; Minkoff and Powell 2006; Jones 2007). But this is only one possibility. Alternatively, a reorientation of goals might involve a process of exchange between a CSO's leadership and its members—or at least proactive communication of the former to the latter—to rationalize and build acceptance for those changes (Lutz Allen et al 2013: 27–8). The latter situation would suggest that a chain of accountability remains intact in terms of justifying modifications of organizational objectives and keeping the organizational base on board. Hence, the extent to which the greater changeability of 'professionalized voluntary organizations' as detected in Chapter 7 is problematic depends on which of the two scenarios we find when looking more closely at how processes underpinning CSO goal orientation evolve in the longer term.

Tracing Change in CSO Goals and Political Engagement Qualitatively

To trace the evolution of NAPA's, SAS's and GPEW's goal orientation and political activities over the course of several decades more than 150 annual reports[1] and newsletters as well as—in the case of GPEW—over 3500 press releases were analysed. These documentary sources were complemented by in-depth interviews.[2] The wealth of these sources is important as it makes it possible to explore both processes of goal reorientation and the evolution of political activities along two complementary empirical dimensions respectively.

Starting with goal reorientation, the qualitative assessments will distinguish between *functional goal reorientation* and *substantive goal orientation*. As argued in Chapter 7, CSOs which transform into professionalized voluntary organizations are expected to become more willing to alter their substantive goals and thus move beyond their traditional issues, beneficiaries

---

[1] Central regulators to which the three CSOs reported were Company House, the Charity Commission of England and Wales, and the Electoral Commission.

[2] Documentation on the primary documents used for each case study and an anonymized list of interviews is provided in the Online Appendix made available on www.oup.co.uk/companion/Bolleyer.

or constituencies. By doing so, they attempt to balance the interests and maintain support of different internal and external, societal and institutional audiences. For the same reason, CSOs might branch out into different areas of activity altogether, e.g. from the provision of services towards political engagement and vice versa. This is referred to as functional goal reorientation. Though both types of change are central to a CSO's identity and interwoven, they approach the question about 'what a CSO is for' in two different ways: substantive goal orientation refers to the nature or content of the interests a CSO actually pursues. Functional goal orientation refers to what type of organization a CSO is meant or wants to be (with implications through which channels or means it pursues its substantive goals). Organizations tend to identify with one primary purpose, but this does not mean that they are exclusively dedicated to this one purpose only. Self-identified interest groups often provide services to members or constituencies. Self-identified service-oriented organizations often engage in advocacy. Self-identified parties employ strategies predominantly associated with interest groups. Hence, the cases studies will trace processes of substantive goal orientation (which directly aligns with Chapter 7's analysis of CSOs' propensity towards changing its core mission or programme). But they will also look at whether, on a more fundamental level, significant shifts towards the template of the 'professionalized voluntary organization' lead to CSOs endorsing of secondary goals (e.g. advocacy in the case of service-providers; service in the case of interest groups; extra-institutional advocacy in the case of parties).

A complete functional reorientation (one primary goal being displaced in favour of another) is not expected as a likely outcome of a CSO's increasing resemblance with the 'professionalized voluntary organization' template. Such transformations are likely to have destabilizing implications as they risk undermining the foundation that drew supporters into the organization in the first place. If so, especially managers concerned about organizational maintenance (who play a central role in increasingly professionalized and bureaucratized organizations) are unlikely to advocate them. That said, CSOs might be internally divided over what their primary goal ought to be to start with. In that case, developments towards the 'professionalized voluntary organization' that tend to benefit most the central organization should tip the balance in favour of the primary goal endorsed by the central leadership.

Moving on to CSO political engagement, also here the qualitative analyses allow exploring two complementary aspects to provide a richer picture than a quantitative operationalization could. A CSO's enhanced political engagement becomes structurally manifest in patterns of staff specialization, i.e. specialization benefiting political engagement finds expression in the creation of paid positions specifically dedicated to political tasks and activities (e.g. campaign manager, director of communications). Alternatively, in organizations that are less well resourced, political activities such as lobbying become part of existing staff's formal responsibilities. Both developments signal the willingness to dedicate scarce resources to keep political rather than other activities going, activities that—depending on the organization—are neither necessarily central to a CSO's success nor its survival.

The second aspect explored is how political activities evolved over time in terms of both their range and intensity. To evaluate this, available documents were analysed with a standardized coding scheme. To ensure coherence between quantitative and qualitative parts of the analysis, the qualitative coding scheme was based on the activity categories used in the survey item capturing CSO political activities in the statistical analyses (see Chapter 3).[3] The scheme allowed to systematically capture basic changes in the range of political activities and their intensity as indicated in CSOs' official reports, newsletters or press releases dedicated to showcase central activities to key audiences.

As explained in Chapter 8, the statistical analysis deliberately treated all types of political activity equally as indications of politicization and aggregated them with equal weight to assess the breadth of CSOs' political action repertoires accordingly. This aimed at ensuring an unbiased analysis across partisan, political and service-oriented CSOs, i.e. across organizations likely to favour towards different activity types. The qualitative analysis was designed to complement this perspective not only by bringing in a temporal dimension, i.e. by establishing whether or not we find a broadening of CSOs' political action repertoires over time as organizations increasingly resemble the 'professionalized voluntary organization' to validate the statistical findings. They also explore whether or not with growing professionalization, bureaucratization and state funding dependency we see non-confrontational insider strategies used at the expense of confrontational strategies. If this was the case, this would somewhat diminish the weight of the finding of Chapter 8 that features of the 'professionalized voluntary organization' are conducive to CSO political engagement. This is important as a 'more wide-ranging'

---

[3] Those were: Contact reporters, write letters to the editor, issue press releases, Paid advertisements in media outlets, Arrange debates/hold press conferences, Encourage members and others to contact decision-makers, Participate in public consultations, Contact government officials, Publish analyses and research reports, Legal direct action (e.g. authorized strikes) and public demonstrations, Civil disobedience and illegal direct action, Electoral and/or referenda campaigns, Donations to political parties, Cooperation with specific interest or advocacy group(s), Cooperation with a political party/parties. To make the scheme more nuanced, educational activities and a residual category of 'Partisan, political, and other news unrelated to specific activity types' were added.

repertoire closely relates to but should not be equated with a 'more diverse' one in terms of the full spectrum of connections to the political process that CSOs might be able to provide.

Before moving to the findings, a few caveats need to be mentioned regarding this part of the analysis. Newsletters (generally the most detailed source) were not available throughout the CSOs' whole existence, with early stages less well covered than more recent ones. Furthermore, with a CSO's growing professionalization the level of detail of newsletters tended to grow. Similarly, coverage through press releases got more extensive. Both tendencies suggest that more activities tended to be reported as organizations matured (which is of course not the same as more activities taking place). This is why a quantification based on 'activity counts' is avoided. Instead, the aim of this qualitative assessment is to capture the basic range of different political activities and to assess whether noticeable shifts occurred at major turning-points of the three CSOs' developments that align with theoretical expectations or not. This qualification is also important as the level of detail of the annual reports differs due to different reporting requirements by the regulators in charge of the three CSOs at different stages of their development. It was thus essential to combine and triangulate a wide range of different documentary sources (both primary and secondary) complemented by in-depth interviews to gain a reliable picture of how political action repertoires evolved across organizations and over time.[4]

Intra-Organizational Dynamics, Goals, and Political Engagement of a Service-Oriented, a Political, and a Partisan Organization

The National Activity Providers Association (NAPA)

While over the course of its lifespan NAPA increasingly resembled a professionalized voluntary organization, GPEW had at its peak more than ten times as many employees than NAPA. SAS had six times as many. Hence, NAPA's

---

[4] This triangulation was also important as the three main document types analysed are partially directed towards different audiences: newsletters, and press releases to the CSO's support base, and official reports to the authorities, which might lead organizations to downplay or stress particular types of activities respectively: a politically active CSO such as SAS might focus in its newsletter more on political activities and initiatives on the ground (e.g. protests, petitions, grass-roots lobbying) to stress its proximity to and mobilize supporters than in its reports to the Charity Commission of England and Wales. In its official reports it might try to put more emphasis on activities demonstrating expertise (e.g. research reports, public consultations), educational achievements, and its collaborations with public institutions. Consequently, to cover different document types to the fullest extent possible in each case study was directed towards achieving a balanced perspective on the range of activities and the latter's evolution.

capacity or willingness to transcend—in terms of organizational activities—its core business (which is the provision of services and support to people working in care homes) in favour of political engagement should be comparatively limited. Among the three organizations studied, NAPA is thus the 'least likely case' for the hypotheses on political engagement detailed in Chapter 8 to hold. Consequently, this case is particularly insightful with regard to whether and, if so, how its professionalization has affected its politicization, its political action repertoire, and its goal orientation. Its in-depth exploration is further telling in light of existing research that mostly treats service-providing organizations as a qualitatively distinct class of organization. This class of organization, so the argument goes, demands a distinct theoretical account of advocacy, different from political organizations such as interest groups, let alone parties (e.g. Almog-Bar and Schmid 2014). Consequently, NAPA is also a 'hard' case regarding whether it is suitable to study political and (supposedly 'non-political') organizations jointly from the same theoretical perspective.

In the following, I first look at NAPA's evolving political engagement and second at how it modified its goals over the course of its history.

As detailed in Chapter 6, up to 2005, NAPA only had part-time staff tied to individual projects. There is no evidence to suggest that political activities formed part of their formal responsibilities. Despite its service orientation on which its resources were (and continue to be) concentrated, we find in a 2002 newsletter the intention to engage in political activities such as campaigning to influence standards in the care sector. This announcement stresses 'the challenge for NAPA to be both practical and down to earth and campaigning and influencing on the other'.[5] Nevertheless, from 2003 onwards, by which time its part-time staff had increased in number from one to four, we find concrete evidence of influence-seeking activities (e.g. through establishing contacts with the National Care Standards Commission, the Department of Health). This shift towards *politicization* associated with the CSO's increasing professionalization intensified post-2005,[6] since when the organization could consolidate a small but permanent staff base. From 2001 to 2003, staff spending tripled from £38,800 to £102,664 and has since not fallen again below £86,600 (staff spending in 2014, the year after the economic crisis). In essence, NAPA's growing financial capacity fuelled its professionalization

---

[5] NAPA, Spring 2002, Volume 5, Issue 3, pp. 1–2.
[6] In 2005, NAPA participated in the House of Commons Breakfast, see NAPA, Winter 2005, Volume 9, Issue 3, p. 3; NAPA also established contacts with the Commission for Social Care Inspection, see NAPA, Spring 2006, Volume 10, Issue 1, p. 1.

CSO Goal Reorientation and the Evolution of Political Engagement   215

(see Chapter 6 for details) which, in turn, facilitated its politicization in terms of pursuing political goals alongside its dominant service orientation.

Since 2005, NAPA had a strategic director and a communications director, indicating an increasing specialization and functional differentiation of its small human resource base. The strategic director—in effect the first paid CEO of the organization—focuses on cooperation with and exercising influence on external stakeholders, including policymakers, and by 2009 was officially recognized as one of the fifty most influential people in the care sector. The communications director is responsible for communication with members and the media to promote the salience of NAPA's concerns in the public domain, as well as to persuade providers, inspectors, policymakers, and other charities to raise the profile of activity providers. Unlike the two (considerably bigger and better resourced) political organizations analysed later, the functional differentiation of NAPA's staff base has remained relatively limited. There is no indication that NAPA has ever hired specialist staff dedicated to political activities (e.g. campaigning) alone. Given its service orientation and small staff size,[7] this is unsurprising. However, the portfolios of the strategic and communications directors (two roles that still exist today) clearly include politically directed activities.[8] The strategic director proactively developed the organization's 'influencer role', trying to counter the fact that the role of activity providers in care homes was not well understood. Nor was NAPA well enough known for its services to be used more widely. Political engagement was directed towards demonstrating the importance of NAPA's concerns and its role in the sector to government authorities, care providers, and the public at large. This was directed towards diversifying available funds and helped to enhance the organization's broader visibility and legitimacy. NAPA's increasing professionalization clearly helped to develop its political profile (politicization) alongside its dominant orientation towards service provision. Furthermore, it supported a diversification of the types of political activities pursued, the breadth of its *political action repertoire*.[9] We find a more developed media strategy (on- and offline) to highlight salient issues, after the hiring of a

---

[7] It had its maximum number of six staff only in 2017, which went down to five, its current staffing level, the year after.

[8] Later documents refer to 'Communications and Project Officer' (NAPA 2015 Financial Statements, p. 5) or 'Communications Manager' (NAPA 2020 Annual Report and unaudited Financial Statement, p. 3) rather than Communications Director.

[9] NAPA engaged in educational and training activities from the start, aligned with its service mission, an engagement that clearly intensified with its professionalization. This was evident in an expanded educational programme, with its first training course formally accredited in 2003, followed by its official recognition as accredited training centre in 2006 (NAPA 2003 Annual Report and Accounts, p. 6; NAPA, Summer 2006, Volume 10, Issue 2, p. 2).

communications director in 2005. While conventional lobbying (i.e. the contacting of government officials) had already become part of the CSO's repertoire in 2003, NAPA's professionalization fed into more frequent participation in national conferences, strategic cooperation with other, increasingly large, organizations to raise awareness in the sector, and the publication of analyses and research to disseminate best practices. The latter increasingly targeted not only the relevant professionals but people involved in care more broadly.

The development of NAPA's political activities happened in the context of significantly altered governance processes including enhanced bureaucratization. Decision-making became easier when in 2004 the attendance quorum for AGMs was reduced to only ten members—effectively, the trustees (i.e. the CSO's national leadership). NAPA's political profile was actively cultivated by increasingly specialized staff from the mid-2000s onwards and publicly recognized in 2009 when NAPA was invited for the first time to take part in a public consultation process by the new Care Quality Commission. Campaigning for changes in care provision and the regulation thereof has remained central to NAPA's awareness-raising activities ever since. Collaboration partners by now not only include government bodies but also Unilever Food Solutions or research institutions such as the College of Occupational Therapists. Such partnering with bigger players in the sector or research institutions in order to exercise influence through them has gained greater importance in recent years, as government has been perceived as increasingly difficult to access directly. Such collaborations were facilitated by the CSO's structural features, essentially its bureaucratization. As detailed in Chapter 6, a major reform in 2014 enhanced efficiency as well as competences and skills of organizational and managerial leaders. This reform contributed to the CSO's ability to engage in a range of distinct activities—both political and service-orientated—simultaneously.

Unlike SAS and GPEW, NAPA formally changed its membership structure by introducing a 'business membership' alongside individual affiliates in 2006. This initiated a change from a predominantly individual membership base (e.g. activity providers) towards more corporate members (e.g. care settings). Former NAPA staff identify this reform as one of the most important steps in NAPA's history, as this move enhanced the continuity of its membership as a core income source. Beforehand, individuals tended to leave the organization when they moved into other jobs (with turnover relatively high). In contrast, ties to care providers, once signed up as members, could be more reliably cultivated, as such providers were likely to remain recipients of NAPA services in the medium and long term.

This change was introduced right after NAPA had professionalized its staff structures. Hence, it formed part of the attempts of the new management to consolidate the organization's support and, relatedly, financial base. The inclusion of political goals in its agenda and attempts to exercise political influence had already occurred prior. Hence, we cannot substantiate a positive link between a reorientation towards corporate members and the CSO's politicization, a connection suggested by the statistical findings. That said, regulatory standards, government policies, and provision of state support for different care settings and activities within them were of greater relevance to institutional members such as care homes, compared to individuals working or living with old people in different capacities (the latter are more likely to be interested in NAPA's support structures and its community work than in its lobbying efforts). Relatedly, the considerable growth in corporate members, encompassing 3000 care homes, that followed the change allowed the organization to invest in 'financially less rewarding activities' such as trying to influence relevant government regulators. At times, this allowed NAPA to become an 'unexpected influencer in the sector' that was heard by government as well as being approached by authorities for information about members. Hence, although NAPA's politicization predated the alteration of its core membership base, the shift towards a corporate membership still benefitted its political engagement.

NAPA's evolving political engagement was closely aligned with the broadening of its mission, bringing us to the dimension of *goal reorientation*. NAPA's initial mission was clearly focused on service, including educational and training activities ('help create a common understanding between older people and those who care for them by providing information, advice and support to those in practice across the UK'[10]). By 2003, however, it had undergone a functional goal reorientation by adding political voice a secondary goal. The CSO's ambitions had broadened to 'standard setting' with regard to appropriate practices in the provision of activities for older people, a change that occurred a year after the CSO had hired its first chief executive officer. From then on, NAPA presented itself as:

> the only national organization that is exclusively dedicated to addressing this vital strand of government policy ... [NAPA] is doing this: practically through its direct support for activity workers [and] strategically, through partnerships on policy work with other campaigning organizations.[11]

---

[10] NAPA, Winter 1997, Volume 1, Issue 2, p. 16.
[11] NAPA 2003 Annual Report and Accounts, p. 3.

Later on, we can detect a substantive broadening of NAPA's target beneficiaries as well as support base. By 2016, a process of mission change was completed that evolved over several years. The CSO's initial beneficiaries were older people and people working in care settings (1997). This focus was successively expanded towards all those involved in the care of older people, to include both professionals and relatives. Since 2013, NAPA's mission statement no longer explicitly focuses on 'older people'. Furthermore, a three-year strategy (2013–15) was put in place. This strategy articulates NAPA's goal to become a professional association as well as a member-led movement for activity providers, older people, and vulnerable adults.

By 2016, NAPA had adopted its current name (National Activity Providers Association), formally replacing National Association For Providers of Activities For Older People (as recognized by the Charity Commission in the same year). 'Older people' was removed 'to expand into other fields of work, in particular "Adults with Learning Disabilities"',[12] which is reflected in NAPA's new mission statement dedicated to 'activities for older persons and adults with learning disabilities'.[13] NAPA further declared that: 'Our new vision and mission points us in the direction we are heading to continue and develop our work as the leading organization in setting the standards and developing meaningful activity in care settings', putting an emphasis on 'every care and support setting'.[14]

Doing so, the organization engaged not only in substantive goal reorientation. It expanded both its corporate and individual membership base respectively. First, it moved beyond its focus on care homes towards also recruiting housing with care providers, for instance. This change was very much informed by experiences of staff who fed back to their organization a need to respond. In the years prior, they had been increasingly approached by other services such as hospitals and day-care centres that did not fit under the heading of 'care for older people'. Second, it developed a 'Family and Friends Stream' to involve a wider circle of people around those needing care beyond those professionals who were NAPA's initial target group.

The management was especially keen to move towards diversifying and attracting members from the wider sector as a necessary step to ensure the organization's long-term survival, displaying an orientation towards organizational self-maintenance often ascribed by paid staff. Though discussions around the need to broaden its support base had started before, the UK economic crisis had put NAPA (and many organizations in the sector) under

---

[12] NAPA 2017 Annual Report and unaudited Financial Statements, p. 2; NAPA, Interview, 30.05 2017.
[13] NAPA 2017 Annual Report and unaudited Financial Statements, p. 5.
[14] NAPA 2016 Financial Statements, p. 6.

pressure to tap into new income sources.[15] Furthermore, the provision in care homes had been improved since the organization's foundation in 1997, and the demand for NAPA training was in decline, which led to the perception that the organization might, if it continued the same way, become a victim of its own success.

The broadening of NAPA's substantive profile was already under way when in 2014 a major reform centralized decision-making and enhanced the influence of paid staff on governance processes (Chapter 6). While staff input was important for the CSO's reorientation that commenced in the 2010s, the process proceeding the 2014 reform involved a major review of procedures as well as central policies, conducted by a senior manager. This process aimed for a reform package able to enhance the overall resilience of the organization. While supporting a further broadening of NAPA's reach in substantive terms, the bureaucratization and staff control the reform invited enabled the CSO to cope with the consequences of such broadening—the diverse demands of new beneficiaries, new care settings, and new members. In this sense, not only professionalization and goal reorientation but also bureaucratization and goal reorientation appear as complementary processes.

Surfers Against Sewage (SAS)

SAS was formed in 1990 as a 'single-issue campaign group' dedicated to the protection of marine life and the coastline, with a focus on water pollution and sewage.[16] This portrayal presented on the organization's own website is echoed by its very first newsletter:

> SAS is a non profitmaking, a political organisation dedicated, for the benefit of all, to the stopping of marine sewage disposal. [...] Our aims and objectives are to increase public awareness of sewage disposal and its effects; to encourage and/or pressurise those responsible to cease all pollution; to explore, find and publicise viable alternatives.[17]

Unlike NAPA, the organization was 'politicized' from its inception. SAS defines itself as a 'pressure group,'[18] a notion central to its self-perception and

---

[15] EESC 2012; Pianta 2013.

[16] See on this, https://www.sas.org.uk/about-us/history/, accessed 21.02.2022.

[17] Pipeline news, 1990, 1, p. 1. This very first issue already presented the initiative to try to develop a programme to monitor sea pollution, in which health authorities worked alongside SAS members who were doctors, with the monitoring being implemented by surfers on the ground, indicating that the CSO indeed tried to pursue actual policy solutions to address environmental problems that were central concerns.

[18] Pipeline news, 1990, 1, p. 2.

220 Civil Society's Democratic Potential

identity. The focus of this case study thus will be the organization's *evolving political action repertoire and mission*, and how those two developments were shaped by the CSO's move towards a 'professionalized voluntary organization'. As with the NAPA case study, the longitudinal analysis of SAS substantiates earlier statistical findings. This is interesting as distinct from NAPA, SAS already started out with a relatively diverse portfolio of political influence. Yet, as the CSO professionalized and bureaucratized, we still see a broadening of its political action repertoire in terms of sustained rather than occasional engagement in (some) political activities, without any central activity types being abandoned. This occurred alongside a broadening of its mission, including a change of its core issue ('Plastic pollution is the new sewage'[19]).

Indicating the diversity of SAS's *political action repertoire* overall, documentary evidence suggests that only two of the thirteen activity categories taken into consideration in the document analysis were not used at all between 1990 and 2020. They are 'Donations to Political Parties' and 'Civil Disobedience and Illegal Direct Action'. Already in its very first newsletter, SAS issued the following item called 'RESPONSIBILITY':

> All members must be aware of the responsibility held to all other members [...] There is a fine line between being an effective hard hitting pressure group (which we hope to be) and *an unpopular extremist organisation (which we must never be)*. A bad move now could lose us the support of the press, private companies and other individuals who would want not to be associated with any bad publicity. An unfortunate event could also dissuade potential members from joining.[20] [italics added]

Striking a balance between using protest to attract media attention without alienating supporters, sympathizers, policymakers and businesses has been central to the CSO's approach to influence-seeking throughout its history. This was the case, despite the early belief within the organization that water companies, the British government, and the environmental agency were 'stacked against' it.[21] As one interviewee who was with the organization from the start explained: 'we were calling [...] Margaret Thatcher a liar. Publicly'.[22] Initial attempts to gain public benefit status in 1990 failed, as reported in its newsletter: 'On applying to the Charities Commission SAS

---

[19] Pipeline news, 2017, 102, p. 4.
[20] Pipeline news, 1990, 1, p.2.
[21] https://www.guggenheim.org/blogs/lablog/grassroots-grown-up-interview-with-chris-hines-of-surfers-against-sewage, 30.06.2012, accessed 7.02.2022.
[22] Interview, SAS, 26.05.2017.

were informed that Charities are not allowed to try to change the stance of government',[23] a legal constraint that was considered incompatible with its activities at the time.

SAS barely had the means to impact on party politics through significant financial contributions anyhow, and generally kept its distance from party politics. In the detailed documentation available, SAS reported active involvement in electoral campaigns only once. In 2008, during the Guernsey local election campaign, it pushed all party candidates to position themselves on the issue of pro-sewage treatment. The same goes for the category 'Cooperation with a Political Party'. Documents only once indicated a collaboration with the Scottish Green Party in 2007 related to the protection of a marine area. While engaging in protest activities throughout its history, the CSO stayed clear of aligning itself with one partisan camp long dominated by the two major parties, Conservative and Labour. Once its leadership recognized that charitable status allowed for political activities in line with its goals, and only prohibited partisan activities, this 'abstention' is likely to have contributed to the organization's smooth transition from pressure group to public charity more than twenty years after its formation.

Starting with a closer look at the development of human resources dedicated to political activities, i.e. staff specialization, it was one of SAS's organizational founders who took over the (paid) role of 'general secretary' early on (see Chapter 6). He was responsible for the organization's financial viability as well as campaigning, essentially combining two roles, organizational maintenance and directing SAS's political activities, which—as the CSO's *raison d'être*—was considered as essential to its survival as was fundraising. It is indicative for how SAS defined itself that these two aspects—internal maintenance and external influence-seeking—remained linked in terms of staff responsibility until 2008, nearly twenty years later. Up to then, SAS was run by a 'campaigns director', a role that (as its first secretary) linked campaign work with the overall running of the organization, though—by that time—the director was supported by a full-time campaign assistant.

Having been threatened by closure in the 2000s, in 2008 a new chief executive, a charity professional, took over. At that point, the organization established the role of 'executive director' alongside a 'campaign manager', a change that allowed the campaign team to fully focus on political work, while shifting resources to ensure the smooth running of the organization. This put a stronger emphasis on the managerial side of maintaining SAS as an organization (favouring bureaucratization). At the same time, the new executive

---

[23] Pipeline news, 1990, 2, pp. 6 and 7.

director functioned as a mouthpiece to communicate SAS's issues and policy proposals to wider audiences, including political elites and the business community. Hence, while separating campaign work from operational issues by having, for the first time, separate leadership roles for the two areas, the 'executive director' has never been a merely inwards-facing, managerial role. Instead, he has been central to communicating and shaping SAS's political message to outside audiences, which benefitted SAS's political engagement.

From 2008 onwards, SAS essentially underwent a period of continuous growth, during which human resources dedicated to political work were successively strengthened. In 2012, SAS hired additional campaign staff, which happened again in 2014, by which time staff numbers had grown to eleven. Human resources personnel further increased to 15.6 in 2017, of which six were campaigners fully dedicated to political work. This development continued when the CSO grew to a staff of twenty in 2020 and thirty in 2022.

As SAS put increasing resources into its political engagement, it changed its communication style and the emphasis on the political activities it pursued (e.g. engaging more in petitions than protest). Though it became more moderate in tone and less confrontational in its activities overall, it still engages in activities such as public protest or grass-roots lobbying when those strategies seem most promising to achieve its goals. Despite a shift in emphasis, we do not see its actual political action repertoire being narrowed in favour of insider strategies. Indeed, with its increasing professionalization, the repertoire of activities SAS is able to perform has broadened as we see a more sustained engagement in some activities SAS had tried to engage in from early on (e.g. public consultation, public education, or lobbying).

Looking at these aspects more closely, SAS has overall become more diplomatic in its political campaigning, especially as compared to its activities in the 1990s, which interviewees identified as one barrier against diversifying its income. In the 1990s, its income came predominantly from membership fees, sponsorships, and merchandise (Wheaton 2007: 269). Had the organization continued its open attacks on the government of the day, according to one interviewee active in SAS early on, the organization would have been unable to access state financial support as it did later.[24] This is echoed by a

---

[24] Illustrating hostility between the CSO and the government of the day, conflict with the Conservative Party was openly reported on in early newsletters: 'TRIPPIER ATTACKS ENVIRONMENTALISTS. At the recent Conservative Party Conference Mr. Trippier, star of Trippier Don't Surf, dubbed environmentalists as "woolly bearded and woolly thinking brigade" [...] Mr. Trippier seems to be making a big mistake if he thinks this way. Environmentalists are doctors, solicitors, builders and people from all walks of life [...] who want a clean world', Pipeline news 1990, 2, p. 6. By 2012, SAS had diverse funding coming from private grant-making foundations and trusts, donations, government agencies, membership fees, and corporate sponsorship. In terms of state funding, the Environmental Agency supported two of SAS's

CSO Goal Reorientation and the Evolution of Political Engagement **223**

current member of staff, who pointed out that by the time SAS had accessed state funding there was the need

> for more constructive dialogue with the key stakeholders around the table, i.e. the water companies, the state; that being DEFRA, the Environment Agency, and others. So you have to turn your tactics from a shouty campaign into a dialogue, discussion, and negotiation to achieve the next stages.[25]

This approach contrasts with that of the early 1990s, when SAS had cultivated a rather confrontational public image as part of its awareness-raising strategy. It was strongly focused on maximizing media attention to enhance the salience of its core issues as a precondition to be heard. This was stressed, for instance, by the 'Media Coverage' section in its newsletter and SAS communications to members: 'THE SAS NEEDS YOU. [...] most importantly we need to be SEEN—attend the AGM, go to the Demos, set up a local SAS Action Group'.[26] As described by an early staff member, 'you would go [to a different beach] and be in a different TV area each day for regional television'.[27] Relatedly, SAS used protest strategically as a means to publicly shame and pressurize relevant actors to reach its policy goals (e.g. in the case of water companies to adopt a full sewage treatment policy) throughout its history. While these activities fitted an 'outsider image', the organization also engaged in lobbying through formal and informal channels from the start. As early as the 1990s, SAS repeatedly gave evidence to the House of Commons, as highlighted by an early SAS staff:

> A lot of people used to say, you are just a bunch of people who jump up and down and you know, gas masks and wetsuits, but absolutely we knew that it was easy to complain about the problem, it's more difficult, but more important thing to do is to come up with solutions. So like in 1994 I wrote some evidence to House of Lords Select Committee, and I was called to go and give an evidence to it on the basis of my written evidence.[28]

This aligns with the active attempts of the organization to mobilize volunteers with expert knowledge and to engage in research relevant to its core issues

---

initiatives with a total of £34,610, which was 6.7 per cent of their total income. SAS also reported financial support from the Environment Agency in 2013, 2014, and 2015 (Ivanovska Hadjievska 2018: 133).

[25] Interview, SAS, 16.06.2017b.

[26] Pipeline news, 1990, 2, p. 5

[27] Interview SAS 26.05.2017.

[28] Interview SAS 26.05.2017. See on SAS's range of political activities also the interview with the SAS cofounder Chris Hines, https://www.guggenheim.org/blogs/lablog/grassroots-grown-up-interview-with-chris-hines-of-surfers-against-sewage, 30.06.2012, accessed 7.02.2022.

from its foundation onwards, as documented in Chapter 6. This was crucial to gain credibility in the policy and business community in order to resolve the water pollution problems that were the organization's central concerns at that time. Using this knowledge, SAS attempted to influence the political agenda. This happened not only through public channels such as parliament but also through informal lobbying at policy conferences involving water companies or meetings with ministers or civil servants from the environment agency. While the organization already started out with a diverse portfolio of political activities that included both 'outsider' and 'insider strategies', its long-term evolution does not reflect a displacement of extra-institutional (outsider) strategies in favour of institutional (insider) strategies as the organization professionalized and bureaucratized. This would have meant that in the longer term a public-facing set of strategies such as protests and petitions should have been replaced by strategies that more quietly targeted policymakers and other 'insiders' in the relevant policy communities. In the case of SAS, this did not happen. Demonstrations and grass-roots lobbying or awareness-raising through public shaming of companies have been used throughout its history and still form part of its repertoire today (e.g. in 2019 directed against water companies; in 2020 against the biggest plastic polluters such as Coca-Cola).

What several interviewees did indicate, though, was a stronger emphasis on less confrontational modes of influence-seeking (i.e. insider strategies) as the organization professionalized. This has not only been reflected in the changing tone of its communication but also in a more sustained engagement in less controversial, public-facing activities such as public education and public consultations, supported by the CSO's enhanced organizational capacity. Early attempts to strengthen its engagement in public education did not take off until the organization was more professionalized. In the late 1990s and early 2000s, SAS tried to engage in educational work by creating a charity linked to its main organization, the 'Clear Water Initiative' (which would have allowed SAS to benefit from charitable benefits without the main organization's political activities being legally constrained). As stressed by staff in charge at the time, this attempt to branch out failed because the organization found educational activities difficult to reconcile with lobbying: 'it never worked well because we did not really concentrate on it particularly [...] what we wanted to do is to affect government decisions'.[29] By 2002, this 'vehicle' had been removed from SAS's Memorandum of Association.

---

[29] Interview, SAS, 26.05.2017.

While SAS engaged in some educational activities in the 2000s, these activities intensified from 2008 to 2011 after it had changed its leadership structure and staff numbers had tripled. This continued as SAS underwent further growth, with community work including the organization's educational work benefiting from both staff growth and specialization. This was supported by a successively stronger regional infrastructure run by increasingly skilled volunteers (Chapter 6). This 'professionalization' of volunteer staff was conducive to a broadening of education initiatives to raise public awareness regarding environmental issues, which were increasingly coordinated across the UK to maximize their impact on the ground as well as their publicity. The patterns of nationally coordinated local activities also showed with regard to beach cleans, a core activity since the organization's foundation that links collective action, awareness-raising, and public education with the hands-on fight against pollution. Relatedly, efforts towards the implementation of best practices were further strengthened. Examples thereof are the Fat, Oils and Greases (FOG) campaign supported by the national environment agency in 2012 which was directed towards individual-level behaviour change. It also showed in sustained attempts to implement policies related to its new core issue of plastic pollution. This included 'Plastic Free Schools', a pupil-led education programme launched in 2017 and the 'Plastic Free Parliament' initiative of 2018.

Especially in the years following 2012, after SAS had become a charity and had broadened its substantive remit (see below), it intensified available channels to exercise influence on policy. We see a more wide-ranging engagement in research and collaboration as well as public consultations in that period.[30] The range of research initiatives broadened in terms of remit as well as partners. This is illustrated by the SAS report on climate change, a collaboration with the University of Exeter to collect data on health consequences of exposure to marine pollution, or the Citizen Science Pilot Programme, a marine litter–monitoring programme supported by the European Environment Agency. While international collaborations such as with the WWF had existed before, these latter initiatives echoed the reorientation towards more international issues announced by the new executive director in 2008 in their welcome statement. Such activities consequently intensified, alongside the forging of connections to organizations inside and outside the voluntary sector, including the United Nations Environment Team; efforts to enhance the evidence base and credibility underpinning SAS's campaign and to broaden

---

[30] See for a joint project with the University of Exeter, Pipeline News, 2018, 105, p. 39.

226 Civil Society's Democratic Potential

the reach of its lobbying work.[31] This was also important as it enabled the CSO to stress the facts-based nature of its policy solutions, important to SAS's public image.[32]

Relatedly, political activities to shape the environmental agenda became 'higher profile' through collaborations with more established organizations such as the National Trust or the Met Office. In the context of the climate coalition, SAS tried to form part of a bigger wave of protest. Simultaneously, SAS forged links to the business community. With the pro bono support of the managing director of M&C Saatchi, an SAS trustee, 2013 saw the launch of a professional advertisement campaign. Similarly, SAS engaged in several years of campaign work with the Iceland Foods Group, a business supporting SAS financially, whose director became its chair in 2021 (see also Chapter 6).

We also find the enhanced use of public consultations and petitions as a strategy of directly influencing political decision-makers. Petitions, as an online form of participation, naturally aligned with the organization's much enhanced social media presence and formed part of the diversification of involvement channels detailed in Chapter 6. Meanwhile, in 2014, a direct channel for exchange with parliamentarians was formalized. With the creation of the Ocean Conservation All-Parliamentary Group, SAS managed to institutionalize its relationships with national decision-makers. This forum involves MPs across party lines, with SAS acting as secretariat. In this capacity, SAS sets the agenda for meetings and details the group's long-term strategy,[33] thereby establishing regular exchanges with politicians, business leaders, and civil servants about environmental threats and campaigns. These more institutionalized communication channels to parliament were used to engage in substantive work on legislation. This included the joint work with MPs to develop the Bathing Water Bill in 2018 and the Sewage (Inland Water) Bill in 2020.

One interviewee summarized the broader development of the CSO in the following way:

> we don't go out and wear gas masks and carry a giant inflatable turtle around with us so much anymore […] We attend more meetings with politicians. Ministers

---

[31] See on how the organization's remit beyond sewage pollution also increased the need to develop broader expertise, the public lecture by Andy Cummins, SAS Campaign Director on 'The Evolution of Surfers against Sewage', 2012, https://vimeo.com/2,108,158, accessed 17.07.2021.

[32] Andy Cummins, SAS Campaigns Director, Lecture on 'The Evolution of Surfers against Sewage', 2012, https://vimeo.com/2,108,158, accessed 17.07.2021. The Exeter Lectures: Hugo Tagholm, Chief Executive, SAS, May 2016.

[33] See, for instance, https://www.oceanconservationappg.org/, accessed 02.03.2022.

and secretaries of state are interested in what we do and see the credibility, the movement we've created. So we do much more. We've got our own all-party parliamentary group, which is our own vehicle—if not the only vehicle—in parliament as an all-party parliamentary group that specifically talks about ocean conservation, and marine plastics, water quality, and personal development as its specific remit. So we've been able to become more sophisticated rather than being on the outside of the—as it were—corridors of power, which we still do. We'll campaign, we'll do marches, we'll do demos, we'll do all those things. But we can also go inside and we can convene people to talk about why we can protect waves, oceans, beaches, and marine wildlife. Not just for surfers, but for everyone.[34]

This self-characterization finally leads us to the connection between SAS becoming a group serving a broader public interest—effectively broadening its substantive remit—and the diversification of political strategies employed. With that, we have arrived at the dimension of *goal reorientation* and the evolution of the CSO's identity. On its website, SAS portrays the substantive reorientation of its goals as its response to new societal and environmental demands, signaling the CSO's responsiveness to external changes. At the same time, it highlights continuity with SAS's long-term history (that SAS 'remain[s] true to its original mandate'[35]):

Surfers Against Sewage doesn't describe exactly what we do anymore! [...] We've made great progress on cleaning up our beaches from sewage and the cleanliness of our seas remains in the DNA of the organisation. But our new priority issue is marine plastic pollution [...] What has always remained though is our unique identity, shaped by the same forces from which we were borne.[36]

Looking at SAS's charitable purposes, the organization is nowadays dedicated to coastal environmental issues including marine litter, sewage pollution, climate change, toxic chemicals, shipping, industry and coastal development through 'community action, campaigning, volunteering, conservation, education and scientific research'[37]. This is a remit in line with but also significantly broader than its initial focus on the 'stopping of marine sewage disposal'. SAS transformed into a public-facing conservation organization that somewhat distanced itself from the more member-focused pressure group it was in the early years. This change shows in a stronger emphasis

[34] Interview, SAS, 16.06.2017a.
[35] Pipeline News, 2012, 89, p. 3.
[36] https://www.sas.org.uk/about-us/history/, accessed 12.9.2022.
[37] SAS Report and Accounts 2012, Companies House, p. 4.

228 Civil Society's Democratic Potential

on activities such as public education and more wide-ranging and diverse collaborations detailed earlier, as well as a wider portfolio of environmental policies pursued.[38] Nowadays, SAS provides a variety of 'services' or 'goods' to the wider community, as detailed above. Its beneficiaries increasingly transcended even its wider support base. Chapter 6 has shown that internal reforms downsized control of members over internal decisions. Since becoming a charity, legal reporting and transparency requirements serve as alternative accountability mechanisms. They help the CSO to signal to relevant audiences that the organization pursues the interests of a range of beneficiaries, yet remains committed to its core mission. They help to signal the pursuit of a public good to enhance the charity's wider, societal legitimacy.

Patterns of goal reorientation and the evolution of SAS's political action repertoire were closely intertwined. As reflected in the quotation above, SAS has presented the broadening of its mission to a wider range of marine conservation issues as a response to its success in the fighting of sewage disposal, which led the organization to move towards tackling new challenges. However, it is important to remember that in the late 2000s leading figures thought of closing the organization (Chapter 6). This uncertainty created pressure to 'modernize' the organization, structurally and substantively. This process pushed for by SAS management was not uniformly welcomed in the organization. But it went ahead nonetheless and led to a significantly altered organization, in terms of governance structure, goals, and activities.[39]

Both political engagement and goal reorientation benefited from SAS increasingly resembling a professionalized voluntary organization. Early on SAS experienced difficulties to reconcile engagement in lobbying with more public-facing influence strategies such as educational initiatives. These difficulties were overcome by the organization's increasing professionalization and bureaucratization as well as (in more recent periods) access to state funding. Enhanced expertise, procedural efficiency, as well as financial capacity strengthened its operations. This broadening of SAS's political activities went hand in hand with the organization reorienting its goals, substantively and, to some extent, functionally. Substantively, it altered its core issue from sewage to plastic pollution, alongside a broadening of its remit in the area of

---

[38] For instance, SAS's #PostPandemicPollution work dealt with rubbish infrastructure in parks as well as pushing for a greater remit for environmental enforcement officers. Pipeline Express No.112—Autumn/Winter 2020, 112, p. 11.

[39] An interviewee described it the following way: '[...] we've had to make sure that we've got all of the systems and are able to cope with modern demands. [...] I think that with any organization, there's always evolution of different phases and stages of how they grow. We're no exception. You have to rise and evolve to the challenges [...]. That's the same whether you're a car manufacturer [...] or a children's charity.' Interview SAS 16.06.2017.

marine conservation. In functional terms, it became more service orientated by expanding its educational and community work. While these changes were considered necessary by managers to maintain the CSO's functioning and enhance its performance, efforts were made to maintain continuity with SAS's core identity in the process.

The Green Party of England and Wales (GPEW)

Similar to the two groups, the GPEW started to increasingly resemble a 'professionalized voluntary organization', yet did so more in terms of its professionalization and bureaucratization than its financial dependencies. Clearly, the relevance to GPEW of direct funding through access to Short Money (granted to opposition parties in the House of Commons[40]) and indirect state resources (e.g. allowances, staff attached to office-holders) grew in absolute terms as the party won more seats on various governmental levels.[41] However, the relative importance of membership fees for the party's budget grew as well. In the decade to 2018, membership income (as a share of the central party's total income) increased by 19.1 per cent, from 25.6 per cent to 44.7 per cent (Thompson and Pearson 2020). While access to indirect funding (e.g. support staff for office-holders) is difficult to quantify, Short Money is not an insignificant source of funding in terms of strengthening the 'party in public office'—whose members ought to be strongly dominated by an orientation towards ensuring re-election—especially as this money is earmarked for carrying out parliamentary business. Clearly, this income source is relevant to the party. Funding losses that followed from the significantly reduced national vote share at the 2017 national election were raised as a concern at the following party conference (Dennison 2017: 132). Nevertheless, compared to the party's income from membership fees (£1,391,630) and fundraising (£1,132,352) in 2021, the Short Money received in 2020/21 of £180,826 constitutes a relatively small amount, underlining the centrality of private income generated from the party's support base.

This is important to mention, as parties' access to state funding tends to be portrayed—at least by party scholars—as particularly pronounced (e.g. Katz 1990; Katz and Mair 1995; van Biezen 2004). That this is not the case makes GPEW not only more comparable to the two groups. It makes all three case studies more representative of the wider sector, as generally only a minority

---

[40] Parties receiving two seats or those receiving one seat plus at least 150,000 votes are eligible.
[41] Short Money income, for instance, increased from 51,300 in 2010/11 to 181,900 in 2021/22. https://commonslibrary.parliament.uk/research-briefings/sn01663/, accessed 10.03.2022.

230 Civil Society's Democratic Potential

of CSOs display a strong dependency on state funding (Chapter 3). It also rationalizes why the following analysis will predominantly focus on the implications of professionalization and bureaucratization as drivers of the party's evolving goal orientation and political engagement patterns.

Starting with the GPEW's *substantive reorientation*, it is well established that political parties strategically adapt their programmes. These processes are strongly driven by inter-party competition (e.g. Meguid 2008), less so by the intra-organizational changes at the centre of this study. Interestingly, the literature has suggested that niche parties such as GPEW are less inclined to adapt their programmatic profile as compared to mainstream parties (e.g. Adams et al 2006), which, to some extent, is challenged by GPEW's programmatic evolution. From the late 2000s onwards, the party underwent significant change, whose specific nature indeed relates to changes in the party system the GPEW operated in. Most crucially, while Labour had moved to the right under Blair's and Brown's leadership (Birch 2009: 55), the Liberal Democrats (traditionally the left-of-centre alternative to Labour) moved into national government with the Conservatives in 2010. Effectively remaining the only credible left-wing alternative in the party system, the GPEW made a significant move towards the left and shifted its message from an environmental to a socio-economic (anti-austerity) message. Distinct from its long-standing post-materialist profile that placed it towards the centre of the ideological spectrum,[42] it made social justice and inequality its primary issues, positioning itself against the Conservative–LibDem government's austerity policies (Dennison 2017: 17–18).

Simultaneously, UKIP polarized the debate around Europeanization and the immigration issue, with Labour taking an ambiguous position. Both UKIP's extremely hostile and Labour's ambiguous stances towards the European Union allowed the GPEW to position itself as a central pro-EU, pro-immigration party before and well after the Brexit referendum, a period during which immigration remained a central issue of contention. By starting to exploit a populist rhetoric not dissimilar to UKIP's, the GPEW managed to effectively appeal to anti-establishment left-wing voters who were frustrated by mainstream parties and unlikely to trust the LibDems after their decision to enter into coalition government with the Conservatives (see for a detailed analysis Dennison 2017: Chapter 2).

---

[42] 'People' was founded in 1972 by former members of the Conservative Party and throughout the 1980s stressed its 'neither left nor right' orientation before slowly moving to the left (Wall 2010: 110; 113). At the 1989 national election, some 60 per cent of those voting Green had previously voted Conservative, Liberals, or Social Democrats (Rootes 1994).

CSO Goal Reorientation and the Evolution of Political Engagement **231**

Clearly, to understand the GPEW's programmatic evolution as a minor party, its relations to its major competitors were key. However, organizational professionalization and bureaucratization (that effectively enhanced the centralization of decision-making, see Chapter 6) still played a facilitating role in the reorientation process just described. They made easier strategically motivated, significant programmatic reorientations that the party leadership—increasingly including career politicians surrounded by professional staff—considered electorally beneficial, even if doing so faced opposition from long-standing activists.

As highlighted by earlier case studies, Caroline Lucas, the party's first national MP and leader, was one driving force of the party's reorientation towards economic issues (Dennison 2017: 15). This is important as the more pronounced economic orientation of the GPEW was contested, especially amongst longer-term members. Green members traditionally saw the environmental movement as their natural constituency. The majority considered themselves as non-socialists (as did members of the green movement) or non-leftist. Ties to social movements were weak (McCulloch 1988: 195; Rüdig and Lowe 1986; Doherty 1992a). Consequently, some long-term members felt the organization's core issues were 'sidelined'. Others even considered the new direction as evidence of the former 'Ecology Party' having been hijacked (Dennison 2017).

Two organizational developments nevertheless facilitated the party's leftward shift. Traditionally there was no systematic development of an eco-socialist perspective in the UK, and radical ecologism tended to be weak (McCulloch 1988: 195; Rootes 1994: 59). Still, 2006 saw the formation of the *Green Left*, 'a network for socialists and other radicals' inside the party and 'as an outreach body that will communicate the party's radical policies to socialists and other anti-capitalists outside'.[43] Leading figures in this group that aimed for the party's move to the left included Derek Wall, Principal Male Speaker of GPEW up to 2007 and opponent to the move to single-party leadership (Chapter 6). Though this socialist current lost the latter battle,[44] it started to exercise increasing influence within the party (Schwartzman 2008: 247; Wall 2010; Dennison 2017). Furthermore, by 2013, traditional, predominantly ecology-oriented party members were outnumbered by a younger generation of members more concerned about left-wing politics (Dennison 2017: 76), a process that had started already in the late

[43] https://web.archive.org/web/20,150,519,182,648/http://www.thegreenleft.co.uk/history.html, accessed 10.03.2022.
[44] Shaughnessy, M., 12 March 2015, 'Britain: A short history of the Green Left current within the Green party', http://links.org.au/node/4335, accessed 10.03.2022.

232 Civil Society's Democratic Potential

2000s (Birch 2009: 12). Reflecting these developments, in 2013 the majority of party members embraced a new preamble to the GPEW's constitution that committed the party to the 'transformation of society for the benefit of the many not the few', a change that highlighted that this shift was not just a 'tweaking' of the party's traditional message (Dennison 2017: 16).

This reorientation towards economics responded to grievances of significant parts of the party's membership and its wider support base. But it also formed part of a strategic attempt of the party leadership to exploit the opportunity that had opened up in the UK party system of the late 2000s to systematically broaden its left-wing oriented support base in terms of voters.

From the perspective of the central party organization, the GPEW's substantive reorientation was directed towards overcoming two long-lasting stereotypes that held the party back as an electoral force: namely that the GPEW is a single-issue party only concerned with the environment[45] and, closely tied to this image, that it could not win elections. It was these stereotypes that leading figures like Lucas and Bennett (former party leader and member of the House of Lords) as well as high-profile candidates in the run-up to the 2010 election tried to proactively overcome (Dennison 2017: 15–17).

A few years later it became evident that the party's substantive reorientation was no simple reflection of intra-organizational changes shifting the party organization leftward. Instead, it was shaped by strategic considerations. Attempts to broaden its support base especially amongst anti-establishment, left-wing, libertarian voters paid off in 2015, when the party more than quadrupled its vote share at the national election compared to 2010 (0.9 per cent) and won (with 3.8 per cent) its best ever result at a national election (Carter 2015: 1055, 1058–9; Dennison 2017: 120–1). When Jeremy Corbyn had taken over the Labour Party in 2015, however, the GPEW lost its position as the only 'truly left-wing' alternative to austerity politics (by the time the LibDems were back in opposition). As a consequence, after suffering significant electoral losses at the 2017 national election,[46] the GPEW put a renewed emphasis on the environment (Dennison 2020: 133–5; Carter and Pearson 2020). Furthermore, while the Greens had in 2017 the most left-wing election manifesto, its 2019 manifesto showed the biggest rightwards movement in the party system. This positioned the party to the right of both Labour

---

[45] The perception of being a single-issue party, GPEW had already tried to overcome in the 1990s, trying to develop and campaign on a green social agenda (Burchell 2000: 148–9), though with limited success.

[46] Its vote share declined to 1.6 per cent in 2017.

and SNP (Allen and Bara 2019: 6; 2021: 7), which again paid off as the party recovered its vote share from 1.9 per cent in 2017 to 2.7 per cent in 2019.

In sum, earlier intra-organizational shifts towards eco-socialism had facilitated a significant substantive reorientation of central party goals towards an economic agenda, but it did not underpin a lasting reorientation 'from below'. Once GPEW had lost its niche as *the* 'anti-austerity party' in the UK, the GPEW showed considerable flexibility to strategically shift back towards environmental issues such as climate change (Dennison 2020: 134). Such display of programmatic flexibility clearly expresses the party leadership's and central staff's determination to maintain the party's electoral performance.

This has brought us to the more fundamental, long-lasting conflict over GPEW's *functional orientation* that has plagued the organization since its inception: the question whether electoral aspirations ought to be its primary goal in the first place. We saw that the party's professionalization is best conceived as a factor favouring programmatic flexibility and thus facilitating substantive reorientations, rather than a driver. In the conflict over its functional goal orientation, the GPEW's changing governance features played a more direct role. These changes impacted on the balance of power between those aiming for electoral success—a group heavily populated by organizational leaders and a growing number of central-level managers—and those preferring a focus on societal activism—predominantly members and volunteer staff active on the subnational level. The conflict between these two groups tended to find expression in divisions over structural reforms, whose implementation would directly impact on each group's ability to shape party activities and processes in their favour.

Conflicts between 'electoralists' and 'decentralists', 'pragmatists' and 'radicals' or 'realists' and 'fundamentalists' have plagued a range of Green parties in Europe, especially in the early stages of their development (e.g. Doherty 1992a; Kitschelt 1989; Poguntke 1993; 2002). In electorally more successful Green parties, this conflict tended to be settled in favour of an electoral orientation. Given the limited electoral success of GPEW, such development has not occurred. The observation that Burchell made in the early 2000s still holds today: namely that since its foundation, the party has been divided over its 'primary goal' (2002: 122).[47]

Relatedly, McCulloch argued already in 1983 that 'different individuals involved in the party have different views of what the party is, how it should be organised, and in what activities the party should involve itself [...]

---

[47] It also meant that despite a range of excellent case studies on GPEW's evolution having been published over the years, the repercussions of this divide has not yet been systematically analysed from its foundation until today.

234 Civil Society's Democratic Potential

the EP can be best understood in terms of these two tendencies and the conflict between them' (1983: 1). To capture these two rival tendencies, McCulloch distinguished a traditional, electorally oriented model of party organization from an alternative model of an organization that—albeit running elections—places more emphasis on societal work employing a 'community and network approach to political organising' directed towards consciousness-raising, education, and personal development (1983: 2; 15; 1992: 424–5). Over time, with the growing prominence of features of the 'professionalized voluntary organization' in GPEW, the balance within the party organization somewhat shifted towards the 'traditional model', with electoral aspirations at its core. Nevertheless, McCulloch's analytical lens to view the evolution of the party in terms of the intra-organizational divide between electorally oriented 'centralists' and campaign-oriented decentralists still applies.

Looking at early conflicts, campaign-oriented decentralists tended to hold the upper hand, as the party was essentially a volunteer-run organization. Many early activists came out of pressure groups and were concerned with affecting social change (McCulloch 1983: 18). Successes of the electoralists in altering the intra-organizational balance of power in their favour tended to be short-lived. In the mid-1970s, only a few years after its formation in 1972, leading party members withdrew from active involvement after intense ideological conflict, allowing a new generation of leaders to take over. This new generation had a more pragmatic outlook and 'understood the party's function in purely electoral terms'. They tried to give the party a national image, including a new logo and new statutes. This led to the party's 1979 electoral success, which was followed by a surge in the party's membership (Rüdig and Lowe 1986: 266–7; 274, see also Chapter 6). Nevertheless, the party remained divided over whether to participate in elections at all (Doherty 1992b: 293) and the balance shifted back in favour of the decentralists soon after. Attempts in 1980 of the national council (NC)—the organ running the organization in between conferences at the time—to professionalize the organization not only failed but backfired, leading to the curtailing of the NC's powers to the point of withdrawing its right to present proposals to the party's conference. As described in a party publication in 1981:

> the annual conference again chucked out the proposal to elect a leader; chucked out a second attempt to lift the three-year limit on holding office; rejected all the National Council proposals to amend the constitution; took away from the National Council the right to make proposals to conference.[48]

---

[48] Undercurrents, 1981, No. 44 (Feb–March: 45) cited in McCulloch (1992: 435).

CSO Goal Reorientation and the Evolution of Political Engagement 235

In the mid-1980s, the chair of the NC (an organizational leader) and the former general secretary—essentially the party's first paid manager—initiated another constitutional reform to streamline the party organization and to enable a more effective leadership. Also this attempt failed and ended with these figures leaving the party. The electoralist wing was heavily discredited in the process, which considerably strengthened the decentralists in turn, because a 'contingency plan' of the electoralists had surfaced in the process. The latter intended—in case the reform would fail—to form a 'private society', which was envisaged as organizationally separate from the party, with its own staff and own policies, which effectively would have split the organization (McCulloch 1983: 18; 1992: 421–2; 430).

Again, things turned (for a brief period), following the electoral success of the 1989 European election. This success allowed the party to hire six full-time staff and enhanced the central leadership's capacity to develop policies. These included an important reform initiative—'Green 2000'—that a group of electoralists including Caroline Lucas actively lobbied for. This reform aimed to create a stronger leadership and a more centralized organization, but actually split the party into two hostile factions (Doherty 1992b: 293–5). Having been initially defeated in 1990, a renewed attempt to pass the reform was made fourteen months later and was successful (McCulloch 1992: 422).[49] As detailed in Chapter 6, it altered the party's leadership organs by creating a national executive (GPEx) that was directly elected by members (which did not exist before) alongside a regional council (GPRC) (which replaced the NC) and removed conference voting rights from rank-and-file members to delegates. Furthermore, the number of its 'principal speakers' was reduced from six to two, while no limits were put on the number of years that executive office could be held. The notable success of the electoralists led key party figures to leave the organization, this time from the decentralist camp (Doherty 1992b: 296–7; Burchell 2000: 145; 2002: 120–3; Faucher 2000: 494; Carter 2008: 232–4; Bennie 2016: 207.

While major elements of the reforms of the early 1990s are still in place today, leading proponents were either dismissed or resigned soon after its implementation. Paradoxically, the newly created regional council (which represented local activists) was used by reform critics against the leadership to obstruct decision-making (Burchell 2000: 145). Almost the entire party leadership resigned as members mobilized against further attempts to turn the CSO into a more election-focused organization. With the party in disarray, the party executive elections in 1992 were consequently won by

---

[49] Despite a highly polarized debate, less than 20 per cent of the membership took part in the decisive vote in 1991 (Doherty 1992b: 295–6).

decentralists (Rootes 1994: 61), and the organization resembled more of an NGO in the subsequent years (Dennison 2017: 14; Burchell 2002; Prendiville 2015). By the end of the decade, in 1999, following a period of disarray during which decentralists were in charge, the number of staff had been reduced to less than three, and the provision to introduce a delegate conference was reversed, only to be reversed again later (see Chapter 6 for details).

In terms of the party's ongoing conflict over its primary goal, still in the late 2000s the GPEW viewed, according to experts:

> elections, representation and even parties somewhat askance, preferring rather to engage in grass-roots consciousness raising activities long after Green parties elsewhere in Europe have reconciled themselves to working within the existing political system [...] No small political organisation can successfully pursue two radically different goals. (Birch 2009: 68)

The pendulum, however, had already started to swing back again at this point as the party started to professionalize from the mid-2000s onwards, while gaining parliamentary representation on various levels of government, notably in the European Parliament (EP), the Scottish Parliament, and the London Assembly. As detailed in Chapter 6, in 2007 the party finally overcame long-standing resistance against being run by a party leader and deputy instead of several 'speakers' (McCulloch 1992: 435). The party fought heavily over moving towards a more election-focused single leader model, favoured by the electoralists around Caroline Lucas, who eventually won the necessary internal referendum (Rüdig 2008: 199; 216; Dennison 2017: 43). Its professionalization had helped to shift the balance in favour of the electoralist camp. Both a growing number of paid staff in central office and Green politicians within the central leadership had become more influential in the organization over time, two groups of actors whose professional careers depend on the GPEW's electoral performance. This, however, did not mean that the 'drawnout internal process of crisis and reform [...] came to an end', as argued, for instance, by Prendiville (2015: 4) and the conflict over the party's functional orientation was finally settled in favour of electoral politics.

In recent years, the traditional divide between (predominantly) centrally located electoralists and local decentralists (Rüdig and Lowe 1986: 277) did not only resurface in the drawn-out process reform process around the 'Holistic Review' reform attempt (Chapter 6). In the run-up to the 2015 national election, the national campaign director of the party tried to implement a uniform electoral strategy on local parties. In response, he was banned by the local party of Bristol West from physically entering the constituency after the latter withheld information from the central party, refusing to give up control over its local campaign. The local party's insistence on its autonomy was later backed up by the party's executive reconfirming the party's commitment to decentralization, at the cost of a coordinated electoral strategy (Dennison 2017: 46; 100). Hence, electoralists have at times won some crucial battles. Yet the issue is far from being settled for good. A quote by the national campaign director cited by Dennison (2017: 48) strikingly echoes McCulloch's depiction of the organization's internal divide presented over thirty years earlier[50]:

> The party's almost split in two. There are quite a few people within the party that in their heart of hearts would still like to be a campaign pressure group. And it kind of winds me up, actually, because I keep hearing every now and then that there are ways to affect change other than through winning elections. That's fine and that's true. Go join Greenpeace. Because we are a political party, this is what we do. We win elections, and that's how we affect change.

With a leading manager's complaint about divisions over the political activities the party ought to engage in, we arrive at the last part of this case study concerned with GPEW's evolving political action repertoire.

As a partisan organization, GPEW was politicized from the start. It engaged in political activity regularly and did so using both insider and outsider strategies. While in the early 1980s many constituency organizations engaged in (conventional) electoral activities, the majority also engaged in campaigning activities unrelated to elections. Many members saw the party as having an important educational role and as helping to unify people who had been involved in ecology-orientated single-issue campaigns. Though engaging with elections, they did not predominantly aim for an involvement in traditional electoral politics (McCulloch 1983: 8, 11). While some constituency organizations cared more about consciousness-raising activities to affect social change, some more about election-related activities, the organization overall engaged in a wide range of political activities aside from running elections. More specifically, constituency organizations encouraged conventional and unconventional forms of participation of members and supporters, including public consultations, the issuing of press releases, as well as

---

[50] More recently a party activist described the division in the following way: 'There is a conflict between members in the party who want a "professional" and exclusive party, much like New Labour, and members who want the Green Party to be radical and democratic—where all members can get involved in decision-making.' https://leftfootforward.org/2019/01/new-reforms-threaten-the-green-partys-internal-democracy/, accessed 08.08.2021.

238 Civil Society's Democratic Potential

protest activities to influence public opinion, formal and informal cooperation with non-party organizations, and educational activities (McCulloch 1983: 11–16; Rüdig and Lowe 1986). This aligns with an assessment of party newsletters covering 1974–90. It indicates that sustained engagement in activities directed towards public institutions and the political process (e.g. electoral activities, seeking media attention for core issues) and those directed towards society (e.g. educational work, activities with like-minded organizations) were relatively balanced.

This is not a matter of course and one might have expected a stronger orientation towards elections, since, unlike other Green parties in Europe, the GPEW neither grew out of social movements nor did it have close connections to a strong anti-nuclear movement or leftist groups (Rüdig and Lowe 1986: 269–71, 278; McCulloch 1983; Doherty 1992a). Yet many members and activists had been involved in environmental organizations and pressure groups prior to joining (Rootes 1994: 63), and leading party members continued their activities in environmental organizations after leaving GPEW.[51] Despite these affinities, repeated attempts to establish formal links with environmental groups had failed.[52] Radical aspirations were pronounced in some local branches. But the GPEW has never been a 'party movement' similar to other members of the Green party family such as the much studied German Greens—neither organizationally nor behaviourally (Rihoux 2016: 301–2).

As detailed in Chapter 6, the party only developed a solid staff base from the late 2000s onwards, by when it had grown to six staff, staff who could as a consequence of such growth be dedicated to particular areas. By then, the party executive was functionally differentiated into offices, several of which dealt with political domains such as elections, campaigns, and policy development. This was echoed by its human resource base, which diversified from five basic categories in 2008 (management, elections, administration, finances, and young greens) to eight categories in 2021. At that point, the party also had staff specializing in fundraising and staff to support local parties, which are electorally central as they control candidate selection. Though finances improved in 2019 and staff spending went up compared to 2018, two staff categories were removed, the ones dedicated to policy and the

---

[51] Paul Ekins, Sara Parkin, and Jonathon Porritt, all three high-profile electoralists who left the party in the context of failed reform aspirations, became principal founding members of prominent environmental think tanks, the New Economics Forum in the early 1980s (Ekins) and the Forum for the Future formed in 1996 (Parkin and Porritt) (Prendiville 2015).

[52] Environmental interest groups had already set up channels to the government of the day. They worked 'from within the system' and were disinclined to enter the electoral arena which might have upset established modes of exercising political influence. Generally, British environmentalists tended to resort to direct action when considered tactically necessary to attract the attention of government, yet were not committed to it as a form of grass-root democratic participation (Rootes 1994: 57–9).

young greens. Instead, election-related posts were strengthened, as this year saw elections on the local, national, and European level. This suggests that while professionalization enhanced the party's overall capacity for political engagement, increasing staff specialization in the central organization particularly benefited election-related activities. This again underlines a stronger orientation of leaders and managers towards elections.

That said, the central tailoring of resources is only one part of the picture. It does not address the question of how the conflict over the organization's primary goal fed into the evolving nature of the party's overall political action repertoire. Did the party's increasing professionalization and bureaucratization lead to a focus on election-related and partisan activities *at the expense of* outsider strategies and unconventional participation?

As already alluded to, in many ways, one would have expected the GPEW to distance itself from confrontative, more controversial engagement in the societal arena more easily than other Green parties in Europe. Unconventional participation was not in the same way a constitutive part of the organization's 'genetic imprint'. This was the case even though early members sought to engage differently in politics, including electoral politics, from conventional political parties. (McCulloch 1983). Available newsletters spanning the period from 1974 to 1990 confirm this. Direct action as an unconventional form of participation was regularly used in the party, especially between the mid- and late 1970s (though civil disobedience appears only once in 1975). However, considering the overall patterns, election-related activities were already more prominent, followed by attempts to seek media attention, the arranging of and participating in debates and workshops, educational work, and cooperation with like-minded organizations. In comparison, reference to direct action was made less consistently than to other activity types and was prominent in a few specific party branches rather than the overall organization.

This is in line with existing in-depth studies of the party. They reveal that the question whether or not to engage in non-violent direct action was an issue of contention even in the very early years. In essence, such forms of participation were considered at odds with the party's aspiration to become a more successful electoral force. The electorally orientated leadership group running the party from the mid- to late 1970s (who mostly left the party after the major clash in the early 1980s detailed above) rejected 'any involvement in non-violent direct action and similar tactics', as it might compromise the party's image from the perspective of voters.

Similarly, while the party in principle supported the activities of protest groups concerned with issues around transport or nuclear power, such

240 Civil Society's Democratic Potential

support remained informal. Only in 1981 did the party explicitly come out in favour of non-violent direct action, coinciding with a backlash of the decentralists against a reform attempt of the party's electoralist central leadership (Rüdig and Lowe 1986: 272–5). That the GPEW remained a marginal actor during the Anti-Poll Tax campaign, a widespread campaign of civil disobedience in the late 1980s, is indicative of its ambivalent stance towards unconventional participation. While being officially opposed to the tax, the party was unwilling to unambiguously endorse non-payment. Hence, while some local parties and members became actively involved, the party overall gained much less prominence than the smaller Socialist Workers' Party (Rootes 1994: 59–60). A bit later, 'Green 2000' reform proposals pushed for by the electoralists in the early 1990s again declared that the party should play 'a specialised role as the political wing of the green movement'. This meant 'concentrating on electoral activities' (Doherty 1992b: 293), a development that was stopped soon enough by internal resistance (see above). Doubts over whether focusing on elections rather than alternative campaign tools was the right way to go remained virulent throughout the 1990s. Consequently salient concerns around BSE (i.e. mad cow disease) or genetically modified food could not be capitalized on by the party but were dominated in the media by movements and protest groups (Burchell 2000: 149–50).

Moving to more recent years, did the stronger position of central leaders and managers since the late 2000s change matters and lead to a more sustained engagement in political activities to enhance the GPEW's influence in national politics? Vice versa, did this lead to a renewed distancing from unconventional politics? The answer to the first question is yes; to the second it is no. GPEW's professionalization (and the bureaucratization reforms that came with it) did not support a narrowing down of the GPEW activity range in favour of conventional, less confrontational methods, substantiating the statistical findings presented earlier.

Starting with the first question, at least in one political activity directed towards enhancing its influence in national (institutional) politics the party engaged in more successfully. It concerns the cooperation with like-minded parties. Generally, incentives towards inter-party cooperation between the smaller players are pronounced under First Past the Post systems that strongly benefit bigger parties. This remained the case even after 1999 when the party started to profit from elections under Proportional Representation on the European and regional level. Early attempts towards cooperation with other—ideologically close—minor parties (e.g. to run joint candidates in some constituencies and to develop joint policy initiatives) had been of limited success. They had triggered intense internal conflict, without generating the expected benefits in terms of national influence (Burchell 2000: 147–8). In contrast, from the national election of 2015 onwards the GPEW engaged in strategic standing down of candidates in constituencies where competition with ideologically similar rivals risked splitting the vote in favour of a major (and therefore from the GPEW's perspective much less desirable) competitor (Carter and Pearson 2020). The strategy was controversially debated at the autumn conference of 2017. Some critics considered it as a reason for the considerable vote losses at the 2017 elections. Yet Caroline Lucas—the party's co-leader at the time—defended it as having prevented a Conservative majority. In 2019, the party forged again a—now more formal—'United to Remain' alliance with the Liberal Democrats and Plaid Cymru, giving the party a free run in eight constituencies, while standing down in forty-three (Dennison 2020: 132–3, 135–6). Hence, while attempts to join forces with other minor parties are not new, we see a more sustained engagement in such cooperation as the party organization professionalized and became more electorally orientated.

Moving to the flipside of the coin, whether GPEW simultaneously distanced itself from unconventional participation, party research would expect this to happen overall. Increasingly professionalized and electorally oriented parties face strong incentives to moderate, not only programmatically but also behaviourally (e.g. Panebianco 1988; Katz and Mair 1995; 2009; Poguntke 2002; McGrane 2019; for critical perspectives see Moens 2022; Aula and Koskimaa 2023). In contrast, the theoretical framework presented earlier suggests that organizations which increasingly resemble the 'professionalized voluntary organization' should lead a CSO to diversify and broaden its political influence strategies. If so, this should also benefit more confrontational strategies.

Considering the GPEW's highly decentralized structure, professionalization, bureaucratization, and state funding can be expected to predominantly affect the operation of central party representatives and the central party as the organizational layer, where electoralist aspirations have traditionally been most pronounced (Rüdig and Lowe 1986: 275; McCulloch 1988: 192, Dennison 2017). *Ceteris paribus*, leading national representatives, e.g. organizational leaders, candidates, and public office-holders, face the strongest incentives towards moderating tendencies in actual political behaviour. They enjoy most media attention and should aspire to be taken seriously as professional politicians by the wider public. Consequently, the most critical test of arguments around the link between professionalization and moderation should focus on the party in central office, including its public representatives.

The GPEW had already started to gain some public exposure when winning seats in the EP and in the devolved assemblies from 1999 onwards. However, 2010 clearly constituted a critical juncture when winning its first and to date only seat in national parliament. Naturally, the media would focus on Caroline Lucas, the party's former leader and MEP, who won and repeatedly defended that seat against the odds of a First Past the Post system.

So how did central figures in the GPEW position themselves towards unconventional participation since then? As the GPEW underwent a process of accelerated professionalization, it deliberately cultivated an anti-establishment image as part of a vote-maximizing strategy (Chapter 6). The Green Left, the party's socialist current, had already committed itself in its launch statement in 2006 to 'work to enhance Green Party contributions to demonstrations, marches and other solidary events', to 'agitate, educate and organise'.[53] Despite being at odds with the electoralists dominating the central party on a range of issues, the latter's vote orientation and the former's inclinations towards direct political action started to align as the party became electorally more ambitious.

Not only did leading electoralists employ populist, anti-establishment rhetoric (Dennison 2017: 28–9; Dodsworth 2017), leading figures actively embrace 'direct action' (Thompson and Pearson 2021). Paradoxically, following a more strategic and centrally coordinated course not only meant more centrally run election campaigns, which clashed with long-standing organizational traditions of local autonomy. It also meant an endorsing of 'direct action' from the top down, as doing so aligned with the vote-maximizing strategy aimed at overcoming the party's 'single-issue image' and helped to highlight the party's economic stances through active involvement in (non-election related) campaigns and protests. Caroline Lucas, who had been firmly located in the electoralist camp of the party since the early 1990s (Doherty 1992b: 294), not only declared herself a 'socialist', she took part in numerous demonstrations against the government's austerity policies, including the initiative 'People's Assembly Against Austerity', which acted against the first Green Party–run council, Brighton & Hove City Council, as the latter was forced to implement public spending cuts opposed by the party. One of her first acts as a new Member of Parliament in 2010 was to speak at a public meeting in solidarity with Greece in the context of the sovereign debt crisis (Wall 2010: 111). She was reprimanded by the House of Commons for campaigning in parliament (Dennison 2017: 16). In 2014, Jenny Jones, a

---

[53] https://web.archive.org/web/20,150,519,182,648/http://www.thegreenleft.co.uk/history.html, accessed 10.03.2022.

Green member of the London Assembly, was arrested at an Occupy London protest, while in 2018 the party's leadership and representatives participated in anti-fracking protests. In 2022, former party leader Natalie Bennett spoke at the #StopTheRot campaign to protest against rights-restrictive legislation passed by the UK government. This emphasis on connecting party and protest politics was underlined by recruiting high-profile activists as electoral candidates.[54]

The 'official' endorsement of unconventional participation can be further illustrated by the activities that the central party advertised in news releases online to members, supporters, and the wider (sympathetic) public in the recent period. Using the same coding scheme on political activity types applied to other publications (see also Chapter 3), this analysis specifically looked at which activity type the headlines of 3533 party online press releases referred to in order to motivate viewers to click on and read the whole article. Available releases covered a period of fourteen years (24 July 2008–25 July 2022). Reflecting the prominence of electoralist aspirations in the central party, the majority of headings referred to electoral campaigning and other partisan or political information (e.g. the critique of rival parties or government and GPEW's central policies and achievements inside and outside public office). Their prominence ranges from 60.3 per cent (2008) up to 90.3 per cent (2012) (the average over the whole period was 87 per cent). Simultaneously, we find regular reference to political activities commonly associated with movement or interest group politics such as different forms of direct action, issuing research reports, and cooperation with other (non-party) organizations spanning the period.

Leaving the dominant election-related/partisan/political news category aside, it is insightful to compare the relative prominence of legal direct action and civil disobedience as unconventional modes of participation to the remaining activity categories (e.g. participate in public consultations, publish analyses/research reports). Over the period, the former were mentioned on average in 3.7 per cent of the press release headings, and only in two years were they not mentioned at all (2020 and 2021). This may not sound particularly prevalent, but amongst the thirteen remaining categories these unconventional forms of participation were most frequently or second most frequently referred to in eight of the fourteen years. Generally speaking, the regular emphasis on the party's involvement in protests challenging conventional politics (alongside other engagement in the extra-institutional

---

[54] In 2010, the party nominated the human rights campaigner Peter Tatchell and the former director of Friends of the Earth Tony Juniper, both of whom have been active campaigners outside the electoral arena.

sphere) can be read as an attempt of the central party organization to present GPEW as an active participant in the societal arena. Noticeably, protest activities were the most frequently advertised activity types in 2009 and 2014, years leading up to general elections, as well as in the election year 2019 (elections took place in December).[55] This implies that participation in protests—rather than being avoided in strategically critical phases—provides a means to gain the attention of potential voters less receptive to tradition campaigning.[56]

To sum up this last case study, regarding the dimension of *substantive goal reorientation* (or programmatic change as referred to in party research), in its most professionalized phase GPEW showed considerable flexibility to adapt its programme to exploit opportunities that emerged thanks to changed dynamics in the national party system. It carved out an anti-austerity niche by moving towards eco-socialism. When this window of opportunity closed, it re-emphasized its environmentalist orientation. The picture is more complex with regard to *functional goal reorientation*, which did not occur, because the party has for decades remained divided over what its primary goal ought to be. This division remains structurally embedded within a highly decentralized organizational structure that active members are keen to protect. This means that the party did not—as it moved towards the 'professionalized voluntary organization template'—transition from 'movement politics' to electoral politics. The increasing weight of professionals (politicians and managers) shifted the balance somewhat in favour of a stronger electoral orientation. Yet, instead of a reorientation, we see recurrent conflicts over organizational reforms aimed at reinforcing the party's ability to operate more efficiently and professionally. These, however, tend to be frustrated by those in favour of grass-roots politics, at least when it comes to constitutional change and thus the support of a supermajority of members, which allows smaller groups of activists who feel strongly about these matters to block reform attempts. Concerning the party's *political action repertoire*, as the party became increasingly professionalized, its ability to engage in a wider range of activities in a sustained fashion was strengthened. This did not go at the cost of outsider strategies. Instead, the central party publicly endorsed direct action, which members of this camp had avoided and traditionally had been associated with the 'decentralists'. As was the case

---

[55] In 2018 they were as often mentioned as the arranging of debates/holding of press conferences, which were together the two most prominent.

[56] Interestingly, we do not find similar tendencies before the 2017 election. This might be due to the party's temporarily reorientation away from its anti-establishment strategy after Jeremy Corbyn became the leader of Labour.

with SAS, professionalization did not incentivize a narrowing down of the organization's political action repertoire in favour of conventional politics.

Conclusion

The long-term trajectories of the three organizations studied in this chapter substantiate the theoretical arguments presented and tested quantitatively to a considerable extent. Evolving patterns of professionalization—bringing a new group of actors with their own interests and aspirations into organizational life—are clearly relevant to understand how CSOs modified their goals, functionally and substantively. The same goes for the three CSOs' political action repertoires which, as staff numbers grew, became more specialized, and thus influential in a growing number of intra-organizational domains.

The qualitative assessments spanning several decades found significant substantive change in all three CSOs, and in all three, professionalization was a facilitating, if not a driving factor. In the two groups, significant reorientation was considered necessary by those running the organizations—organizational leaders and managers—to ensure the ongoing survival of their organizations—a central concern of these two sets of actors. Regarding both SAS and NAPA, interviewees pointed to worries that their organization might become a 'victim of its own success', which facilitated reform. In all three CSOs, the experience of crisis—financially, in terms of identity or both—were catalysts for change. In none of the organizations such change was uniformly welcomed. While being careful to maintain continuity, both groups' agendas broadened significantly to make their organization attractive to new constituencies. In order to serve more diverse constituencies, they required a broader range of expertise and the capacity to handle a wider range of issues, which were ensured by the organizations' professionalization and the bureaucratization that tended to follow it. The GPEW deviated from this picture insofar as its programmatic reorientation towards economic issues—facilitated by its professionalization—was less a 'negative' response to what was perceived as a crisis by leaders and managers. It was their attempt to strategically exploit a window of opportunity that opened thanks to significant changes in the party system and the national government in charge at the time, an interpretation that was substantiated as the party shifted back to environmental issues later on when circumstances had changed.

All three case studies emphasized the close entanglement of structural reforms and CSOs' evolving goal orientations. This was most evident in the GPEW, where over the course of the organization's history, a divide over the party's primary goal (winning elections and affecting national politics versus achieving change through societal activism) manifested itself time and time again in conflicts over structural reforms. These reforms repeatedly shifted the balance back and forth between electoralists who wanted an organization able to achieve the former (pushing for more efficiency and centralization) and decentralists who preferred an organization designed to realize the latter (favouring a party structure maximizing member control). Electoralists in the central party, where most paid staff are located, pushed for and were strengthened by the GPEW's transition to a 'professionalized voluntary organization'. But the increasing professionalization and bureaucratization of party structures did not allow for this conflict to be finally settled in the latter's favour. One reason is its constitutive set-up. Unlike the two groups, the powers of subnational units are constitutionally enshrined and actively used and defended by activists (i.e. volunteer staff) and members. The centralization of these rights would require the agreement of not only them but a significant part of the party membership who feel strongly about the principles of intra-party democracy and subsidiarity, even though many of them use those rights only occasionally. The fact that candidate selection—essential for the party's electoral success—is controlled locally reinforces the need for the central leadership to ensure the ongoing cooperation of activists and volunteer staff maintaining activities on the subnational level.

In contrast to GPEW, the primary goals of the two groups were uncontested throughout. NAPA has always been focused on service; SAS on advocacy. Nevertheless, we found significant modifications were supported by the two CSOs' professionalization. Essentially, their functional goal orientation became more complex by adding secondary goals. NAPA added political goals to its service mission and broadened its political action repertoire. SAS transformed from a pressure group concerned with sewage pollution to a conservation charity. It nowadays not only deals with a much broader range of marine conservation issues but also engages more widely in educational and community work, two forms of public good provision. Both groups started to resemble 'multipurpose organizations' (e.g. Minkoff 2002; Hasenfeld and Gidron 2005), a shift that allowed them to appeal to wider constituencies and a broader variety of audiences.

Professionalization and bureaucratization driven by managers (Chapter 6) increased the ability of all three organizations to engage in a broader range of activities in a sustained fashion. This included, irrespective of the CSO's primary goal, political activities. In early periods, SAS found it challenging to reconcile educational work with lobbying. Similarly, NAPA stressed the difficulties of reconciling advocacy with service provision. Meanwhile,

GPEW found it more difficult to engage in inter-party cooperation early in its career. In terms of the motivations underpinning these developments, leaders' and managers' shared concerns around the long-term viability of their organization led to investments in different political strategies to simultaneously engage different types of audiences inside and outside the organization to broadly communicate the importance of the organization's goals. While in none of the three organizations state funding has become a dominant income source, the chance to access these funds strengthened attempts by the two groups—especially of managers—to cultivate channels with public authorities. In GPEW, it contributed to an orientation towards electoral success prevalent amongst professional politicians and managers in the central leadership.

There is no evidence that the transition toward a 'professionalized voluntary association' led to a downsizing or moderating of CSOs' political engagement, in fact, the opposite is true, at least in the context of the three cases studied. In SAS—which in the early years was best known for its confrontational strategies (though it employed insider strategies right from the start)—we find a moderation in tone in terms of communication style and a diversification and strengthening of (already used) conventional channels. Yet unconventional methods such as protest have remained part of its repertoire and are still used today. Indeed, one interviewee suggested that in the most recent period, after the group had consolidated its insider status with the creation of the Ocean Conservation All-Parliamentary Group, SAS had become more confrontational. Almog-Bar (2017) observed similar tendencies in human services organizations that started to use outsider strategies more forcefully *after* their relationship with government was well established. We find similar tendencies in the GPEW. The party has traditionally been divided between those on the one hand sceptical of direct action (which might bring the party in disrepute) and focused on electoral performance, and on the other hand those embracing direct action to evoke societal change. However, while undergoing accelerated professionalization and gaining more public visibility through parliamentary representation, extra-institutional direct action was proactively embraced by its leadership, instead of being avoided.

10
Disaggregating the Transmission Belt and the Study of CSOs' Democratic Contributions

This concluding chapter integrates the overall findings—both quantitative and qualitative—presented in this study. This synthesis brings us back to the beginning, to the three normative yardsticks—participation, representation, and societal responsiveness—hence to the overall framework proposed to assess CSOs' diverse democratic contributions. The classical notion of CSOs as a transmission belt assumes that membership organizations can deliver on all three fronts simultaneously. Ideal-typically, CSOs are politically engaged and their leaders are held accountable by an active membership. But this is not what we find in reality. Indeed, as highlighted in Chapter 1, research on parties, interest groups, and non-profits has long been concerned with the challenges confronting CSOs in individualizing societies that rationalize why CSOs fall short of this image. What this study has done to address this important theme is to 'disaggregate' the transmission belt into its basic components, both analytically and empirically. This was essential to theorize and analyse the various discrepancies between the democratic potentials that scholars, policymakers, and the public tend to ascribe to CSOs and the actual and very diverse contributions that materialize on the level of individual membership organizations. Returning to the bigger picture, the overall findings of this study allow me to now review some widespread assumptions about the deficiencies of professionalized voluntary organizations as a 'new form of organizing' in contemporary civil societies and about the virtues of associations as the 'traditional form'. Inevitably, the findings also raise new questions which future research needs to address to further advance our understanding of how organized civil society operates and evolves and how it matters for contemporary democracy.

Civil Society's Democratic Potential. Nicole Bolleyer, Oxford University Press. © Nicole Bolleyer (2024).
DOI: 10.1093/oso/9780198884392.003.0010

The Democratic Contributions of Voluntary Associations and Professionalized Voluntary Organizations: An Overview

Table 10.1 summarizes what, according to the statistical analyses, the five organizational characteristics of the 'voluntary association' and the three characteristics of the 'professionalized voluntary organization' implied for CSOs' 'performance' on the four analytical dimensions used to capture their democratic contributions empirically. To recap, separate analyses dealt with the cultivation of member activism, indicating organizations' participatory contributions to democracy (distinguishing member control over decision-making from member involvement in CSO activities more generally) (Chapter 4), with the organizational accountability of CSO decision-making (whose weakening was captured through the presence and scope of staff control over decision-making) and the cultivation of a stable CSO identity (captured through CSOs' relative propensity to reorient central goals) as two complementary indications of whether organizational behaviour is likely to be responsive to societal concerns (Chapters 5 and 7); and finally, with CSOs' political engagement patterns as indication of their contribution to processes of interest representation (Chapter 8). The 'plus' and 'minus' signs for each variable displayed in Table 10.1 indicate when I found a robust (positive or negative) significant relationship in the respective analysis.[1] Alongside the findings about the central features of the two governance templates, the table also includes findings on four further variables: membership instability, size, age, and CSO type. Drawing on existing research, they were expected to be relevant for membership-based CSOs' functioning and behaviour generally and therefore included in all models.

Most importantly, Table 10.1 shows that nearly all of the characteristics associated with the same governance template relate to the four dimensions in the theoretically expected (i.e. the same) direction. This pattern underlines that each governance template embodies a distinct behavioural logic, as generated by its constitutive features, which incentivizes similar organizational responses with regard to the four dimensions relevant to CSOs' democratic contributions. Comparing the findings across different dimensions capturing CSOs' democratic performance instead, it is noteworthy that the implications

---

[1] To inform a general discussion, the results for staff control do not distinguish between presence and scope of staff control, nor do the results on political engagement distinguish CSO politicization from the breadth of CSOs' political action repertoires (the implications of these two distinctions were discussed in detail in Chapters 5 and 8).

Table 10.1 Summary of the Statistical Findings on How CSO Features Relate to Their Democratic Contributions

Normative Yardstick		Participation		Societal Responsiveness		Interest Representation
		Member Activism		Organizational Accountability of Decision-Making (Absence of Staff Control)	A Stable CSO Identity (Disinclinations against Goal Reorientation)	Political Engagement
	Analytical Dimensions	Member Control	Member Involvement			
Features of the Voluntary Association	Individual Membership		−		+	−
	Orientation towards Member Interests		+			−
	Multi-Tier Structure		+	+		
	Volunteer Staff		+	+		−
	Membership Fees					
Features of the Professionalized Voluntary Organization	Bureaucratization		+	−	−	+
	Professionalization	−	+	−	−	+
	State Funding				−	+
Features Generally Relevant to CSO Behaviour	Membership Instability			−		+
	Membership Size	−	−	−		+
	Organizational Age	+				−
	Being a Party vs. an Interest Group/ Service-Oriented CSO		+			+

Note: Includes only significant effects robust across different model specifications: '−' indicates negative relationship; '+' a positive relationship; cells are empty when there is no robust significant relationship (at least on 0.05 level).

of the characteristics belonging to the same governance template run parallel when looking at their implications for organizational accountability of decision-making and the stability of CSO identities. This substantiates the decision to conceptualize them as complementary indications of the same dimension—the societal responsiveness of CSO behaviour.

Considering the findings across all three normative yardsticks, it becomes clear that neither the 'voluntary association' nor the 'professionalized voluntary organization' is uniformly beneficial or detrimental in terms of CSOs' democratic contributions. This is widely confirmed on the level of individual variables. Of the eight variables forming part of the two governance templates, only one has unambiguous (either negative or positive) implications with regard to CSOs' democratic contributions. Having a multi-tier structure—an association feature—is conducive to member involvement and helps to contain staff control.

More generally, association features only 'outperform' the features of the professionalized voluntary organization in terms of societal responsiveness, i.e. by inviting goal commitment and helping to contain staff control. Applying the representation yardstick instead, CSOs resembling the professionalized voluntary organization 'do better' as they support (rather than disincentivize) CSO political engagement. Moving to the participation yardstick, the picture is mixed. Only CSO professionalization impacts on member control negatively, while none of the other features of either template seem to matter for whether members control decision-making, either positively or negatively. Involvement is unambiguously supported by professionalization and bureaucratization as key features of professionalized voluntary organizations. Association features, except for individual membership, have the same positive effect.

It strengthens confidence in these findings that other features long considered central to organizational dynamics impacted on several analytical dimensions in line with earlier research. Those variables are membership instability, membership size, age, and CSO type. Interestingly, as the features of the two governance templates, all of them except for CSO type have contradictory repercussions for CSOs' democratic contributions. This further reinforces the importance of analytically separating different dimensions of how CSOs might contribute to democracy. Among these variables, membership size, relevant to CSO performance on three of four dimensions, stands out. Only CSO professionalization has more wide-ranging significant effects in the context of the framework overall. Growing size is central to patterns of member activism (hence CSOs' participatory contribution), the organizational accountability of CSO decision-making (hence their societal responsiveness), and political engagement (interest representation). Considering internal dynamics, the bigger the organization, the more passive are its members and the easier it is for member control to be reduced and for staff to gain control over a wider range of domains. This, of course, is much in line with a long tradition of research on the oligarchic tendencies in organizations with a mass membership (Michels 1915).

To some extent, the case studies echoed this by showing that, even in comparatively small organizations, growth constituted an important challenge and catalyst for changes in decision-making procedures. This underlines the pervasiveness of this factor beyond large mass organizations. At the same time, the organizations studied addressed the challenge of growth very differently and showed that especially the (formal) reduction of member control is not inevitable. In GPEW, reforms were stalled as membership votes were not quorate because an insufficient number of members participated in conferences, a problem that was also brought up by SAS management to justify the removal of voting rights from its considerably increased membership. This, however, does not explain why SAS directly transferred voting rights to trustees (essentially a complete centralization of decision-making to the CSO's executive organ), rather than going for an intermediate solution maintaining indirect member control through elected member representatives, for instance. It also does not explain why GPEW, having briefly resorted to such representative structure in the form of a delegate conference in response to its significant growth, moved back to a member conference despite the difficulties related to this format in the context a considerably grown organization. Overall, the case studies indicated that how the challenges of growth are addressed has less to do with 'objective functional pressures' than the prevalent intra-organizational dynamics between members, leaders, and managers and their respective priorities.

Returning to the statistical findings, compared to other variables relevant to several dimensions of the theoretical framework, the implications of growing size for CSOs' democratic contribution were negative in terms of both member activism and the likely societal responsiveness of CSO behaviour. In contrast, political engagement benefited from growth in terms of the diversity of influence strategies that CSOs could afford to invest in (while, interestingly, politicization—whether political activity is enough of a priority to invest resources in to start with—was unaffected by size).

As with membership size, organizational age and membership instability align with distinct analytical dimensions in opposite ways. Importantly, age is the only CSO characteristic that has positive implications for members being directly in charge of decision-making, suggesting that the institutionalization of internal procedures might help to enshrine and protect member rights, as already discussed in Chapter 4. Age further impacts negatively on CSO political engagement, echoing classical arguments about maturing organizations' growing orientation towards selective incentive provision to ensure organizational maintenance (e.g. Panebianco 1988). In terms of membership instability, the analysis in Chapter 5 showed that organizations struggling with retaining or recruiting members show a higher propensity to allow staff to assume responsibility for decision-making. This process of enhancing staff control was illustrated by the case studies, as difficulties in member recruitment and retainment led both SAS and GPEW to professionalize member admissions and their volunteer management, processes that tended to be actively driven by paid staff. Simultaneously, membership instability seems to invite a broader political action repertoire, since the diversification of influence strategies can help to signal the importance of organizational issues to a wider range of members and supporters.

Proposing an 'organization-centred perspective' on CSOs' democratic contributions broadly applicable to different types of membership organizations, this study placed a deliberate emphasis on those organizational features *unrelated to* CSOs' primary goals to account for their internal dynamics and behaviour. Yet, CSOs' activities can be mainly directed towards running elections, influencing public policy, or providing services, three orientations widely used to distinguish political parties, interest groups, and service providers. And clearly, an organization's primary functional orientation does matter. Being a party is, on average, associated with a more involved membership, while parties are, on average, more likely to engage in political activities regularly and in a wider range thereof than groups are.

As highlighted in Table 10.1, being a party is—alongside having a multi-tier structure—the only other variable relevant across several analytical dimensions examined whose significant effects were uniformly positive in terms of CSOs' democratic contributions. This provides evidence towards political parties' special status among membership organizations both as participatory venues and vehicles for interest representation. The positive association between party status and member involvement is particularly important in an era in which parties are generally unpopular and their importance as societal organizations is frequently questioned (e.g. Katz 1990; Biezen 2004; Dalton and Weldon 2005).

That parties are, on average, more likely to be politicized and have a wider political action repertoire than service providers seems obvious in comparison, especially when using service organizations as reference group. This is less the case when contrasting them with interest groups that are, like parties, defined by a political mission (e.g. Wilson 1973; Fraussen and Halpin 2018). The literature on politicization has pointed out that—on the organization level—politicization can become manifest in an organization's goals (denoting intention) and its political action repertoire (denoting behaviour), two aspects that do not always go together (e.g. Zamponi and Bosi 2018). The findings imply that having political goals more consistently translates into sustained political activity in the case of organizations that consider themselves as parties than those that consider themselves as interest groups. If so, (self-declared) parties are more likely to *actually* function as vehicles for political interest representation than (self-declared) interest groups (this is the case even though a significant minority of parties engage in sustained political activity that is not election-related, see Chapter 8).

This line of argument gains weight given parties' (on average) broader political action repertoires, suggesting that parties tend to provide more varied channels into politics. Given the prominence of the notion of parties as 'electoral vehicles' in party research, this is no matter of course either. Instead, this finding complements the well-established characterization of parties as programmatically more broad-ranging organizations than issue-specific interest groups on the behavioural level, again underscoring the central role of parties in contemporary democracies. This is the case despite this study's sole focus on parties' democratic potential 'as organizations', leaving aside—from the start—their important contributions to democracy from 'within government' (Dalton et al. 2011: 6) that parties themselves consider increasingly paramount (Aula and Koskimaa 2023: 5). Relatedly, parties tend to mobilize individual citizens whose voice is commonly considered more relevant (and less problematic) to the democratic process than the mobilization of corporate members (especially firms) (Beyers et al. 2008). This is important as the association feature of individual membership as such has negative implications for both member involvement and for political engagement, which being a party is conducive to.[2]

CSOs as Changing Configurations of Participation and Representation and the Growing Importance of Hybridization

The cross-sectional picture provided in Table 10.1—reflecting an attempt to empirically disaggregate the transmission belt across a wide range of CSOs—

---

[2] See Bolleyer (forthcoming) for a discussion of these findings from the perspective of party scholarship.

is now complemented by an overview of the three case studies' long-term evolution. This overview returns to the six configurations of participation and representation—one of them the 'Transmission Belt Scenario'—formulated at the very start of this study to systematize different CSOs' (likely) democratic contributions (see Table 1.1).

By connecting one of the most abstract elements to the most specific part of this study, we see that only one of the organizations studied in-depth—the GPEW—matched one of the configurations depicted in Table 1.1 throughout its history. Still today it meets the conditions for the 'Transmission Belt Scenario' (member control, political engagement), the category with the most diverse (direct and indirect) potential to contribute to democracy. SAS, an interest group, moved category from the 'Transmission Belt Scenario' to 'Consultative Representation' (member involvement, political engagement) which suggests fewer participatory benefits than in the phase before it had professionalized and bureaucratized. Service-oriented NAPA transited through two categories—the 'Democratic Emulation Scenario' (member control, no political engagement) in the very early years and then briefly the 'Internal Responsiveness Scenario' (member involvement, no political engagement) before also ending up in the 'Consultative Representation' category. Hence, in the course of NAPA's professionalization and bureaucratization, its participatory contribution declined, when considering member control as a normatively more relevant form of member activism. At the same time, however, its contribution in terms of interest representation was enhanced.

Both SAS and GPEW started out as falling under the 'Transmission Belt Scenario' of politically engaged CSOs that grant member control over central decisions. Active members keen to keep direct control over central decisions in the GPEW repeatedly fought off reform attempts to downsize their power, or won such power back through counter-reform. This was the case despite some important shifts of the organization towards a more centralized governance model (essentially leading to the formation of a central organization able to operate as a counterpart to local branches that initially did not exist). Nevertheless, the party has remained in the same overall category throughout its existence, one in which participatory mechanisms keep its political engagement activities responsive, despite professionalization and bureaucratization supporting centralization and having created leeway for staff control.

SAS, in contrast, moved from the 'Transmission Belt Scenario' to the 'Consultative Representation Scenario' by formally removing member control. When this happened, members had already ceased to actively use their decision-making rights, meaning the CSO was already reliant on consultation mechanisms rather than using formal democratic mechanisms central to the 'Transmission Belt Scenario' in practice. Importantly, the (first informal and then formal) move away from the traditional model of a democratically organized CSO did not imply a move towards 'Assumed Representation' in terms of the detachment of the CSO leadership from its membership base. Even though nowadays management tends to dominate decision-making, managers continue to consult those members and supporters who actively contribute to organizational work and activities on the regional and local levels. These supporters care both about the organization's political cause and about being listened to by the central office when policies and activities concern their local areas. However, unlike GPEW activists, they do not seem to want to be formally 'in charge' of decision-making. In the opposite, management's ability to determine the overall strategic direction of the organization is considered central to SAS's success.

Though many studies on CSOs' democratic contributions or benefits would not examine service-orientated CSOs such as NAPA, studying its evolution proved insightful. This case moved from the 'Democratic Emulation Scenario' in the very early years, through a transition stage when it corresponded to the 'Internal Responsiveness Scenario', to end up like SAS in the 'Consultative Representation' category. At its inception, NAPA was not politically active. Moreover, the early period saw attempts to couple member involvement and member control by integrating regional groups and central organization and to co-opt regional members in central governance organs ('Democratic Emulation Scenario'). However, already a few years after its foundation, members made very little use of their formal rights to select the board and shape the CSO's programmatic priorities. Hence, while member control was only formally removed in 2014, for a long period member control had not been exercised in practice. Before NAPA started to become politically engaged in the mid-2000s, the CSO is therefore best placed in the 'Internal Responsiveness' category, characterized by member involvement but not control. Post-2005, when the CSO started to rely on full-time staff, NAPA politicized, despite its primary orientation towards service, which coincided with a departure from regional organization-building. While professionalization contributed to a shift from member control towards 'only' member involvement, it was instrumental to developing the CSO's political role, placing NAPA finally in the 'Consultative Representation' category. NAPA thus illustrated how professionalization can help a social organization to generate political 'voice'.

As with SAS, we do not find tendencies towards 'Assumed Representation' in NAPA but an (increasingly) active and diverse use of consultation mechanisms to solicit feedback from members about its activities keeping the latter involved. Consultations further address concerns of its (by now predominantly corporate) membership around standard setting in the care sector central to NAPA's political activities. Direct forms of consultation are complemented by elements of 'Surrogate Representation' with regard to some beneficiaries. They traditionally include old people and, more recently, people with learning disabilities. While these beneficiaries' ability to voice their interests and concerns can be curtailed, their needs are still experienced by staff working in different care facilities on a daily basis, thereby feeding back into organizational activities.

Both NAPA's and SAS's development (though moving away from the 'Transmission Belt Scenario' by the formal downsizing of member control) indicate that the cultivation of member involvement provides an important alternative mechanism preventing the detachment of a CSOs' leadership from members. Clearly, that both NAPA and SAS—when structurally moving towards the professionalized voluntary organization—ended up in the same 'quadrant' of 'Consultative Representation' does not mean that their political engagement is similar in scale or in nature. But the in-depth analyses of the two case studies—one organization, at its inception, clearly a social one; the other, clearly political— evidence the positive implications of professionalization for both political engagement and member involvement within very different organizational contexts.

Another interesting parallel between the three very different organizations studied in depth is the recruitment of organizational affiliates or activists into leading management posts. This connection between members and paid staff as two supposedly separate groups puts the emergence of staff control—deemed more problematic than mere centralization to organizational leaders—into perspective, an issue to which I will return below. With regard to the two groups (in which members have lost their formal channels to exercise control) it raises the question whether the replacement of managerial leaders by 'outside recruits' without any organizational affiliation would invite a shift towards 'Assumed Representation'. If so, this might displace the informal consultative practices currently assuring the two CSOs' societal responsiveness. The qualitative analyses suggest that this is unlikely if current dependencies between membership base and organizational leadership otherwise remain intact. SAS staff are likely to continue to cultivate informal channels to regional volunteers whose work is essential to maintain a bulk of central SAS activities and whose effective nationwide coordination has become more strategically important to showcase organizational achievements on a national stage. In this sense, its by now institutionalized regional infrastructure maintained by trained volunteers in itself is likely to provide a 'vertical counterweight' against the detachment of management from the CSO's active base. In NAPA, we are likely to find a 'horizontal counterweight' through the board instead. NAPA trustees—different from those of SAS—still tend to bring with them an organizational affiliation as well as knowledge about the care sector. They can be expected to remain keen to ensure that NAPA management remains responsive to the needs of its core constituencies and committed to its core mission. At the same time, the latter constitute a crucial source of expertise for the CSO's small staff team. The resulting mutual dependency between paid and voluntary leadership (i.e. managers and leaders) is likely to contain the risk of staff detachment.

Despite moving away from the classical 'Transmission Belt Scenario', intra-organizational accountability and CSO–constituency linkages in SAS and NAPA have remained intact. This might be ensured through different and less formal channels than anticipated and maybe weaker ones than would be desirable in an 'ideal world'. Meanwhile, in terms of political engagement, this development created benefits as well. These mixed repercussions for democracy of such organizational change away from the traditional 'ideal type' clearly are of wider importance and deserve further study, especially since deviations from the classical transmission belt scenario are less the exception than the rule. Amongst the over 3000 CSOs examined in this study (Chapter 3), we find member control over leader selection and constitutive rules *as well as* regular recourse to political activity (politicization) only in 36.4 per cent. Hence, approximately 36 per cent of CSOs match the notion of the transmission belt to the extent that they function as venues for participation and vehicles of representation at the same time (e.g. Skocpol 2013; Maloney 2012; Lang 2013; Albareda 2018); 14.4 per cent fall short of either of these two benchmarks that are most prominently discussed in existing research.[3] Nearly half, 49.2 per cent, meet only one of two basic benchmarks to start with. This—the most populated category—is the one in which SAS and NAPA are located. As societal individualization in Europe progresses, the number of CSOs that deviate from 'traditional forms' is bound to rise, reflecting the increasing diversity of civil societies and growing pressures towards hybridization in them (e.g. Minkoff 2002; Minkoff et al. 2008; Hasenfeld and

---

[3] For the sake of parsimony, member involvement (often viewed as a 'thin' form of participation) is not considered here. Neither are indications of social responsiveness as the third normative yardstick used in this study. Suffice to say that the share of CSOs meeting basic normative expectations would go down further if additional benchmarks were applied.

Gidron 2005; Smith 2010; Sadiq et al. 2022). While further organizational diversification might make it even more complex to pin down such a development's democratic ramifications, this study suggests that these ramifications might be less problematic than often assumed.

This does not only refer to political engagement, i.e. that more CSOs might end up being politically active in a more professionalized civil society sector. The findings (both quantitative and qualitative) suggested that professionalization and bureaucratization support member involvement. In line with the statistical findings, none of the three case studies evolved into an organization with 'only' passive members (hence two of the six configurations distinguished in Table 1.1 remained unoccupied when tracing the case studies' long-term evolution). None of the case studies suggested a detachment of CSO leaders and managers, as problematized by notions such as 'NGOization', 'astroturf representation', or 'astroturf participation' (e.g. Lang 2013; Kohler-Koch 2010; Maloney 2015; Lits 2020).

Of course, one caveat needs to be highlighted again returning to the influence of an increasing membership size, a factor with widely negative implications for intra-organizational dynamics. None of the three case studies has grown into a large mass organization, likely to reveal the 'pathologies' long highlighted in the literature, such as the growing detachment of professionals underpinned by widely passive members best understood as 'subscribers'. This focus was deliberate, since, numerically, most regionally or nationally active political parties, interest groups, and service providers are relatively small (Chapter 3). This means the findings might travel to the biggest players in the civil society sector to only a limited extent. It also means they are likely to have broader relevance for a wider range of small to medium-sized CSOs constitutive of civil society in established democracies. The widespread disillusionment with CSOs' inability or unwillingness to fulfil their democratic functions might be less warranted, after all. It might be—at least partially—more a result of looking at those cases most likely to disappoint than being a response to what is actually prevalent in the wider civil society sector.

The Professionalized Voluntary Organization: Better Than Its Reputation

These relatively optimistic conclusions about the transformation of organized civil society derived from the case studies are further substantiated by the statistical findings about the two governance templates, when assessed in more detail.

The two association features with the most far-fetching implications are individual membership and reliance on volunteer staff, each relevant across all three normative yardsticks underpinning the theoretical framework of this study. The findings on individual membership (as compared to corporate members) underline the importance of this characteristic that has long been considered as constitutive for 'real' associations, traditionally defined as associations of individual citizens (e.g. Sills 1959; 1968; Smith and Freedman 1972). Yet at odds with normative preconceptions, its repercussions in terms of CSOs' likely democratic contributions were mostly negative. Echoing classical, incentive-theoretical arguments (e.g. Wilson 1973), of the dimensions relevant for CSOs' democratic contributions, individual membership has a significant negative relationship with two: member involvement and political engagement.[4] At the same time, it favours the cultivation of stable organizational identities by disincentivizing goal reorientation, thereby providing a reliable foundation for constituency linkages.

A similar discrepancy showed with regard to CSOs' reliance on volunteer staff. As with individual membership, this factor disincentivizes political engagement, while helping to contain staff control and being conducive to member involvement. Though volunteer staff fares better than individual membership, features associated with the 'voluntary association' have overall less straightforward implications regarding CSOs' actual democratic contributions than one might expect in light of their usually positive portrayal in a range of works. In some sense, one might argue that the finding that individual membership and reliance on volunteer staff (as well as member interest orientation) have significant negative relationships with CSO political engagement offsets the finding that association features help encourage stable identities and support the organizational accountability of CSO decision-making by containing staff control. By pitting engagement in interest representation and societal responsiveness against each other, resembling an association implies that voice in the political process and responsiveness to societal needs might not be easily reconciled. Only multi-tier structure stands out, as mentioned earlier, which unlike any other significant association feature has only positive implications. Facilitating member mobilization,

---

[4] The negative implications for member involvement align with Barakso and Schaffner's insightful study of voluntary organizations in the US (2008). Building on Hirschman's seminal study (1970), they found that citizen associations are less likely to provide internal voice than professional groups because to members of the former, exit is less costly, which reduces demands for participatory channels (Barakso and Schaffner 2008: 203–4).

it not only supports member involvement but also helps to maintain the organizational accountability of decision-making by containing staff control.

With regard to the implications of association features, it is finally noteworthy that dependence on membership fees seems not to matter for CSOs' democratic contributions as conceptualized here, despite recent work finding positive repercussions of this factor for related aspects (e.g. Bolleyer and Weiler 2018; Heylen et al. 2020; Bolleyer 2021a). This finding contrasts with all other theorized organizational characteristics (irrespective of template), each relevant to how CSOs perform with regard to at least two of the three normative yardsticks. The measure used to capture CSOs' dependence on membership fees in the analyses might be one reason for its 'non-effect'. The membership fees variable captures—in line with resource dependency theory (e.g. Pfeffer and Salancik 1978; Nienhüser 2008)—whether a significant dependence of an organization to a particular income source was given or not (Chapter 3). It does not capture the specific proportion of membership fees in a CSO's budget (e.g. Heylen et al. 2020). This, however, does not explain why state funding dependency (operationalized in the same fashion) has significant associations with two dimensions of the theoretical framework, and why the same measure of fee dependence was a significant variable in other analyses of CSO behaviour (Bolleyer 2021a). Hence, while examinations with more nuanced financial measures would definitely be desirable in future research, the respective proxies used in this study seemed to have captured relevant differences in CSOs' financial dependencies in a meaningful fashion.[5]

This is underlined by the case studies, which suggest that the 'non-findings' with regard to CSO membership fees might to some extent rather complement than contradict existing quantitative findings. Heylen et al. found that reliance on membership fees and member influence on CSOs' public policy positions are positively related (2020: 1237). Especially in organizations 'that aggregate and represent the political interests of their members and supporters' (Heylen et al. 2020: 1231), members who strongly care about the political activities of the organization are likely to be vocal, and their voice is likely to gain internal weight from the perspective of a CSO's leadership if member fees are essential for organizational maintenance (see, for a similar argument, Bolleyer and Weiler 2018). This dynamic, however, is likely

---

[5] Note that the dependency measures chosen mitigate problems of reverse causation, as they refer to the budget of the past five years (i.e. current income through membership fees might be higher because an organization cultivates more involvement or invests in a more diverse political action repertoire, rather than membership fees impacting on these activities).

to be less pronounced in membership organizations generally (which members join for all sorts of reasons other than political interest) than interest groups, rationalizing the finding that dependence on membership fees and member control have no significant association. More importantly, the concept and measure of 'member control' used in this study captured members' say over domains central to CSOs' authority structures (e.g. selection of leaders, change of statutes) akin to notions of intra-organizational democracy. It deliberately did not capture control over substantive policy positions. As we saw in the SAS case study, active members might care about their impact on the latter (visible in informal consultations between central organization and regionally and locally active volunteer staff), without necessarily caring about control over organizational governance (which was abolished without triggering resistance). If so, dependence on membership fees might as well increase leaders' concern around member demands. But this will not feed into the granting of member control simply if this is not what members want in the first place (Chapter 2).

Indeed, in all three case studies, membership fees remained an important income source, and maintaining membership numbers remained an important strategic consideration for leaders and managers throughout these CSOs' history. This had implications not only for the nature of member involvement cultivated but also for how CSOs' mission and target constituencies were modified over time. And this was the case despite the fact that in only one of them—the GPEW—did members proactively use their powers to hold their leadership to account and resisted reforms that tried to curtail their rights. The case studies further showed that though financial dependency on members was a relevant consideration of those in charge of running the organization, the fees of rank-and-file members were not the only and not necessarily the main member contribution that CSO leaders and managers were keen to maintain. This observation has broader implications which I return to further below. Here the crucial point is that these observations further rationalizes why dependence on membership fees *in itself* might have appeared in the statistical analyses as less relevant than expected.

Returning to the broader picture and applying the three normative yardsticks of participation, representation, and societal responsiveness to the 'professionalized voluntary organization', the statistical analyses indicated that CSO professionalization and bureaucratization are empirically relevant for all three. Indeed, both impact on all four analytical dimensions used to capture CSOs' diverse democratic contributions. They further shape each dimension in the theoretically expected direction, i.e. in line with the hypotheses derived from the four fundamental trade-offs confronting

CSOs on each dimension: the trade-off between member control and leader autonomy; between efficient as well as expertise-based and organizationally accountable decision-making; between the cultivation of long-term commitment and the maximization of short-term support; and finally between the provision of inwards-oriented selective incentives to members and the provision of collective incentives to external audiences.

Making a comparison across all template features theorized (Table 10.1), organizational professionalization is the characteristic that has the most wide-ranging implications for membership-based voluntary organizations' democratic contributions, followed by bureaucratization, which does not have implications for member control but whose effects parallel professionalizationotherwise.

Focusing initially on the most prominent yardsticks of participation and representation, professionalization is negatively related to member control and positively to both member involvement and political engagement. Similarly, bureaucratization is positively associated to member involvement and political engagement generally, while state funding positively relates to CSO politicization specifically. The qualitative case studies underlined this considerably more positive verdict about these features' implications than is common in the literature. Looking at intra-organizational processes and dynamics in depth, members might have little interest in having a say in decision-making, while managers and leaders might be keen to enhance their autonomy. Neither means that members become unimportant in organizational life. As CSOs increasingly transform into professionalized voluntary organizations, they cultivate a more involved but less powerful (rank-and-file) membership. In terms of decision-making control, these developments favour the influence of those actors actively contributing to organizational maintenance, not only the influence of organizational leaders and managers but also of volunteer staff in key roles. This also means that the formal disempowerment of passive members might be partially compensated by the granting of informal influence to the subset of active members who contribute—from the perspective of leaders and managers—valuable organizational work. They need to be listened to in order to maintain their contributions to the running of the organization and the successful implementation of core activities.

That professionalized CSOs are more forceful advocates as compared to amateur-run associations is already well established. Yet, this is rarely considered a positive. The nature and contents of advocacy are assumed to change as CSOs professionalize, bureaucratize, and rely on state funding. This is associated with institutionalized insider-lobbying that relies less on grass-roots involvement, refrains from confrontational methods, and shies away from controversial issues. This is because confrontational methods might upset government, funders, or donors, external audiences whose ongoing support these organizations are more focused on than pushing for their constituencies' concerns. The argument goes that, while their interest representation activities are more likely to be heard in the institutional arena, they are less likely to provide an authentic voice for, and actively involve, their societal constituencies in political action (e.g. Lang 2013; Maloney 2012; Alexander and Ferndandez 2021).

Bringing together the quantitative and qualitative findings again qualifies such verdicts. For one thing, CSOs with features of the 'professionalized voluntary organization' are more likely to politicize, i.e. engage in sustained political activity to start with. This is most relevant regarding CSOs that are predominantly oriented towards service and do not consider themselves as political as such. They are more likely, in terms of capacity and motivation, to channel their constituencies' interests in the political process, if they can rely on staff, receive state support, and can rely on procedures enhancing skills and efficiency. The case study of NAPA, a service provider, documented this positive connection between increased professionalization and efforts to become a political voice in the care sector, despite this organization not having more than a handful of staff for most of its history. The positive implications of this should not be downplayed, as many service-oriented CSOs are dedicated to meet the needs of marginalized groups who might find it difficult to articulate and proactively advocate for their own interests (e.g. LeRoux and Feeney 2015; Almog-Bar 2017).

A similar observation can be made with regard to the positive relationship between professionalization and bureaucratization and CSOs' political action repertoires, i.e. the propensity to regularly exercise influence through a wider range of channels. This makes it not only more likely that the organization reaches different audiences but also that actual policy change might be achieved (e.g. Halpin and Fraussen 2017). At the same time, tendencies towards engaging in a broader repertoire - as detected in Chapter 8 - could mean a broader repertoire of insider strategies (e.g. lobbying, consultations, research reports) at the cost of controversial or participatory strategies. To address this issue, the qualitative case studies examined the evolving nature of CSOs' political action repertoires. As NAPA's political action repertoire never included either controversial or participatory modes of influence-seeking, the two political organizations SAS and GPEW were the critical cases in that regard. In line with earlier studies, as the two CSOs increasingly resembled 'professionalized voluntary organizations' this benefited political activities targeting the institutional arena. Yet neither organization stopped using protest or grass-roots activism as means to influence politics. On the contrary, key figures in GPEW seem to engage in unconventional participation more visibly in the course of its professionalization. Meanwhile, there were suggestions that SAS became more assertive and confrontational, after having consolidated its 'insider status', a pattern observed by Almog-Bar (2017) regarding service-oriented CSOs. These tendencies need to be examined in a wider range of organizations to assess how generalizable they are. At the least, the statistical findings on the drivers of political engagement in conjunction with the two case studies put into question suggestions that the benefits of professionalization and bureaucratization come at the cost of engagement that is conducive to societal activism.

While the repercussions of the features of the 'professional voluntary organization' in terms of CSO participation and representation are complex, the negative image of 'staff-driven organizations' seems most clearly confirmed when applying societal responsiveness as a separate, normative yardstick. According to the statistical findings, professionalization and bureaucratization show a significant positive relationship with staff control and with a propensity towards goal reorientation. This suggests that in CSOs that resemble a professionalized voluntary organization, the organizational accountability of decision-making is likely to be weakened and a CSO's core identity is more likely to be altered. Both indicate, according to earlier research, an increased risk of societal detachment. Concretely, this might mean activities of interest representation being flexibly adapted in light of the changing public salience of central issues. It might mean the provision of services not tailored to the most urgent needs of constituents but driven by funders' priorities. Yet again, this is not quite the portrayal the case studies provided us with.

Starting with patterns of goal commitment and reorientation, in NAPA and SAS (the two organizations in which the primary goal orientation was not contested as such) we saw that professionalization facilitated the broadening of these organizations' remit in terms of issues, constituencies, and beneficiaries. While diversifying these CSOs' income streams was one important consideration, especially among managers, these changes were also reactions to societal and political changes. Central issues of the early years had been addressed to a considerable extent (e.g. through improved sewage management), while related areas gained in importance (e.g. plastic pollution). The initially aspired and later implemented reorientation of goals was proactively rationalized and communicated by leaders and managers accordingly. The latter showed awareness that moving away too much from their CSOs' core identity as seen by its long-term supporters could have a destabilizing effect. They therefore addressed the tensions between broadening their CSOs' (societal and institutional) support base and maintaining the commitment of more traditional members and volunteers by stressing the consistency and continuity between their traditional priorities and their altered agendas. More generally, the findings indicate that a meaningful linkage can be maintained by an organization's leadership making an effort to convince its more involved members that a reorientation of organizational activities towards different or a wider range of goals is the right thing to do in light of altered circumstances (e.g. Lutz Allen et al. 2013). Responsiveness, then, consists in the leadership knowing to what extent the CSO's identity can change without detrimental effects regarding its traditional support base. Neither the notion of 'goal displacement' nor of 'mission drift' suitably captures the three organizations' long-term evolution. In contrast, they illustrate the pressure on CSO leaders and managers to maintain continuity so as to prevent losing their credibility, especially in the eyes of those members and supporters whose contributions and input the leadership still depends on.

Consequently, the constraints generated by the need to sustain a voluntary membership *as such* continue to operate as CSOs professionalize and bureaucratize. As long as member support is valued, leaders and managers are likely to try not to upset more committed and involved members and to reconcile their needs with changes necessary to exploit emerging opportunities to widen external support. Importantly, for these constraints to operate, a CSO does not have to be politically active. Its members need not be ideologically driven, nor do they need to control decision-making. These observations lead us back to one central claim of this study, namely that the very nature of membership-based voluntary organizations generates fundamental trade-offs. 'Professionalized voluntary organizations' and 'voluntary associations'—representing different configurations of leaders, managers, and members—address these trade-offs differently. But neither template can ever fully resolve them, except of course by transforming into memberless organizations or organizations solely reliant on 'checkbook members' who are only valued for the fees they pay (e.g. Bosso 2003; Jordan 2012; Painter and Paxton 2014; Schlozman et al. 2015).

Clearly, an important question for future research is which membership-based organizations undergo such transformations and why. But it is also important to recognize that changing from a membership model with formal voting rights to one without is no sufficient indication of such transformation. Both SAS and NAPA downsized on member control, but their leadership still tried to keep their members on board when altering organizational objectives to avoid alienation or even resistance. The critical condition of 'being a membership-based organization as such' that continued to constrain CSO leaders and managers despite considerable internal change boiled down to the following: a leadership relying on members and/or supporters for something *other than* fees, something which requires a level of voluntary commitment on behalf of those members and supporters that must be proactively cultivated by those running the organization. This 'something' could be the provision of competent input on how to improve the quality or provision of services offered, as in the case of NAPA; joining a beach clean, as in the case of SAS; or running for public office without a chance of winning, as in the case of GPEW. As alluded to earlier, the dependency on these non-financial member contributions might be one reason why dependence on membership fees *in itself*—unlike all other theorized organizational features—had no implication in the statistical findings covering mostly small and medium-sized organizations. Big, wealthy mass organizations can outsource more demanding tasks to employees or provide careerist or other selective incentives to volunteer staff in exchange for their efforts. Smaller organizations dominating the civil society cannot afford this. They have to listen to their active members and supporters to sustain their commitment beyond a contribution of membership fees.

Moving to the dimension of staff control, both the quantitative findings as well as the case studies showed that the idea that CSOs, once relying on paid staff, are simply taken over by the latter, needs qualification (see on this also Heylen et al. 2020). The quantitative analysis in Chapter 5 showed that many organizations with staff do not grant staff control. Meanwhile, professionalization 'only' seems to increase the propensity for staff control to be present in a CSO but not to support its expansion to wider domains. It is bureaucratization, a governance principle directed towards ensuring efficient and expertise-based decision-making, which seems to favour decisions being made by managers more generally. The qualitative findings added nuance by tracing how spaces for staff control emerged and how this was supported by the presence of managers. This happened officially through reforms introducing a division of labour between leaders and managers or unofficially by the informal shifting of subject matters away from member-controlled fora.

The Three Faces of Membership Organization and Avenues for Future Research

As already alluded to, the case studies led me back to this study's very foundations and forced me to critically review some of the assumptions about the relationships between members, leaders, and managers I started out from. Inspired by different literatures, I conceptualized staff control as decision-making by actors—i.e. managers—driven by professional rather than organizational values and, relatedly, following an instrumental rationale rather than being driven by organizational loyalty. On that basis, the interests, priorities, and motivations of managers—envisaged as 'outside recruits' in line with Panebianco's notion of the independent professional (1988)—and those of members were conceptualized as least likely to align. Organizational leaders, in contrast, were considered as 'sitting in between', sharing with members a (non-instrumental) organizational affiliation and with managers functional responsibilities for CSO maintenance. Managers' (assumed) detachment as well as autonomy from the organization, in turn, underpinned the normative claim that staff control is more problematic than the centralization of decision-making power to organizational leaders. All this rationalized staff control as a suitable proxy for CSOs' weakened societal responsiveness.

Challenging this line of argument, the qualitative case studies showed that in all three CSOs, leading managerial positions were or are occupied by former affiliates, suggesting an overlap between managers and these CSOs' membership base. Moreover, while managers themselves might be recruited from a CSO's membership, organizational leaders in central governance organs might not. As detailed in Chapter 6, in SAS, organizational commitment is no longer a central consideration in the recruitment of trustees (the members of its executive board). Instead, as the CSO is currently operating, SAS seems to turn on its head the claim that managers (former activists) are likely to make decisions that put organizational accountability at risk, while organizational leaders (outside recruits) are likely to keep it intact.

To what extent does this inductive finding force us to rethink the framework this study rests upon? One might reject that line of reasoning simply because decision-making control of paid employees remains problematic in CSOs, whether or not they are outside recruits. Unlike with leaders, their authority is not derived from being representatives of the organization, neither procedurally nor substantively, which in itself is problematic in terms of democratic control (e.g. Wallander and Molander 2014; Mellquist 2022). This is because these actors are recruited in a competitive process, selected predominantly for their competences and skills, especially when it comes to high-level managerial positions in a CSO's leadership team (e.g. Moens 2021; Norris-Tirrell et al. 2018). This leaves aside that legal forms adopted by CSOs in European democracies tend to allocate governing responsibilities to volunteer actors (e.g. Hopt and von Hippel 2010; van der Ploeg et al. 2017), which sits uneasily with a de facto takeover of decision-making by staff (Hoye and Cuskelly 2003: 70). Supporting this angle, Laube et al. (2020) have shown that the contributions to policy formulation of support staff working for MPs is deliberately hidden to maintain the legitimacy of the representative process, which assigns this responsibility to elected officials. Even if leaders, managers, and members are more closely intertwined than envisaged, the expansion of staff control remains a contentious phenomenon and thus problematic with regard to CSOs' democratic contributions.

This, however, only resolves the issue of whether staff control can serve as a proxy for decision-making conflicting with normative expectations about intra-organizational processes that ought to be in the hands of actors recognized as organizationally accountable. It does not address the issue that managers—if recruited from within CSOs—might operate differently than theorized in Chapter 2, as basic assumptions about their motivations and priorities might be flawed. Illustrating the problem, Holland points out the following with regard to a local grass-roots movement in the US:

> In the modern movement model professional staff are in charge with manufacturing grievances. This claim suggests that professional staff are more interested in job security than the goals of the movement. Once again, this was not the case [...] members carefully chose staff according to their ideological commitment to the goals of the group [...] Rather than hindering democratic decision-making processes, staff provided the framework that allowed the grassroots membership base to pursue their goals aggressively. (2004: 119)

Though the constraints of CSO professionalization might well be less pronounced in small, local CSOs than those operating on a broader scale, this depiction underlines the relevance of the following question: if managers in the civil society sector were predominantly organizational affiliates, should we expect their motivations and priorities to align with those of members or leaders, rather than constituting a third group of actors with a separate profile from either? Clearly, CSOs' recruiting of managers from their own membership base—whether or not it is a frequent phenomenon—would blur the boundaries between the three actor types theorized as staff cannot be simply assumed to emphasize the 'cash nexus of an employment contract' instead of organizational loyalty (Katz and Mair 2009: 759). If so, increasing reliance

270 Civil Society's Democratic Potential

on paid staff as opposed to volunteer labour—whether by groups or political parties—cannot be assumed to lead to a marginalization of the organization's membership base either.

Taking a closer look, in the party literature we do not find agreement on this issue. According to what Aula and Koskimaa recently called 'the perils-of-professionalization' narrative (2023: 3), party staffers have been traditionally considered as apolitical, suggesting that the ways in which party members and staffers engage with their organization are clearly distinct (e.g. Mair and Katz 2009: 759; Panebianco 1988). In contrast, Karlsen and Saglie (2017: 1347–8) argue that if political parties put their own members in paid positions—a frequent occurrence in Norway—this might prevent a detachment of leaders from the grass roots by preventing 'employees from becoming uncritical yea-sayers for the leadership' (see for a similar interpretation Moens 2021). This reading, however, raises its own questions. Why—if an organizational affiliation is given for leaders as well (which is likely to be the case for many CSOs, even if not required[6])— should managers' interests and priorities align with those of members rather than those of leaders? Similarly, it is unclear why organizational leaders should be more detached from members than managers as paid employees, if both groups are recruited from within the organization. The argument implicitly suggests that an organizational affiliation would affect managers' behaviour more than that of organizational leaders, even though leaders' positions depend more strongly on continuous member support than those of managers (whether or not they are elected by members). This suggestion seems counterintuitive.

A long tradition going back to Michels (1915) has conceptualized organizational leaders as a group distinct from rank-and-file members. There is plenty of work criticizing the dichotomy as such (e.g. Katz and Mair 1993) or claims derived from this perspective. Michels' 'iron law of oligarchy' is a prime example (e.g. Leach 2005; Diefenbach 2019). Still, there is little doubt that theorizing leader–member relations as an interplay of two sets of actors with different (and potentially conflicting) motivations and priorities has been helpful to gain a more systematic understanding of intra-organizational dynamics, behaviour, and change in different types of organization across a variety of contexts (e.g. Ganz 2014; Ahlquist and Levi 2014; Han 2014; Bentancur et al. 2019; McAlevey 2016). Managers, defined in this study as paid employees forming part of a CSO's leadership, tend to share all the characteristics that also rationalize the treatment of leaders as a group distinct from members. This includes a high-level position within the organization, as well

---

[6] As these positions do not bring a lot of prestige or any material advantages to the average CSO, organizational commitment is likely to be a central motivation to assume such an unpaid role, even if those running a CSO are open to recruiting outsiders.

as superior skills and access to more information as compared to members. In addition, and unlike both leaders and members, they tend to bring with them professional expertise from advanced training which allows them to earn a living from their role in the organization. These characteristics are likely to remove them further from members, while still sharing the responsibility for running the organization with leaders. Hence, if we are concerned about the detachment of organizational leaders from the grass-roots, the same concern should apply even more so when managers start influencing or making decisions. This also holds when managers have been – as leaders – recruited from within the organization, which has been illustrated by the case studies. In all three, managers with volunteer backgrounds pushed for or even initiated reforms that deliberately reduced member control, which empirically substantiates the assumptions about staff control that this study started out from.

Consequently, organizational ties of paid employees—rather than indicating an overlooked affinity with rank-and-file members (Karlsen and Saglie 2017; Moens 2021)—suggest that managers might resemble organizational leaders more than is often assumed. This makes two scenarios relevant, as specified by Webb and Fisher (2003) in an earlier analysis of the overlap between party staffers and party members in UK Labour. The first scenario aligns with the theoretical arguments put forward in Chapter 2. The second suggests a slightly different take on how to theorize staff control, putting a stronger emphasis on the responsibilities that employees share with leaders than the implications of their competences and skills.

First, the increased reliance on paid professionals—stressing their autonomy in terms of competences and skills—might risk undermining the managerial control of party elites, irrespective of managers' prior or current affiliations, at the cost of leaders as well as members (Webb and Fisher 2003: 23). This scenario echoes the trade-off conceptualized in Chapter 2 between organizational accountability that is important to members and leaders as organizational affiliates and efficient decision-making based on expert knowledge favoured by managers (Table 2.1, Chapter 2). Second, if the similarities in the functional responsibilities of managers and leaders in the organization are more relevant for actors' orientations and behaviour (who might also share a commitment to the organization), the increased reliance on paid staff might enhance the leadership's grip on the organization—at the cost of members, including volunteer staff—instead (Webb and Fisher 2003: 23). In both scenarios, members lose out as power shifts to the leadership. But in the latter scenario organizational accountability is more likely to remain intact, if only in a mediated fashion, even if staff takes over decision-making in some areas (given staff's proximity to leaders).

Which of these two closely related scenarios is more likely to materialize within an organizational setting depends on the answers to three basic questions: first, whether managers are recruited from a CSO's member or support base or whether they are outside recruits; second, whether—if they have a prior organizational affiliation—managers are more strongly driven by the priorities of their employers (organizational leaders) and the functional responsibilities they share with the latter or their own expert status; and third, whether and when the two orientations are likely to clash. While further research is necessary to answer them, this study's findings—in conjunction with recent work—offer some initial suggestions.

Clearly, managers' detachment seems less likely if leaders and managers are both organizational affiliates, since organizational leaders might find staff control less problematic as a consequence. This is what the case studies in this study suggested. Organizational leaders who for most of these CSOs' history were recruits from within the CSO or its closer network tended to support reforms establishing a clearer division of labour, usually allowing staff to assume responsibility for certain areas in which their expertise was particularly valuable. These reforms were initiated or actively supported by managers to enhance organizational performance and functioning, often at the cost of, and sometimes despite the active resistance of, members. While organizational leaders were less sceptical towards staff control than theoretically expected, these reforms simultaneously aimed to improve the capacity of organizational leaders to hold management to account, especially in substantive areas. This is important as it suggests that the closer proximity between leaders and managers was not uniformly or exclusively beneficial to managers.

In the GPEW, of course, the more fundamental conflict centred around whether organizational leaders ought to have more control over the party than members, which relegated the importance of the issue of the appropriate level of staff control. The contrast between GPEW and the two groups generally implies that the propensity of organizations to try to combine professional qualification and organizational attachment within their staff is likely to be more pronounced in CSOs that are ideologically driven. We thus should expect the prevalence of organizational recruits in parties rather than groups, as parties generally tend to be underpinned by a shared ideology (Husted et al. 2022),[7] making party staffers' value commitments

---

[7] This is probably one reason why classical studies essentially assumed that paid party positions would be filled by members (e.g. Michels 1915; May 1973). This leaves aside that when these were written, fewer posts overall and fewer posts that could attract outside professionals without any affiliation were available.

more important to leaders.[8] That GPEW staff cannot be members of another party and must endorse the party's values underlines this expectation. While groups can also be ideological, the average group leader faces stronger incentives to keep her CSO's profile sufficiently neutral to be able to solicit support for its core issues across the political spectrum (e.g. Halpin 2014). For leaders of service-orientated groups, the quality and efficiency of service provision are central considerations (e.g. Grønbjerg 1993; Grohs 2014; Almog-Bar 2018). Hence, organizational commitment should be less of a recruitment priority in groups than in parties.

Irrespective of CSOs' varying desires to reconcile organizational commitment with expertise, their capacity to do so is likely to differ depending on the nature of the posts to be filled as well as the number of posts that need filling. Approaching the hiring of employees as an attempt to balance loyalty and expertise, Moens shows that paid employees in Dutch and Belgian parties that require greater extra-political expertise (which enhances their autonomy from their organization and the political domain generally) are more likely to be unaffiliated to the party they work for (2021: 10). This not only suggests that more demanding positions are more likely to be filled with outside recruits, but also that when the two demands conflict, expertise wins out. The need to fill more and increasingly specialized posts makes the reconciliation of loyalty and the required skills more difficult, which leads us back to the challenges of organizational growth. Even in the GPEW, a highly ideological organization, recruitment from its activist base has become weaker as the party's human resources have expanded.[9] Specialization is likely to shift the balance towards prioritizing expertise further. While leading managers in NAPA and SAS had prior links to the organization, this is not the case for their teams. In SAS, whose human resources have grown much more than those of NAPA, not even an interest in the organizations' core issues is relevant anymore. Managers' professional identity seems to win out when they try to strengthen their organization's competence base through new hirings.

---

[8] There is little systematic evidence on party staffers' relations with their party beyond a few party systems in Europe. They suggest, however, that employees working for party organizations tend to share an organizational affiliation with members, hence are not solely attached to their organization in an instrumental fashion (Webb and Fisher 2003; Karlsen and Salgie 2017; Moens 2021; 2022). Looking at groups, it is well established that many non-profit workers have a background in volunteering, and many non-profit leaders have been active as volunteers in the sector, such as positions on CSOs' governing boards (e.g. Norris-Tirrell et al. 2018; Stewart and Kuenzi 2018). Similarly, movement research has long stressed that staff members tend to be associated with their organizations' cause (e.g. McCarthy and Zald 1977; Staggenborg 1988; Holland 2004). That said, it is not clear to what extent membership organizations that are not parties tend to recruit their own volunteers into leading positions, though there are indications that organizations use their pool of volunteers to screen talented people suitable for paid positions (e.g. Nelson 2018).

[9] This aligns with Moens' finding that the mainstream parties who hire most staff are more likely to hire staff without an affiliation (Moens 2021: 10), even though they have more members in absolute terms to recruit from than smaller organizations.

274 Civil Society's Democratic Potential

This, yet again, substantiates the usefulness of theorizing managers, members, and leaders as three distinct faces of membership organizations, in order to gain an understanding of why CSOs address the challenges confronting them in modern societies the way they do.

Some Final Remarks

Where does this leave us in terms of the democratic potential attributed to CSOs by external audiences—academics, politicians, the public—and its various realizations in contemporary democracies? If decision-making power shifts from the 'many' to the 'few' as CSOs move away from the traditional 'association model' towards the 'professionalized voluntary organization' (or organizations are increasingly formed as such), how these few decision-makers relate to the organization they run and what drives their behaviour becomes a crucial question, regardless of whether they are organizational leaders or paid managers.

The growing importance of studying the increasing diversity and hybridization of organizational forms in contemporary civil societies and its consequences for democracy—and of applying multiple yardsticks in this process—become apparent just from reading the news. Last Generation (*Letzte Generation*) is an organization of German climate activists formed in 2021 that has received a lot of publicity in different circles (good and bad).[10] It is dedicated to the mobilization and nationwide coordination of civil disobedience to force the federal government to adopt immediate measures to address the challenges of climate change. To highlight the urgency of the climate emergency, Last Generation activists have blocked roads, disrupted airports, and desecrated artwork. By doing so, they deliberately provoked severe conflict with the state authorities and political establishment more generally. Essentially, Last Generation is a protest movement falling in a class of organizations whose members tend to be characterized by often very fluid infrastructures, which this study excluded from the outset.[11] In many ways, we might expect Last Generation to be a least likely case for the transformation this study is concerned with. After all, organizational professionalization

---

[10] Information on the sources used for this brief case study can be found in the Online Appendix available here: www.oup.co.uk/companion/Bolleyer.

[11] Social movement organizations (SMOs) with fluid infrastructures and highly permeable boundaries would not fall under the notion of membership-based voluntary organization used in this study, as they were expected to generate different intra-organizational dynamics than those theorized in Chapter 2. In contrast, SMOs or protest movements that adopt a formalized infrastructure fall under the proposed framework, as CSOs' primary purpose was no criterion used to include/exclude organizations from the study.

and bureaucratization are often associated with close state entanglement and dependency, and the 'professionalized voluntary organization' as an ideal type embodies this. It not only clashes with the traditional 'movement image' but sits uneasily with an organization whose primary purpose is illegal direct action. However, if we take a closer look at how Last Generation is organized, and how it operates, this expectation is not substantiated by the facts.

Rather than corresponding to the classical movement image of a loose, permeable grouping, to maximize its political impact, Last Generation has deliberately adopted a form of organizing that effectively integrates central features of the professionalized voluntary organization. That the organization's primary purpose (civil disobedience) prevents it from attracting state support again underlines earlier arguments that elements constitutive for the professionalized voluntary organization (and their implications) should be considered in isolation. Last Generation also highlights that some of these elements might be adopted by organizations we least expect this from.

For the year 2022, Last Generation reported donations of over 900,000 euros[12], which allowed it to pay those working for them who found it increasingly difficult to reconcile their activism with earning an income. Through an affiliated public benefit association with legal recognition,[13] Last Generation can receive support from private foundations[14] and pay out salaries. As of March 2023, it had seventy (full- or part-time) staff. Receiving a small salary allowed activists, including some members of its national leadership, to fully focus on their societal and political work. This sparked controversy, as media reports implied that the organization had advertised this in recruitment seminars as an incentive to join. Echoing traditional expectations towards 'voluntary associations' as well as classical 'social movements', the question was raised whether such organization ought not to be volunteer run instead. This was the case even though the salaries paid out are on a subsistence level ('*Verein bezahlt Aktivisten*';[15] '*Beruf Klimaaktivist*'[16]).

Taking an organization-centred perspective, such critique seems to somewhat miss the point. From its inception, Last Generation favoured leader autonomy over member control and valued efficient decision-making

---

[12] https://letztegeneration.de/transparenzbericht/, accessed 15.03.2023.
[13] Though not receiving any direct or indirect state support (e.g. subsidies or tax credits), the organization actively collaborates with organization that do. A pre-existing legally recognized public benefit organization was willing to integrate an initiative to support Last Generation's educational work (e.g. information campaigns about climate justice) in its structures.
[14] A main sponsor is the US-based organization 'Climate Emergency Fund'.
[15] https://www.welt.de/politik/deutschland/plus242956621/Letzte-Generation-Geld-fuer-den-Aufstand-Verein-bezahlt-Aktivisten.html, accessed 15.03.2023.
[16] https://www.sueddeutsche.de/wirtschaft/letzte-generation-aktivismus-gehalt-fuehrungsriege-1.5765989?reduced=true, accessed 15.03.2023.

over building or maintaining organizational accountability structures. Its organization has local groups of activists throughout Germany, but decision-making is highly centralized. It is run by a 'core group' of six leaders with a mandate to set the organization's national strategy. The purpose of its infrastructure is to implement this strategy as effectively as possible, with channels for vertical communication that do not serve bottom-up control. The core group of six people is connected through another small group in charge of coordination, with several working groups focused on areas such as 'mobilization', 'press', 'legal support', 'finances', 'values', and 'logistics'. Member involvement is pronounced, with an estimated 800–900 people active in the organization. Those interested in joining need to complete a form and indicate their belonging to one of three types of members—those willing to go to prison, those willing to be held in temporary custody, and those willing to only provide logistical support such as help with fundraising, recruitment and organizational activities or the provision of childcare. Doing so is clearly oriented towards making most efficient use of the member involvement that is on offer. Meanwhile, the CSO has developed a support structure for its activists, including a point of contact for those put into custody to receive legal advice, or for those in need of psychological counselling.

Given a, by now, functionally differentiated infrastructure in the form of working groups embedded in a clear hierarchy (emulating classical bureaucratic structures), different forms of member involvement are directed into domains central to ensure organizational maintenance as well as key activities, depending on what different members are willing to do and what not. This maximizes the forcefulness of its political engagement and thus its external political and societal impact. If this is further advanced by more leaders and activists earning a living by working full time for the CSO and this is affordable, so be it. While this is substantiated by reports that Last Generation aspires to further professionalization, those organizational leaders who have become employees are unlikely to have changed their orientation towards how their organization ought to operate. Judging from the organization they built up, their priority had been the formation of a functional hierarchy for supporting acts of civil disobedience, while building an infrastructure to systematically recruit more members willing to engage in such acts despite the risk of suffering severe consequences. Notions around *Basisdemokratie* central to Green and anti-nuclear activism of the 1960s and 1970s, especially in Germany—and indeed central to the ideology of the GPEW—do not come into this.

In terms of its democratic contributions to date, the impact of its political engagement is hard to dispute. Those citizens who run and sustain the organization and its controversial activities are unified in their commitment to jointly force the government to address the climate emergency. Further professionalization and bureaucratization are unlikely to lead to a more moderate modus operandi. On the contrary, it has been suggested that its increasing professionalization—which distinguishes the CSO from similar movements such as Fridays for Future—enabled Last Generation to engage in even more drastic acts, such as disrupting major airports. This runs parallel to its engagement in a wider range of conventional political activities, including public education to raise awareness about climate change. Meanwhile, the CSO's contribution to political activism as a participatory practice favouring self-determination, individual agency, and supporting self-governance can be debated, as allowing for or even cultivating member control is not an issue. However, member involvement is intense and, whatever one's opinion on the subject matter or the CSO's methods, those at the forefront of its political activities are willing to pay a high price to exercise political voice in a way that attracts as much public attention as possible. Clearly, member involvement in organizational activities as generated by this hierarchical organization cannot be downplayed as a form of low-cost participation.

This brief glance at Last Generation illustrates that the analytical framework and distinctions proposed in this study can help us to systematically assess CSOs that are in the public eye right now. They are relevant to the analysis of membership organizations that were only established a few years ago, and that on the surface seem unlikely to be affected by the broader trend towards a more professionalized civil society.

Furthermore, Last Generation's story underlines one of this study's most central implications. Rather than regarding the growing number of CSOs that resemble professional voluntary organizations (one way or the other) as a problematic endpoint in the story of membership organizations' contributions to democracy, this development is better understood as an evolution. This evolution is likely to find expression in membership organizations choosing organizational elements that they believe best suit their particular purposes when trying to balance the need to assure their own functioning while—as forcefully as possible—pursuing their goals. Organizational attempts to address this fundamental balancing act and the various tensions resulting from it are likely to lead to a growing diversity of organizational forms, whose complex repercussions can strengthen as well as weaken democracy. Indeed, they might do both at the same time. Above all else, one thing should have become clear over the course of this study. To consider membership organizations, a collective form of organizing shared societal concerns, as 'outdated' in individualizing societies is likely to underestimate their capacity for renewal and change and thus the important role they are still able to play in contemporary democracies.

Bibliography

Adams, J., Clark, M., Ezrow, L., & Glasgow, G. (2006) Are Niche Parties Fundamentally Different from Mainstream Parties? The Causes and the Electoral Consequences of Western European Parties' Policy Shifts, 1976–1998, *American Journal of Political Science* 50(3): 513–529.

Aggeborn, L., Lajevardi, N., & Nyman, P. (2021) Disentangling the Impact of Civil Association Membership on Political Participation: Evidence from Swedish Panel Data, *British Journal of Political Science* 51(4): 1773–1781.

Ahlbäck, Ö., S. & Bringselius, L. (2015) Professionalism and Organizational Performance in the Wake of New Managerialism, *European Political Science Review* 7(4): 499–523.

Ahlquist, J. S. & Levi, M. (2014) *In the Interest of Others: Organizations and Social Activism.* Princeton: Princeton University Press.

Ahrne, G. (1996) Civil Society and Civil Organizations, *Organization* 3(1): 109–210.

Albareda, A. (2018) Connecting Society and Policymakers? Conceptualizing and Measuring the Capacity of Civil Society Organizations to Act as Transmission Belts, *Voluntas: International Journal of Voluntary and Nonprofit Organizations* 29(6): 1216–1232.

Albareda, A. & Braun, C. (2019) Organizing Transmission Belts: The Effect of Organizational Design on Interest Group Access to EU Policy-making, *Journal of Common Market Studies* 57(3): 468–485.

Albert, S. & Whetten, D. A. (1985) Organizational Identity, *Research in Organizational Behavior* 7: 263–295.

Alexander, D. T., Barraket, J., Lewis, J. M., & Considine, M. (2012) Civic Engagement and Associationalism: The Impact of Group Membership Scope versus Intensity of Participation, *European Sociological Review* 28(10): 43–45.

Alexander, J. & Fernandez, K. (2021) The Impact of Neoliberalism on Civil Society and Nonprofit Advocacy, *Nonprofit Policy Forum* 12(2): 367–394.

Allen, N. & Bara, J. (2019) Marching to the Left? Programmatic Competition and the 2017 Party Manifestos, *The Political Quarterly* 90(1): 124–133.

Allen, N. & Bara, J. (2021) Clear Blue Water? The 2019 Party Manifestos, *The Political Quarterly* 92(3): 531–540.

Allern, E. H. (2010) *Political Parties and Interest Groups in Norway.* Colchester: ECPR Press.

Allern, E. H. & Bale, T. (2012) Political Parties and Interest Groups: Disentangling Complex Relationships, *Party Politics* 18(1): 7–25.

Almog-Bar, M. (2017) Insider Status and Outsider Tactics: Advocacy Tactics of Human Service Nonprofits in the Age of New Public Governance, *Nonprofit Policy Forum* 8(4): 411–428.

Almog-Bar, M. (2018) Civil Society and Nonprofits in the Age of New Public Governance: Current Trends and Their Implications for Theory and Practice, *Nonprofit Policy Forum* 8(4): 343–349.

Almog-Bar, M. & Schmid, H. (2014) Advocacy Activities of Nonprofit Human Service Organizations: A Critical Review, *Nonprofit and Voluntary Sector Quarterly* 43(1): 11–35.

Alter, C. (1998) Bureaucracy and Democracy in Organizations: Revisiting Feminist Organizations. In Powell, W. W. & Clemens, E. S. (eds.) *Private Action and the Public Good.* New Have: Yale University Press.

280   Bibliography

Alvarez, S. E. (2009) Beyond NGO-ization? Reflections from Latin America, *Development* 52(2): 175–184.

Andeweg, R. B. & Thomassen, J. J. A. (2005) Modes of Political Representation: Toward a New Typology, *Legislative Studies Quarterly* 30(4): 507–528.

Andrews, K. T. & Edwards, B. (2004) Advocacy Organizations in the U.S. Political Process, *Annual Review of Sociology* 30(1): 479–506.

Andrews, K. T., Ganz, M., Baggetta, M., Han, H., & Lim, C. (2010) Leadership, Membership, and Voice: Civic Associations That Work, *American Journal of Sociology* 115(4): 1191–1242.

Anheier, H. (2000) *Managing Non-Profit Organisations: Towards a New Approach.* Civil Society Working Paper series (1). Centre for Civil Society. London School of Economics and Political Science, http://eprints.lse.ac.uk/29022/1/cswp1.pdf, accessed 02.10.2022.

Ansolabehere, S., Gerber, A., & Snyder, J. (2002) Equal Votes, Equal Money: Court-Ordered Redistricting and Public Expenditures in the American States, *American Political Science Review* 96(4): 767–777.

Arda, L. & Banerjee, S. B. (2021) Governance in Areas of Limited Statehood: The NGOization of Palestine, *Business & Society* 60(7): 1675–1707.

Aula,V. & Koskimaa, V. (2023) The Imperative of Expertise: Why and How the Professionalisation of Policymaking Transforms Political Parties?, *Party Politics*, Online First, 1–12.

Baer, D. (2007) Voluntary Association Involvement in Comparative Perspective. In Trägårdh, L. (ed.) *State and Civil Society in Northern Europe: The Swedish Model Reconsidered.* New York: Berghahn Books, 67–125.

Bandara, Y. S., Arosha S. A., & Kumudinei, D. (2021) Multiple Perspectives of Measuring Organisational Value Congruence, *Asian Journal of Business Ethics* 10(2): 331–354.

Barakso, M. (2004) *Governing NOW: Grassroots Activism in the National Organization for Women.* Ithaca: Cornell University Press.

Barasko, M. & Schaffner, B. F. (2008) Exit, Voice and Interest Group Governance, *American Political Research* 36(2): 186–209.

Barberà, O., Sandri, G., Correa, P., & Rodríguez-Teruel, J. (2021) *Digital Parties. The Challenges of Online Organisation and Participation.* Cham: Springer.

Barbieri, D., Galli, D., Fedele, P., & Ongaro, E. (2013) Drivers of Autonomy of Public Agencies in Italy, *Financial Accountability & Management* 29(1): 26–49.

Barberis, P. (2013) The Managerial Imperative: Fifty Years' Change in UK Public Administration, *Public Policy and Administration* 28(4): 327–345.

Baroni, L., Carroll, B. J., Chalmers, A., Muñoz Marquez, L. M., & Rasmussen, A. (2014) Defining and Classifying Interest Groups, *Interest Groups and Advocacy* 3(2): 141–159.

Bauer, M. W. & Ege, J. (2016) Bureaucratic Autonomy of International Organizations' Secretariats, *Journal of European Public Policy* 23(7): 1019–1037.

Baumgartner, F. R. & Leech, B. L. (1998) *Basic Instincts: The Importance of Groups in Politics and in Political Science.* Princeton: Princeton University Press.

Baumgartner, F. R. & Leech, B. L. (2001) Interest Niches and Policy Bandwagons: Patterns of Interest Group Involvement in National Politics, *Journal of Politics* 63(4): 1191–1213.

Bawn, K. et al. (2012) A Theory of Political Parties: Groups, Policy Demands and Nominations in American Politics, *Perspectives on Politics* 10(03): 571–597.

Behrens, M. (2018) Structure and Competing Logics: The Art of Shaping Interests within German Employers' Associations, *Socio-Economic Review* 16(4): 769–789.

Bekkers, R. (2012) Trust and Volunteering: Selection or Causation? Evidence from a 4 Year Panel Study, *Political Behavior* 34(2): 225–247.

Ben-Ner, A. & Ren, T. (2010) A Comparative Study of Allocation of Decision-Making across Stakeholder Groups: The Case of Personal Care Industries. *Annals of Public and Cooperative Economics* 81(4): 611–630.

Bennet, R. J. (2000) The Logic of Membership of Sectoral Business Associations, *Review of Social Economy* 58(1): 17–42.

Bennett, R. & Savani, S. (2011) Surviving Mission Drift: How Charities Can Turn Dependence on Government Contract Funding to Their Own Advantage, *Nonprofit Management and Leadership* 22(2): 217–231.

Bennie, L. (2016) Greens in the United Kingdom and Ireland: Weak but Persistent. In van Haute, E. (ed.) *Green Parties in Europe*. Milton Park: Taylor and Francis.

Bentancur, V. P., Rodríguez, R. P. & Rosenblatt, F. (2019) *How Party Activism Survives: Uruguay's Frente Amplio*. Cambridge: Cambridge University Press.

Berker, L. E. & Pollex, J. (2021) Friend or Foe? Comparing Party Reactions to Fridays for Future in a Party System Polarised between AfD and Green Party, *Zeitschrift für Vergleichende Politikwissenschaft* 15: 1–19.

Berkhout, D. J. (2010, May 6) Political Activities of Interest Organizations: Conflicting Interests, Converging Strategies. Retrieved from https://hdl.handle.net/1887/15347, accessed 29.08.2022.

Berkhout, J. (2013) Why Interest Organizations Do What They Do: Assessing the Explanatory Potential of 'Exchange' Approaches, *Interest Groups & Advocacy* 2: 227–250.

Berkhout, J., Beyers, J., Braun, C., Hanegraaff, M., & Lowery, D. (2018) Making Inference across Mobilization and Influence Research: Comparing Top-Down and Bottom-Up Mapping of Interest Systems, *Political Studies* 66(1): 43–62.

Berkhout, J. Hanegraaff, L., & Statsch, P. (2021) Explaining the Patterns of Contacts between Interest Groups and Political Parties: Revising the Standard Model for Populist Times, *Party Politics* 27(3): 418–429.

Berkhout, J., Hanegraaff, M., & Braun, C. (2017) Is the EU Different? Comparing the Diversity of National and EU-level Systems of Interest Organisations, *West European Politics* 40(5): 1109–1131.

Bernhagen, P. & Maloney, W. A. (2010) Civil Society Organizations as 'Little Democracies?' In Maloney, W. A. & van Deth, J. W. (eds.) *Civil Society and Activism in Europe: Contextualizing Engagement and Political Orientations*. London: Routledge.

Berry, D. (1969) Party Membership and Social Participation, *Political Studies* 17(2): 196–207.

Berry, J. M. (1993) Citizen Groups and the Changing Nature of Interest Group Politics in America, *The ANNALS of the American Academy of Political and Social Science* 528(1): 30–41.

Berry, J. M. & Arons, D. F. (2003) *A Voice for Nonprofits*. Washington, DC: Brookings Institution Press.

Bértoa, F. & Rama, J. (2021) Mainstream Parties in Crisis: The Antiestablishment Challenge, *Journal of Democracy* 32(1): 37–51.Beyers, J. (2004) Voice and Access: Political Practices of European Interest Associations, *European Union Politics* 5(2): 211–240.

Beyers, J. et al. (2016) Comparative Interest Group Survey Questionnaire, University of Antwerp.

Beyers, J., Bonafont, L. C., Dür, A., Eising, R., Fink-Hafner, D., Lowery, D. L., Mahoney, C., Maloney, W., & Naurin, D. (2014) The Intereuro Project: Logic and Structure, *Interest Groups and Advocacy* 3(2): 126–140.

Beyers, J., Eising, R., & Maloney, W. A. (2008) Researching Interest Group Politics in Europe and Elsewhere: Much We Study, Little We Know?, *West European Politics* 31(6): 1103–1128.

Beyers, J. & Kerremans, B. (2007) Critical Resource Dependencies and the Europeanization of Domestic Interest Groups, *Journal for European Public Policy* 14(3): 460–481.

282   Bibliography

Biela, J., Kaiser, A. & Hennl, A. (2013) *Policy Making in Multilevel Systems: Federalism, Decentralisation, and Performance in the OECD Countries.* Colchester: ECPR Press.

Biezen, I. van & Kopecký, P. (2017) The Paradox of Party Funding: The Limited Impact of State Subsidies on Party Membership. In Scarrow, S. E., Webb, P. D., & Poguntke, T. (eds.) *Organizing Political Parties: Representation, Participation, and Power.* Oxford: Oxford University Press.

Billis, D. (1991) The Roots of Voluntary Agencies: A Question of Choice, *Nonprofit and Voluntary Sector Quarterly* 20(1): 57–69.

Billis, D. (2010) *Hybrid Organizations and the Third Sector: Challenges for Practice, Theory and Policy.* London: Palgrave.

Binderkrantz, A. (2005) Interest Group Strategies: Navigating between Privileged Access and Strategies of Pressure, *Political Studies* 53(4): 694–715.

Binderkrantz, A. (2008) Different Groups, Different Strategies: How Interest Groups Pursue Their Political Ambitions, *Scandinavian Political Studies* 31(2): 173–200.

Binderkrantz, A. (2009) Membership Recruitment and Internal Democracy in Interest Groups: Do Group-membership Relations Vary between Group Types?, *West European Politics* 32(3): 657–678.

Binderkrantz, A. S., Christiansen, P. M., & Pedersen, H. H. (2015) Interest Group Access to the Bureaucracy, Parliament, and the Media, Governance: *An International Journal of Policy, Administration, and Institutions* 28(1): 95–112.

Birch, S. (2009) Real Progress: Prospects for Green Party Support in Britain, *Parliamentary Affairs* 62(1): 53–71.

Bischoff, C. S. (2006) *Political Competition and Contestability: A Study of the Barriers to Entry in 21 Democracies*, PhD Thesis, Department of Political and Social Sciences, European University Institute, Florence.

Bloodgood, E. & Tremblay-Boire, J. (2017) Does Government Funding Depoliticize NGOs? Examining Evidence from Europe, *European Political Science Review* 9(3): 401–424.

Bob, C. (2011) Civil and Uncivil Society. In Edwards, M. (ed.) *The Oxford Handbook of Civil Society.* Oxford: Oxford University Press.

Bolleyer, N. (2012) New Party Organization in Western Europe: Of Hierarchies, Stratarchies and Federations, *Party Politics* 18(3): 315–336.

Bolleyer, N. (2013a) *New Parties in Old Party Systems: Persistence and Decline in 17 Democracies.* Oxford: Oxford University Press.

Bolleyer, N. (2013b) The Rise and Decline of the Irish Green Party. In Clark, A. & Weeks, L. (eds.) *Radical or Redundant? Minor Parties in Irish Politics.* Gloucestershire: The History Press.

Bolleyer, N. (2018) *The State and Civil Society: Regulating Interest Groups, Parties and Public Benefit Organizations in Contemporary Democracies.* Oxford: Oxford University Press.

Bolleyer, N. (2021a) State Funding Pressure in Interest Groups, Political Parties and Service-oriented Membership Organizations, *West European Politics* 44(7): 1577–1603.

Bolleyer, N. (2021b) Civil Society—Politically Engaged *or* Member-serving? A Governance Perspective, *European Union Politics* 22(3): 495–520.

Bolleyer, N. (forthcoming) How to Study Political Parties: From Civil Society to the State and Back, forthcoming with *Irish Political Studies.*

Bolleyer, N. & Correa, P. (2020a) Self-Maintenance versus Goal Attainment—Drivers of Mortality Anxiety in Organized Civil Society, *European Political Science Review* 12(3): 271–288.

Bolleyer, N. & Correa, P. (2020b) Why Parties Narrow Their Representative Profile: Evidence from Six European Democracies, *Politische Vierteljahresschrift*, 29–57.

Bolleyer, N. & Correa, P. (2022a) Member Influence and Involvement in Civil Society Organizations: A Resource Dependency Perspective on Groups and Parties, *Political Studies* 70(2): 519–540.

Bolleyer, N. & Correa, P. (2022b) Advocacy in European Civil Societies: Organizational Trade-offs between Selective and Collective Incentive Provision, *Social Forces*, Online First: 1–26.

Bolleyer, N., Gauja, A. & Correa, P. (2020) Legal Regulation and the Juridification of Party Governance, *The Journal of Comparative Politics* 52(4): 1–22.

Bolleyer, N., Little, C., & von Nostitz, F. (2015) Implementing Democratic Equality in Political Parties. Organizational Consequences in the Swedish and the German Pirate Parties, *Scandinavian Political Studies* 38(2): 158–178.

Bolleyer, N. & Ruth, S. (2018) Elite Investments in Party Institutionalization in New Democracies: A Two-Dimensional Approach, *Journal of Politics* 80(1): 288–302.

Bolleyer, N. & Trumm, S. (2014) From Parliamentary Pay to Party Funding: The Acceptability of Informal Institutions in Advanced Democracies, *European Journal of Political Research* 53(4): 784–802.

Bolleyer, N. & Weiler, F. (2018) Why Groups Are Politically Active: An Incentive-Theoretical Approach, *Comparative Political Studies* 51(12): 1628–1660.

Bonotti, M. (2011) Conceptualising Political Parties: A Normative Framework, *Politics* 31(1): 19–26.

Borbáth, E. & Hutter, S. (2021) Protesting Parties in Europe: A Comparative Analysis, *Party Politics* 27(5): 896–908.

Borchgrevink, K. (2020) NGOization of Islamic Charity: Claiming Legitimacy in Changing Institutional Contexts, *Voluntas: International Journal of Voluntary and Nonprofit Organizations* 31(5): 1049–1062.

Bosso, C. J. (1995) The Color of Money: Environmental Groups and the Pathologies of Fund Raising. In Cigler, A. J. & Loomis B. A. (eds.) *Interest Group Politics*, fourth edition. Washington, DC: Congressional Quarterly Press.

Bosso, C. J. (2003) Rethinking the Concept of Membership in Nature Advocacy Organizations, *Policy Studies Journal* 31(3): 397–411.

Bovaird, T. (2007) Beyond Engagement and Participation: User and Community Coproduction of Public Services, *Public Administration Review* 67(5): 846–860.

Brandsen, T., Trommel, W., & Verschuere, B. (2014) *Manufacturing Civil Society: Principles, Practices and Effects.* London: Palgrave Macmillan.

Broadbridge, A. & Parsons, E. (2003) *Still Serving the Community? The Professionalisation of the UK Charity Retail Sector, International Journal of Retail and Distribution Management* 31 (8): 418–427.

Bunea, A. (2019) Reconciling the 'Logic of Influence' and the 'Logic of Membership' in the EU: The Case of Lobbying Networks in Environmental Consultations. In Dialer, D. & Richter, M. (eds.) *Lobbying in the European Union: Strategies, Dynamics and Trends.* Cham: Springer.

Burchell, J. (2000) Here Come the Greens (Again): The Green Party in Britain during the 1990s, *Environmental Politics* 9(3): 145–150.

Burchell, J. (2002). *The Evolution of Green Politics: Development and Change Within European Green Parties.* London: Routledge.

Burstein, P. & Linton, A. (2002) The Impact of Political Parties, Interest Groups, and Social Movement Organizations on Public Policy: Some Recent Evidence and Theoretical Concerns, *Social Forces* 81(2): 380–408.

Butschi, D. & Cattacin, S. (1993) The Third Sector in Switzerland: The Transformation of the Subsidiarity Principle, *West European Politics* 16(3): 362–379.

284 Bibliography

Cairns, B., Harris, M., & Young, P. (2005) Building the Capacity of the Voluntary Nonprofit Sector: Challenges of Theory and Practice, *International Journal of Public Administration* 28 (9–10): 869–885.

Cairns, B., Hutchison, R., & Aiken, M. (2010) 'It's Not What We Do, It's How We Do It': Managing the Tension between Service Delivery and Advocacy, *Voluntary Sector Review* 1(2): 193–207.

Carter, N. (2008) The Green Party: Emerging from the Political Wilderness?, *British Politics* 3: 223–240.

Carter, N. (2015) The Greens in the UK General Election of 7 May 2015, *Environmental Politics* 24(6): 1055–1060.

Carter, N. & Pearson, M. (2020) A 'Climate Election'?: The Environment and the Greens in the 2019 UK General Election, *Environmental Politics* 29(4): 746–751.

Chatelain-Ponroy, S., Eynaud, P., & Sponem, S. (2015) Civil Society Organisation Governance: More than just a Matter for the Board. In Laville, J., Young, D., & Eynaud, P. (eds.) *Civil Society, the Third Sector and Social Enterprise Governance and Democracy*. New York: Routledge.

Chaves, M., Stephens, L., & Galaskiewicz, J. (2004) Does Government Funding Suppress Nonprofits' Political Activity?, *American Sociological Review* 69(2): 292–316.

Child, C. D. & Grønbjerg, K. A. (2007) Nonprofit Advocacy Organizations: Their Characteristics and Activities, *Social Science Quarterly* 88 (1): 259–281.

Choudry, A. & Kapoor, D. (eds.) (2013) *NGOization: Complicity, Contradictions and Prospects*. London: Zed Books.

Christenson, D. P., Lin, J., & Makse, T. (2021) Ask Only What Your Country Can Do for You: Group Interests, Constituency Characteristics and Demands for Representation, *American Politics Research* 49(1): 17–29.

Cinalli, M. & Guigni, M. (2014) The Impact of Political Opportunity Structures on the Politicization of Civil Society Organizations in the Field of Unemployment and Precarity. In Baglioni, S. & Guigni, M. (eds.) *Civil Society Organizations, Unemployment, and Precarity in Europe*. London: Palgrave Macmillan.

Clarence, E. L., Jordan, G., & Maloney, W. A. (2005) Activating Participation: Generating Support for Campaign Groups. In Rossteutscher, S. (ed.) *Democracy and the Role of Associations Political, Organisational and Social Contexts*. London: Routledge.

Clark, P. B. & Wilson, J. Q. (1961) Incentive Systems: A Theory of Organizations, *Administrative Science Quarterly* 6(2): 129–166.

Close, C., Kelbel, C., & van Haute, E. (2017) What Citizens Want in Terms of Intra-Party Democracy: Popular Attitudes towards Alternative Candidate Selection Procedures, *Political Studies* 65(3): 646–664.

Cnaan, R. (1991) Neighborhood-representing Organizations: How Democratic Are They? *Social Service Review* 65(4): 614–634.

Cohen, J. & Arato, A. (1992) *Civil Society and Political Theory*. Cambridge: MIT Press.

Cohen, J. & Rogers, J. (eds.) (1995) *Associations and Democracy*. London: Verso.

Cornforth, C. (2003) *The Governance of Public and Non-Profit Organisations: What Do Boards Do?* Oxford: Routledge.

Cornforth, C. (2012) Nonprofit Governance Research: Limitations of the Focus on Boards and Suggestions for New Directions, *Nonprofit and Voluntary Sector Quarterly* 41(6): 1116–1135.

Cornforth, C. & Edwards, C. (eds.) (1998) *Good Governance: Developing Effective Board-Management Relations in Public and Voluntary Organizations*. London: CIMA Publishing.

Cross, W. & Blais, A. (2012) Who Selects the Party Leader?, *Party Politics* 18(2): 127–150.

Cross, W. & Katz, R. S. (eds.) (2013) *The Challenges of Intra-Party Democracy*. Oxford: Oxford University Press.

Daalder, H. (2007) A Crisis of Party?, *Scandinavian Political Studies* 15(4): 269–288.

Dalton, R. J., Farrell, D. M., & McAllister, I. (2011) *Political Parties and Democratic Linkage: How Parties Organize Democracy*. Oxford: Oxford University Press.

Dalton, R. J., Recchia, S., & Rohrschneider, R. (2003) The Environmental Movement and the Modes of Political Action, *Comparative Political Studies* 36(7): 743–771.

Dalton, R. J. & Weldon, S. J. (2005) Public Images of Political Parties: A Necessary Evil?, *West European Politics* 28(5): 931–951.

Dalziel, R. (2010) Interest and Pressure Groups. In Anheier, H. K. & Toepler, S. (eds.) *International Encyclopedia of Civil Society*. New York: Springer.

De Bruycker, I. (2017) Politicization and the Public Interest: When Do the Elites in Brussels Address Public Interests in EU Policy Debates?, *European Union Politics* 18(4): 603–619.

Dekker, P. (2009) Civicness: From Civil Society to Civic Services? *Voluntas: International Journal of Voluntary and Nonprofit Organizations* 20(3): 220–238.

Della Porta, D. (2020) Building Bridges: Social Movements and Civil Society in Times of Crisis, *Voluntas: International Journal of Voluntary and Nonprofit Organizations* 31(5): 938–948.

Demker, M., Heidar, K., & Kosiara-Pedersen, K. (2019) *Nordic Party Members: Linkages in Troubled Times*. Colchester: ECPR Press.

Dennison, J. (2017) *The Greens in British Politics*. London: Palgrave Macmillan.

Dennison, J. (2020) How Niche Parties React to Losing Their Niche: The Cases of the Brexit Party, the Green Party and Change UK, *Parliamentary Affairs* 73(1): 125–141.

De Vries, C. & Hobolt, S. (2020) *Political Entrepreneurs: The Rise of Challenger Parties in Europe*. New Haven: Princeton University Press.

Diamond, L. (1994) Rethinking Civil Society: Toward Democratic Consolidation, *Journal of Democracy* 5(3): 4–17.

Diefenbach, T. (2019) Why Michels' 'Iron Law of Oligarchy' Is Not an Iron Law—And How Democratic Organisations Can Stay 'Oligarchy-Free', *Organization Studies* 40(4): 545–562.

Dodsworth, A. (2017) The Advantages of Opposition: Fracking and the Greens. In Atkins, J. & Gaffney, J. (eds.) *Voices of the UK Left: Rhetoric, Ideology and the Performance of Politics*. London: Palgrave Macmillan.

Doherty, B. (1992a) The Fundi-Realo Controversy: An Analysis of Four European Green Parties, *Environmental Politics* 1(1): 95–120.

Doherty, B. (1992b) The Autumn 1991 Conference of the UK Green Party, *Environmental Politics* 1(2): 292–298.

Doyle, J. L. (2018) Government Co-Option of Civil Society: Exploring the AKP's Role within Turkish Women's CSOs, *Democratization* 25(3): 445–463.

Driskell, R. & Wise, J. (2017) Voluntary Associations. In Turner, B. S. (eds.) *The Wiley-Blackwell Encyclopedia of Social Theory*. Hoboken: Wiley-Blackwell.

Du Gay P. & Pedersen K. Z. (2020) Discretion and Bureaucracy. In Evans, T. & Hupe, P. (eds.) *Discretion and the Quest for Controlled Freedom*. Cham, Switzerland: Springer.

Dür, A. (2018) How Interest Groups Influence Public Opinion: Arguments Matter More Than the Sources, *European Journal of Political Research* 58(2): 514–535.

Dür, A. & Mateo G. (2013) Gaining Access or Going Public? Interest Group Strategies in Five European Countries, *European Journal of Political Research* 52(5): 660–686.

Dür, A. & Mateo, G. (2016) *Insiders versus Outsiders: Interest Group Politics in Multilevel Europe*. Oxford: Oxford University Press.

Duverger, M. (1964) *Political Parties: Their Organization and Activity in the Modern State*, third edition. London: Methuen.

286 Bibliography

Edwards, C. & Cornforth, C. (2003) What Influences the Strategic Contribution of Boards?. In Cornforth, C. (ed.) *The Governance of Public and Non-Profit Organisations What Do Boards Do?* London: Routledge.

EESC (European Economic and Social Committee) (2012) The Impact of the Crisis on Civil Society Organisations in the EU Risks and Opportunities. Retrieved from https://www.eesc.europa.eu/sites/default/files/resources/docs/qe-30-13-200-en-c.pdf, accessed 29.8.2022.

Eikenberry, A. M. (2009) *Giving Circles: Philanthropy, Voluntary Association, and Democracy.* Bloomington: Indiana University Press.

Eikenberry, A. M. & Kluver, J. D. (2004) The Marketization of the Nonprofit Sector: Civil Society at Risk? *Public Administration Review* 64: 132–140.

Einolf, C. J. (2015) The Social Origins of the Nonprofit Sector and Charitable Giving. In Wiecking, P. & Handy, F. (eds.) *The Palgrave Handbook of Global Philanthropy.* Basingstoke: Palgrave Macmillan, 509–529.

Eliasoph, N. (2013) *The Politics of Volunteering.* Cambridge/Malden: Polity Press.

Enos, R. D. & Hersh, E. D. (2015) Party Activists as Campaign Advertisers: The Ground Campaign as a Principal-Agent Problem, *American Political Science Review* 109(2): 252–278.

Evans, G. (1993) Hard Times for the British Green Party, *Environmental Politics* 2(2): 327–333.

Evers, A. (2014) Changes in Work and Human Services: On the Risks and Chances they Entail for Volunteering. In Freise, M. & Hallmann, T. (eds.) *Modernizing Democracy: Associations and Associating in the 21st Century.* New York: Springer, 121–131.

Farrell, D. & Webb, P. (2000) Political Parties as Campaign Organizations. In Dalton, R. J. & Wattenberg, M. P. (eds.) *Parties without Partisans.* Oxford: Oxford University Press.

Farrell, D. & Webb, P. (2002) Political Parties as Campaign Organizations. In Dalton, R. J. & Wattenberg, M. P. (eds.) *Parties without Partisans.* Oxford: Oxford University Press.

Farrer, B. (2017) *Organizing for Policy Influence. Comparing Parties, Interest Groups and Direct Action.* London: Routledge.

Faucher, F. (1999) Party Organisation and Democracy—A Comparison of Les Verts and the British Green Party, *GeoJournal* 47(3): 487–496.

Ferlie, E. & Geraghty, K. J. (2007) Professionals in Public Service Organizations: Implications for Public Sector 'Reforming'. In Ferlie, E., Lynn Jr, L. E., & Pollitt, C. (eds.) *The Oxford Handbook of Public Management.* Oxford: Oxford University Press.

Fisker, H. M. (2015) Dead or Alive? Explaining the Long-Term Survival Chances of Interest Groups, *West European Politics* 38(3): 709–729.

Fitzpatrick, J. (2018) *Digital Civil Society: Wie zivilgesellschaftliche Organisationen im Web 2.0 politische Ziele verfolgen.* Wiesbaden: Springer VS.

Foley, M. W. & Edwards, B. (2002) How Do Members Count? Membership, Governance, and Advocacy in the Nonprofit World. In Reid, E. J. & Montilla, M. D. (eds.) *Nonprofit Advocacy and the Policy Process: Exploring Organizations and Advocacy.* Washington: The Urban Institute.

Ford, R. & Jennings, W. (2021) The Changing Cleavage Politics of Western Europe, *Annual Review of Political Science* 23: 295–314.

FRA (European Union Agency for Fundamental Rights) (2021) Protecting Civic Space in the EU. Retrieved from https://fra.europa.eu/sites/default/files/fra_uploads/fra-2021-protecting-civic-space_en.pdf, accessed 29.08.2022.

Franke, J. L. & Dobson, D. (1985) Interest Groups: The Problem of Representation, *Western Political Quarterly* 38(2): 224–237.

Frankland, G., Lucardie, P., & Rihoux, B. (eds.) (2008) *Green Parties in Transition: The End of Grass-Roots Democracy?* London: Routledge.

Fraussen, B. (2014) The Visible and of the State: On the Organizational Development of Interest Groups, *Public Administration* 92(2): 406–421.

Fraussen, B. & Halpin, D. (2018) Political Parties and Interest Organizations at the Crossroads: Perspectives on the Transformation of Political Organizations, *Political Studies Review* 16(1): 25–37.

Freeman, J. (1974) The Tyranny of Structurelessness, *Second Wave* 2(1). Reprinted in Jaquette, J. (ed.) *Women in Politics.* New York: Wiley, 202–214.

Froelich, K. A. (2005) Diversification of Revenue Strategies: Evolving Resource Dependence in Nonprofit Organizations, *Nonprofit and Voluntary Sector Quarterly* 28(3): 246–268.

Frumkin, P. (2002) *On Being Nonprofit: A Conceptual Policy Primer.* Cambridge: Harvard University Press.

Frumkin, P. & Andre-Clark, A. (2000) When Missions, Markets, and Politics Collide: Values and Strategy in the Nonprofit Human Services, *Nonprofit and Voluntary Sector Quarterly*: 29(1): 141–163.

Frumkin, P. & Kim, M. (2002) The Effect of Government Funding on Nonprofit Administrative Efficiency: An Empirical Test. Innovations in American Government Program, Harvard University.

Fung, A. (2003) Associations and Democracy: Between Theories, Hopes, and Realities, *Annual Review of Sociology* 29(1): 515–539.

Fyall, R. (2017) Nonprofits as Advocates and Providers: A Conceptual Framework, *Policy Studies Journal* 45(1): 121–14.

Ganz, M. (2014) *Why David Sometimes Wins: Leadership, Organization, and Strategy in the California Farm Worker Movement.* Oxford: Oxford University Press

Gauja, A. (2015) The Construction of Party Membership, *European Journal of Political Research* 54(2): 232–248.

Gauja, A. (2017) *Party Reform: The Causes, Challenges and Consequences of Organisational Change.* Oxford: Oxford University Press.

Gerbaudo, P. (2019) *The Digital Party: Political Organisation and Online Democracy.* London: Pluto Press.

Geys, B. (2012) Association Membership and Generalized Trust: Are Connections between Associations Losing Their Value?, *Journal of Civil Society* 8(1): 1–15.

Gioia, D., Patvardhan, S., Hamilton, A., & Corley, K. (2013) Organizational Identity Formation and Change, *The Academy of Management Annals* 7(1): 123–192.

Golensky, M. (1993) The Board-Executive Relationship in Nonprofit Organizations: Partnership or Power Struggle?, *Nonprofit Management and Leadership* 4(2): 177–191.

Grant, W. (2000) *Pressure Groups and British Politics.* London: Palgrave Macmillan.

Gray, V. & Lowery, D. (1995) The Demography of Interest Organization Communities: Institutions, Associations, and Membership Groups, *American Politics Research* 23(1): 3–32.

Gray, V. & Lowery, D. (1996) *The Population Ecology of Interest Representation. Lobbying Communities in the American States.* Ann Arbor: University of Michigan Press.

Grohs, S. (2014) Hybrid Organizations in Social Service Delivery in Quasimarkets: The Case of Germany, *American Behavioral Scientist* 58(11): 1425–1445.

Grömping, M. & Halpin, D. (2019) Does Group Engagement with Members Constitute a 'Beneficial Inefficiency'?, *Governance* 32(3): 511–529.

Grønbjerg, K. A. (1993) *Understanding Nonprofit Funding: Managing Revenues in Social Services and Community Development Organizations.* San Francisco: Jossey-Bass.

288   Bibliography

Gunther, R. & Diamond, L. (2001) Types and Functions of Parties. In Diamond, L. & Gunther, R. (eds.) *Political Parties and Democracy*. Baltimore: Johns Hopkins University Press, 3–39.

Guo, C. & Musso, J. A. (2007) Representation in Nonprofit and Voluntary Organizations: A Conceptual Framework, *Nonprofit and Voluntary Sector Quarterly* 36(2): 308–326.

Guo, C. & Saxton, G. (2020) *The Quest for Attention: Nonprofit, Advocacy in a Social Media Age*. Stanford, CA: Stanford University Press.

Hall, R. H. (1968) Professionalization and Bureaucratization, *American Sociological Review* 33(1): 92–104.

Halpin, D. (2006) The Participatory and Democratic Potential and Practice of Interest Groups: Between Solidarity and Representation, *Public Administration* 84(4): 919–940.

Halpin, D. (2010) *Groups, Representation and Democracy: Between Promise and Practice*. Manchester: Manchester University Press.

Halpin, D. (2014) *The Organization of Political Interest Groups*. London: Routledge.

Halpin, D. & Daugbjerg, C. (2015) Identity as Constraint and Resource in Interest Group Evolution: A Case of Radical Organizational Change, *The British Journal of Politics and International Relations* 17(1): 31–48.

Halpin, D. & Fraussen, B. (2015) *Survey of National Advocacy Groups, The Organised Interest System in Australian Public Policy Project*. Canberra: Australian National University.

Halpin, D. & Fraussen, B. (2017) Conceptualising the Policy Engagement of Interest Groups: Involvement, Access and Prominence. *European Journal of Political Research* 56(3): 723–732.

Halpin, D. & Thomas, H. (2012) Interest Group Survival: Explaining Sources of Mortality Anxiety, *Interest Group & Advocacy* 1(2): 215–238.

Han, H. (2014) *How Organisations Develop Activists: Civic Associations and Leadership in the 21st Century*. Oxford: Oxford University Press.

Hanegraaff, M., Beyers, J., & De Bruycker, I. (2016) Balancing Inside and Outside Lobbying: The Political Strategies of Lobbyists at Global Diplomatic Conferences, *European Journal of Political Research* 55(3): 568–588.

Hanegraaff, M. & Poletti, A. (2019) Public Opinion and Interest Groups' Concerns for Organizational Survival, *European Political Science Review* 11: 125–143.

Hannan, M. T. & Freeman, J. (1984) Structural Inertia and Organizational Change, *American Sociological Review* 49(2): 149–164.

Harlan, S. & Saidel, J. (1994) Board Members' Influence on the Government-Nonprofit Relationship, *Nonprofit Management and Leadership* 5(2): 173–196.

Harris, M. (1989) The Governing Body Role: Problems and Perceptions in Implementation, *Nonprofit and Voluntary Sector Quarterly* 18(4): 317–333.

Harris, M. (1998) Doing It Their Way: Organizational Challenges for Voluntary Associations, *Nonprofit and Voluntary Sector Quarterly* 27(2): 144–158.

Hasenfeld, Y. & Gidron, B. (2005) Understanding Multi-purpose Hybrid Voluntary Organizations: The Contributions of Theories on Civil Society, Social Movements and Non-Profit Organizations, *Journal of Civil Society* 1(2): 97–112.

Hazan, R. Y. & Rahat, G. (2010) *Democracy within Parties: Candidate Selection Methods and Their Political Consequences*. Oxford: Oxford University Press.

Healy, A. & Malhotra, N. (2009) Myopic Voters and Natural Disaster Policy, *American Political Science Review* 103(3): 387–406.

Heaney, M. T. (2010) Linking Political Parties and Interest Groups. In Maisel, L. S., Berry J. M. & Edwards, G. C. (eds.) *The Oxford Handbook of American Political Parties and Interest Groups*. New York: Oxford University Press.

Heclo, H. (1978) Issue Networks and the Executive Establishment. In King, A. (ed.) *The New American Political System*. Washington: American Enterprise Institute of Public Policy Research.

Heelas, P., Scott, L. & Morris, P. (1996) *Detraditionalization*. Hoboken: Wiley-Blackwell.

Heimovics, R. & Herman R. (1990) Responsibility for Critical Events in Nonprofit Organizations, *Nonprofit and Voluntary Sector Quarterly* 19(1): 59–72.

Heimovics, R., Herman, R., & Jurkiewicz, C. (1995) The Political Dimension of Effective Nonprofit Executive Leadership, *Nonprofit Management and Leadership* 5(3): 233–248.

Heinze, A. S. & Weisskircher, M. (2022) How Political Parties Respond to Pariah Street Protest: The Case of Anti-Corona Mobilisation in Germany, *German Politics* 10, Online First March 2022.

Herzog H. (1987) Minor Parties: The Relevancy Perspective, *Comparative Politics*, 19(3): 317–329.

Heylen, F., Fraussen, B., & Beyers, J. (2018) Live to Fight Another Day? Organizational Maintenance and Mortality Anxiety of Civil Society Organizations, *Nonprofit and Voluntary Sector Quarterly* 47(6): 1249–1270.

Heylen, F., Willems, E. & Beyers, J. (2020) Do Professionals Take Over? Professionalisation and Membership Influence in Civil Society Organisations, *Voluntas: International Journal of Voluntary and Nonprofit Organizations* 31: 1226–1238.

Hirschman, A. O. (1970) *Exit, Voice and Loyalty: Responses to Decline in Firms, Organizations, and States*. Cambridge: Harvard University Press.

Hoch, K. (2008) Rethinking Voluntary Associations: Visions of Democracy and Communicative Practices, *Journal of Civil Society* 4(3): 233–253.

Höijer, B. (2011) Social Representations Theory, *Nordicom Review* 32(2): 3–16.

Holland, L. (2004) Movement Professionalization: A Positive Force for the Grassroots SMO? *Free Inquiry in Creative Sociology* 32 (2): 109–120.

Holyoke, T. T. (2013a) A Dynamic Model of Member Participation in Interest Groups, *Interest Groups & Advocacy* 2(3): 278–301.

Holyoke, T. T. (2013b) The Interest Group Effect on Citizen Contact with Congress, *Party Politics* 19(6): 925–944.

Holyoke, T. T. (2014) *Interest Groups and Lobbying: Pursuing Political Interests in America*. New York: Routledge.

Honaker, J., King, G., & Blackwell, M. (2011) Amelia II: A Program for Missing Data, *Journal of Statistical Software* 45(7): 1–47.

Hood, C. (1991) A Public Management for All Seasons? *Public Administration* 69(1): 3–19.

Hooghe, M. (2003) Voluntary Associations and Democratic Attitudes: Value Congruence as a Causal Mechanism. In Hooghe, M. & Stolle, D. (eds.) *Generating Social Capital: Civil Society and Institutions in Comparative Perspective*. New York: Palgrave Macmillan.

Hooghe, M. (2008) Voluntary Associations and Socialization. In Castiglione, D., van Deth, J. W., & Wolleb, G. (eds.) *The Handbook of Social Capital*. Oxford: Oxford University Press.

Hooghe, M. & Kölln, A. (2020) Types of Party Affiliation and the Multi-Speed Party: What Kind of Party Support is Functionally Equivalent to Party Membership?, *Party Politics* 26(4): 355–365.

Hopt, K. & von Hippel, T. (2010) *Comparative Corporate Governance of Non-Profit Organizations*. Cambridge: Cambridge University Press.

Houtzager, P. P. & Gurza Lavalle, A. (2009) Participatory Governance and the Challenge of Assumed Representation in Brazil, *IDS Working Papers* 321.

Hoye, R. & Cuskelly, G. (2003) Board–Executive Relationships within Voluntary Sport Organisations, *Sport Management Review* 6(1): 53–73.

Hu, M., Pavlicova, M., & Nunes, E. (2011) Zero-Inflated and Hurdle Models of Count Data with Extra Zeros: Examples from an HIV-Risk Reduction Intervention Trial, *American Journal of Drug and Alcohol Abuse* 37: 367–375.

Husted, E., Moufahim, M., & Fredriksson, M. (2022) Political Parties and Organization Studies: The Party as a Critical Case of Organizing, *Organization Studies* 43(8): 1327–1341.

Hustinx, L. (2014) Volunteering in a Hybrid Institutional and Organizational Environment: An Emerging Research Agenda. In Freise, M. & Hallmann, T. (eds.) *Modernizing Democracy: Associations and Associating in the 21st Century*. New York: Springer.

Hustinx, L., Cnaan, R. A., & Handy, F. (2010) Navigating Theories of Volunteering: A Hybrid Map for a Complex Phenomenon, *Journal for the Theory of Social Behaviour* 40(4): 410–434.

Hwang, H. & Powell, W. (2009) The Rationalization of Charity: The Influences of Professionalism in the Nonprofit Sector, *Administrative Science Quarterly* 54(2): 268–298.

Ignazi, P. (2021) The Failure of Mainstream Parties and the Impact of New Challenger Parties in France, Italy and Spain, *Italian Political Science Review/Rivista Italiana Di Scienza Politica* 51(1): 100–116.

Imig, D. (1996) Advocacy by Proxy: The Children's Lobby in American Politics, *Journal of Children and Poverty* 2(1): 31–53.

Ivanovska Hadijevska, M. & Stavenes, T. (2020) Maintaining Registration and Tax Benefits: Consequences for Professionalisation of Voluntary Membership Organisations in Norway and the UK, *Journal of Civil Society* 16(12): 1–23.

Ivanovska Hadjievska, M. (2018) *Exploring the Link between Non-Profit Law and the Internal Governance of Non-Profit Membership Organisations: Legal Forms and Maintaining Indirect Benefits in the UK and the Netherlands*, PhD Thesis, University of Exeter.

Jankowski, R. (1998) Preference Aggregation in Political Parties and Interest Groups: A Synthesis of Corporatist and Encompassing Organization Theory, *American Journal of Political Science* 32(1): 105–125.

Jentges, E., Brändli, M., Donges, P., & Jarren, O. (2013) Die Kommunikation politischer Interessengruppen in Deutschland. SCM *Studies in Communication and Media* 1(3–4): 381–409.

Jones, M. (2007) The Multiple Sources of Mission Drift, *Nonprofit and Voluntary Sector Quarterly* 36(2): 299–307.

Jordan, G. (2012) Professionalized Supply-Side Mobilization. Are Financial Contributors 'Meaningful Participants'?. In van Deth, J. W. & Maloney, W. A. (eds.) *New Participatory Dimensions in Civil Society: Professionalization and Individualized Collective Action*. London: Routledge.

Jordan, G. & Greenan, J. (2012) The Changing Contours of British Representation: Pluralism in Practice. In Halpin, D. & Jordan, G. (eds.) *The Scale of Interest Organization in Democratic Politics: Data and Research Methods*. Basingstoke: Palgrave Macmillan.

Jordan, G., Halpin, D., & Maloney, W. A. (2004) Defining Interests: Disambiguation and the Need for New Distinctions?, *British Journal of Politics and International Relations* 6(2): 195–212.

Jordan, G. & Maloney, W. A. (1997) *The Protest Business: Mobilizing Campaign Groups*. Manchester: Manchester University Press.

Jordan, G. & Maloney, W. A. (2007) *Democracy and Interest Groups: Enhancing Participation?*. London: Palgrave Macmillan.

Junk, W. M., Crepaz, M., Hanegraaff, M., Berkhout, J., & Aizenberg, E. (2022) Changes in Interest Group Access in Times of Crisis: No Pain, No (Lobby) Gain, *Journal of European Public Policy* 29(9): 1374–1394.

Karl, B. D. (1998) Volunteers and Professionals: Many Histories, Many Meanings. In Clemens, E. S. & Powell, W. W. (eds.) (1998) *Private Action and the Public Good.* New Haven: Yale University Press.

Karlsen, R. & Saglie, J. (2017) Party Bureaucrats, Independent Professionals or Politicians? A Study of Party Employees, *West European Politics* 40(6): 1331–1351. '

Karthikeyan, S. I., Jonsson, S. & Wezel, F. C. (2016) The Travails of Identity Change: Competitor Claims and Distinctiveness of British Political Parties, 1970–1992, *Organization Science* 27(1): 106–122.

Katz, R. S. (1990) Party as Linkage: A Vestigial Function?, *European Journal of Political Research* 18(1): 143–161.

Katz, R. S. & Mair, P. (1993) The Evolution of Party Organizations in Europe: The Three Faces of Party Organization, *American Review of Politics* 14(4): 593–617.

Katz, R. S. & Mair, P. (eds.) (1994) *How Parties Organize: Change and Adaptation in Party Organizations in Western Democracies.* London: SAGE.

Katz, R. S. & Mair, P. (1995) Changing Models of Party Organisation and Party Democracy: The Emergence of the Cartel Party, *Party Politics* 1(1): 5–28.

Katz, R. S. & Mair, P. (1996) Cadre, Catch-All or Cartel? A Rejoinder, *Party Politics* 2 (4): 525–534.

Katz, R. S. & Mair, P. (2002) The Ascendancy of the Party in Public Office: Party Organizational Change in 20th-Century Democracies. In Gunther, R., Montero, J. R., & Linz, J. J. (eds.) *Political Parties: Old Concepts and New Challenges.* Oxford: Oxford University Press.

Katz, R. S. & Mair, P. (2009) The Cartel Party Thesis: A Restatement, *Perspectives on Politics* 7(4): 753–766.

Kaur, M. & Verma, R. (2016) Social Media: An Emerging Tool for Political Participation, *International Journal of Social and Organizational Dynamicsin IT* 5(2): 31–38.

Kikulis, L. M., Slack, T., & Hinings, B. (1995) Does Decision Making Make a Difference? Patterns of Change within Canadian National Sport Organizations, *Journal of Sport Management* 9(3): 273–299.

Kimberlin, S. E. (2010) Advocacy by Nonprofits: Roles and Practice of Core Advocacy Organizations and Direct Service Agencies, *Journal of Policy Practice* 9(3–4): 164–182.

King, D. (2017) Becoming Business-Like: Governing the Nonprofit Professional, *Nonprofit and Voluntary Sector Quarterly* 46(2): 241–260.

King, G., Honaker, J., Joseph, A., & Scheve, K. (2001) Analyzing Incomplete Political Science Data: An Alternative Algorithm for Multiple Imputation, *American Political Science Review* 95(1): 49–69.

Kirchheimer, O. (1965) Der Wandel des westeuropäischen Parteisystems, *Politische Vierteljahresschrift* 6(1): 20–41.

Kitschelt, H. (1989) *The Logics of Party Formation: Ecological Politics in Belgium and West Germany.* Ithaca: Cornell University Press.

Kittilson, M. & Scarrow, S. (2003) Political Parties and the Rhetoric and Realities of Democratization. In Cain, B. E., Dalton, R. J., & Scarrow, E. S. (eds.) *Democracy Transformed? Expanding Political Opportunities in Advanced Industrial Democracies.* Oxford: Oxford University Press.

Kleidman, R. (1994) Volunteer Activism and Professionalism in Social Movement Organizations, *Social Problems* 41(2): 257–276.

Klitzke, J. (2017) Membership or Influence Logic? The Response of Organized Interests to Retirement Age Reforms in Britain and Germany. In Ebbinghaus, B. & Naumann, E. (eds.)

Welfare State Reforms Seen from Below, Comparing Public Attitudes and Organized Interests in Britain and Germany. New York: Palgrave Macmillan.

Klüver, H. & Saurugger, S. (2013) Opening the Black Box: The Professionalization of Interest Groups in the European Union, *Interest Groups & Advocacy* 2(2): 185–205.

Knoke, D. (1990) *Organizing for Collective Action. The Political Economies of Associations.* New York: Aldine de Gruyter.

Kohler-Koch, B. (2010) Civil Society and EU Democracy: 'Astroturf' Representation?, *Journal of European Public Policy* 17(1): 100–116.

Kohler-Koch, B. & Buth, V. (2013) The Balancing Act of European Civil Society: Between Professionalism and Grass Roots. In Kohler-Koch, B. & Quittkat, C. (eds.) *De-Mystification of Participatory Democracy: EU-Governance and Civil Society.* Oxford: Oxford University Press.

Kölln, A. (2015) The Value of Political Parties to Representative Democracy, *European Political Science Review* 7(4): 593–613.

Koole, R. (1996) Cadre, Catch-All or Cartel? A Comment on the Notion of Cartel Party, *Party Politics* 2(4): 507–523.

Kopecký, P. & Mudde, C. (2003) *Uncivil Society? Contentious Politics in Post-Communist Europe.* London: Routledge.

Kreutzer, K. & Jäger, U. (2011) Volunteering versus Managerialism: Conflict Over Organizational Identity in Voluntary Associations, *Nonprofit and Voluntary Sector Quarterly* 40(4): 634–661.

Kriesi, H. (1996) The Organizational Structure of New Social Movements in a Political Context. In McAdam, D., McCarthy, J. D., & Zald, M. N. (eds.) *Comparative Perspectives on Social Movements: Political Opportunities, Mobilizing Structures, and Cultural Framings.* Cambridge: Cambridge University Press.

Kriesi, H. (2006) Organizational Resources: Personnel and Finances. In Maloney, W. A. & Roßteutscher, S. (eds.) *Social Capital and Associations in European Democracies: A Comparative Analysis.* London: Routledge.

Kriesi, H. & Baglioni, S. (2003) Putting Local Associations into Their Context, *Schweizerische Zeitschrift für Politikwissenschaft* 9(3): 1–34.

Kriesi, H., Tresch, A. D., Jochum, C., & Margit, T. (2007) Going Public in the European Union: Action Repertoires of Western European Collective Political Actors, *Comparative Political Studies* 40(1): 48–73.

Krouwel, A. (2003) Otto Kirchheimer and the Catch-All Party, *West European Politics* 26(2): 23–40.

Lang, S. (2013) *NGOs, Civil Society, and the Public Sphere.* Cambridge: Cambridge University Press.

Larsson, O. S. (2011) *Standardizing Civil Society.* Stockholm: Santérus Press.

Laube, S., Schank, J., & Scheffer, T. (2020) Constitutive Invisibility: Exploring the Work of Staff Advisers in Political Position-Making, *Social Studies of Science* 50(2): 292–316.

Lawson, K. (1980) *Political Parties and Linkage: A Comparative Perspective.* New Haven: Yale University Press.

Lawson, K. & Merkl, P. (eds.) (1988) *When Parties Fail: Emerging Alternative Organizations.* Princeton: Princeton University Press.

Leach, D. K. (2005) The Iron Law of *What* Again? Conceptualizing Oligarchy across Organizational Forms, *Sociological Theory* 23(3): 312–337.

Lee, Y. et al. (2020) Charity Advertising: Congruence between Political Orientation and Cause of Need, *International Journal of Advertising* 39(7): 943–962.

LeRoux, K. & Feeney, M. K. (2015) *Nonprofit Organizations and Civil Society in the United States.* New York: Routledge.

LeRoux, K. & Goerdel, H. T. (2009) Political Advocacy by Nonprofit Organizations, *Public Performance & Management Review* 32(4): 514–536.

Lipset, S. M., Trow, M., & Coleman, J. S. (1956) *Union Democracy: The Internal Politics of the International Typographical Union.* Glencoe: The Free Press.

Lisi, M. & Oliveira, R. (2020) Standing Alone? Towards a More Unified View of Party-Group Relations in Contemporary Democracies, *European Review* 30(1): 58–78.

Lits, B. (2020) Detecting Astroturf Lobbying Movements, *Communication and the Public* 5 (3–4): 164–177.

Lowery, D. (2007) Why Do Organized Interests Lobby? A Multi-Goal, Multi-Context Theory of Lobbying, *Polity* 39(1): 29–54.

Lu, J. (2015) Which Nonprofit Gets More Government Funding? Nonprofits' Organizational Attributes and Their Receipts of Government Funding, *Nonprofit Management and Leadership* 25(3): 297–312.

Lu, J. (2018a) Fear the Government? A Meta-Analysis of the Impact of Government Funding on Nonprofit Advocacy Engagement, *The American Review of Public Administration* 48(3): 203–218.

Lu, J. (2018b) Organizational Antecedents of Nonprofit Engagement in Policy Advocacy: A Metaanalytical Review, *Nonprofit and Voluntary Sector Quarterly* 47(4): 177–203.

Lu, J. & Park, J. (2018) Bureaucratization, Professionalization, and Advocacy Engagement in Nonprofit Human Service Organizations, Human Service Organizations: Management, *Leadership & Governance* 42(4): 380–395.

Lucardie, P. (2000) Prophets, Purifiers and Prolocutors: Towards a Theory on the Emergence of New Parties, *Party Politics* 6(2): 175–185.

Lupu, N. (2017) *Party Brands in Crisis: Partisanship, Brand Dilution, And The Breakdown Of Political Parties In Latin America.* Cambridge: Cambridge University Press.

Lutz, A. et al. (2013) Leadership Style in Relation to Organizational Change and Organizational Creativity: Perceptions from Nonprofit Organizational Members, *Nonprofit Management & Leadership* 24(1): 23–42.

Lynn, T., Rosati, P., Conway, E., Curran, D., Fox, G., & O'Gorman, C. (2022) Digital Technologies and Civil Society. In Lynn, T., Rosati, P., Conway, E., Curran, D., Fox, G., & O'Gorman, C. (eds.) *Digital Towns.* London: Palgrave Macmillan.

Mahmood, T. (2016) Government Funding to the NGOs: A Blessing or a Curse?, *International Journal of Research in Business and Social Science* 51(6): 51–61.

Maier, F. & Meyer, M. (2011) Managerialism and Beyond: Discourses of Civil Society Organization and Their Governance Implications, *Voluntas: International Journal of Voluntary and Nonprofit Organizations* 22(4): 731–756.

Maier, F., Meyer, M., & Steinbereithner, M. (2016) Nonprofit Organizations Becoming Business-Like: A Systematic Review, *Nonprofit and Voluntary Sector Quarterly* 45(1): 64–86.

Mair, P. (1994) Party Organizations: From Civil Society to the State. In Katz, R. S. & Mair, P. (eds.) *How Parties Organize: Change and Adaptation in Party Organizations in Western Democracies.* London/Thousand Oaks: SAGE.

Mair, P. (1997) *Party System Change: Approaches and Interpretations.* New York: Oxford University Press.

Mair, P. (2002) Populist Democracy vs. Party Democracy. In: Meny, Y. & Surel, Y. (eds.) *Democracies and the Populist Challenge.* Basingstoke: Palgrave.

Mair, P., Müller, W. C., & Plasser, F. (2004) *Political Parties and Electoral Change.* London: SAGE Publications Ltd.

Bibliography

Mair, P. & Mudde, C. (1998) The Party Family and its Study, *Annual Review of Political Science* 1: 211–229.

Malkopoulou, A. & Kirshner, A. (eds.) (2021) *Militant Democracy and Its Critics: Populism, Parties, Extremism*. Edinburgh: Edinburgh University Press.

Maloney, W., Jordan, G., & McLaughlin, A. (1994) Interest Groups and Public Policy: The Insider/Outsider Model Revisited, *Journal of Public Policy* 14(1): 17–38.

Maloney, W. A. (2009) Interest Groups and the Revitalization of Democracy: Are We Expecting Too Much?, *Representation* 45(3): 277–287.

Maloney, W. A. (2012) The Democratic Contribution of Professionalized Representation. In van Deth, J. W. & Maloney, W. A. (eds.) *New Participatory Dimensions in Civil Society: Professionalization and Individualized Collective Action*. London: Routledge.

Maloney, W. A. (2015) Organizational Populations: Professionalization, Maintenance and Democratic Delivery. In Lowery, D., Halpin, D., & Gray, V. (eds.) *The Organization Ecology Of Interest Communities: Assessment and Agenda*. Basingstoke: Palgrave Macmillan.

Maloney, W. A. & Rossteutscher, S. (2005) Welfare through Organizations. In Rossteutscher, S. (ed.) *Democracy and the Role of Associations*. London: Routledge.

Mansbridge, J. (2003) Rethinking Representation, *American Political Science Review* 97(4): 515–528.

Margetts, H., John, P., Hale, S., & Yasseri, T. (2015) *Political Turbulence: How Social Media Shape Collective Action*. Princeton: Princeton University Press.

Martin, N., de Lange, S. L., & van der Brug, W. (2022a) Staying Connected: Explaining Parties' Enduring Connections to Civil Society, *West European Politics* 45(7): 1385–1406.

Martin, N., de Lange, S. L., & van der Brug, W. (2022b) Holding on to Voters in Volatile Times: Bonding Voters through Party Links with Civil Society, *Party Politics* 28(2): 354–364.

Mason, D. (1996) *Leading and Managing the Expressive Dimension*. San Francisco: Jossey-Bass Publishers.

May, J. D. (1973) Opinion Structure of Political Parties: The Special Law of Curvilinear Disparity, *Political Studies* 21(2): 135–151.

Mc Alevey, J. F. (2016) *No Shortcuts: Organizing for Power in the New Gilded Age*. New York: Oxford University Press.

McCarthy, J. & Zald, M. (1977) Resource Mobilization and Social Movements: A Partial Theory, *American Journal of Sociology* 82(6): 1212–1241.

McCulloch, A. (1983) The Ecology Party and Constituency Politics: The Anatomy of a Grass-roots Party, Paper presented at the Political Studies Association Conference at Newcastle-upon-Tyne, April 1983.

McCulloch, A. (1988) Shades of Green: Ideas in the British Green Movement, *Teaching Politics* 17(2): 186–207.

McCulloch, A. (1992) The Green Party in England and Wales: Structure and Development: The Early Years, *Environmental Politics* 1(3): 418–436.

McGrane, D. (2019) *The New NDP: Moderation, Modernization, and Political Marketing: Communication, Strategy, and Politics*. Vancouver: University of British Columbia Press.

McLaverty, P. (2002) Civil Society and Democracy, *Contemporary Politics* 8(4): 303–318.

Meguid, B. (2008) *Party Competition between Unequals*. Cambridge: Cambridge University Press.

Mellquist, J. (2022) The Game of Influence: Policy Professional Capital, *Journal of Civil Society* 18(1): 105–123.

Meyer, M. & Maier, F. (2015) The Future of Civil Society Organisation Governance: Beyond Managerialism. In Laville, J., Young, D., & Eynaud, P. (eds.) *Civil Society, the Third Sector and Social Enterprise Governance and Democracy*. London: Routledge.

Michels, R. (1915) *Political Parties a Sociological Study of the Oligarchical Tendencies of Modern Democracy*. London: Routledge.

Miller-Millesen, J. (2003) Understanding the Behavior of Nonprofit Boards of Directors: A Theory-Based Approach, *Nonprofit and Voluntary Sector Quarterly* 32(4): 521–547.

Milligan, C., & Fyfe, N. R. (2005) Preserving Space for Volunteers: Exploring the Links Between Voluntary Welfare Organisations, Volunteering and Citizenship, *Urban Studies* 42(3), 417–433.

Minkoff, D. C. (2002) The Emergence of Hybrid Organizational Forms: Combining Identity-Based Service Provision and Political Action, *Nonprofit and Voluntary Sector Quarterly* 31(3): 377–401.

Minkoff, D. C., Aisenbrey, S., & Agnone, J. (2008) Organizational Diversity in the U.S. Advocacy Sector, *Social Problems* 55(4): 525–548.

Minkoff, D. C. & Powell, W. W. (2006) Nonprofit Mission: Constancy, Responsiveness, or Deflection?. In Powell, W. W. & Steinberg, R. (eds.) *The Nonprofit Sector: A Research Handbook*, second edition. New Haven: Yale University Press.

Moe, T. M. (1980) *The Organization of Interests: Incentives and the Internal Dynamics of Political Interest Groups*. Chicago: The University of Chicago Press.

Moens P. (2021) Professional Activists? Party Activism Among Political Staffers in Parliamentary Democracies, *Party Politics*, Online First June 2021.

Moens P. (2022) Are Political Staffers out of Touch with Grassroots Party Members? Assessing Congruence between Professionals and Volunteers, *Political Studies*, Online First July 2022.

Moore, M. H. (2000) Managing for Value: Organizational Strategy in for-Profit, Nonprofit, and Governmental Organizations, *Nonprofit and Voluntary Sector Quarterly* 29(1): 183–204.

Mosley, J. E. (2010) Organizational Resources and Environmental Incentives: Understanding the Policy Advocacy Involvement of Human Service Nonprofits, *Social Service Review* 84(1): 57–76.

Mosley, J. E. (2011) Institutionalization, Privatization, and Political Opportunity: What Tactical Choices Reveal about the Policy Advocacy of Human Service Nonprofits, *Nonprofit and Voluntary Sector Quarterly* 40(3): 435–447.

Moufahim, M., Reedy, P., & Humphreys M. (2015) The Vlaams Belang: The Rhetoric of Organizational Identity, *Organization Studies* 36(1): 91–111.

Mudde, C. (2007) The Single-Issue Party Thesis: Extreme Right Parties and the Immigration Issue, *West European Politics* 22(3): 182–197.

Muldoon J. & Rye, D. (2020) Conceptualizing Party-Driven Movements, *British Journal of Politics and International Relations* 22(3): 485–504.

Murray, V., Bradshaw, P., & Wolpin, J. (1992) Power in and around Nonprofit Boards: A Neglected Dimension of Governance, *Nonprofit Management and Leadership* 3(2): 165–182.

Nass, C. I. (1986) Bureaucracy, Technical Expertise, and Professionals: A Weberian Approach, *Sociological Theory* 4(1): 61–70.

Nelson, E. (2018) They Pay People to Work Here? The Role of Volunteering on Nonprofit Career Awareness and Interest, *Journal of Public and Nonprofit Affairs* 4(3): 329–349.

Nesbit, R., Brudney, J. L., & Christensen, R. (2012). *Exploring the Limits of Volunteerism in Public Service Delivery: Substituting Volunteer Labor For Paid Labor*. Working Paper. New York: Center for Nonprofit Management and Strategy, The City University of New York.

Nesbit, R., Christensen, R., & Brudney, J. L. (2017) The Limits and Possibilities of Volunteering: A Framework for Explaining the Scope of Volunteer Involvement in Public and Nonprofit Organizations, *Public Administration Review* 78(4): 502–513.

296   Bibliography

Netting, F. E., Nelson W., Borders K., & Huber, R. (2004) Volunteer and Paid Staff Relationships, *Administration in Social Work* 28(3–4): 69–89.

Nienhüser, W. (2008) Resource Dependence Theory—How Well Does It Explain Behavior of Organizations?, *Management Revue* 19(1/2): 9–32.

Norris, P. (2002) *Democratic Phoenix: Reinventing Political Activism*. Cambridge: Cambridge University Press.

Norris-Tirrell, D., Rinella, J., & Pham, X. (2018) Examining the Career Trajectories of Nonprofit Executive Leaders, *Nonprofit and Voluntary Sector Quarterly* 47(1): 146–164.

O'Regan, K. & Oster, S. M. (2005) Does the Structure and Composition of the Board Matter? The Case of Nonprofit Organizations, *Journal of Law, Economics, and Organization* 21(1): 205–227.

O'Reilly, D. & Reed, M. (2011) The Grit in the Oyster: Professionalism, Managerialism and Leaderism as Discourses of UK Public Services Modernization, *Organization Studies* 32(8): 1079–1101.

Offe, C. & Wiesenthal, H. (1980) Two Logics of Collective Action: Theoretical Notes on Social Class and Organizational Form, *Political Power and Social Theory* 1: 67–115.

Olson, M. (1965) *The Logic of Collective Action: Public Goods and the Theory of Groups.* Cambridge: Harvard University Press.

Otjes, S. & Rasmussen, A. (2017) The Collaboration between Interest Groups and Political Parties in Multi-Party Democracies: Party System Dynamics and the Effect of Power and Ideology, *Party Politics* 23(2): 96–109.

Paine, A., Ockenden, N., & Stuart, J. (2010) Volunteers in Hybrid Organizations: A Marginalized Majority? In Billis, D. (ed.) *Hybrid Organisations and the Third Sector: Challenges for Practice, Theory and Policy*. London: Palgrave Macmillan, 93–113.

Painter, M. A. & Paxton, P. (2014) Checkbooks in the Heartland: Change over Time in Voluntary Association Membership, *Sociological Forum* 29(2): 408–428.

Panagopoulos, C. (2016) All about That Base: Changing Campaign Strategies in U.S. Presidential Elections, *Party Politics* 22(2): 179–190.

Panebianco, A. (1988) *Political Parties: Organization and Power*. Cambridge: Cambridge University Press.

Patsiurko, N., Campbell, J. L. & Hall, J. A. (2012) Measuring Cultural Diversity: Ethnic, Linguistic and Religious Fractionalization in the OECD, *Ethnic and Racial Studies* 35(2): 195–217.

Paxton, P. and Ressler, R. W. (2018) Trust and Participation in Association. In Uslaner, E. (ed.) *The Oxford Handbook of Social and Political Trust*. Oxford: Oxford University Press.

Pedersen, K., Bille, L., Buch, R., Elklit, J., Hansen, B., & Nielsen, H. J. (2004) Sleeping or Active Partners? Danish Party Members and the Turn of the Millennium, *Party Politics* 10(4): 367–338.

Pedersen, M. N. (1982) Towards a New Typology of Party Lifespans and Minor Parties, *Scandinavian Political Studies* 5: 1–16.

Pekkanen, R. J. & Smith, S. R. (2014) Nonprofit Advocacy: Definitions and Concepts. In Pekkanen, R. J., Smith, S. R., & Tsujinaka, Y. (eds.) *Nonprofits and Advocacy, Engaging Community and Government in an Era of Retrenchment*. Baltimore: Johns Hopkins University Press.

Peng et al. (2015) Is There a Nonprofit Advantage? Examining the Impact of Institutional Context on Individual—Organizational Value Congruence, *Public Administration Review* 75(4): 585–596.

Pestoff, V., Brandsen, T., & Verschuere B. (eds.) (2012) *New Public Governance, the Third Sector, and Co-Production*. London: Routledge.

Pfeffer, J. & Salancik, G. R. (1978) *The External Control of Organizations: A Resource Dependence Perspective*. New York: Harper & Row.

Pianta, M. (2013) Democracy Lost: The Financial Crisis in Europe and the Role of Civil Society, *Journal of Civil Society* 9(2): 148–161.

Pitkin, H. F. (1967) *The Concept of Representation*. Berkeley: University of California Press.

Plesner, U. & Husted, E. (2019) *Digital Organizing: Revisiting Themes in Organization Studies*. London: Bloomsbury Publishing.

Poguntke, T. (1993) *Alternative Politics: The German Green Party*. Edinburgh: Edinburgh University Press.

Poguntke, T. (2002) Green Parties in National Governments: From Protest to Acquiescence?, *Environmental Politics* 11(1): 133–145.

Poguntke, T. et al. (2016) Party Rules, Party Resources and the Politics of Parliamentary Democracies: How Parties Organize in the 21st Century, *Party Politics* 22(6): 661–678.

Poguntke, T. & Webb, P. (2005) *The Presidentialization of Politics. A Comparative Study of Modern Democracies*. Oxford: Oxford University Press.

Polk, J., Rovny, J., Bakker, R., Edwards, E., Hooghe, L., Jolly, S., Koedam, J., Kostelka, F., Marks, G., Schumacher, G., Steenbergen, M., Vachudova, M., & Zilovic, M. (2017) Explaining the Salience of Anti-Elitism and Reducing Political Corruption for Political Parties in Europe with the 2014 Chapel Hill Expert Survey Data, *Research & Politics* 4(1): 1–9.

Pollitt, C. (1990) Doing Business in the Temple? Managers and Quality Assurance in the Public Services, *Public Administration* 68(4): 435–452.

Prendiville, B. (2015) The Green Party: 'Green Surge' or Work in Progress?, *Revue Française de Civilisation Britannique* XX-3: 1–18.

Putnam, R. D. (2000) *Bowling Alone: The Collapse and Revival of American Community*. New York: Simon and Schuster.

Quintelier, E. (2008) Who is Politically Active: The Athlete, the Scout Member or the Environmental Activist? Young People, Voluntary Engagement and Political Participation, *Acta Sociologica* 51(4): 355–370.

Rahat, G., Hazan, R., & Katz, R. S. (2008) Democracy and Political Parties: On the Uneasy Relationship between Participation, Competition and Representation, *Party Politics* 14(6): 663–683.

Rangan, V. K. (2004) Lofty Missions, Down-to-Earth Plans. Retrieved from https://hbr.org/2004/03/lofty-missions-down-to-earth-plans, accessed 10.05.2022.

Rasmussen A. (2020) How has Covid-19 changed lobbying activity across Europe?. Retrieved from https://blogs.lse.ac.uk/europpblog/2020/06/17/how-has-covid-19-changed-lobbying-activity-across-europe/, accessed 29.08.2022.

Rasmussen, A. & Lindeboom, G.-J. (2013) Interest Group–Party Linkage in the Twenty-First Century: Evidence from Denmark, the Netherlands and the United Kingdom, *European Journal of Political Research* 52(2): 264–289.

Rasmussen, A. & Reher, S. (2019) Civil Society Engagement and Policy Representation in Europe, *Comparative Political Studies* 52(11): 1648–1676.

Reid, E. J. (1999) Nonprofit Advocacy and Political Participation. In Boris, E. T. & Steuerle, C. E. (eds.) *Nonprofit and Government*. Washington, DC: The Urban Institute Press, 291–308.

Renzsch, W., Detterbeck, K., & Kincaid, J. (2015) *Political Parties and Civil Society in Federal Countries*. Oxford: Oxford University Press.

Rihoux, B. (2016) Green Party Organisations: The Difficult Path from Amateur-Activist to Professional-Electoral Logics. In van Haute, E. (eds.) *Green Parties in Europe*. London: Routledge (Taylor & Francis), 298–314.

Rogers, B. (2005) From Membership to Management? The Future of Political Parties as Democratic Organisations, *Parliamentary Affairs* 58(3): 600–610.

298 Bibliography

Romzek, B. S. & Utter, J. A. (1997) Congressional Legislative Staff: Political Professionals or Clerks?, *American Journal of Political Science* 41(4): 1251–1279.

Rootes, C. (1994) Greens in a Cold Climate. In Richardson, D. and Rootes, C. (eds.) *The Green Challenge: The Development of Green Parties in Europe*. London and New York: Routledge (Taylor & Francis), 48–65.

Rosenblum, N. L. (1998) *Membership and Morals: The Personal Uses of Pluralism in America*. Princeton: Princeton University Press.

Rosenblum, N. L. (2000a) Political Parties as Membership Groups, *Columbia Law Review* 100(3): 813–844.

Rosenblum, N. L. (2000b) Primus Inter Pares: Political Parties and Civil Society, *Chicago-Kent Law Review* 75(2): 493–529.

Rüdig, W. (2008) Green Party Organization in Britain: Change and Continuity. In Rüdig, W., Frankland, E. G., Lucardie, P., & Rihoux, B. (eds.) *Green Parties in Transition*. Farnham: Ashgate Publishing.

Rüdig, W., Franklin, M. N., & Bennie, L. G. (1996) Up and Down with the Greens. Ecology and Party Politics in Britain 1989–1992, *Electoral Studies* 15(1): 1–20.

Rüdig, W. & Lowe, P. D. (1986) The Withered 'Greening' of British Politics: A Study of the Ecology Party, *Political Studies* 34(2): 262–284.

Ruzza, C. & Sanchez Salgado, R. (2021) The Populist Turn in EU Politics and the Intermediary Role of Civil Society Organisations, *European Politics and Society* 22(4): 471–485.

Sadiq, T., van Tulder, R., & Maas, K. (2022) Building a Taxonomy of Hybridization: An Institutional Logics Perspective on Societal Impact, *Sustainability* 14 (10301): 1–22.

Saidel, J. R. & Harlan, S. L. (1998) Contracting and Patterns of Nonprofit Governance, *Nonprofit Management and Leadership* 8(3): 243–259.

Salamon, L. M. (1994) The Rise of the Nonprofit Sector, *Foreign Affairs* 73(4): 109–122.

Salamon, L. M. (1995) *Partners in Public Service: Government–Nonprofit Relations in the Modern Welfare State*. Baltimore: Johns Hopkins University Press.

Salamon, L. M. & Anheier, H. K. (1998) Social Origins of Civil Society: Explaining the Nonprofit Sector Cross-Nationally, *Voluntas: International Journal of Voluntary and Nonprofit Organizations* 9(3): 213–248.

Salamon, L. M. & Flaherty, S. (1997) Nonprofit Law: Ten Issues in Search of Resolution. In Salamon, L. M. (ed.) *The International Guide to Nonprofit Law*. New York: Wiley.

Salamon, L. M. & Lessans-Geller, S. (2008) Nonprofit America: A Force for Democracy (Communiqué no. 9). Baltimore, MD: Center for Civil Society Studies, Johns Hopkins University Institute for Public Policy.

Salgado, R. (2010) NGO Structural Adaptation to Funding Requirements and Prospects for Democracy: The Case of the European Union, *Global Society* 24(4): 507–527.

Salisbury, R. H. (1969) An Exchange Theory of Interest Groups, *Midwest Journal of Political Science* 13(1): 1–32.

Salisbury, R. H. (1984) Interest Representation: The Dominance of Institutions, *The American Political Science Review* 78(1): 64–76.

Salvatore, D. & Numerato D. (2018) Governance and Professionalism. In Farazmand, A. (ed.) *Global Encyclopedia of Public Administration, Public Policy, and Governance*. Cham: Springer.

Sartori, G. (1965) *Democratic Theory*. New York: Frederick A. Praeger.

Sartori, G. (1976) *Parties and Systems: A Framework for Analysis*. Cambridge: Cambridge University Press.

Saurugger, S. (2008) Interest Groups and Democracy in the European Union, *West European Politics* 31(6): 1274–1291.

Saurugger, S. (2012) The Professionalization of EU's Civil Society. A Conceptual Framework. In van Deth, J. W. and Maloney W. A. (eds.) *New Participatory Dimensions in Civil Society, Professionalization and Individualized Collective Action.* London: Routledge.

Sayan, P. & Duygulu, Ş. (2022) NGOization, Politicization and Polarization of Roma Civil Society in Turkey, *Southeast European and Black Sea Studies* 22(3): 419–440.

Saz-Gil, I., Bretos, I., & Díaz-Foncea, M. (2021) Cooperatives and Social Capital: A Narrative Literature Review and Directions for Future Research, *Sustainability* 13(2): 534–551.

Scarrow, S. E. (1994) The 'Paradox of Enrollment': Assessing the Costs and Benefits of Party Memberships, *European Journal of Political Research* 25(1): 41–60.

Scarrow, S. E. (1996) *Parties and Their Members: Organizing for Victory in Britain and Germany.* New York: Oxford University Press.

Scarrow, S. E. (2005) *Implementing Intra-party Democracy: Political Parties and Democracy in Theoretical and Practical Perspectives.* Washington, DC: National Democratic Institute.

Scarrow, S. E. (2015) *Beyond Party Members: Changing Approaches to Partisan Mobilization.* New York: Oxford University Press.

Scarrow, S. E. & Webb P. (2017) Investigating Party Organization: Structures, Resources, and Representative Strategies. In Scarrow, S. E. Webb, P., and Poguntke, T. (eds.) *Organizing Political Parties: Representation, Participation, and Power.* Oxford: Oxford University Press.

Scarrow, S. E., Webb, P., & Poguntke, T. (2017) *Organizing Political Parties: Representation, Participation and Power.* Oxford: Oxford University Press.

Schattschneider, E. (1942) *Party Government.* New York: Farrar & Rinehart, Inc.

Schattschneider, E. (1960) *The Semisovereign People: A Realist's View of Democracy in America.* New York: Holt, Rinehart and Winston.

Schlozman, K. L. (2010) Who Sings in the Heavenly Chorus?: The Shape of the Organized Interest System. In Maisel L. S., Berry, J. M., & Edwards, G. C. (eds.) *The Oxford Handbook of American Political Parties and Interest Groups.* New York: Oxford University Press.

Schlozman, K. L., Jones, P. E., You, H. Y., Burch, T., Verba, S., & Brady, H. E. (2015) Organizations and the Democratic Representation of Interests: What Does It Mean When Those Organizations Have No Members?, *Perspectives on Politics* 13(4): 1017–1102.

Schmid, H., Bar, M. & Nirel, R. (2008) Advocacy Activities in Nonprofit Human Service Organizations: Implications for Policy, *Nonprofit and Voluntary Sector Quarterly* 37(4): 581–602.

Schmitter, P. C. & Streeck, W. (1999) The Organization of Business Interests: Studying the Associate action of Business in Advanced Industrial Societies. MPIfG, Discussion Paper 1999/01.

Schoenefeld, J. J. (2021) Interest Groups, NGOs or Civil Society Organisations? The Framing of Non-State Actors in the EU, *Voluntas: International Journal of Voluntary and Nonprofit Organizations* 32(3): 585–596.

Schouten, B., Coben, F., & Bethlehem, J. (2009) Indicators for the Representativeness of Survey Response, *Survey Methodology* 35(1): 101–113.

Schulz, T. (2010) Mobilising Voluntary Work: The Interplay between Organisations and Municipalities. In Maloney, W. A. & van Deth, J. W. (eds.) *Civil Society and Activism in Europe: Contextualizing Engagement and Political Orientations.* London: Routledge.

Schwartzman, D. (2008) Review of Babylon and Beyond: The Economics of Anti-Capitalist, Anti-Globalist and Radical Green Movements by Derek Wall, *Science & Society* 72(2): 247–250.

Scott, R. (1967) The Factory as a Social Service Organization: Goal Displacement in Workshops for the Blend, *Social Problems* 15(2): 160–175.

Shepherd, S. (2018) Managerialism: An Ideal Type, *Studies in Higher Education* 43(9): 1668–1678.

Sills, D. L. (1959) Voluntary Associations: Instruments and Objects of Change, *Human Organization* 18(1): 17–21.

Sills, D. L. (1968) Voluntary Associations. II. Sociological Aspects. In Sills, D. L. (ed.) *International Encyclopedia of the Social Sciences* Volume 16. New York: Macmillan and Free Press.

Skocpol, T. (2013) *Diminished Democracy: From Membership to Management in American Civic Life.* Oklahoma: University of Oklahoma Press.

Skocpol, T., Ganz, M., Munson, Z., Camp, B., Swers, M., & Oser, J. (1999) How Americans Became Civic. In Skocpol, T. & Fiorina, M. P. (eds.) *Civic Engagement in American Democracy.* Washington, DC: The Brookings Institute.

Smith, C. E. & Freedman A. E. (1972) *Voluntary Associations: Perspectives on the Literature.* Cambridge: Harvard University Press.

Smith, S. R. (2010) Hybridization and Nonprofit Organizations: The Governance Challenge, *Policy and Society* 29(3): 219–229.

Smith, S. R. & Lipsky, M. (1993) *Non-Profits for Hire: The Welfare State in the Age of Contracting.* Cambridge: Harvard University Press.

Solon, G., Haider, S. J., & Wooldridge, J. (2013) What Are We Weighting For?, NBER Working Papers 18859, National Bureau of Economic Research, Inc.

Staggenborg, S. (1988) The Consequences of Professionalization and Formalization in the Pro-Choice Movement, *American Sociological Review* 53(4): 585–605.

Staggenborg, S. (1991) *The Pro-Choice Movement: Organization and Activism in the Abortion Conflict.* New York: Oxford University Press.

Stavenes, T. & Ivanovska Hadjievska, M. (2021) Insider Status-Membership Involvement Offer Trade Off? The Case of Green Parties and Environmental Organisations, *Political Studies,* Online First August 2021.

Stewart, A. J. & Kuenzi, K. (2018) The Nonprofit Career Ladder: Exploring Career Paths as Leadership Development for Future Nonprofit Executives, *Public Personnel Management* 47(4): 359–381.

Stolle, D. & Rochon, T. R. (1998) Are All Associations Alike?: Member Diversity, Associational Type, and the Creation of Social Capital, *American Behavioral Scientist* 42(1): 47–65.

Stone, M. (1996) Competing Contexts: The Evolution of a Nonprofit Organization's Governance System in Multiple Environments, *Administration & Society* 28(1): 61–89.

Striebing, C. (2017) Professionalization and Voluntary Transparency Practices in Nonprofit Organizations, *Nonprofit Management and Leadership* 28(1): 65–83.

Strolovitch, D. Z. & Forrest, M. D. (2010) Social and Economic Justice Movements and Organizations. In Maisel, L. S., Berry J. M., & Edwards G. C. (eds.) *The Oxford Handbook of American Political Parties and Interest Groups.* New York: Oxford University Press.

Suarez, D. (2010a) Collaboration and Professionalization: The Contours of Public Sector Funding for Nonprofit Organizations, *Journal of Public Administration Research and Theory* 21(2): 307–326.

Suarez, D. (2010b) Street Credentials and Management Backgrounds: Careers of Nonprofit Executives in an Evolving Sector, *Nonprofit and Voluntary Sector Quarterly* 39(4): 696–716.

Svallfors, S. (2017) "Most MPs Are Not All That Sharp." Political Employees and Representative Democracy, *International Journal of Public Administration* 40(7): 548–558.

Thomassen, J. & van Ham, C. (2014) Failing Political Representation or a Change in Kind? Models of Representation and Empirical Trends in Europe, *West European Politics* 37(2): 400–419.

Thompson, L. & Pearson, M. (2021) Exploring Party Change: The Professionalisation of the UK's Three Green Parties Crossing the Representation Threshold, *Environmental Politics* 30(6): 938–957.

Toepler, S. (2010) Government Funding Policies. In Seaman, B. & Young, D. R. (eds.) *Handbook of Research on Nonprofit Economics and Management*. Cheltenham, UK: Edward Elgar, 320–334.

Toren, N. (1976) Bureaucracy and Professionalism: A Reconsideration of Weber's Thesis, *Academy of Management Review* 1(3): 36–46.

Tschirhart, M. & Gazley, B. (2014) Advancing Scholarship on Membership Associations: New Research and Next Steps, *Nonprofit and Voluntary Sector Quarterly* 43(2S): 3S–17S.

Uhlin, A. (2009) Which Characteristics of Civil Society Organizations Support What Aspects of Democracy? Evidence from Post-communist Latvia, *International Political Science Review* 30(3): 271–295.

van der Meer, T. & van Ingen, E. (2009) Schools of Democracy? Disentangling the Relationship between Civic Participation and Political Action in 17 European Democracies, *European Journal of Political Research* 48: 281–308.

van Biezen, I. (2004) Political Parties as Public Utilities, *Party Politics* 10(6): 701–722.

van Biezen, I., Mair, P., & Pogunkte, T. (2012) Going, Going, ... Gone? The Decline of Party Membership in Contemporary Europe, *European Journal of Political Research* 51: 24–56.

van der Ploeg, T., van Veen, W., & Versteegh, C. (2017) *Civil Society in Europe: Minimum Norms and Optimum Conditions of its Regulation*. Cambridge: Cambridge University Press.

van Deth J. W. & Maloney W. A. (2010) Introduction: Contextualizing Civil Societies in European Communities. In Maloney, W. A. & van Deth, J. W. (eds.) *Civil Society and Activism in Europe: Contextualizing Engagement and Political Orientations*. London: Routledge, 1–16.

van Deth J. W. & Maloney, W. A. (eds.) (2012) *New Participatory Dimensions in Civil Society: Professionalization and Individualized Collective Action*. London: Routledge.

van Haute, E. & Gauja, A. (2015) *Party Members and Activists*. London: Routledge.

van Puyvelde, S., Cornforth, C., Dansac, C., Guo, C., Hough, A., & Smith, D. (2016) Governance, Boards, and the Internal Structure of Associations. In Smith, D., Stebbins, R., & Grotz, J. (eds.) *The Palgrave Handbook of Volunteering, Civic Participation, and Nonprofit Associations*. London: Palgrave.

Waardenburg, M. & van de Bovenkamp, H. (2014) Civil Society Organisations as a Government Steering Mechanism: A Comparison between Sport Associations and Patient Organisations in the Netherlands. In Brandsen, T., Trommel, W., & Verschuere, B. (eds.) *Manufacturing Civil Society: Principles, Practices and Effects*. London: Palgrave Macmillan.

Walker, E., McCarthy, J., & Baumgartner, F. (2011) Replacing Members with Managers? Mutualism among Membership and Nonmembership Advocacy Organizations in the United States, *American Journal of Sociology* 116(4): 1284–1337.

Walker E. T. (2008) Contingent Pathways from Joiner to Activist: The Indirect Effect of Participation in Voluntary Associations on Civic Engagement, *Sociological Forum* 23(1): 116–143.

Walker, E. T. & McCarthy, J. D. (2010) Legitimacy, Strategy, and Resources in the Survival of Community-Based Organizations, *Social Problems* 57(3): 315–340.

Walker, J. L. (1983) The Origins and Maintenance of Interest Groups in America, *American Political Science Review* 77(2): 390–406.

Wall, D. (2010) Ecosocialism, the Left, and the U.K. Greens, *Capitalism Nature Socialism* 21(3): 109–115.

Wallander, L. & Molander, A. (2014) Disentangling Professional Discretion: A Conceptual and Methodological Approach, *Professions and Professionalism* 4(3): 1–19.

Ward, S. C. (2011) Commentary: The Machinations of Managerialism: New Public Management and the Diminishing Power of Professionals, *Journal of Cultural Economy* 4(2): 205–215.

Warner, W. K. & Havens, A. E. (1968) Goal Displacement and the Intangibility of Organizational Goals, *Administrative Science Quarterly* 12(4): 539–555.

Warren, M. E. (2001) Democracy and Association, *International Journal of Retail & Distribution Management* 31(8): 418–427.

Warren, M. E. (2008) The Nature and Logic of Bad Social Capital. In Castiglione, D. & van Deth, J. W. (eds.) *The Handbook of Social Capital*. Oxford: Oxford University Press.

Webb, P. (1994) Party Organizational Change in Britain: The Iron Law of Centralization?. In Katz, R. S. & Mair, P. (eds.) *How Parties Organize*. London: Sage.

Webb, P. & Fisher, J. (2003) Professionalism and the Millbank Tendency: The Political Sociology of New Labour's Employees, *Politics* 23(1): 10–20.

Webb, P. D. & Keith, D. (2017) Assessing the Strength of Party Organizational Resources. In Scarrow, S. E., Webb, P. D., & Poguntke, T. (eds.) *Organizing Political Parties*. Oxford: Oxford University Press.

Webb, P. & Kolodny, R. (2006) Professional Staff in Political Parties. In Katz, R. S. & Crotty, W. J. (ed.) *Handbook for Party Politics*. Thousand Oaks: SAGE Publications Ltd.

Webb, P., Scarrow, S., & Poguntke, T. (2019) Party Organization and Satisfaction with Democracy: Inside the Blackbox of Linkage, *Journal of Elections, Public Opinion and Parties*, Online First December 2019.

Weisbrod, B. A. (1997) The Future of the Nonprofit Sector: Its Entwining with Private Enterprise and Government, *Journal of Policy Analysis and Management* 16(4): 541–555.

Welzel, C., Inglehart, R., & Deutsch, F. (2005) Social Capital, Voluntary Associations and Collective Action: Which Aspects of Social Capital Have the Greatest 'Civic' Payoff?, *Journal of Civil Society* 1(2): 121–146.

Werner, A. (2020) Representation in Western Europe: Connecting Party-Voter Congruence and Party Goals, *The British Journal of Politics and International Relations* 22(1): 122–142.

Wheaton, B. (2007) Identity, Politics, and the Beach: Environmental Activism in Surfers Against Sewage, *Leisure Studies* 26(3): 279–302.

Whiteley, P. (2011) Is the Party Over? The Decline of Party Activism and Membership across the Democratic World, *Party Politics* 17(1): 21–44.

Whiteley, P. & Seyd, P. (1998) The Dynamics of Party Activism in Britain: A Spiral of Demobilization?, *British Journal of Political Science* 28(1): 113–137.

Wilderom, C. P. M. & Miner B. J. (1991) Defining Voluntary Groups and Agencies within Organization Science, *Organization Science* 2(4): 366–378.

Wilensky, H. L. (1964) The Professionalization of Everyone?, *American Journal of Sociology* 70(2): 137–158.

Williams, R. (2009) Using Heterogenous Choice Models to Compare Logit and Probit Coefficients across Groups, *Sociological Methods & Research* 37(4): 531–559.

Williams, R. (2010) Fitting Heterogeneous Choice Models Using OGLM, *Stata Journal* 10(4): 540–567.

Willis, E. (1978) Professionalism and Bureaucracy. The Changing Context of Primary Medical Care, *Community Health Studies* 2: 1–12.

Wilson, J. Q. (1973) *Political Organizations*. New York: Basic Books.

Witko, C. (2015) Case Study Approaches to Studying Organization Survival and Adaptation. In Lowery, D., Halpin, D., & Gray, V. (eds.) *The Organization Ecology of Interest Communities: Assessment and Agenda*. Basingstoke: Palgrave Macmillan.

Wollebæk, D. & Selle, P. (2010) Social Capital. In Taylor, R. (ed.) *Third Sector Research*. New York: Springer.

Wood, M. (1992) Is Governing Board Behavior Cyclical? *Nonprofit Management and Leadership* 3(2): 139–163.

Zald, M. N. & McCarthy, J. D. (1987) *Social Movements in an Organizational Society: Collected Essays*. New Brunswick: Transaction Publishers.

Zamponi, L. & Bosi, L. (2018) Politicizing Solidarity in Times of Crisis: The Politics of Alternative Action Organizations in Greece, Italy, and Spain, *American Behavioral Scientist* 62(6): 796–815.

Zeileis, A., Kleiber, C., & Jackman, S. (2008) Regression Models for Count Data in R., *Journal of Statistical Software* 27(8): 1–25.

Zimmer, A. & Pahl, B. (2018) Barriers to Third Sector Development. In Bernard, E., Lester, M. S., Sivesind, K. H., & Zimmer, A. *The Third Sector as a Renewable Resource for Europe: Concepts, Impacts, Challenges and Opportunities*. London: Palgrave Macmillan.

Index

Advocacy. *See* Political advocacy

Advocacy activities 6, 10, 29, 40.
  See also Political engagement, Political activities, Politicization

Advocacy group. *See* Interest group

Aggregation challenge
  Effects of 181–184
  Measurement of 73

Association. *See* Voluntary association

Association template. *See* Voluntary association

Astroturf lobbying. *See* Representation

Audiences. *See* Organizational audiences

Bad civil society 18–20, 102

Bureaucratization. *See also* Functional differentation, Manager, Professionalization, Staff control
  Definition of 85
  Difference to professionalization 109–111
  Efficiency-enhancing reform 33–34, 52, 56, 63, 68, 85–87, 98, 109–111, 118–125, 134–136, 143, 160–168, 176, 199, 208, 216, 228, 244–246, 267, 272
  Measurement of 68–69
  Normative evaluation of 6, 11, 32
  Provision of training 56, 85–86, 109, 140–142, 155, 158, 163, 168
  Tendencies associated with 6, 33, 85–87, 106, 169, 205
  Theoretical expectations regarding CSOs' democratic contributions 58

Case selection
  Case studies for longitudinal analysis 62–64, 78–81, 124–170, 207–247
  Countries for surveys 59–61

Citizen. *See also* Representation
  Preferences of 15–16, 23, 27, 175

Civil society. *See also* Bad civil society
  Definition of 1, 8, 206
  Diversity in 1, 8, 18, 44–55, 81

Functions of 1–9, 19–20, 103–104
  Normative expectations towards 2, 5, 32, 36–38, 44, 57–58, 89, 100–101, 105, 190

Civil society organization (CSO). *See* Membership-based voluntary organization

Civil society organizations (CSOs). *See also* Membership-based voluntary organization, Democratic potential of CSOs, Democratic performance of CSOs
  As systems of goverance 82–83
  Deficits of 2, 5, 31, 173, 207, 210, 209–210, 259, 266
  Normative expectations towards 3, 8–10, 18, 26–32, 36–38, 41–42, 65–67, 248–251, 260–265

Competition. *See also* Competition density, Market pressure, Resource competition
  Ideology-based/issue-based 27, 72, 178
  Inter-party 12, 230
  Inter-group 72, 178–185, 204

Competition density 72, 178, 181–183, 200, 204. *See also* Competition, Niche, Resource competition
  Effects of 182
  Measurement of 72

Conflicting priorities of leaders, members, and managers 26–27, 44–52, 85–86, 114, 118, 184–185, 197, 266–273. *See also* Leader, Manager, Member

Congruence 26–27. *See also* Societal responsiveness

Constituency linkage 6, 10, 23–24, 27–31, 36–37, 65–67, 104, 180, 207, 258, 260. *See also* Constituency pressure

Constituency pressure 178–186. *See also* Constituency linkage, Societal responsiveness

Control variables 70–71, 77, 204, 250. *See also* Model choices, Multiple imputations, Surveys

Corporate members. *See also* Individual membership, Member
  As part of civil society 39–42
  Definition of 39
  Instrumental orientation/behaviour of 41, 91–92, 99, 113, 178, 183, 196, 208
Crisis
  Covid-19 1–4, 131, 161
  Financial 1, 134–135, 214, 218
CSO type. *See also* Political party, Service-oriented organization, Interest group
  Distinction between CSO types 43, 196
  Effects of 74–78, 92–100, 116, 198–205
  Measurement of 59, 70–71

Decentralization 45, 55, 119, 126, 168. *See also* Multi-tier structure
Democracy
  Intra-organizational 12, 89, 105, 165, 262
  Intra-party 12, 82, 99, 156, 246
Democratic contributions of CSOs 8, 27, 32–33, 35–38
Democratic performance of CSOs 33–35, 57, 78, 205, 249–251. *See also* Democratic potential of CSOs
  Dimensions to measure the 47
Democratic potential of CSOs 3–35, 38–40, 44, 254, *See also* Democratic performance of CSOs
  Discrepancies between democratic potential and reality 3–35, 36–58, 207, 248–277
  Normative yardsticks defining the 27–31
Digitalization 1–3
  Digital campaining 153, 189
Division of labour. *See* Functional differentiation
Donor dependency. *See also* Financial income sources
  Effects of 116, 181–182, 200
  Measurement of 71
  Private donation 75

Ecology Party 149, 231. *See also* GPEW
Exit threat 22, 39, 84, 135, 145. *See also* Membership instability, Organizational exit

Financial income sources 45, 54–56, 69, 71–75, 87–88, 176–178, 181, 195, 208, 247, 261–265. *See also* Donor dependency, membership fees, state funding, state funding dependency
  Sales and services 75
Focus group 24
Functional differentiation 112, 118–119, 128, 136–137, 162, 169, 215, 267, 272

Goal commitment 171–186. *See also* Organizational loyalty, Organizational identity, Organizational values
  Definition of 67
  Normative relevance of 30–31, 57
  Relation to organizational identity 51
Goal displacement 173, 209–210, 266. *See also* Mission drift
Goal reorientation 171–186. *See also* Organizational identity, Goal commitment
  Instrumental *vs.* responsive 175–179, 183, 185
  Functional *vs.* substantive 185, 210–211
  Mission change and programmatic change 173–174, 181
  Normative evaluation of 70
  Quantitative Measurement of 67
  Qualitative Measurement of 77–78, 210–211
Governance
  Definition of 125
Governance characteristics 34, 53–56, 68–70, 178, 250
  Theoretical expectations related to central governance characteristics 57–58
Governance domains 12, 30, 64–66, 110–111, 114, 117–122, 126, 132, 136, 147, 164, 169, 173, 176, 198, 238, 245, 277
Governance template
  Distinction between voluntary association and professionalized voluntary organization 53, 68, 92, 115
  Distinct theoretical expectations regarding two templates 36, 55–56, 58, 75–76, 85, 88, 92, 103, 175, 179–185, 188, 199, 201, 249–251

306 Index

GPEW (Green Party of England and Wales)
Brexit 230
Candidate recruitment/selection 151, 154–155, 162–163, 166–167, 232, 238, 240, 243, 246
Centralization 150, 152, 159, 163–166, 169, 231, 234–235, 246, 252–255, 257
Conflict/divide over primary goal 233–234, 236–239, 244–246
Conservatives/Conservative Party 230, 241
Corbyn, Jeremy 232, 244
Crisis 157, 236, 245
Decentralization; subsidiarity 151, 163, 165, 168, 233–237, 240–241, 244, 246, 252
Direct action; protest 213, 238–240, 242–244, 247, 265
European Parliament (EP) 233–236, 242
Evolution of functional goal reorientation 210, 229–233, 244–247
Evolution of member control and involvement 149–152, 156–160, 164–165, 169, 208, 234–240, 246, 252–256, 262, 267, 272
Evolution of politicization and political action repertoire 237, 244–245, 253–255
Evolution of substantive goal reorientation 210, 229–233, 244–247
Evolution of staff control 150–151, 158, 162–164, 168, 208, 253, 255
Finances 152–155, 159, 163–164, 208, 229, 238
Identity 229, 245, 273
Inter-party cooperation 240–243, 247
Intra-party democracy 150, 156, 165, 246
Labour Party; Labour 230–232, 237, 244
Lucas, Caroline 231, 235–236, 241–242
Membership size/growth/decline 150–157, 231, 234, 252, 274
Parliamentary representation 166, 208, 236, 242, 247
Post-materialism 230
Professionalization of volunteers/volunteering 163, 168–169, 208
Programmatic/ideological development 230–233, 240–245
Relations to government 229, 230, 232, 236, 242–243, 247

SNP 233
Staff specialization in 155, 161, 164, 167, 238–239, 245, 273
State funding 125, 155, 208–209, 229–230, 241, 247, 263
Subnational organization/activities 151–152, 155, 158, 162, 165–166, 168, 233, 235, 240, 246
UKIP 230
Green Party. *See* GPEW
Green Party of England and Wales (GPEW). *See* GPEW
Group type 70, 73, 93, 99, 190, 202, 205. *See also* CSO type, Interest group, Service-orientated organization

Hybridization/hybrid organizational forms 8, 53, 57, 157, 191, 254–259, 278

Incentive. *See also* Incentive theory
Careerist 48, 154, 166, 267
Collective 37, 49, 196–197, 263
Material 196, 270
Selective 34, 47, 49, 91, 132, 193–204, 253, 262, 267
Solidary 90–91, 173, 183, 196, 206
Incentive theory 37–38, 43–45, 47, 49, 55, 91, 99, 101, 103, 193–194, 197–198, 204, 253, 260
Individualization of society 1–4, 73, 179, 187, 258
Individual Membership. *See also* Corporate member, Member
Effects of 96, 98, 116, 182, 250
Non-instrumental/emotional affiliation/attachment of 49–51, 120, 173, 178, 183, 268–271
Theoretical expectations regarding CSOs' democratic contributions 58
Interest group. *See also* Group type, Interest representation, Political Advocacy
Characteristics of being an 9, 17, 26, 73–75, 93–94, 173
Definition of 40
Effects of being a 96, 116, 182, 191, 200, 203, 211, 250
Functions of a 9, 11, 16, 41, 171–172
Measurement of 70
Public 12
Sectional 26, 93

Interest representation. *See also* Political activity, Political engagement, Political action repertoire
   As behavioural activity 8, 43, 189, 192, 198, 206
   Definition of 104, 192
   Measurement of interest representation behaviour 67–68
Intermediary function/structure 2, 20, 24. *See also* Constituency linkage, Goal commitment, Society responsiveness
Intra-organizational decision-making
   Centralization of decision-making 11, 30, 50–51, 11, 30, 98–102, 106, 119–127, 145, 149–150, 163–169, 231, 258, 269. *See also* Staff control
   Leader-dominated 30, 66, 135
   Member-controlled 11, 66, 143–144
   Staff-driven 31, 54, 95, 265. *See also* NGOization, Staff control
Intra-organizational dynamics 43, 63, 82, 95–97, 124–171, 191, 207–247, 252, 259, 270, 274
Intra-organizational efficiency 30–33, 37, 46–56, 85–86, 106–111, 113, 118, 122, 201
Intra-organizational/internal participation. *See also* Member activism, Member control, Member involvement
   As normative yardstick for CSOs' democratic contribution 11–15
   Normative relevance of 5, 9–10, 12–13, 19, 26–28
Intra-organizational trade-off 44–58
   Balancing act related to 5–6, 37–38, 277
   Configurations of 46–51
   Relevant to CSOs' democratic contributions 37–38, 46–51
   Trade-off between leader autonomy and member control 47–50
   Trade-off between demands for expertise/ efficiency and organizational accountability 47–50
   Trade-off between organizational loyalty and maximization of support 47, 51
   Trade-off between selective and collective incentive provision 47, 51
Issue salience. *See* Salience

Last Generation (*Letzte Generation*) 274–277
Leader. *See also* Conflicting priorities of leaders, members, and managers
   Definition of 44–46
   Priorities/orientations/interests of leaders as compared to members, managers 44–51, 109–110, 266–273
Leader autonomy 37, 43, 46–50, 86, 95, 165, 262, 275
Leadership. *See also* Conflicting priorities of leaders, members, and managers, Leader autonomy
Letzte Generation. *See* Last Generation
Lobbying
   Astroturf 23, 259
   Grass-roots 23, 93, 140, 213, 222, 224, 265
Logic of influence 37, 187–206
Logic of membership 187–206

Manager. *See also* Conflicting priorities of leaders, members, and managers, Efficiency, Leader, Staff control
   Definition of 44–46
   Priorities/orientations/interests of managers as compared to members, leaders 44–51, 109–110, 268–273
   The professional identity of 48, 273
Managerial competences/skills 37, 45, 48, 68, 114, 118–119, 142, 145, 160, 163, 170, 208, 216, 268, 270–273
Market pressure 72, 111, 178–180, 183–184, 204. *See also* Competition, Competition density, Marketization, Resource competition
Marketization. *See also* Financial income sources, Market pressure
   Measurement of 71
   Effects of 116
Mass organization 79, 100, 252, 259, 267. *See also* Membership size
Member. *See also* Conflicting priorities of leaders, members, and managers, Leader, Manager
   Checkbook 266
   Definition of 84
   Members/membership as a resource 56, 75, 91, 93, 97, 100, 104–105, 153, 204

308   Index

Member. *See also* Conflicting priorities of leaders, members, and managers, Leader, Manager (*Continued*)

Orientation of individual versus corporate members 40–42, 91–92, 98, 113, 178, 183, 196, 208

Passive 5, 11, 18, 21–22, 84–85, 87, 90, 105. *See also* Member activism

Priorities/orientations/interests of members as compared to managers, leaders 44–51, 109–110, 267–273

Socialization of 13–14, 106

Member activism 82–105. *See also* Intra-organizational participation, Member control, Member involvement

Definition of 84–85

Measurement of 64–65

Normative relevance of 14–16, 19, 21

Two forms of 13–14, 33, 82

Member control 11–12, 82–105. *See also* Democracy, Intra-organizationa participation, Member activism

Definition of 28, 84–85

Difference to member involvement 13–14, 84–85

Drivers of 97

Measurement of 64

Member control over policy 73, 181

Member interest orientation. *See also* Member

Effects of 96, 116, 179, 182, 201, 205, 250

Measurement of 68

Theoretical expectations regarding CSOs' democratic contributions 58

Member involvement 13–14, 82–105. *See also* Intra-organizationa participation, Member activism

As a resource 91, 93, 97, 100, 104–105, 204

Definition of 14, 85

Democratic effects of 14–16, 19

Difference to member contro 13–14, 84–85

Drivers of 97

Measurement of 65

Need to cultivate 83

Member, Organization, Organizational Exit

Definition of 38–39, 43, 53

Three faces of 63, 77, 268–274

Vulnerability of 4, 118. *See also* Exit threat, Organizational dilemma, Membership instability

Member support 34, 70, 83, 163, 193, 196–197, 266–267

Memberless organization 39, 104, 266

Membership. *See* Member

Membership base 70, 93, 103, 112, 179, 197, 257, 269

Membership-based voluntary organization. *See also* Civil society organizations (CSOs), Exit threat

Membership fees 53, 56, 58, 74–75, 90, 113, 176, 260–262, 267. *See also* GPEW Finances, NAPA Finances, SAS Finances

Effects of 96, 98, 116, 182, 200, 250, 261–262

Measurement of 69

Theoretical expectations regarding CSOs' democratic contributions 58

Membership instability

Measurement of 70

Effects of 96, 116, 120, 182, 184–186, 200, 250, 204, 249–253

Membership organization. *See* Membership-based voluntary organization

Membership size. *See also* Organizational capacity, The iron law of oligarchy

Measurement of 70–71

Effects of 74, 96, 100, 116, 119, 135, 182, 200, 250–252, 259

Missing values. *See* Multiple imputations

Mission drift 5, 27, 173, 210. *See also* Goal displacement, Goal commitment, Goal reorientation

Mixed-methods design 33, 59, 62–64, 77–78

Model choices

Heterogeneous choice models 95, 96

Logistic regressions 181, 182, 199

Zero-inflated models 115, 116, 199

Multi-tier structure. *See also* Decentralization

Measurement of 69

Effects of 76, 90, 96, 98, 101, 116, 119, 121, 125, 138–139, 197, 200, 250–251

Theoretical expectations regarding CSOs' democratic contributions 58

Two types of 126–128

Multiple imputations 62, 96, 116, 182, 200

NAPA (National Activity Providers Association)
Centralization 165, 257–258
Charity Commission 137, 218
Crisis 134–135, 214, 218–219, 245
Corporate membership 131, 137, 208–209, 216–218
Evolution of functional goal reorientation 210, 217, 245
Evolution of member control and involvement 134–137, 168, 208, 256–257
Evolution of politicization and political action repertoire 213–217, 245
Evolution of staff control 125, 135–136, 169, 208, 219, 256
Evolution of substantive goal reorientation 210, 219, 245
Identity 245, 265, 273
Finances 128–130, 134–135, 208, 216–219, 262, 265
Membership size/growth/decline 128–129, 131, 134, 216–218, 259
Organization-building 131, 168, 208, 213–219, 273
Recruitment of personnel 134–135, 170, 257, 273
Regional tier 128–131, 168
Relations with government/state authorities 209, 215–217, 246–247, 264
Service provision 125, 128–133, 167–168, 214–218, 246, 265–267
Staff specialization in 167, 215–216, 245, 273
National Activity Providers Association. See NAPA
NGO 8, 9, 106, 209, 236. See also Membership-based Voluntary Organization
NGOization 2, 31, 207, 259
Niche. See also Competition density
Competition 199
Ideological/programmatic 72, 173, 233, 244, 199
Substantive 72, 183
Non-profit. See also Membership-based Voluntary Organization

Definition of 1, 38–39, 191
Organization 4–11, 13, 16, 27, 30, 39, 54, 68, 71, 87, 106, 109, 171, 173, 182–183, 191, 209, 248

Organization
Definition of 1
Organizational accountability. 29–31, 106–121. See also Staff control, Constituency linkage, Societal responsiveness
Organizational age
Effects of 96, 100, 116, 182, 200, 249, 250, 252
Measurement of 71
Organizational audience
External 51, 72, 171, 175, 194, 204, 210, 262–263
Organizational capacity 97, 192–193, 197, 202, 204, 224. See also Financial income sources, Membership size, Professionalization, Staff specialization
Organizational change. See Goal reorientation
Organizational commitment 12–13, 27, 37, 44–48, 137, 142, 154, 266–267, 270–273. See also Organizational loyalty
Organizational dilemma 55, 179, 192. See also Intra-organizational trade-off
Organizational exit 7, 10, 22, 39, 48, 70, 84–85, 135, 145, 160
Organizational governance. See Governance characteristics, Governance domains, Governance template
Organizational identity. 30–31, 51, 198, 206, 211, 245, 249, 265–266. See also Goal commitment
Organizational values
Change of. See Goal reorientation
Definition of 31, 171–172
Function of 171–3
Organizational institutionalization. 39, 100, 140, 252–253. See also Organizational age
Organizational integration 130, 139, 149, 156
Organizational linkage. See Constituency linkage, Organizational accountability, Societal responsiveness

310 Index

Organizational loyalty 13, 107, 142, 170, 179, 268–273. *See also* Organizational commitment, Organizational values

Organizational model. *See* Governance template

Organizational self-maintenance 2, 6, 15, 28, 31, 39, 47, 50, 52, 70, 83, 87, 102, 218. *See also* Organizational survival

Organizational survival 46, 51, 107, 124, 176–178, 195, 218. *See also* Organizational self-

Maintenance

Organizational values 27, 30–37, 107, 113, 267. *See also* Goal commitment, organizational identity, Organizational loyalty

Paid employee/staff. *See* Manager

Party. *See* Political Party

Party system 17, 62, 230–232, 244–245. *See also* Political party

Low-cost 277

Participation 54, 99, 103, 189, 198. *See also* Intra-organizational/internal participation Electoral

Thin 102

Partisan Organization. *See* Political Party

Party Organization

Cartel party model of 54, 93, 155

Political action repertoire. *See also* Political activities

Analyzing changes in CSOs' 212–213

Definition of 29, 192

Drivers of 192–198, 200–203, 289

Insider strategies 209, 212, 222–244, 247, 264

Outsider strategies 35, 209, 223–224, 237, 239, 244

Political activities 187–206. *See also* Interest representation, Politicization, Political action repertoire

Analyzing changes in CSOs' 212–213

Types of 28–29, 67–68

Political advocacy 7, 29, 193, 195. *See also* Interest representation, Political action repertoire, Political activities

As primary or secondary goal 18, 190, 205

Political engagement. *See* Political activity, Politicization, Political action repertoire, Interest representation

As normative yardstick for CSOs' democratic contribution 28–29

Political Party

Crisis of 7–8, 103–104

Definition of 54, 61, 188

Effects of being a 96, 99–100, 116, 182, 200, 250, 253

Functions of a 9–10

Party in central office 241

Party in public office 80–81, 229–234, 238, 270–271

Measurement of 70

Membership/ members 9, 99–100, 102, 246

Niche/minor party 18, 100, 154–155, 230, 240–241

Politicization 187–205. *See also* Political action repertoire, Political activities

Definition of 29, 192

Drivers of 35, 194–205, 214–217, 258, 263

Populism 2, 80, 231, 242

Professionalization. *See also* Staff specialization, Staff control, Professionalized voluntary organization, Volunteer management

Definition of 56

Difference to bureaucratization 109–111

Effects of 96–98, 116–117, 181–184, 199–201, 250–252, 262–267

Normative assumptions about 2, 32, 106–107, 122–123, 207–208, 248, 260–269

Theoretical expectations regarding CSOs' democratic contributions 58

Qualitative Measurement of 124–126

Quantitative Measurement of 68–69

Professionalized voluntary organization. *See also* Governance template, Manager, Professionalization, Staff specialization, Volunteer management

Behavioural/internal logic/tendencies of 52–56

Characteristics of 53

Detachment from constituencies 30, 106, 170, 123, 205, 258–260, 265

Theoretical expectations regarding CSOs' democratic contributions 58

Qualitative case studies. *See also* GPEW, Mixed-methods design, NAPA, SAS
Comparability of the trajectories of parties and groups 80–81
Data collection 62–63, 210–213
Interviews 63, 210, 213
Methodological advantages of 62–64, 77–78, 98, 103, 123–126, 209–210
Quantitative findings further explored by 103, 117–120, 167–169, 245–246, 252–243, 266–267
Selection of 77–78, 128, 229–230
Theoretical implications of the 169–170, 268–273

Representation. *See also* Interest representation
Assumed 18–25, 208, 256–7
Astroturf 23, 259
Consultative 18–25, 255–257, 262
Democratic 23–4
Detached 30–31, 170. 203, 205, 210, 256–8
Resource competition. *See also* Competition, Competition Density, Market pressure
Surrogate 22–25, 226, 257
Types of representation 18–25
Measurement of 72, 181, 199
Effects of 34, 116, 182, 183, 185, 200, 204
Resource dependency theory 37, 43, 44, 69, 101, 261. *See also* State dependency

Salience 1, 7, 23, 25, 44, 51, 73, 127, 174, 178, 183–184, 189, 195, 206, 265. *See also* Competition, Visibility challenge
SAS (Surfers Against Sewage)
Charity Commission 143–144
Crisis 138, 245
Evolution of functional goal reorientation 210, 227–229, 245
Evolution of member control and involvement 138–146, 149, 168–169, 208, 228, 255–256
Evolution of politicization and political action repertoire 168, 210–213, 219–224, 226–228, 245–247

Evolution of staff control 138–139, 143–149, 168–169, 208, 252–253
Evolution of substantive goal reorientation 210, 219–220, 225–228, 245
Finances 140–147, 208, 221–223, 226, 228, 262
Identity 144, 219–220, 227–229, 245, 265–266, 273
Insider/strategies 222–224, 247, 264
Membership size/growth/decline 138, 140, 143–144, 208, 252–253
Outsider/Outsider strategies 35, 223–224, 247
Professionalization of volunteers/volunteering 138–142, 145–149, 168, 225–228, 265–266
Protest and unconventional political activities 220–226, 244–247
Recruitment of personnel 138–149, 167–168, 220–222, 257, 273
Relations with government/state authorities 143, 222, 224, 226–227, 247
Regional organization/activities 139–142, 145–148, 168, 223, 225, 256–258, 262
Staff specialization in 140–142, 145–149, 167, 221, 225, 273
Territorian expansion/development 139–142

Service organization. *See* Service-oriented organization

Service-oriented organizations. *See also* CSO type, NAPA
Characteristics of 73–75, 94, 135, 174, 190–191
Deficiencies of 27
Definition of 18, 43
Effects of being a 96, 104, 116, 182, 200, 203, 250
Functions of 11, 42, 191
Measurement of 70
Political activities of 16–17, 18, 190–191, 195, 211
Priorities of a 18, 195, 211, 265

Social capital 5, 11, 14

Social integration 11, 19

312 Index

Societal responsiveness. *See also* Constituency linkage, Goal reorientation
  As separate, normative yardstick to evaluate CSOs' democratic contributions 20, 22–27
  Definition of 10, 23–24, 26
  Empirical expressions of 29–31
Staff. *See* Manager
Staff control 106–122, *See also* Manager, NGOization, Professionalized voluntary organization, Staff specialization
  And accountability of organizational behaviour 30–31, 106–108
  Definition of/difference to staff influence 109
  Detachment from constitutencies 30, 106, 170, 122–123, 205–206, 258–260, 265
  Difference to centralization 106–107. *See also* Intra-organizational decision-making
  Mangerial control versus professional discretion 109–111
  Normative repercussions of 30, 109, 267–273
Staff specialization 140–141, 145, 147–149, 161, 167, 210–211, 215, 225, 239, 273. *See also* Manager, Staff control
State dependency 1, 2, 35, 54, 121. *See also* State funding dependency
State funding 5–7, 53–58, 60, 69, 74–76, 88, 96–98, 116–117, 125, 135, 155, 177, 182, 195, 200–201, 208–209, 222–223, 229, 241, 247, 250, 263
State funding dependency. *See also* State dependency, State funding
  Effects of 34, 37, 58, 76, 88–89, 97–98, 110–111, 177, 181–183, 195, 201–207, 212, 266
  Measurement of 69, 261
  Normative evaluation regarding 87–88
  Theoretical expectations regarding CSOs' democratic contributions 58
Subnational unit/level/branch 5, 119, 126, 127, 168, 233, 246. *See also* Decentralization, Multi-tier structure
Surfers Against Sewage. *See* SAS
Surveys. *See also* Mixed-methods design, Multiple imputations

  Countries selected for 59–61
  Data collection 59–62

The iron law of oligarchy 100, 106, 119, 270
The tyranny of structurelessness 100
Trade-off. *See* Intra-organizational trade-off
Transmission belt. *See also* Constituency linkage, Representation
  As a configuration of participation and representation 19–21, 253–259
  Central components of the 8–10, 26–27, 248
  The classical notion of the 24, 26–27, 32, 188, 206, 248

Uncivil society. *See* Bad civil society

Visibility challenge 178, 181, 183. *See also* Salience
  Measurement of 73
  Effects of 182
Voluntary association. *See also* Governance template
  Behavioural/internal logic of 52, 112–114, 125, 177–180, 185–188, 195, 206
  Defining characteristics of 33–34, 55–58, 69, 73, 76, 101, 116, 175–176, 182, 200
  Normative assumptions about 44, 89–90, 102
  Theoretical expectations regarding CSOs' democratic contributions 58
Voluntary member. *See* Membership-based voluntary organization, Exit threat, Voluntary membership
Voluntary membership 1–2, 7, 46, 75, 53, 193, 266, *See also* Exit threat, Membership-based voluntary organization
Voluntary membership organisation. *See* Membership-based voluntary organization
Volunteer 13–14, 45, 55, 85, 125, 197. *See also* Volunteer management, Volunteer staff
Volunteer management 87–88, 97, 120, 147, 163, 169, 253. *See also* Volunteer staff
Volunteer staff 33, 52, 73–75, 112, 126, 140, 149, 151, 246, 250
  Definition of 13–14, 45–46

Effects of 58, 76–77, 96–100, 113–120, 125, 127, 150, 182, 197–205, 259–267

Measurement 69

Professionalization of 86, 87, 88, 145, 225

Theoretical expectations regarding CSOs' democratic contributions 58

Training of 141, 146